MOSSES OF THE SOCIETY ISLANDS

MOSSES OF THE SOCIETY ISLANDS

Henry O. Whittier

A FLORIDA TECHNOLOGICAL UNIVERSITY BOOK

THE UNIVERSITY PRESSES OF FLORIDA
GAINESVILLE / 1976

Library of Congress Cataloging in Publication Data

Whittier, Henry O   1937–
   Mosses of the Society Islands.

   "A Florida Technological University book."
   Bibliography: p.
   Includes index.
   1. Mosses—Society Islands.   I. Title.
QK548.S6W44   588′.2′099621   75-23309
ISBN 0–8130–0521–3

PRINTED BY STORTER PRINTING COMPANY, GAINESVILLE, FLORIDA

CONTENTS

CONTENTS

PREFACE

More than ever before the scientific community is oriented toward rapid publication and communication of research. With good reason, published reports are often only parts of larger, more comprehensive research programs, presented in "serialized" form. The researcher who holds his data to the conclusion of his program may find all or part developed and published by others before he is finished. Countless and painstaking hours of research may be effectively lost by this duplication. At the least, results become dated while the final drafts are prepared and edited, or equally serious, while the manuscript awaits publication. High publication costs for long papers or books cannot be borne by most journals or irregular publications if they are to be sold at reasonable prices, unless the author can provide at least part of the expenses.

With the foregoing in mind, it is with most especial thanks that I here recognize the generous financial support provided by the Donald Richards Bryological Publication Fund, established to aid in the publication of bryological research, which has made possible the publication of *Mosses of the Society Islands*.

I wish also to thank Clark Rogerson, Arthur Cronquist, William C. Steere, and the other members of the editorial board of the *Memoirs of the New York Botanical Garden*, who originally accepted the manuscript for publication in 1972, and when that proved financially impossible, recommended support by the Florida Technological University Press for its subsequent publication. Special thanks are due Roland Browne, who, as director of the F.T.U. Press, made final arrangements for publication by the University Presses of Florida.

My studies of Society Islands mosses began in mid-Pacific, on board the 124-foot schooner *Collegiate Rebel*, when in 1960 I worked as a member of the crew and as field collector for Harvey

A. Miller during the Miami University Expedition to the Galápagos, Polynesia, and Micronesia. Field expenses and travel assistance in 1960 and in 1964 were provided in part from National Science Foundation grants G-7115 and GB-1236 to Miami University, Harvey A. Miller, principal investigator. I was also assisted in 1964 by a Grant-in-Aid of Research from Sigma Xi-RESA. Further field support was provided by the New York Botanical Garden through its director, William C. Steere. This publication is derived in part from my doctoral dissertation, completed under the cooperative program between the New York Botanical Garden and Columbia University. Professor Steere directed the dissertation and provided assistance and encouragement in a variety of ways for which I am deeply grateful.

Those who should be recognized for their help while I taught at the University of Hawaii and conducted research at the Bernice P. Bishop Museum include the late Marie C. Neal, curator of the herbarium of the Bernice P. Bishop Museum; Alvin K. Chock, an assistant curator and close friend who helped with the 1964 expedition plants; Margaret Titcomb, librarian of the Bishop Museum; Bryce and Shirley Decker, who collected bryophytes for me in Tahiti and in the Marquesas Islands; and Charles Lamoreaux, chairman of the Department of Botany, who provided friendly advice and research facilities.

In the Society Islands, I found the traditional hospitality which contributed immeasurably to the success of my field work, and for their contributions I owe especial thanks to Mme Aurora Natua, curator of the Museum of Papeete; Cambridge Shiu of Manuia Imports-Exports, whose help went far beyond expediting specimens; and Maurice and Henri Jay, whose advice and guidance concerning my work in the field made it possible for me to visit otherwise inaccessible localities.

Thanks are owed a number of the staff of the New York Botanical Garden, including Pierre Dansereau for advice regarding ecological aspects and for reading early drafts; Gary Smith, for help in resolving systematic problems especially within the Polytrichaceae; Clark Rogerson, for unlimited use of herbarium facilities; Mulford Martin, for continued interest and concern; John Reed and his library staff for long-standing support; and especially to Arthur Cronquist, for his encouragement over a long period of time.

Winona Welch and Marie-Heléne Sachet kindly sent personal

collections from the Society Islands. MacKenzie Lamb, curator of the Farlow Herbarium, Harvard University, and Harold Robinson, curator of bryophytes, U.S. National Herbarium, allowed me to review specimens in their collections. Howard Crum lent collections sent to him for study. M. M. J. van Balgooy collected bryophytes, forwarding them to me for study, and his contribution is marked by the number of new insular records contained in his collections.

It is with especial fondness that I thank Prof. E. J. Bonnot, of the University of Lille, France, who introduced me to the bryologists of Europe, most notably to Mme Jovet-Ast, and to Mlle Heléne Bischler of the Museum National de Histoire Naturelle, in Paris, who showed me many kindnesses during my brief visit in 1973, and who gave me access to the rich Bescherelle herbarium materials housed there.

I wish to thank Sally McDonough and Bonnie Simmons, who helped with early stages of typing. Illustrations for some species were prepared by H. A. Miller, indicated by "*del.* HAM."

Most of all, my love and thanks go to my wife, Barbara, who has contributed immeasurably to the final completion of this research. An especial appreciation is recognized here for my parents, Grace and Robert Whittier, who helped support my travel and educational expenses for many years.

It seems fitting to dedicate this work, not to one person, but to several, living and dead: to Dr. J. Nadeaud, eminent naturalist and surgeon, to Emile Bescherelle, outstanding French bryologist, and to the late Edwin Bunting Bartram, who so warmly encouraged my early studies of Pacific Islands mosses; among the living are W. C. Steere, whose guidance, help, and encouragement enabled completion of a dissertation and its later publication, and to Harvey A. Miller, who initiated my bryological career and stimulated its development through the last fifteen years as friend and mentor; and lastly, to those whom I do not, and may never know . . . the students of natural history who will use this work.

The moss flora of the Society Islands may contain approximately 200 taxa. My own studies have reduced the some 400 taxa previously ascribed to the Society Islands to approximately 175, but this can be only considered an approximation of the true flora which is far from thoroughly known. In fact, the bryophyte flora of the Society Islands archipelago is known primarily from collections made on Tahiti, from a few hundred specimens collected on

Moorea, about 100 specimens from Raiatea, fewer than 20 from
Bora Bora, Mopelia, and a single collection on Scilly. To the best
of my knowledge, the collections I made on Tahiti and Moorea
are the first made by a trained bryologist working in the field in
the Society Islands, and include 1800 numbered collections of both
mosses and hepatics, with some individual collection numbers represented by over 20 species . . . whole bryophyte microecosystems.
As far as possible, associated taxa have been reported along with
locality data in specimen citations in the text. A Thomen pocket
altimeter was used to provide altitudinal data which I consider
accurate to within about 20 meters. In the hope that this work will
stimulate further study of the bryophytes of fragile insular ecosystems, I have provided diagnostic keys and have illustrated every
species at my disposal, selecting type or authentic material whenever possible, and designating the specimens illustrated in nearly
every instance.

INTRODUCTION

The Society Islands extend in a southeast to northwest direction from 148° to nearly 155° west longitude, and from about 16° to 18° south latitude in the south-central Pacific Ocean. They are typically treated as two groups, the windward archipelago (Iles du Vent), and the leeward archipelago (Iles sous le Vent). The windward group is comprised of six islands, including Tahiti, the capital of French Oceania, Moorea (Eimeo), and three low islands or atolls: Mehetia with a low peak and a central, undissected crater, Maiao iti, and Tetiaroa. Makatea, an uplifted limestone island geographically a part of the Tuamotu archipelago, is floristically linked to Tahiti. In his research on the snail genus *Partula*, Crampton (1916) included Makatea with the Society Islands. The leeward islands include Raiatea and Tahaa (which are enclosed within the same reef and are separated only by a narrow channel), Huahine, Bora Bora, Maupiti, Motu iti, Mopelia, Scilly, and Bellingshausen, a total of nine islands. Maupiti has a low peak, but Motu iti, Scilly, and Bellingshausen are true atolls. The other islands are distinctly volcanic (Fig. 1).

The total land area of the volcanic islands has been estimated as 1750 square kilometers. Tahiti, the largest of the group, has an area of approximately 1036 square kilometers, Moorea about 130, Raiatea, 155, Tahaa, 83, and Huahine about 49 (Crampton, 1916).

Tahiti

Tahiti is botanically one of the most interesting and diverse of all the Pacific islands, for to find the nearest comparable areas and elevations, one must look to Hawaii, to the Americas, New Zealand, New Caledonia, and New Guinea. The nearest land masses are the Marquesas Islands, the Austral Islands, Samoa, Fiji, and Australia.

Tahiti, at 17°38' south latitude and 149°25' west longitude, oriented in a northwest to southeast direction, is composed of two almost separate islands, the deeply dissected cones of two ancient volcanos. *Tahiti nui* (big Tahiti) forms the largest northwestern

1

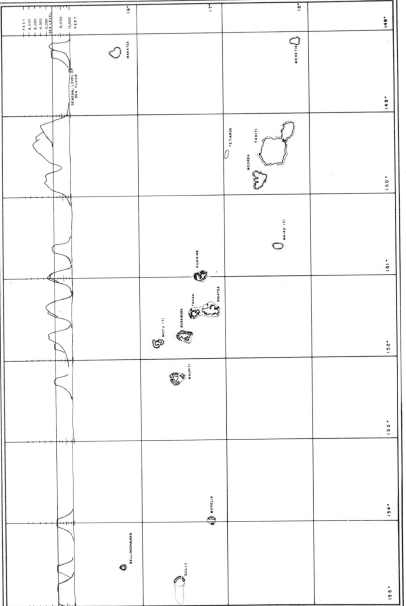

FIG. 1. Map and profile of Society Islands and Makatea.

area and *Tahiti iti* (little Tahiti) the southeastern part (Fig. 2), joined by the low Isthmus of Taravao. Tahiti nui is about 30 km long and 27 km wide; the road along its narrow coastal plain is about 120 km long. Tahiti iti (the Taiarapu Peninsula) is nearly 18 km long and about 9 km wide, with a circumference of about 70 km. Roads extend onto the Taiarapu Peninsula from the isthmus along the north shore to Tautira, and a second road follows the south coast to Teahupoo. Foot trails continue beyond these points, but travel in this remote end of Tahiti iti is commonly by sea.

Howell Williams (1933) described Tahiti as an excellent example of a youthfully dissected cone, the deep, narrow, V-shaped valleys separated by knife-edge ridges, the conical shape of the island and the very narrow coastal plains testifying to the comparatively recent origin of the island. The last volcanic eruptions probably occurred in the Recent period, though well before the arrival of man. The westernmost islands are the oldest; the easternmost islands are the most recent. The detailed study of the older, western islands of the archipelago may yield much of interest to the biogeographer, despite the smaller land areas and the lower elevations of these islands.

Many of the valleys of Tahiti have nearly vertical sides 1000 m high. The ridges separating them are so narrow that erosion has formed small "windows" in the decomposing basaltic rock. Typical of the valleys are small streams, many permanent, occupying the entire width of the valley floor. Toward the upper elevations in the valleys are numerous waterfalls. At lower, drier elevations, erosion has proceeded at a slower pace, and the knife-edge ridges have become flattened slopes or sloping plateaus, terminating in numerous rounded buttresses that extend to the coastal plain or to the sea.

The one freshwater lake on Tahiti is Lake Vaihiria, situated at the head of the Vaihiria Valley on the south side of Tahiti nui. The lake, about 600 m long, is at an elevation of about 400 m, surrounded by cliffs rising nearly 1000 m. Its depth was determined by G. P. Wilder as less than 30 m (Williams, 1933). Williams' suggestion that the lake originated when landslides blocked the stream is supported by my own observation. The sides of the valley form a huge amphitheater around the lake; there are indications that large masses of rock have broken loose from the steep cliffs surrounding the site to form a natural dam. Access to the lake is by day-long

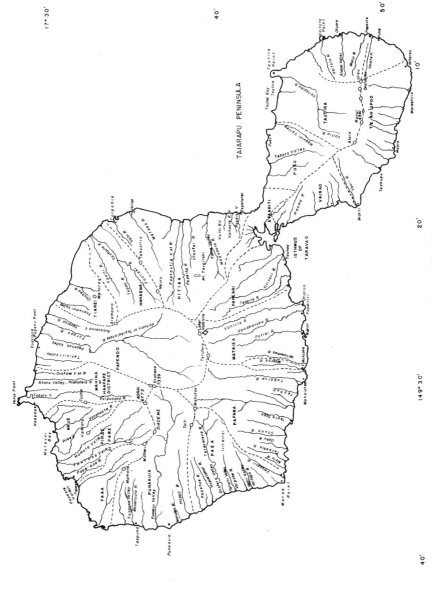

Fig. 2. Map of Tahiti.

hike up the stream bed from the coastal plain at Mataiea, or by a two- or three-day trek from the north side of the island, following the Papenoo River and tributaries through the crater of the ancient volcano that formed Tahiti nui.

A coastal plain seldom more than a mile wide extends around most of Tahiti nui and a part of Tahiti iti. Cliffs several hundred feet high rise from the ocean along the north shore of Tahiti nui, and in the Pari district on the Taiarapu Peninsula the cliffs may exceed 300 m.

There are fourteen mountains on Tahiti higher than 1000 m, and of these, five exceed 1500 m: Mt. Orohena (2237 m), Mt. Aorai (2045 m), Mt. Hahutea (1585 m), Mt. Ivirairai, and Mt. Tetufera. To my knowledge, bryophyte collections have been made only at the summit of Mt. Aorai. Mt. Orohena was first climbed by Europeans in 1953, and the only plant collected there seems to have been a sedge, *Oreobolus*, apparently a species new to science and a new generic record for the Society Islands.

The northeastern and eastern windward portion of Tahiti is much wetter than the opposite side which lies in the rain shadow of the high central mountain ridges (see Fig. 3). Countless waterfalls occur all over the island. Many exceed 300 m, although the volume of water which passes over them is often so small that the slender thread of silver may vanish into mist before it reaches the bottom of the cliffs. The volcanic rock provides a tremendous reservoir which is constantly replenished, so that from the summit of Mt. Aorai, one can see a dozen or more cascades originating close to the summit of Mt. Aorai's larger sister peak, Orohena, and continuing long after rains have passed. Among the most famous waterfalls are the Cascade de Faone, in the Hitiaa District, and the Cascade de Fautaua in the Pirae District.

One of the few roads that extends inland leads to the beginning of trails to the Cascade de Fautaua and scenic points near the falls, the trail above the falls leading ultimately to the famous crown-like ridge known as the Diademe. Another leads up a long, tortuous incline to Fare Rau Ape, and from there a trail leads to the summit of Mt. Aorai. Another road, near the airport at Faaa, leads inland to a point overlooking Papeete from an elevation of about 300 m. In the Afaahiti District, on the Isthmus of Taravao, a paved road extends inland onto the peninsula to an elevation of about 300 m. Above this point jeep roads continue to about 800 m where they

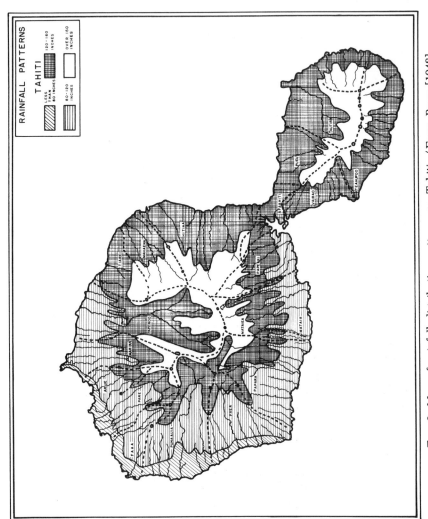

FIG. 3. Map of rainfall distribution patterns on Tahiti. (From Papy [1948], with permission of the publisher.)

enter a forest of *Metrosideros, Aleurites, Cyathea,* and *Miconia.* Undeveloped roads lead into the Papenoo Valley on the north side of Tahiti nui, and into the Haavini Valley on the north side of the Taiarapu Peninsula. More and more such roads appear, as valley lands are developed for vegetable farms by Chinese or Tahitian farmers.

MOOREA

Moorea, less than 19 km north and west of Tahiti, is shaped like the track of a three-toed bird, its toes pointing north. Two deep indentations on the north side, Paopao Bay and Papetoai Bay, are responsible for this distinctive outline. The highest mountain is Mt. Tohivea (1212 m). Other prominent peaks are Mauna Roa and Mt. Rotui, both about 600 m high. To my knowledge, none of these peaks has been explored botanically. A road approximately 64 km long follows the coastline, and numerous trails extend into the island interior. Williams (1933) suggested that because of its high degree of dissection, Moorea must be four to six times older than Tahiti, which perhaps dates back as far as the Pleistocene. Mehetia, nearest Tahiti to the east, is the only member of the Society Islands archipelago which still possesses an intact volcano crater. The absence of any recent volcanic activity, such as barren lava flows, steam vents, or hot springs, suggests that the volcano has been dormant a long time.

RAIATEA AND TAHAA

Raiatea is the third best-known and -explored for bryophytes among the Society Islands archipelago, thanks to the field work of Moore (Bartram, 1931). The island, together with its unexplored sister island Tahaa, lies surrounded by a common reef, about 200 km west northwest of Tahiti. The total land area has been reported as 238 km², with the greatest elevation, 1033 m, in the northwest part of the island near Faaroa, and lesser altitudes reaching 820 m at the southeast end of the mountain chain. A distinctive, eroded volcano crater is located near the central part of the island. An elevated plateau (300–750 m) near Uturoa is inhabited by *Apetahia raiateensis* (Tiare apetahi), a native gardenia, and should prove interesting to future field workers. Papy (1948) provides further comparisons to Tahiti and Moorea in geology and climate. Tahaa, separated only by a narrow channel from Raiatea, has an area of approximately 82 km², with a maximum altitude of 590 m on Mt. Ohiri and 549 m on Mt. Purauti in one mountain chain, and in a secondary chain, of 460 m on Mt. Fareura. To my knowledge, there are no collections from Tahaa.

BORA BORA

Bora Bora (Pora-Pora) has an area of about 38 km², and is located about 12 km west of Tahaa. A single large peak of 725 m gives Bora Bora a pyramidal shape known to navigators around the world. The north-south dimension of Bora Bora is approximately 9 km, and the east-west about 4 km, according to Papy (1948). Stark and Howland (1941) reported on the geology of Bora Bora and provided an interesting general background for the island geography, history, vegetation, physiography, and geology. The sole collections known to this author are those of Phillips (1947) and of van Balgooy (reported in part herein).

Descriptions of the other islands in the archipelago are provided by Papy (1948), but as they are presently represented by few or no bryological collections, no further mention seems necessary here.

Miller (personal communication) and others have advanced the idea that the geological history of island archipelagoes such as the Hawaiian and Society chains which show sequential volcanic formation and subsequent subsidence, a natural progression through time and space, form natural, living laboratories for the study of biological processes. The Society Islands archipelago is represented in the west by geologically older islands such as Bora Bora, Scilly, and Bellingshausen, and in the east by younger islands such as Tahiti and Moorea. Hopefully, as new collections are introduced to better represent all the islands of the archipelago, the bryophytes will yield to the investigator additional data enabling the construction of more highly refined models for island biogeography, evolution, and speciation.

HISTORY OF EXPLORATION AND BRYOLOGICAL NOTES

1762   One of the islands in the Society archipelago was discovered by the Dutch. Jacob Roggeveen landed on "Recreation Island" (either Raiatea or Makatea) on his voyage with the *Eagle* and the *Thienhoven*. No reports or collections have been found.

1767   On June 17, Captain Samuel Wallis of the British ship *Dolphin* discovered the easternmost island of the archipelago, Meetia (Mehetia), and named it Osnaburgh. He sighted Tahiti the next day, named it King George III Island, and anchored in Matavai Bay. Although Wallis stayed over a month, no anchorages were made at Tahiti's sister island Moorea, which Wallis named Duke of York Island. No reports of any collections made by this expedition are known.

1768   Captain Louis De Bougainville, in command of *L'Etoile* and the frigate *Boudeuse*, landed on Tahiti in April, and named the island La Nouvelle Cythère. Philibert Commerson accompanied the expedition, and although his collections are deposited in several herbaria, no bryophytes have been reported.

1769   Captain James Cook, commanding H.M. Bark *Endeavour,* landed on Tahiti on April 10. Among the scientists were two botanists, Joseph Banks and Dr. Charles Solander. Sydney Parkinson served as Banks' draftsman. As they visited nearby islands, a native guide identified the islands by names which were recorded as Huahine, Ulietea (Raiatea), Otahau (Tahaa), Bola Bola (Bora Bora), and Maurua or Maowrooah (Maupiti). Cook named the leeward islands, which he discovered, the Society Islands, supposedly in honor of the Royal Society of London, although according to other reports, he so named them because they lay contiguous to each other. Buck (1953) argued that Cook retained the name of Georgian Islands for Tahiti and the windward group in deference to Wallis, but that with the passage of time, the entire group came to be known as the Society Islands. Original collections are in the British Museum; *Index Herbariorum* lists other herbaria in which collections are deposited. Banks' moss collections were reported upon by Hedwig (1801), Hooker (1818), and Bridel (1826). Among them were: *Dicnemon banksii* (*D. rugosum*), *Syrrhopodon banksii, Leptostomum macrocarpum,* and *Entodon solanderi.*

1773   Captain Cook's first voyage was so successful that shortly after his return to England a second expedition was proposed. Banks' twelve assistants proved too many for Cook to accommodate on the *Resolution,* so Banks and his group went instead on an expedition to Iceland. Accompanying Cook as botanists were John Reinhold Forster, his young son George Forster, and a Swedish botanist, Dr. Anders Sparrman, who joined the expedition at Capetown. On this voyage, Captain Cook sailed through the Marquesas, landing on several islands before returning to Tahiti. Specimens collected by the Forsters and by William Anderson are in the British Museum Herbarium. Only one moss, *Leptostomum macrocarpum,* was reported from the Forsters' Tahitian collections (Guillemin, 1836).

1777   As a result of Cook's great contribution to the prevention of scurvy, he was made a Fellow of the Royal Society, and when a third expedition was planned, it naturally followed that he must lead it. David Nelson was botanist for this expedition, but there is no record that he collected any bryophytes. His vascular plants are at Kew, the Linnean Society of London Herbarium, and the British Museum Herbarium. This voyage proved to be Cook's last, for he was killed during a sudden attack on his landing party while the expedition visited the island of Hawaii.

1788   Captain William Bligh, who accompanied Cook as a lieutenant on his last voyage, was sent by the British Admiralty to collect living breadfruit trees for merchants in the British West Indies who sought a cheap food for slaves. The ill-fated H.M.S. *Bounty* reached Tahiti in October and remained nearly six months, leaving in April. In that same month, Bligh and eighteen loyal crew members were seized by mutineers and set adrift in the ship's launch. After a remarkable voyage of thousands of miles, Bligh and his crew reached Timor. David Nelson, botanist on the expedition, survived the arduous trip but succumbed to a jungle fever not long after his rescue. The *Bounty* was destroyed and any collections which had been made were lost. Bligh was able to make a later voyage to Tahiti and to successfully collect breadfruit, but apparently no bryophyte collections were made.

1791   Archibald Menzies, a surgeon in the British Navy, collected bryophytes during Captain Vancouver's expedition with the *Discovery* and the *Chatham*. His collections from the Galápagos, Hawaii, and Tahiti were reported by Hooker (1818); two were later reported by Guillemin (1836), *Holomitrium vaginatum* and *Neckera pennata*. In 1895, Emile Bescherelle reported the following Menzies collections: *Holomitrium vaginatum, Macromitrium menziesii, M. incurvifolium,* and *Entodon pallidus*; collections are in the British Museum, Kew, and the New York Botanical Garden Herbarium.

1795   Under the command of Captain W. R. Broughton, the *Providence* stopped at Tahiti while doing survey work in the North Pacific. If any collections were made, they are unknown today.

1822   M. Lesson and J. d'Urville accompanied Captain Louis Isadore Duperrey on the corvette *Coquille* on a three-year voyage which included stops in Tahiti and Bora Bora. Some bryophytes were collected; reports were made by Guillemin (1836) and by Jardin (1860).

1823   Captain Otto von Kotzebue, a Russian, stopped in Matavai Bay, Tahiti, during his second voyage into the South Seas, with the *Predpriatie*. Johan Friedrich Gustav von Escholtz collected botanical specimens and sent the original set to Leningrad; if mosses were collected they have not been reported.

1826   Captain Frederick W. Beechey sailed from England for the South Pacific on the H.M.S. *Blossom* with George T. Lay and Alexander Collie as naturalists. The few bryophytes collected in Tahiti were studied by Hooker and Arnott and reported upon in *The Botany of Captain Beechey's Voyage* (1830), and by Guillemin (1836) in *Zephyritis Taitensis*. Most of the original collections are in the Geneva and the Kew herbaria, although some of the moss specimens are in the herbarium of the New York Botanical Garden.

1828   Moerenhout, the French consul in Tahiti, made several trips to nearby islands and collected with C. G. L. Bertero in 1830–31. The collections were sent to herbaria in Paris, Kew, and Geneva, but Guillemin's report (1836) included no mosses.

1834   The *Tuscan* anchored at Tahiti and Raiatea. Collections made by Fred D. Bennett, a Fellow of the Royal College of Surgeons, who accompanied the expedition as a naturalist, were apparently sent to Berlin. No mosses have been reported.

1835   The *Beagle*, commanded by Captain Fitz-Roy, stopped in Tahiti. No bryophytes were reported for the Society Islands by Darwin or by Hooker.

1836   The frigate *Venus*, commanded by Abel Du Petit-Thouars, landed in Tahiti. Collections of cryptogams are in the Paris Museum.

1837 The Reverend J. Diell collected in Tahiti; the date given here indicates the receipt of his collections at Kew. No mosses have been reported from these collections.

1838 Jules Sebastien César Dumont d'Urville spent a short time in Tahiti and visited nearly all the Society Islands during his second voyage with the corvettes *Astrolabe* and *Zelée*. While there, d'Urville encountered Du Petit-Thouars and Moerenhout. The *Zelée* was commanded by Captain Jacquinot, who, together with Dr. Hombron, collected the cryptogams reported by J. F. C. Montagne in a series of papers beginning in 1842. The original collections are deposited in Paris and in Geneva.

The United States Exploring Expedition, commanded by Captain Charles Wilkes, visited Tahiti and Moorea. William Rich was botanist on the expedition, but bryophyte collections bear Wilkes' name. Charles Pickering and T. R. Peal were naturalists, and J. D. Brackenridge served the expedition as horticulturist. The mosses collected during the expedition were studied by William Starling Sullivant, who reported upon them in a series of papers (1854, 1857, 1859). These specimens are in the U.S. National Herbarium, Farlow Herbarium, and the New York Botanical Garden.

1846 On this date, specimens collected in Tahiti by John Carne Bidwill were received at Kew. His bryophyte collections were reported upon by Mitten in 1871.

1848 Jules Lépine, a naval pharmacist, collected in Tahiti; his bryophyte collections were first reported upon by Montagne in 1848, who honored him with *Neckeropsis lepineana*.

Collections were made by Vesco, surgeon on the *Uranie*, in Tahiti, and reported by Mitten (1871) and by Emile Bescherelle (1895a).

1849 Carl Mueller listed many Society Islands mosses in his *Synopsis Muscorum* (1849–51).

1852 M. Edèlestan Jardin, a naval inspector, collected bryophytes on Tahiti between 1852 and 1855. His mosses were reported upon by Bescherelle (1895a).

Nils Johan Andersson was botanist on the Swedish frigate *Eugenie* during a voyage of exploration around the world. His collections were examined and reported upon by Aongstrom (1872, 1873, 1876), and the original specimens were placed in the herbarium of the Museum of Natural History in Stockholm, Sweden. Twenty-six taxa were reported.

Bryophytes were collected in Tahiti by the Reverend R. P. Ponten and reported upon by S. O. Lindberg (1864) and by Bescherelle (1895a).

1855 Vieillard and Pancher collected mosses on Tahiti; these were reported upon by Bescherelle (1895a).

1857 The frigate *Novara*, commanded by Commodore B. von Wullerstorf-Urbair, stopped in Tahiti. Reichardt (1868a, b; 1870) published the reports of the collections made during the expedition, including bryophytes.

1864 Jules Nadeaud, a surgeon, eminent naturalist, and resident of Tahiti for several years (1856–59), published his doctoral (medical) dissertation on the medicinal plants of Tahiti, listing one bryophyte, a species of *Anthoceros* (1864). Bryophyta were treated in a later paper (1873). That Nadeaud had to work under restrictive conditions is indicated by the fact that Bescherelle (1895a) changed four out of five names for the forty-nine taxa Nadeaud listed, but this does not diminish in the least the importance of his contribution.

1867   George Ritter von Frauenfeld collected on Tahiti and sent Musci to Berlin, the other specimens to Vienna. This date marks receipt of the mosses in Berlin.

1870   M. Jelinek collected in Tahiti. His specimens were reported by Bescherelle (1895a).

1871   William Mitten reported on a number of Society Islands mosses in Berthold Seemann's *Flora Vitiensis*.

1875   Anatole Freiherr von Hugel collected on "Duke of York Island" partly with C. Walter. This island may be Moorea, listed under the name given by Wallis in 1767. Specimens are in Cambridge Herbarium, England. I have seen no reports of mosses from these collections.

1877   Dr. Savatier collected in Tahiti during the voyage of the *Magicienne*. Mosses from his collections were listed by Bescherelle (1895a).

1878   Specimens collected by Richard W. Coppinger on Tahiti, during the cruise of the *Alert* are at Kew, but it is not known whether bryophytes are represented in his collections.

1895   Emile Bescherelle published the first major report on mosses from Tahiti and Moorea, with a summary and annotation of most previous works, and descriptions of many new species.

1896   Nadeaud returned to Tahiti and made new collections of mosses which were sent to Bescherelle, who published on them in 1898. These collections are in the Paris Museum Herbarium, but at least fifteen sets of duplicates were sold. Some of these appear in herbaria at Farlow, the Bishop Museum, and the New York Botanical Garden; a number appear to be isotypes.

1899   Nadeaud made additional collections with his Tahitian son and recorded his expeditions in an unpublished diary which I examined while in Tahiti in 1964. Unfortunately, Nadeaud died shortly after field work in 1899, and Temarii Nadeaud, who also collected on Moorea, sent their collections to Bescherelle, who reported upon them in 1901. T. W. N. Beckett collected on Tahiti and sent his specimens to Copenhagen, Denmark. Mosses, if any were collected, are unreported.

1909   Josephine Tilden collected mosses and algae on Tahiti. Her collections were sold as a series to many herbaria, including Farlow and the Bishop Museum. Although a set of algae was purchased by the New York Botanical Garden, it seems that no mosses were included.
Temarii Nadeaud collected on Tahiti and Moorea, sending his collections to Paris. Some duplicates of these apparently unreported mosses appear in the Bishop Museum Herbarium.

1911   M. Larminat collected on Tahiti. His collections were reported on by Potier de la Varde (1912).

1922   W. B. Jones and E. P. Mumford collected in the Marquesas and on Makatea. Their collections were reported by Bartram (1933a).
Mosses of the W. A. Setchell and H. E. Parks expedition to Tahiti were sent to Brotherus, who reported on them in 1924. Original specimens are in Helsinki; duplicates may also have been sent to the University of California and to the California Academy of Sciences. Some specimens are in the Bishop Museum Herbarium and the New York Botanical Garden Herbarium. Setchell (1926) also published on Tahitian phytogeography.

E. H. Quayle collected bryophytes on Tahiti and Makatea during the Whitney Expedition. Notably, Quayle used a barometer to determine elevations during field work. A report on these collections was made by Bartram (1933a).

1924 F. B. H. Brown, botanist for the Bishop Museum–Bayard Dominick Expedition, collected bryophytes in the Marquesas, Tahiti, and Raiatea. These collections appear to be unreported and are deposited in the Bishop Museum Herbarium.

Miss Lucy Evelyn Cheesman, who collected on Tahiti, sent her specimens to the British Museum. Bryophytes were not recorded among the collections.

1926 John W. Moore collected ninety-two specimens on Raiatea and sent them to Bartram. Bartram's report (1931) listed fifty-one species, including three which were apparently new to science, and one new variety. Duplicates and type specimens are in the Bishop Museum Herbarium and in Bartram's private collection, now in the Farlow Herbarium at Harvard.

1927 L. H. MacDaniels collected in Tahiti; his mosses were reported upon by Bartram (1933a).

1930 Martin L. Grant collected pteridophytes on most of the islands of the Society archipelago. No bryophytes were collected (personal communication, 1963).

1932 Gerritt Parmile Wilder collected vascular plants on Makatea. His report (1934) listed no bryophytes.

1934 F. R. Fosberg and Harold St. John collected bryophytes and vascular plants on Tahiti and on adjacent archipelagos. Most noteworthy of their Tahitian collections is that they are apparently the first from higher elevations on the slopes of Mt. Orohena, the highest peak in south-central Polynesia. Their collections were reported upon by Bartram (1940).

1947 Edwin A. Phillips collected mosses on Bora Bora, the westernmost high island of the archipelago. His five specimens represent the first collections known to me to have ever been made on that island. Determinations were made by Bartram and the results reported by Phillips (1947); a set of the specimens was deposited in the Bishop Museum and duplicates from Bartram's herbarium are at Farlow.

1952 Professor Guillaumin and M. G. Bauman-Bodenheim made a research expedition to New Caledonia, collecting bryophytes in west Australia, Fiji, Tonga, and Tahiti. The mosses were determined by Bartram and reported upon by Hans Hürlimann (1963).

1956 Maxwell S. Doty and Jan Newhouse collected plants in the Society Islands but ignored bryophytes (personal communication, 1962).

1960 Hans Hürlimann collected bryophytes in Fiji, Tonga, and Tahiti. His specimens were identified by Bartram together with specimens collected by Guillaumin and Bauman-Bodenheim and were reported by Hürlimann in 1963. Hürlimann kindly sent me a manuscript copy of his paper, and Bartram loaned duplicates to me for study. Following Bartram's death in 1964 the specimens were sent to the Farlow Herbarium at Harvard to be placed with the Bartram Herbarium.

Henry Whittier landed at Papeete, Tahiti, in June, on board the schooner *Collegiate Rebel,* on an expedition directed by Harvey A. Miller for Miami University. The mosses collected during the two-week stay are reported here. The original collections are at Miami University.

Duplicates were distributed from the herbarium for deposit in the herbaria of the New York Botanical Garden, Bishop Museum, Geneva, Paris, and in Japan.

1961 Beatrice Krauss collected bryophytes in Tahiti and deposited the unidentified specimens in the Bishop Museum Herbarium. These are reported here.

1964 Bryce and Shirley Decker collected bryophytes on Tahiti and in the Marquesas at my request. Specimens of mosses collected in the Marquesas were reported by me in an earlier publication (1973); those collected on Tahiti are reported herein. Their collections of hepatics were sent to H. A. Miller for study.

Henry Whittier spent the months from September through November collecting bryophytes on Tahiti and Moorea, making nearly 1500 mixed collections of both mosses and hepatics. Hepatics were sent to Miller for study; the mosses are reported here. The original collection is deposited in the herbarium of the New York Botanical Garden. In addition to other American herbaria, duplicates were prepared for European and Japanese herbaria.

1966 Winona Welch collected mosses in the Society Islands and on other Pacific islands. Duplicates were kindly forwarded to me by her and by Howard Crum. The Society Islands collections are reported here.

1968 Rudolf Schuster collected hepatics on Tahiti during a brief visit. No mosses were collected (personal communication, 1968).

1971 M. M. J. van Balgooy collected on Tahiti and on Bora Bora in September, sending bryophyte specimens to me for determination. Most noteworthy of these collections is that they provide valuable additional specimens from Bora Bora, including such interesting new records as *Rhizogonium spiniforme* and *Leucobryum tahitense* as well as several other taxa hitherto unreported from that island.

EPILOGUE

In December, 1972, I traveled to Lille, France, to present a paper on the bryogeography of southeastern Polynesia at the First International Bryological Colloquium. On the advice of W. C. Steere and H. A. Miller, I visited the Museum National d'Histoire Naturelle in Paris, in search of the type specimens of species described by Bescherelle, reported by some to be elsewhere. I was kindly received by Mme V. Allorge and Mme S. Jovet-Ast, and to my great pleasure, Mme Jovet-Ast was able to produce Bescherelle's notebooks containing his reprints complete with personal annotations, critical correspondence, original pencil illustrations (some colored), and mounted specimens representing the species he described! Other important specimens from the Bescherelle herbarium were located without difficulty. The limited time at my disposal permitted the illustration and redescription of only one species, *Rhacomitrium papeetense,* known from a single collection on Tahiti. Now that the location of Bescherelle's type and authentic specimens is certain, I hope to return to Paris at some future date to complete the redescription and illustration of key taxa for a supplement to this present work.

ECOLOGICAL OBSERVATIONS AND NOTES

Papy's (1948) monograph on Society Islands ecology provides considerable climatological data. Rainfall varies markedly around Tahiti, both near sea level and at higher elevations. The most reliable data come from a weather station near Papeete, where the annual rainfall averages near 1900 mm, and may be as much as 2800 mm. However, Papeete is in a drier region of the island, but inland and more toward the windward side, and the annual rainfall averages over 2500 mm. Toward the interior of the island, where no long-term measurements have been made (to my knowledge), Papy estimated the rainfall to be in excess of 4500 mm. There are no records for the wettest localities—the windward mountain ridges and upper slopes of Mt. Orohena and the central portion of the island. Crampton (1916) estimated over 2500 *cm* a year, based upon the known rainfall of Papeete and the number of cloudy, rainy days in the island interior as viewed from near sea level. Williams (1933) estimated a rainfall of 1750 cm a year. A nearly continuous cloud cover (almost every day, between ten o'clock in the morning and three in the afternoon) exerts a marked effect upon temperature, relative humidity, and light intensity. Vegetation can trap large quantities of moisture in cloud or mist zones, effectively doubling or tripling the actual measurable rainfall, rendering rainfall data for such regions only partially useful as an ecological consideration.

The relative humidity at Papeete seldom reaches 80 per cent. Temperatures rarely exceed 32°C or fall below 21°C, averaging about 25–27°C. Of course, the data for Papeete do not reflect accurately the conditions on the windward side of the island, the interior of the island, or elevations far above sea level. Changes in temperature and humidity produce marked vegetational changes around the circumference and in the altitude on Tahiti. These changes are not always abrupt, but in general one can observe increased lushness in the vegetation as humidity and rainfall increase. Lichens and bryophytes provide the most obvious indicators. East of Venus Point in the northern Mahina District of Tahiti nui, for example, there is a sudden almost magical appearance of small, pendent tufts of *Usnea* (old man's beard lichen) on the trunks of the ubiquitous coconut palms. As one continues eastward through the Papenoo District of north-central Tahiti, mosses become more obvious as tufts or loose cushions on the trunks of *Artocarpus* (breadfruit) trees and coconut palms. At first there is an increase in the numbers of crustose lichens and small, turf-forming corticolous mosses such as *Calymperes* or *Macromitrium*. Farther along the coastline, into the wet, windward region of the island, cushions of *Thyridium constrictum*, 5–10 cm thick, form on the trunks of coconut palms (this is especially obvious in the northern Hitiaa District). Here also, *Syrrhopodon banksii* appears in tight cushions almost in the salt spray zone along the abbreviated shoreline, together with pendent festoons of the lichen *Usnea*, often more than 30 cm long. The southern and eastern parts of the peninsula are only a little drier than the northern side, despite an intervening backbone of mountains 1200 m high. The atmosphere becomes warmer and drier west of Papeari, and the waterfalls so evident near the coast on the northeast side of the island are located far from the shore in the recesses of deep valleys on the south and southwest sides of the island where the coastal plain reaches its maximum width.

The effect of variation in rainfall is also noticeable as one climbs inland and toward higher elevations on ridges. Here, not only the altitude but the orientation of the island to prevailing winds is important. On the Taiarapu Peninsula and in Hitiaa, tree ferns (*Cyathea*) appear within 500 m of sea level; on the northwest side of Tahiti, on the lower slopes of Mt. Aorai, tree ferns do not appear much below 1000 m. A similar variation occurs in the low altitude *Gleichenia* (*Dicranopteris*) and *Lantana* savanna. Near Papeete and Faaa, this savanna begins near sea level and extends to above 300 m, covering the gradual slopes or inclined plateau regions and lower ridges. Toward the east, however, this belt is compressed until the total vertical extent of the savanna is less than 200 m, as in the western Hitiaa District.

The extreme minimum temperature recorded at Papeete is about 17°C and the extreme high about 35°C. More typical temperature ranges are the 21°C–28°C recorded at Hamuta. A series of records for Hamuta has been compared with a similar series from the greater elevation at Fare Rau Ape, and indicate the nature of the decrease in temperature with increase in elevation. Papy (1948) estimated that the temperature drops about 0.5°C for each 100 m increase in elevation up to 800 m. Above this elevation the rate of decrease is more rapid. Above 1600 m, the temperature decrease is estimated at over 0.8°C per 100 m. It might be inferred that the temperature at the summit of Mt. Aorai and Mt. Orohena could be as much as 16°C colder than the temperature at Papeete. There is no evidence to indicate that freezing temperatures occur at the peaks of these mountains, but minimum temperatures may frequently drop below 11°C.

Papy (1948) reported that the humidity decreases markedly toward the mountain summits. On the high peaks and exposed ridges, the vegetation must be capable of withstanding rapid and extreme changes in humidity. Within a brief period, the 100 per cent humidity under cloud cover can change to less than 60 per cent when the clouds dissipate. The high peaks and exposed ridges are structurally and floristically quite distinct from the lower and more sheltered regions.

Relatively little literature exists on the ecology of Pacific islands bryophytes. Miller (1953, 1954, 1960) published brief accounts on bryophyte associations, societies, and succession in the Hawaiian Islands. Horikawa (1951, 1954), Hosokawa (1952), and others have reported on the ecology of certain Micronesian islands, including Kusaie, Ponape, and Yap, emphasizing the bryophytes.

The topography of islands such as Tahiti is so varied that different climatic zones are represented in distinctive vegetation patterns, from tropical-oceanic to subalpine in the horizontal distance of less than 2 km or in a vertical range of 1500–2000 m (Fig. 4). Papy (1948, pp. 189–239) classed the original vegetation of Tahiti and neighboring high islands, especially Raiatea, into three major levels or zones, some subdivided into subzones or belts (Table 1). These include: the *Maritime Zone*, comprising, according to Papy, a submangrove belt, a littoral belt, and an adlittoral belt; the *Mesotropical Zone*, which Papy had some difficulty in delimiting because its width varies considerably with the orientation and topography of the island; and the *Hygrotropical Zone*, which corresponds, according to Papy, with Egler's (1939) Pluviotropical Zone on Oahu in the Hawaiian Islands, and which is subdivided into four major belts: the plateaus and middle slopes, the forested lower valleys, the humid forest or "rain forest" with limited sunlight, and the summit regions over 1500 m high. The middle

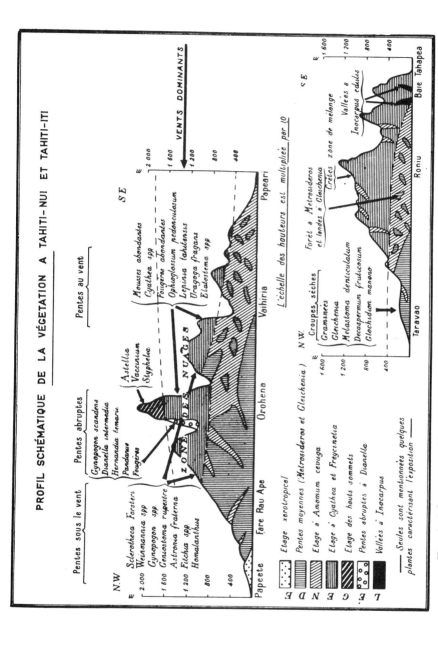

Fig. 4. Schematic profile of the vegetation of Tahiti nui and Tahiti iti. (From Papy [1948], reproduced with permission of the publisher.)

slopes and plateaus were further subdivided into the forest of *Metrosideros* and *Dodonea*; scrub *Metrosideros* and *Gleichenia* (*Dicranopteris*) pseudosavanna; and abrupt slopes, at 700–1000 m. The Hygrotropical Zone is comprised of wet regions with annual rainfall exceeding 2000 mm. Lower valley forests are relatively consistent in vegetational composition and community structure. The upper slopes and ridges Papy treated as having distinctive windward and leeward aspects. The middle and upper valleys, from about 200–600 m to over 2000 m, are unique. At the upper limits, what has been called "humid forest" or "rain forest" by various authors, is characteristic, but a more proper designation is "cloud

TABLE 1. Ecological Zonation[a]

Maritime Zone
    Submangrove
    Littoral
    Adlittoral
Mesotropical Zone
Hygrotropical Zone
    Plateaus (xerophytic) and middle slopes
        Forest of *Metrosideros* and *Dodonea*
        Scrub of *Metrosideros*, pseudosavanna of *Dicranopteris*
        Abrupt slopes 700–1000 m (2000–3000 feet)
    Lower Valley Forests of *Amomum* and Guava
    Humid, High Elevation Forests
        Middle and upper valleys, 200–600 m (to over 2000 feet)
        Wet upper slopes and ridges, 900–1500 m (3000–5000 feet and over)
            Windward slopes
            Leeward slopes
    High Summits of Tahiti, Moorea, and Raiatea, 1500–2065 m (about 4500–7339 feet)

a. Modified from Papy, 1948.

forest," in keeping with the characteristic cloud cover, constant high humidity, and the low, gnarled, moss-covered miniature trees.

MARITIME ZONE

This major zone occupies the lowermost tier of vegetational belts and extends from sea level to about 30–50 m elevation. It is this region which is most important to man and most affected by him.

The prevailing climatic condition is dry (Papy, 1948–1958, p. 142). The maritime zone encompasses the low islets of coral on the south side of Tahiti and the basaltic islets on the north side, as well as the beach or littoral belt and the coastal plain.

Submangrove

The mangrove swamp, with its characteristic species, does not exist in the Society Islands. The genus *Rhizophora* does grow on Moorea, but it is of recent introduction as it is in the Hawaiian Islands. Although *Rhizophora* is not present, *Barringtonia* and *Hibiscus* form associations in which one or the other may be dominant, and which, to a limited extent, duplicate the mangrove ecosystem (Papy, 1948). Plants in this ecosystem have a high degree of tolerance to seawater or to brackish water; mineral nutrients are in excellent supply. Mosses are rare in this belt. Represented are members of wide-ranging groups such as the Calymperaceae (*Calymperes* and *Syrrhopodon*), Leucobryaceae (*Leucophanes*) on bark, Bryaceae (*Brachymenium*, *Bryum*) on coral sand or rocks, and Hypnaceae (*Ectropothecium*, *Isopterygium*) on coral sand and rocks, on bark, or on decaying wood.

Littoral

The beach ecosystem varies considerably, depending upon the orientation of the island and upon the nature of the parent material. Exposed basalt shelves extend into the sea and in places black sand beaches are present. In Hitiaa the littoral community may extend to the sea, with the adlittoral or beach community completely absent (see Fig. 5). On white coral beaches, plants are typical strand species such as *Ipomoea pes-caprae*, *Vigna lutea*, and some grasses and sedges. Just behind this association, but within the confines of the littoral belt, are *Pemphis acidula*, *Tournefortia* and *Scaevola*, and *Hibiscus tiliaceus* together with *Cocoloba uvifera* and *Casuarina*, which are frequently planted. The beaches of black basaltic sand are represented by an association which has developed apparently in response to higher moisture levels and a more acid pH. The sedges are the dominant graminoid forms, among them *Cyperus pennatus*, *C. polystachyus*, *C. flabelliformis*, and *Fimbristylis cymosa* (Papy, 1948). Bryophytes usually are absent because they seem to lack the physiological tolerance for the saline conditions, the dry atmospheric conditions, and the intense light which is characteristic of the beaches.

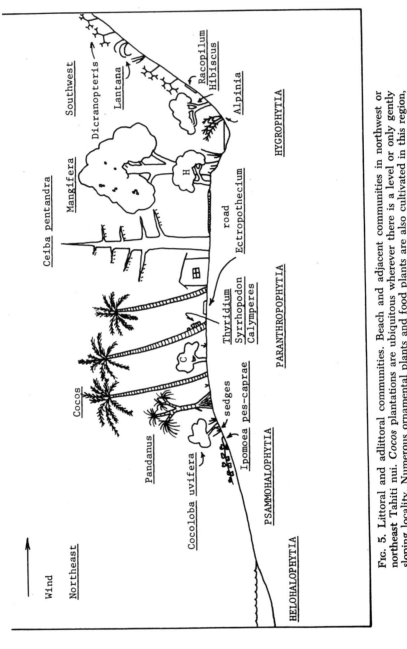

Fig. 5. Littoral and adlittoral communities. Beach and adjacent communities in northwest or northeast Tahiti nui. *Cocos* plantations are ubiquitous wherever there is a level or only gently sloping locality. Numerous ornamental plants and food plants are also cultivated in this region, which suggests the use of the term "paranthropophytia" to denote man's influence. The lower slopes which touch the adlittoral belt are a part of the Mesotropical Zone.

Adlittoral

Adjacent to the beach communities, this belt includes the coastal plain and the lowest slopes of Tahiti. In some regions, notably the north side of Tahiti, this belt may also be much abbreviated wherever the eroded slopes extend directly into the ocean and the prevailing winds bring such an abundance of water that the Mesotropical or even the Hygrotropical zones may extend nearly to sea level (see Fig. 6).

On the south side of Tahiti, especially toward the west, a more protected shoreline and a reduced rate of erosion, determined by the rain shadow, has permitted the development of a broad coastal plain. At the upper limit of the adlittoral belt, perhaps 75–100 m elevation in this region, the belt is met by a broad Mesotropical Zone.

In pre-European days, the Tahitians and the residents of the neighboring islands lived, not in discrete communities, but in almost randomly spaced homes dispersed along the coastal plains around the islands, and on Tahiti, extending up into the major valleys such as the Papenoo or Vaihiria for some miles. The vegetation, apparently once forest which extended right to the littoral belt, has been profoundly modified by the Polynesians, but it must have presented Wallis, when he arrived on the *Dolphin* in 1767, with a far different aspect than it has today. An ever increasing commerce transformed the coastal plain into a nearly continuous series of copra plantations, and the residents have introduced ornamental plants from the Old World and New World Tropics. Increasing population pressure has forced man's habitations up onto the lower slopes, especially near Papeete, and communities have arisen here and there along the western and southern shores of Tahiti nui. There is little or no land in this belt that does not show the effects of man's influence, and del Villar has appropriately provided for this perturbing biotic factor with a classification of *Paranthropophytia*. Were it not for man's influence, this belt might be classed better under his *Subhygrophytia*, for the land once supported forest vegetation; for practical purposes, the copra plantations might be considered a proper forest formation-type. The dry portions (*Mesoxerophytia*) along the southwestern and the western coasts parallel to some extent a kind of Mediterranean forest. Intermediate regions are difficult to classify because of vegetation zone compression

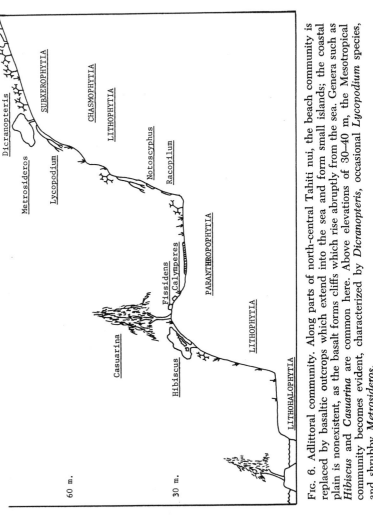

FIG. 6. Adlittoral community. Along parts of north-central Tahiti nui, the beach community is replaced by basaltic outcrops which extend into the sea and form small islands; the coastal plain is nonexistent, as the basalt forms cliffs which rise abruptly from the sea. Genera such as *Hibiscus* and *Casuarina* are common here. Above elevations of 30–40 m, the Mesotropical community becomes evident, characterized by *Dicranopteris*, occasional *Lycopodium* species, and shrubby *Metrosideros*.

toward the windward side and the modification of the original vegetation.

The presence of the lichen *Usnea* on the trunks of coconut palms is a response to higher and more constant humidity levels accompanying increased rainfall on the north and northeast side of Tahiti nui; the appearance of *Thyridium constrictum*, a moss forming thick cushions on *Cocos* trunks, indicates a still higher rainfall. Other mosses found in the same region are *Macromitrium, Calymperes, Syrrhopodon, Leucobryum*, and *Ectropothecium*. Mosses of this belt are limited in number and endemism is negligible. They may be classed as *Ectobiophytia* when they appear on living tree trunks, as *Pezosaprophytia* when the substratum is decaying wood, or as *Chasmophytia* when they appear in rock crevices.

MESOTROPICAL ZONE

Papy (1948) characterizes the climate of this zone using Thornthwaite's formula BIA'a', and compares it to the region of Oahu described by Egler (1939) as having a rainfall between 250 and 1250 mm. This zone begins at the upper limit of the adlittoral belt and extends to, or slightly beyond, 300 m elevation, depending upon the orientation of the island. It is in this zone on Oahu that *Prosopis chilensis* is common. In Tahiti as in Hawaii, the genus is introduced, and it is not common on Tahiti. Among the plants typical of this zone are *Abrus, Alphitonia, Buettneria, Wickstroemia*, and *Glochidion*. The fern genus *Gleichenia*, which extends into the adlittoral belt of the Maritime Zone, appears together with *Lycopodium* in cleared areas. This zone, markedly controlled by man, has predominantly introduced plants such as *Lantana camara, Citrus* spp., *Mangifera, Eugenia, Eucalyptus*, and other common species. Structurally the communities of this zone may be classed as forest, savanna, scrub, meadow, and prairie. The associations of this zone have been broadly outlined by Papy. Near Papeete, in the Fautaua Valley, del Villar's mesophytic classification of *Subhygrophytia* or of *Mesoxerophytia* is well applied. Mosses show a low degree of endemism, under 25 per cent, but higher than in the adlittoral belt of the Maritime Zone. Members of the Calymperaceae are more common in the Mesotropical Zone, and the genus *Fissidens*, which appears in or near stream beds, in rock crevices, among tree roots, or on banks where moisture is relatively constant, is also much more common, together with members of the Orthotrichaceae, Hypnaceae, and Sematophyllaceae.

HYGROTROPICAL ZONE

Papy subdivided this zone into several belts and regions, the first described as *Plateaus and Middle Slopes*. A complex of communities, primarily determined by rainfall, are represented in this category. Papy recognized three basic community groups within this belt: *Metrosideros–Dodonea* forest, *Metrosideros* scrub–*Gleichenia* pseudosavanna, and one not designated by a plant association, but called simply *Abrupt Slopes*, 700–1000 m.

Metrosideros–Dodonea Forest

This low forest or woodland is markedly altered by man for cultivation of *Coffea* and *Vanilla* (Fig. 7), and might thus be classed as *Paranthropophytia*, especially as it may be seen in the Hitiaa District of northeast Tahiti nui, at an elevation between 100 and 500 m. Some of the basic forest structure, which includes *Dodonea* and *Metrosideros* as characteristic genera, is still intact. At the exposed heads of ridges leading to this sloping plateau area, the forest is dominated by *Metrosideros* of tree size (to, or exceeding, 8 m), and by *Pandanus*. *Dodonea* is not very common in the areas I visited, and the understory is comprised mainly of *Coffea* (cultivated) and *Hibiscus tiliaceus*, which, together with an occasional *Aleurites* (candle nut) and frequent *Cordyline terminalis* (ti), strongly suggests similar forests in the Hawaiian Islands. *Asplenium nidus*, the bird's nest fern, is common on the ground and on tree trunks and crotches. The characterization *Subhygrophytia* applies well to the lower limits of this woodland, and *Hygrophytia* to the better developed forest where water is abundant in depressions and at higher elevations. The mosses of this belt are interesting, and epiphytic forms are especially abundant. Among them are the relatively rare *Syrrhopodon ciliatus*, one of the most beautiful of mosses, intermixed with *Rhizogonium*, *Leucobryum*, and *Exodictyon dentatum*, forming restricted associations on tree trunks or decaying wood, characterized as *Pezosaprophytia*. The novel moss *Calomnion schistostegiellum* is found here on *Cyathea* trunks. On long-lived leaves and stable bark surfaces, rather sizable communities or associations may develop. In especially wet localities even

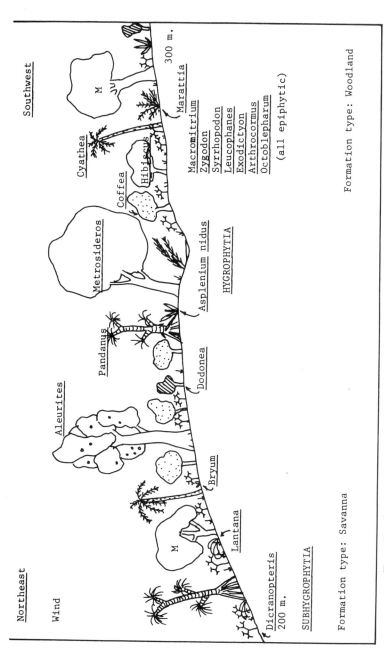

Northeast

Wind

Southwest

Aleurites

Metrosideros

Cyathea

M

300 m.

Pandanus

Coffea

Hibiscus

Marattia

Lantana

Bryum

Dodonea

Asplenium nidus

Macromitrium
Zygodon
Syrrhopodon
Leucophanes
Exodictyon
Arthrocormus
Octoblepharum

(all epiphytic)

Dicranopteris
200 m.

SUBHYGROPHYTIA

HYGROPHYTIA

Formation type: Savanna

Formation type: Woodland

Fig. 7. The region that is depicted in this plate is the *Metrosideros–Dodonea* forest described by Papy (1948), and is a continuation of the scrub-pseudosavanna which at higher elevations becomes a woodland, characterized by low trees of *Metrosideros, Aleurites,* and *Hibiscus,* with occasional tree ferns, *Cyathea,* and the screw pine, *Pandanus.* In the Hitiaa District on windward Tahiti nui, where this hypothetical transect is placed, *Coffea* and *Vanilla* are cultivated in partially cleared areas.

Psidium, the guava, which has a bark that scales off in sheets (rather like *Platanus*), may support corticolous epiphytes, especially hepatics. Watercourses which drain the sloping plateau have their own associations comparable in some respects to those of the upper valleys. *Amomum* or *Alpinia* is common in such wet environments. The moss genus *Fissidens*, especially *F. mangarevensis* and *F. nadeaudii*, which are large, robust taxa, is common, but curiously *Thuidium*, which would certainly be expected in similar habitats in the Hawaiian Islands and elsewhere, seems rare. When the genus is present, the plants are quite reduced in form and seem somewhat atypical.

Metrosideros Scrub–*Gleichenia* Pseudosavanna

The variation in habit and distribution of *Metrosideros* is quite wide. In this belt, the formation type used by Dansereau (1966) is *scrub* or *savanna*. In the former, *Metrosideros* would have only to be more than 0.1 m tall and occupy at least 25 per cent of the cover. The two types intergrade with a transition between responses which can be identified as *Subxerophytia* and *Mesoxerophytia*. The scrub and savanna belt forms, on the lower slopes, the transition between the Mesotropical Zone and the Hygrotropical Zone.

The flora of this belt is monotonous, and the vegetational structure relatively uniform (Fig. 8). Edaphic conditions are poor; the soil is lateritic, gravelly to clayey, brown to bright red, with excellent drainage. The belt is subjected to periodic fire and to high rainfall at irregular intervals during the dry season and for continuous periods during the wet summer season. It seems debatable whether water deficiency or temperature excess, or even edaphic conditions might prove to be the controlling or limiting factor. This type of community or vegetation structure has elements which extend along ridges to high elevations on Mt. Aorai, where the decrease in temperature is such that high extremes rarely occur, so the classification of *Subxerophytia* does not always apply; fluctuations in relative humidity may be great at the higher elevations, so the classification *Mesoxerophytia* may be appropriate. The low organic content of the soil, coupled with mineral loss through leaching, suggests that *Chersophytia* might also be considered.

In addition to *Gleichenia* and *Metrosideros*, scrubby *Dodonea* and *Lantana* are common together with *Paspalum* and *Fimbristylis*.

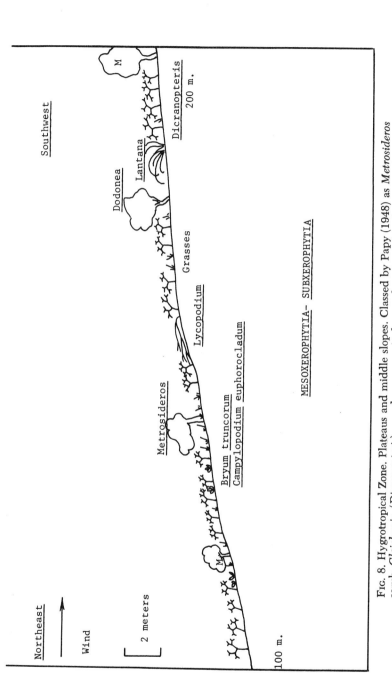

FIG. 8. Hygrotropical Zone. Plateaus and middle slopes. Classed by Papy (1948) as *Metrosideros* scrub–*Gleichenia* (*Dicranopteris*) pseudosavanna. At lower elevations the plateaus and middle slopes are characterized by *Dicranopteris* and grasses, with occasional shrubby *Dodonea* and *Metrosideros*; *Lantana camara* may form extensive patches. Mosses are rare and are usually limited to small turfs of *Bryum billardieri* (formerly *B. truncorum*) under the dense fern growth, or to *Campylopodium euphorocladum* in exposed localities.

Lycopodium cernuum is relatively common. Among the limited number of moss taxa in this belt are *Bryum billardieri*, appearing frequently in the shade of *Gleichenia* ferns, and in exposed locations, *Campylopodium euphorocladum*, *Trematodon*, and *Wilsoniella*, together with the hepatic *Notoscyphus paroicus* on soil and rocks.

Abrupt Slopes (700–1000 m)

In the ecosystems of the abrupt slopes, *Gleichenia* and *Metrosideros* exist wherever there is a foothold. In addition to these, Papy reports *Celtis paniculata*, *Dianella intermedia*, and *Ficus tinctoria* as representative plants. Graminoid genera such as *Paspalum* are common. All but the most impossibly steep or rocky slopes are 60–75 per cent covered by vegetation, but large barren areas testify to masses of vegetation and earth scaling off during periods of high rainfall. The prime controlling factor is the rocky substratum on which plants must grow: *Lithophytia*. Secondarily, depending upon water availability, *Subhygrophytia* or *Mesoxerophytia* would apply. Formation types range from crusts of lichens or bryophytes, to tundra, desert, or steppe, depending upon the degree of slope. Mosses of this region are *Campylopus*, *Racopilum*, *Campylopodium*, *Pogonatum*, *Trematodon*, and *Wilsoniella*. The hepatic *Porella*, capable of withstanding extremes of desiccation, forms massive, loose sheets over otherwise barren rock surfaces in the Fautaua Valley.

Lower Valley Forests of *Amomum* and Guava

A wide variety of associations occurs in the broad, lower valley forests. At the lower end of the Vaihiria Valley on the southeastern side of Tahiti nui, and near the mouth of the Haavini Valley on the north side of the Taiarapu Peninsula, extensive associations restricted to *Amomum* or to bamboo appear within a community dominated by mapé, *Inocarpus edulis* or Tahitian chestnut, and by *Barringtonia asiatica*. At the lowest levels, this forest is partially replaced by cultivated coconut, coffee, and vanilla. Under natural stands of *Amomum*, a ginger, little can grow, and even shade-tolerating bryophytes are excluded. *Angiopteris* and *Marattia* are two of the largest ferns and are found frequently on the valley floor of the less disturbed areas. The side slopes are commonly inhabited by *Asplenium nidus,* and at the transition to higher altitude forest, the tree fern *Cyathea* appears. Epiphytes abound, including small ferns such as *Trichomanes omphalodes*—with bizarre peltate leaves pressed tightly against their substrates—lycopods, and orchids, all associated with deep tufts of mosses, especially *Acroporium,* on tree branches. A welcome food for the camper who has time to roast plantains, is *Musa fehi,* common to the valleys. Other common mosses of the Lower Valley Forest are *Macromitrium, Leucophanes, Leucobryum, Taxithelium, Trichosteleum, Isopterygium, Vesicularia, Ectropothecium, Calymperes,* and *Syrrhopodon,* all forming associations or unions whose ultimate order of response might be termed *Ectobiophytia* or *Pezosaprophytia.* Few taxa grow on bare soil, but among these are *Homaliodendron exiguum, Distichophyllum,* and *Pogonatum.* When light is insufficient for vascular plants to compete successfully for territory on the wet valley floor, the darkness or some biotic factor also inhibits soil-inhabiting bryophytes that thrive in the moist, shaded environments on stream banks.

The basic response of this forest community is properly *Hygrophytia* or *Subhygrophytia,* depending upon the elevation and the location of the valley. The stream beds harbor separate associations classed in del Villar's system as *Limnophytia.* The basic formation type, following Dansereau's (1966) usage, is forest; less frequently, or at higher elevations, woodland (Fig. 9).

HUMID, HIGH ELEVATION FORESTS

Middle and Upper Valleys

The middle and upper valleys are especially interesting in their floristics and biogeography. The relatively undisturbed associations seen in these forests and woodlands (scrub, at highest elevations), are extensions or continuations of the lower elevation communities in a structural sense, but differ in floristic content. Endemism is highest in the middle and upper valleys.

Water availability is constant in this belt and the humidity is always high: *Hygrophytia* applies well. Epiphytes are prominent, especially on *Hibiscus tiliaceus,* which may form the entire canopy. *Inocarpus edulis* is not a significant member of the upper valley communities but is prominent in the middle valleys. At higher

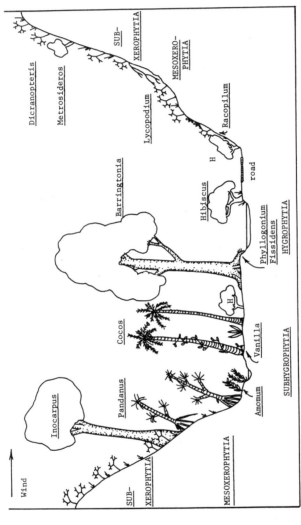

FIG. 9. Mesotropical Zone. Lower valley forest of *Amomum* and *Hibiscus*. Papy (1948) used *Guava* as characteristic of this forest, and it is, but guava is of recent origin, and it might be more appropriate to use *Hibiscus* and *Amomum* or *Inocarpus*. The valley sides are often covered with *Dicranopteris*, and *Lycopodium* appears frequently. *Amomum* is restricted to the dampest portion of the valley floor but is usually not immediately adjacent to the streams. In this belt, *Racopilum* and *Rhynchostegium* may be common on vertical rock faces. In the streams, *Marchantia* appears on rocks in sunny places, and *Dumortiera* in shaded localities, especially on mud banks at stream edges. The Haavini Valley, Taiarapu Peninsula, about 100 m, is typical of this zone.

elevations, the entire valley floor is occupied by stream bed, and slopes begin immediately on either side. Large ferns such as *Marattia* and *Angiopteris* are much more common than in the lower valleys, and the tree fern *Cyathea* appears first as a plant already of good size, perhaps 1–2 m tall. The few small plants suggest that *Cyathea* is today extended beyond its optimum environmental range and that the area now occupied may gradually decrease in the future. Tree ferns seldom grow directly on the exposed ridges and appear most commonly on the sheltered leeward slopes; some are more than 10 m tall.

Epiphytic mosses are most abundant and diverse in the middle and upper valleys. *Spiridens*, with stems more than 0.4 m long, forms large golden tufts which are nearly always restricted to *Cyathea* trunks, but it is rarely found at the limits of the range of this tree fern, because it is apparently more sensitive to humidity fluctuations than is *Cyathea*. Moss genera such as *Fissidens, Ectropothecium, Calomnion,* and *Papillaria* are common on tree trunks and on *Cyathea*.

The central crater of Tahiti nui might well be placed within the province of the upper valleys, although in many respects it is unique. More correctly an elevated, dissected plateau, exposed to the north by the extreme breadth of the ancient volcano crater, to sunlight, wind, and to a high rainfall, the plateau has a superficial water table resulting from the capture of rainwater by the surrounding ridges and a combination of relatively impermeable (or saturated) rock and organic material at its floor. Much of the vegetation of the crater forms a community which can be classed structurally as savanna, with segments of prairie dominated by large grassy expanses interrupted by *Asplenium nidus* and patches of the ubiquitous *Gleichenia*. At intervals, groups of *Metrosideros* or isolated *Pandanus* appear in the community. Along watercourses, *Amomum* forms limited associations. Almost nothing is known of the bryophytes of the central crater.

Wet Upper Slopes and Ridges

The upper slopes and ridges are dominated by a scrub association of *Gleichenia* and *Metrosideros*, with the upper ridges especially characterized by an occasional *Weinmannia*, a small tree, or more rarely, by *Santalum*, the sandlewood. The fern genus *Elaphoglossum* is common on tree trunks together with the moss genera *Acro-*

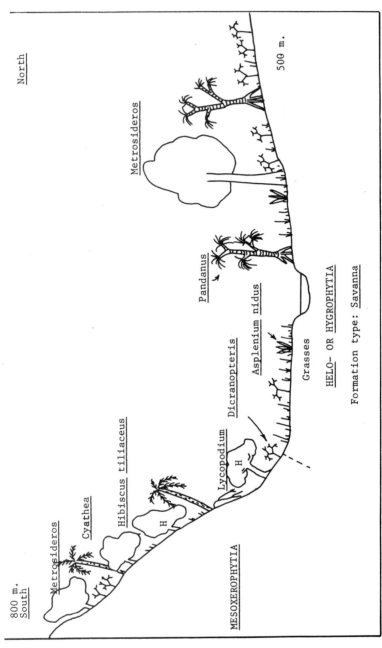

FIG. 10. Hygrotropical Zone. A representative transect from the south-central portion of the volcano crater of central Tahiti nui, where the elevated dissected floor is approximately 500 m above sea level. At the left is the 800 meter-high ridge which separates Papenoo from Vaihiria. The vegetation structure is essentially that of the formation type classified by Dansereau (1957) as "savanna" and has scattered *Metrosideros* and *Pandanus*, with grasses, *Asplenium nidus*, and *Dicranopteris* covering the ground.

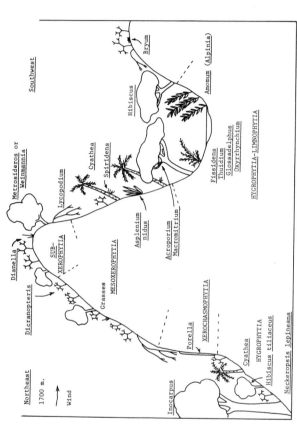

Fig. 11. Hygrotropical Zone. Upper slopes and ridges. Sheltered slopes and upper valleys have trees 5–10 meters tall, with grasses, *Marattia*, and *Asplenium* ferns forming a lower story. *Dicranopteris* grows wherever there is sufficient light; where protected, *Cyathea* also appears. The exposed ridges and slopes are almost exclusively the domain of *Dicranopteris* and shrubby *Weinmannia* or *Metrosideros*. *Lycopodium* species are common. Among the mosses are *Dicranoloma*, *Dicnemon*, *Macromitrium*, and *Acroporium*. On the sheltered slopes, especially associated with *Cyathea*, are the moss genera *Calomnion*, *Garovaglia*, and *Spiridens*, the last of these especially prominent, with stems up to 18–20 in. long, standing erect from the tree fern trunks.

porium, Macromitrium, and *Ptychomnion.* On the ground, the moss *Dicnemon rugosum* is frequent. Essentially *Mesoxerophytic,* the vegetation is regularly exposed to intense sunlight, but the constant trade winds and extreme elevation combine to keep temperatures cool and moderate in fluctuation. Humidity may vary considerably, but during periods of cloud cover the vegetation intercepts water to effectively multiply the amount of rainfall measured in conventional terms (Figs. 10, 11). Endemism for mosses is estimated at 35–40 per cent in the middle and upper valleys, but on the wet upper slopes and ridges it is lower, more nearly 20 per cent.

High Summits

The limited scrub or steppe formations of the summit are dominated by species of *Vaccinium, Metrosideros,* and *Dicranopteris. Styphelia (Cyathodes), Weinmannia, Dianella,* and *Lycopodium* are common. Two species of *Dicranopteris,* one with a broad range, the other restricted to the uppermost elevations, are present together with two species of *Lycopodium* which demonstrate a similar distribution pattern. The extent of this subalpine zone is variable and dependent upon the orientation of the island. According to Maurice Jay (personal communication, 1964), one of the few people to have visited Mt. Aorai's larger sister peak, Mt. Orohena, the summit of Orohena is much wetter and colder. Although Orohena is only about 200 m higher than Aorai, the mountain lies to the windward of Aorai, and is subject to the full force of the trade winds (Fig. 12).

The best designation for the high summit vegetation may be *Subxerophytia,* but at the summit of Mt. Aorai, the vegetation has been stripped and several feet of the actual peak removed to permit the construction of a rest house. This has also been done at the summit of Mt. Orohena, but visitors are rare, and it is to be hoped that the vegetation there is less disturbed. Aorai is a tourist attraction for hundreds of visitors each year. Dansereau (1966) compared the Puerto Rican montane scrub vegetation with Madeira and New Zealand, in the simplicity of its composition, the well-marked dominance by a few species, and the importance of mosses. I have no data for the accumulation of fibrous organic matter, but judging from the springiness of the trail, there is a fairly large mass of organic material in the less disturbed areas adjacent to the summit of Mt. Aorai. Immediately beneath the summit, the scrub vege-

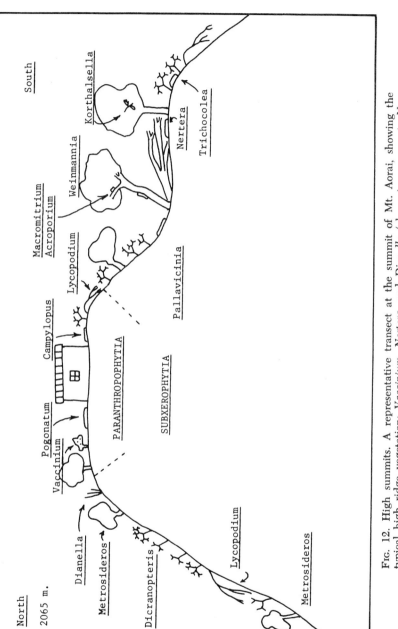

Fig. 12. High summits. A representative transect at the summit of Mt. Aorai, showing the typical high ridge vegetation: *Vaccinium*, *Nertera*, and *Dianella* (elements common to New Zealand, the Society Islands, and the Hawaiian Islands). Mosses of the summit are *Pogonatum* and *Campylopus introflexus*, but many more taxa appear in the less disturbed, slightly lower ridge just beyond the summit.

tation has some of the structural aspects of the "elfin" or scrub cloud forest at the summit of Mt. Kaala on Oahu, Hawaii (1300 m), but it is quite limited in extent.

Although certain vascular plants represent interesting endemics, the general level of endemism is low and the floristic affinities with Hawaii, New Zealand, the Marquesas, and other high Pacific Islands are quite clear. For mosses, endemism is below 20 per cent.

SYSTEMATIC TREATMENT

The genera and species reported herein have been derived from previous records and from herbarium specimens deposited in the Bernice P. Bishop Museum, the Farlow Herbarium, the U.S. National Museum, the Conservatoire et Jardin Botaniques, Geneva, the Museum National et d'Histoire Naturelle, Paris, and the New York Botanical Garden Herbarium. Included are the results of studies made on specimens from my own collections, those in the private herbarium of Harvey A. Miller, and those sent to me by helpful field collectors around the world. My own collections, made in 1960 and in 1964, are deposited in the herbaria of Miami University and the New York Botanical Garden.

The history of bryological collection and exploration shows that reports of mosses from the Society Islands have been based upon collections by transient sailors, amateur naturalists, ship's surgeons, and botanists specializing in flowering plants, and are scattered in the publications of Bescherelle (1895, 1898, 1901), Brotherus (1924), Bartram (1931, 1933a, 1940, 1950), and others. Nearly two hundred years have elapsed since the first recorded collection was made on Tahiti, and in that time, the only comprehensive bryological study with a review of past collections, and a report of unpublished new collections, was made by Emile Bescherelle (1895a). Since that time, major publications treating critical regions such as Java (Fleischer, 1904–1923), the Philippines (Bartram, 1939), New Zealand (Sainsbury, 1955), Micronesia (Miller, Whittier, and Bonner, 1963; Smith, 1969), and Hawaii (Bartram, 1933b), have appeared together with numerous small papers reporting new collections or providing up-dated species catalogs from the Pacific area. These include, in part, the publications of Bartram (1936, 1938, 1943, 1944, 1948, 1950, 1953, 1956), Brotherus (1910, 1918, 1924), Brotherus and Watts (1915), Cardot (1901, 1908, 1912), Dixon (1919, 1922, 1927), Hürlimann (1963, 1965), Miller (1953, 1954, 1957, 1959, 1960, 1967), Potier de la Varde (1912), Whittier (1973), Whittier and Miller (1967), Whittier and Whittier (1975), Schultze-Motel (1963a, 1963b, 1973), van Zanten (1964), Hoe (1974), and others.

Brotherus' treatment of the mosses in the second edition of Engler and Prantl's *Natürliche Pflanzenfamilien* (1924–1925) provides diagnostic keys, illustrations, and geographical information. A useful contemporary overview of moss families and their respective genera was provided by Harvey A. Miller, who allowed the author to examine the manuscript of his text (in final preparation) on this subject.

Each species is cited as fully as possible. Whenever possible, illustrations have been prepared from authentic specimens. Diagnostic treatments are not always complete, and in some instances are based upon a translation or are constituted by a reproduction of the original description to avoid possible confusion. The author considers this regrettable, but hopes that as teaching duties permit, and as travel opportunities become available, herbaria where authentic specimens are housed can be visited, allowing new descriptions and original illustrations to be prepared as a supplement to this work. Many groups will require more intensive study under the eye of the monographer before their position in the Society Islands flora will become clear. The *Index Muscorum* (van der Wijk, Margadant, and Florschutz, 1959–1969) has been used as the authority for nomenclatural recombinations, epithets, and bibliographic citations, except where indicated.

Collection numbers not otherwise identified are those of the author (160–400 [1960], 2000–3500 [1964]).

KEY TO FAMILIES OF SOCIETY ISLANDS MOSSES

1. Leaves in 2 opposite rows (distichous), apparently in 2 opposite rows (but with attachment around stem), or in 3 distinct rows, with 2 rows of larger lateral leaves and a third row, either dorsal or ventral, of smaller leaves
   2. Leaves strictly in 2 rows
      3. Leaf blade doubled near the base on the side of the costa (rib) nearest the stem and single on the opposite, lower side ....I. Fissidentaceae.
      3. Leaf blade simple, not doubled near the base ....XXIII. Phyllogoniaceae.
   2. Leaves apparently in 2 opposite rows or in 3 distinct rows with 2 rows of larger lateral leaves

3. Leaves apparently in 2 opposite rows, undulate or wrinkled at right angles to the leaf axis___XXIV. Neckeraceae.
3. Leaves in 3 distinct rows, with 2 rows of larger lateral leaves
    4. Leaves unbordered; upper row of leaves differentiated, smaller than lateral leaves; plants prostrate_____
_____XVIII. Racopilaceae.
    4. Leaves bordered; lower row of leaves differentiated, plants with secondary stems erect or inclined
        5. Underleaves plane, unspecialized; leaf borders distinct; plants usually (although not always) branched, frondose, with the appearance of a flattened tree_____XXX. Hypopterygiaceae.
        5. Underleaves not plane, modified into inflated "water sacs" near their bases; leaf borders indistinct, of 1 cell layer; plants usually not branched____
_____XXXI. Cyathophoraceae.
1. Leaves obviously in more than 2 rows as they originate on the stem (but may be compressed into one plane—complanate)
    2. Leaves black below; apices blunt, cells linear, sinuose_____
_____VI. Grimmiaceae.
    2. Leaves not black below, may be variously colored, green or hyaline, apices and cells variable
        3. Leaf cross section near base shows 3 or more layers of cells, with hyaline cell layers above and below a median layer of chlorophyllose cells_____IV. Leucobryaceae.
        3. Leaf cross section near base shows 1 layer of cells or lacks median chlorophyllose cell layer
            4. Inner basal cells adjacent to the costa hyaline, empty, sharply differentiated and enlarged in contrast to the chlorophyllose cells of the upper lamina_____
_____V. Calymperaceae.
            4. Inner basal cells not markedly differentiated from outer lamina cells, but may be hyaline or colored
                5. Leaves with longitudinal lamellae 3–8 cells high on lamina upper surface___XXXIX. Polytrichaceae.
                5. Leaves lacking lamellae on upper surface of lamina
                    6. Stems usually erect, dichotomously branched, seta terminal on main or lateral branches (Acrocarpous mosses)

7. Calyptra large, campanulate to cucullate, often pilose............XVII. Orthotrichaceae.
7. Calyptra small, cucullate, usually hairless and smooth
   8. Peristome single
      9. Peristome teeth divided into 32 filiform, papillose branches....................
         ....VII. Pottiaceae.
      9. Peristome teeth broad at base, entire or cleft above
         10. Leaves linear-lanceolate, unbordered, or if bordered, then cells nearly isodiametric and not porose
             ....III. Dicranaceae.
         10. Leaves ovate, bordered by a broad band of cells lacking chlorophyll; lamina cells porose....................
             ....II. Dicnemonaceae.
   8. Peristome double
      9. Leaves broad, abruptly pointed to broadly rounded, cells large, mostly more than 20 μ wide
         10. Leaves firm, cells isodiametric to less than 2 times longer than broad
             ....X. Mniaceae.
         10. Leaves soft, cells 2–3 times longer than broad, leaf tips broadly rounded....VIII. Splachnobryaceae.
      9. Leaves narrow, lanceolate, acuminate, cells narrow and elongate, usually less than 10 μ wide
         10. Capsules approximately spherical, striate to furrowed when dry........
             ....XV. Bartramiaceae.
         10. Capsules elongate, ovoid to cylindric, usually not striate or furrowed when dry
             11. Upper leaf cells elongate, 4–6-sided, thin-walled

12. Cell length:width ratio to 7–8:1............IX. Bryaceae.

12. Cell length:width ratio not more than 2:1........................ ....XI. Leptostomaceae.

11. Upper leaf cells quadrate, iso-diametric, thick-walled

12. Leaves arranged uniformly around the stem, seta on short, lateral basal branch ....XII. Rhizogoniaceae.

12. Leaves arranged in 3 distinct ranks, seta terminal.... ....XIII. Calomniaceae.

6. Stems usually prostrate, forming mats or tangled wefts, frequently and irregularly branched, seta lateral on stem (Pleurocarpous mosses)

7. Stems with leaves 3-ranked, lateral leaves asymmetrical with either a lower row or an upper row of differentiated, symmetrical leaves

8. Leaves unbordered; all stems prostrate, upper row of leaves differentiated, smaller than lateral leaves........................ ....XVIII. Racopilaceae.

8. Leaves bordered; secondary stems erect or inclined, frondose (branching in 1 plane) or unbranched, lower row of leaves (amphigastria) symmetrical, differentiated

9. Underleaves plane, undifferentiated; leaf borders distinct; plants usually but not always branched, frondose, with the appearance of a flattened tree............ XXX. Hypopterygiaceae.

9. Underleaves modified into inflated "water sacs"; leaf borders indistinct, of 1 cell layer; plants usually not branched, not frondose........................ ....XXXI. Cyathophoraceae.

7. Leaves in more than 3 ranks (may be complanate), leaves not markedly differentiated
8. Costa single, conspicuous
   9. Leaves conspicuously bordered
      10. Plants 10–30 cm tall, robust, stems stiff, golden to reddish, leaves golden, rigid, lanceolate-acuminate borders strongly toothed........ ....XVI. Spiridentaceae.
      10. Plants less than 5 cm long, usually prostrate, stems slender, yellow-green, leaves short-pointed, borders 1 cell-layer thick
         11. Plants prostrate, to 5 cm long, leaves somewhat flattened or complanate................ .....XXVII. Distichophyllaceae.
         11. Plants erect, less than 1 cm tall, leaves erect-spreading............. ....XXVIII. Daltoniaceae.
   9. Leaves not bordered, or border inconspicuous
      10. Plants frondose or dendroid (like miniature trees); costa toothed on lower side in upper leaf
         11. Dendroid habit; leaf margins spinose-serrate; capsules may be ribbed.................... ....XIV. Hypnodendraceae.
         11. Frondose habit; leaf margins with small teeth; capsules smooth, not ribbed........ ....XXI. Pterobryaceae.
      10. Plants not frondose or dendroid, mostly forming mats or tangled masses; costa smooth on lower side in upper leaf
         11. Leaf cells papillose
            12. Stems prostrate, stiff, branching pinnate to tripin-

nate, stem and branch leaves dimorphous................
................XXXII. Thuidiaceae.

12. Stems long-pendulous or ascending, branching irregular; primary stem and branch leaves similar, although branch leaves may be slightly smaller................
................XXII. Meteoriaceae.

11. Leaf cells smooth

12. Stems pinnately branched, branching irregular to frondose, leaves complanate......
................XXIV. Neckeraceae.

12. Stems irregularly branched, not frondose; leaves may be slightly laterally compressed but not truly complanate

13. Stems erect; capsules hidden by perichaetial leaves; upper lamina cells short, walls irregularly thickened................
......XIX. Cryphaeaceae.

13. Stems prostrate; capsules on elongated setae, not hidden by perichaetial leaves; upper lamina cells elongate, walls uniformly thickened

14. Leaves with alar cells well defined......
XXXVI. Plagiotheciaceae.

14. Leaves with alar cells few or poorly defined

15. Leaves ovate-lanceolate, acuminate, erect-spreading _____ XXXIV. Brachytheciaceae.

15. Leaves ovate, broadly acuminate, pressed against the stem, slightly flattened or compressed____ XXXIII. Amblystegiaceae.

8. Costa double, or costa not present

  9. Plants erect, often frondose, leaves plane to transversely undulate_____ _____XXIV. Neckeraceae.

  9. Plants prostrate or pendent, irregularly branched, not frondose; leaves plane but not undulate or wavy

    10. Capsules ribbed; plants pendent, forming tangled masses; stems reddish_____XX. Ptychomniaceae.

    10. Capsules smooth; plants prostrate, stems not reddish

      11. Alar cells sharply defined, often large and inflated

        12. Alar cells more than 2–3 on each side of the leaf base, not markedly inflated, not colored; capsules erect_____ _____XXXV. Entodontaceae.

        12. Alar cells fewer than 3 on each side, often colored and markedly inflated; capsules inclined to horizontal_____ XXXVII._____ Sematophyllaceae.

11. Alar cells indistinctly defined, inconspicuous, usually not much enlarged or inflated
12. Costa double
13. Costae strong, extending more than half the length of the leaf............
........XXVI. Hookeriaceae.
13. Costae faint, extending less than one-quarter the length of the leaf....
........XXV. Pilotrichaceae.
12. Costa none
13. Leaves bordered............
........XXVI. Hookeriaceae.
13. Leaves unbordered
14. Leaf cells more than 10 μ wide
15. Plants whitish; operculum long-beaked, peristome with median furrow on teeth ....
XXIX. Leucomiaceae.
15. Plants green; operculum short-beaked (the beak not longer than the base of the operculum), peristome teeth not furrowed with a fine zigzag line....
XXXVIII. Hypnaceae.
14. Leaf cells linear, narrow, less than 8 μ wide

15. Leaves with basal angle (alar) cells decurrent (extending) onto the stem; cells smooth .... XXXVI. Plagiotheciaceae.

15. Leaves with basal angle (alar) cells not decurrent; cells smooth or with a single papilla formed by projecting upper cell end wall. XXXVIII. Hypnaceae.

I. FISSIDENTACEAE

Fissidens Hedwig
  Spec. Musc. 152. 1801.

The family Fissidentaceae is represented in the Society Islands by the genus *Fissidens,* with a total of thirteen species. Even though recently reviewed (Whittier and Miller, 1967), the data for this genus are restricted to Tahiti, Moorea, and Raiatea. Undoubtedly many of the species of *Fissidens* reported from these islands will also appear on the other high, volcanic islands and atolls of the archipelago in wet, humid localities, as bark-inhabiting epiphytes or on damp basaltic and calcareous rocks.

Key to Species of *Fissidens*

1. Leaves bordered on the distal lamina and the duplicate blades
   2. Laminal border 1–3 cells wide and typically 1 cell thick, with the outer row of cells linear to vermiform
      3. Leaves lanceolate to linear-lanceolate, cells along the costa one-third below the tip about the same size as those adjacent to the border ....12. *F. dixonianus.*
      3. Leaves oblong-elliptic, broadly to rounded acute, cells along the costa one-third below the tip nearly twice the diameter of those adjacent to the border
         4. Leaves 5–6 times longer than broad, to ca 3 mm, with rounded acute apices, sometimes with a small apiculus, the leaves overlapping, inserted at an angle of less than 45° ....
            ....13. *F. nanobryoides.*
         4. Leaves 3–4 times longer than broad, to ca 2.5 mm, with acute to broadly acute apices, the leaves distant to slightly overlapping, inserted at an angle of 45° or more ....11. *F. zollingeri.*
   2. Laminal border 3–4 cells wide and 1–2 cells thick, with the outer rows of cells shortened and rhomboidal ....10. *F. raiatensis.*
1. Leaves unbordered or bordered only on the duplicate blades
   2. Leaves bordered to or beyond the middle of the duplicate blades with a broad band of elongate cells
      3. Leaves gradually tapered to an acuminate tip, laminal cells rounded-papillose ....3. *F. clarkii.*
      3. Leaves abruptly acuminate from a rounded tip, laminal cells pluri-papillose ....2. *F. philonotulus.*
   2. Leaves unbordered on the duplicate blades or with a short border only on the upper and perichaetial leaves
      3. Laminal cells smooth or nearly so

49

    4. Leaf apex rounded, lamina 2 or 3 cells thick, costa ends 8–15 cells below the leaf apex_____1. *F. jaiorum.*
    4. Leaf apex acute, lamina 1 cell thick, costa ends just below the apex or percurrent_____8. *F. mooreae.*
  3. Laminal cells pluripapillose or strongly rounded to conic-papillose
    4. Laminal cells pluripapillose
      5. Margin in the upper third of the leaf irregularly crenulate-papillose, the apical cell sharp and longer than broad, the dorsal (lower) lamina abruptly rounded to the stem at the base of the costa_____9. *F. aoraiensis.*
      5. Margin in the upper third of the leaf regularly crenate by projecting angles of the cells, the apical cell blunt and as long as broad, the dorsal lamina decurrent (tapered) to the costa or to the stem_____6. *F. fautauae.*
    4. Laminal cells unipapillose
      5. Costa percurrent, cells conic-papillose_____7. *F. taiarapuensis.*
      5. Costa ends 4–9 cells below the apex, cells rounded-papillose
        6. Free margin of the duplicate blade extending to, or nearly to, the costa, apex broadly acute to obtuse_____
_____5. *F. nadeaudii.*
        6. Free margin of the duplicate blade ends less than midway to the costa, apex acute to abruptly acute_____
_____4. *F. mangarevensis.*

1. *Fissidens jaiorum* Whittier & Miller
   Bryologist 70(1): 78–81. f. 1–9. 1967.

   Plants yellow-green, to 3–7 × 1–2 mm, with 6–14 pairs of leaves; leaves lingulate, 1.1–2.1 × 0.16–0.22 mm; costa ends 8–15 cells below the rounded or rounded-acute leaf apex; leaf margins smooth to crenulate. Upper lamina with 2–3 layers of cells nearly to the margins and the apex; vaginant lamina from one-third to one-half the length of the leaf, the free margin attached distally one-fourth to one-half the way between the margin and the costa. Cells of the lamina thin-walled, quadrate to irregularly hexagonal, isodiametric to elongate, 7–(12)–17 μ in the upper leaf, smaller, 3–8 × 3–4 μ, and more regular toward the margins, and larger, 17–28 × 12–17 μ, and more quadrate near the costa, especially in the base near insertion. Cells of the vaginant lamina margin small and elongate near the base. Dorsal (lower) lamina decurrent onto the stem. Plants sterile.

   ILLUSTRATIONS. Figure 13A–I.

   TAHITI. Pirae District: Mt. Aorai, ca 1700 m, in deep shaded valley W of Chalet Fare Ata, associated with *Rhynchostegium* and *Thuidium tahitense, 2936* (holotype, NY; isotypes, MU, BISH).

   Distribution.—Society Islands (Tahiti), endemic.

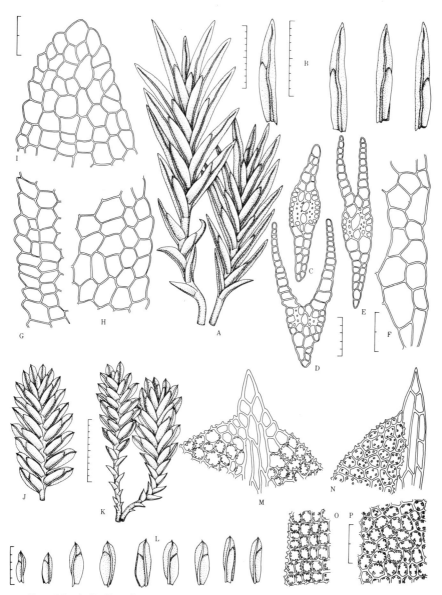

Fɪɢ. 13. A–I. *Fissidens jaiorum.* (*HOW 2936.*) A. Habit, scale 1 mm. B. Leaves, scale 1 mm. C. Cross section, upper lamina. D. Cross section, near midleaf through conduplicate blade. E. Cross section, near leaf base. C–E, scale 50 μ. F. Dorsal lamina cells, leaf base. G. Margin, conduplicate blade. H. Margin and median cells, upper lamina. I. Apex. F–I, scale 20 μ. J–P. *Fissidens philonotulus.* (*HOW 2384.*) J, K. Habit, scale 1 mm. L. Leaves, scale 0.5 mm. M, N. Leaf apex. O. Marginal cells, upper lamina. P. Median cells, upper lamina. M–P, scale 20 μ. (Reproduced with permission of *The Bryologist.*)

The lamina has 2 layers (sometimes 3) of cells on either side of the costa as in the subgenus *Pachyfissidens,* previously unknown from the Pacific Islands. This species is named in honor of Maurice and Henri Jay, father and son, ardent naturalists who provided invaluable advice and assistance in the field.

2. *Fissidens philonotulus* Bescherelle
Bull. Soc. Bot. France 48: 13. 1901.

Plants to 5 × 0.7 mm; leaves in about 20 pairs, elliptical, 0.39–0.57 × 0.13–0.16 mm, rounded, abruptly acute above; percurrent costa ends in a short apiculus. Vaginant lamina extends from two-thirds to three-fourths the leaf length, at its upper end attached from the costa almost to the margin; lower lamina decurrent to the costa. Cells small, moderately thick-walled, quadrate to irregularly rounded-hexagonal, 3–6 μ in diameter, minutely pluripapillose, smaller and more obscure toward the leaf apex. Fruiting material unknown.

ILLUSTRATIONS. Figure 13J–P.

TAHITI. Hamuta District: Hamuta Valley, *Nadeaud sn* (Bescherelle, 1901, NY, P). Papenoo District: 17 km E of Papeete, 25–30 m, on dry rocks along highway, associated with *Calymperes, Fissidens clarkii,* and *Vesicularia, 2383; 2384; 2389.* Hitiaa District: 1 km E of church opposite Bougainville's anchorage, 10–15 m, on soil banks, with *Fissidens* and *Taxithelium, 3190; 3196.*

Distribution.—Society Islands (Tahiti), endemic.

Bescherelle (1901) commented, "au premier abord cette Mousse offre l'aspect des petites espèces du genre *Philonotula,* mais elle diffère totalement des espèces de ce genre par la constitution des feuilles," an observation appropriate for the slender, delicate, pale green plants.

3. *Fissidens clarkii* Bartram
Bishop Mus. Occ. Pap. 15: 324. 1940.

Plants green, 4–7 mm tall and 1.25–(1.5)–1.75 mm wide; leaves in 5–10 pairs, oblong-lanceolate, 1.1–(1.2–1.3)–1.4 × 0.19–(0.23)– 0.26 mm; costa ends 2–4 cells below the acute apex. Margin of the vaginant lamina bordered by 1–3 rows of elongate cells, the upper and lower laminae unbordered and crenulate; lower lamina abruptly rounded to the stem or occasionally to the costa base, but in the lowermost leaves the lamina may be decurrent onto the stem. Leaf cells thin-walled, rhomboid to hexagonal, 5–(7–8)–10 μ in diameter, usually twice as large adjacent to the costa as in the margin, rounded to once-papillose. Sporophytes to 3 mm long; deoperculate capsules 0.5 × 0.2 mm; seta smooth. Spores smooth, green, 10–11 μ in diameter.

ILLUSTRATIONS. Figure 14A–K.

TAHITI. Pirae District: Mt. Aorai, 1700 m, in valley W of Chalet Fare Ata, with *Fissidens aoraiensis, Cyclodictyon blumeanum* var. *vescoanum,* and *Metzgeria, 3128;* Fautaua Valley, 80 m, on vertical rock face, with *Fissidens fautauae, 2327.* Taiarapu Peninsula: Taravao, above experiment station, 640–650 m, on rocks, with *Leucomium aneurodictyon, 2281;* Pueu District, Haavini Valley, 115 m, on roots exposed in bank, with *Callicostella, 2488;* 130 m, with *Fissidens nanobryoides, F. zollingeri, Vesicularia, Leucomium aneurodictyon,* and *Anthoceros, 2538;* 200 m, with *Fissidens nanobryoides, 2559.* Papenoo District: Papenoo Valley, W side, 140 m, on soil, with *Riccardia, 2462.* Mataiea District: Vaihiria Valley, ca 50–100 m, *3109.*

Distribution.—Society Islands (Tahiti, a new record), Pitcairn Island, Marquesas (Nuku Hiva).

Bartram (1940) compared this species with *Fissidens scabrisetus* Mitt., from Samoa, which has a scabrous seta and wider leaves, and with *F. philonotulus* Besch., which differs markedly in the much shorter leaf blades and in the entire margins. Bartram noted further that even the lower stem leaves of *F. clarkii* are constantly bordered on the duplicate blades.

4. *Fissidens mangarevensis* Montagne
Ann. Sci. Nat. Bot. ser. 3, 4: 113. 1845.

Plants dark to yellow-green, erect, branched or unbranched, to 10–14 × 2.4–3.4 mm tall; leaves in 14–20 pairs, 1.5–2.5 × 0.25–0.30 mm. The vaginant lamina extends to midleaf or slightly beyond and is confluent with the ventral lamina one-half to three-fourths the distance from the costa to the margin. Dorsal lamina abruptly rounded at base; leaf apices acute to abruptly so; costa vanishing 6–10 cells below apex; margins unbordered, rounded-crenulate. Cells thick-walled, rounded hexagonal, rounded-papillose, 3.5–7 μ diameter, slightly larger, more nearly quadrate adjacent to the costa, especially toward the base of vaginant lamina, to 14–17 × 10 μ; cells of the lower lamina similar. Sporophytes to about 6 mm tall;

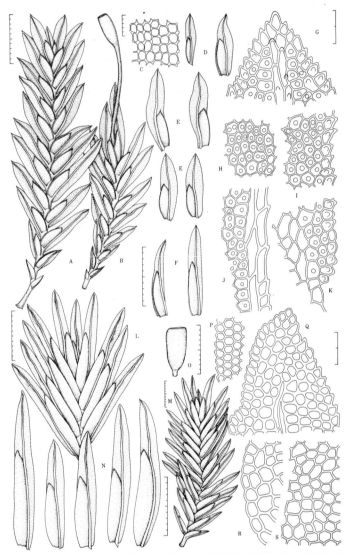

FIG. 14. A–K. *Fissidens clarkii.* A. Habit (*HOW 3128*). B. Habit (*HOW 2488*). A, B, scale 1 mm. C. Exothecial cells, capsule, scale 50 μ. D. Leaves (*HOW 2327*). E. Leaves (*HOW 2488*). F. Leaves (*Nadeaud 320*). D–F, scale 1 mm. G. Leaf apex. H, I. Median and margin cells. J. Margin, conduplicate blade. K. Dorsal lamina, leaf base. G–K, scale 20 μ (*HOW 2488*). L–S. *Fissidens mangarevensis.* (*HOW 2351*.) L. Habit, scale 1 mm. M. Habit, scale 1 mm. N. Leaves, scale 1 mm. O. Capsule, scale 1 mm. P. Margin, upper lamina. Q. Leaf apex. R. Dorsal lamina, leaf base. S. Median cells. P–S, scale 20 μ. (Reproduced with permission of *The Bryologist.*)

operculate capsules about 1–1.5 × 0.2–0.3 mm. Spores green, smooth, 14–18 μ. No antheridia observed. The abundant fruiting material suggests that this species is autoicous or pseudodioicous. ILLUSTRATIONS. Figure 14L–S.

TAHITI. Taiarapu Peninsula: Taravao, above experiment station, 400–500 m, along new water conduit, on tree fern, *Hürlimann T 1160* (Hürlimann, 1963, det. Bartram); Pueu District, N side, Haavini Valley, 150 m, on damp rocks, *2481.* Pirae District: Fautaua Valley, 240 m, below Cascade de Fautaua, on wet rocks, *2083, 2347, 2353, 2356;* 390 m, with *Fissidens fautauae, Calyptothecium crispulum* and *Lejeunea, 2359; 2355;* above Cascade de Fautaua, 400 m, on rocks and tree roots, with *Bryum billardieri, Hypopterygium,* and *Pinnatella keuhliana, 3153, 3157.* Papenoo District: Papenoo Valley, 150 m, on wet rocks, with *Homaliodendron exiguum, Calymperes,* and *Radula, 2401, 2438.* Arue District: Mt. Aorai–One Tree Hill trail, 180 m, on rocks, *2838.* Mataiea District: Vaihiria Valley, 200–400 m, on rocks, with *Hypopterygium, Porella,* and *Radula, 3058;* on tree branches, with *Racopilum, Hypopterygium, Homaliodendron exiguum,* and *Plagiochila, 3061.*

MOOREA. Without locality: *Nadeaud sn* (Bescherelle, 1901, P! NY!). Paopao Bay: Lower slopes of Mt. Matanui, 30–100 m, above Haring Plantation, in *Hibiscus-Inocarpus* forest, on rocks, with *Neckeropsis lepineana, 3398, 3399;* with *Hypopterygium, Racopilum,* and *Vesicularia, 3411;* with *Homaliodendron exiguum* and *Calymperes tahitensis, 3415.* Mt. Rotui: Lower slopes, 150–200 m, on rocks, *3437, 3438.*

Distribution.—Society Islands (Tahiti, Moorea), Tonga, Mangareva, Austral Islands (Raivavae, Rapa), Samoa, Fiji.

Typical on roots, branches, and wet rocks, common in moist places to about 500 m.

This large and conspicuous species becomes immediately distinct under the microscope, by the unbordered leaves, the acute apices, and the rounded, thick-walled cells. The type specimen was collected by Hombron on Mangareva in the Gambier Archipelago on wet rocks at 220 m. Bescherelle (1895a) described *F. mangarevensis* var. *tahitensis* as "a typo tantum differt habitu minore, caulibus pleurumque simplicibus foliis dimidio brevioribus." Dixon and Greenwood (1930) wrote that the variety did not seem of importance, being only a small form. Apparently no one since Bescherelle has recognized the variety and nothing in our collections suggests that any of the Tahitian plants are distinctive. Dixon and Greenwood also examined authentic specimens of *F. samoanus* C. Muell. and found no satisfactory distinction between it and *F. mangarevensis*. *Fissidens nadeaudii* may immediately be distinguished from *F. mangarevensis* by its broadly acute apices and the vaginant laminae with distal margins arching free nearly to the costa.

5. *Fissidens nadeaudii* Bescherelle
   Ann. Sci. Nat. Bot. ser. 7, 20: 22. 1895a.

Plants green, 12 × 2–2.5 mm tall; leaves in up to 20 pairs, linear, abruptly acuminate or rounded-obtuse, nerve ending 5–9 cells below the apex. Vaginant lamina extends from one-half to two-thirds the length of the leaf, distally free or nearly so, arching to the costa. Margins irregularly crenulate throughout, the base of the lower lamina decurrent to the nerve, or more rarely, to the stem. Margins of the vaginant laminae unbordered but often with a narrow triangle of thin-walled, elongate-rectangular cells at the basal angles. Lamina cells thick-walled, irregular-quadrate to rounded-hexagonal, 4–7 μ in diameter. Sporophytes unknown.

ILLUSTRATIONS. Figure 15A–H.

TAHITI. Without locality: *Nadeaud 44*, "Au milieu des torrents des hautes vallées" (Bescherelle, 1895a, NY!); *Nadeaud 231*, "Sur les rochers inondés à Pute, vallée de Temarua" (Bescherelle, 1898a, NY); *Quayle 212a, 213a* (Bartram, 1933a, BISH). Taiarapu Peninsula: Taravao, above experiment station, 640 m, on tree trunks, with *Rhizogonium spiniforme* and *Leucobryum*, *2278*. Pueu District: Haavini Valley, 255 m, on rocks, *2593*. Papenoo District: Papenoo Valley, 140 m, W side on wet banks, with *Calymperes* and *Radula*, *2465*; 60–80 m, on rocks in river bed, *2981, 2986, 2988*. Pirae District: Mt. Aorai, 1700 m, in valley W of Chalet Fare Ata, with *Glossadelphus tahitensis*, *Trichocolea*, and *Plagiochila*, *2912*; in stream bed, with *Fissidens jaiorum* and *Distichophyllum*, *2937*.

Distribution.—Society Islands (Tahiti), Samoa.

Fissidens nadeaudii is easily separated from *F. mangarevensis*, which it superficially resembles, by its broad, abruptly acuminate or wedge-shaped apices and the vaginant lamina which remains separate in its upper portion nearly to the nerve. The frequency of this species suggests that, like *F. mangarevensis*, it should be expected on all the high islands of the archipelago. Bescherelle

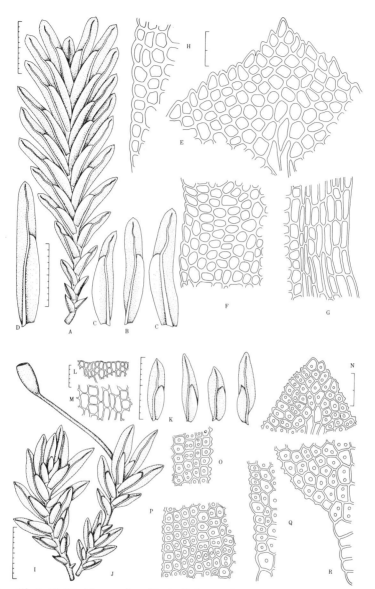

Fig. 15. A–H. *Fissidens nadeaudii*. A. Habit, scale 1 mm (*HOW 2465*). B–D. Leaves, scale 1 mm (*HOW 2465, 2988*). E. Leaf apex. F. Margin and median cells, upper leaf. G. Margin, duplicate blade at leaf base. H. Margin, decurrent lower lamina. E–H, scale 20 μ (*HOW 2988*). I–R. *Fissidens fautauae*. (*HOW 396*.) I, J. Habit, scale 1 mm. K. Leaves, scale 1 mm. L, M. Subannular and exothecial cells, capsule jacket, scale 50 μ. N. Leaf apex. O. Margin, vaginant lamina. P. Margin, upper lamina. Q, R. Dorsal lamina, leaf base. N–R, scale 20 μ. (Reproduced with permission of *The Bryologist*.)

(1895a) considered Nadeaud's report of *F. genunervis* C. Muell. to be an incorrect identification for *F. nadeaudii*.

6. *Fissidens fautauae* Whittier & Miller
   Bryologist 70(1): 83. 1967.

Plants 3–6 × 1–1.5 mm; leaves in 6–7 pairs, ovate-lanceolate, apices rounded-acute; costa ends 6–7 cells below apex. Lower lamina decurrent to costa or stem, sometimes gradually rounded to stem; vaginant lamina extends one-half the length of the leaf, its upper margin joined one-fourth to one-half the distance from costa to margin. Leaves unbordered or with marginal or submarginal row of elongate cells in the vaginant laminae of upper leaves especially. Cells strongly rounded on free surfaces or uni- to bipapillose even on costa, isodiametric, quadrate to hexagonal, 5–8 μ, typically smaller toward margins. Sporophytes terminal, 2.5–3 mm tall; urn 0.58 × 0.23 mm. Operculum, peristome, calyptra, and spores not seen.

ILLUSTRATIONS. Figure 15I–R.

TAHITI. Pirae District: Fautaua Valley, 80 m, in dry forest of *Cocos* and *Inocarpus* (mapé), on rocks with hepatics, *2326* (holotype, NY); 80 m, on vertical weathered rock face near trail to Bain Loti, with *Fissidens clarkii*, *2327*; 390 m, on rocks near trail, with *F. mangarevensis* and *Neckeropsis lepineana*, *2359*; 80–100 m, in forest behind Papeete, on rocks, *396*.

Distribution.—Society Islands (Tahiti), endemic.

Similar to *Fissidens taiarapuensis*, this species differs in the more irregularly crenulate margins and the low, rounded, uni- or bipapillose cells.

7. *Fissidens taiarapuensis* Whittier & Miller
   Bryologist 70(1): 85. 1967.

Plants green, 5–6 × 1.5 mm; leaves in 12–14 pairs (in fruiting specimens), 1.4–1.6 × 0.19–0.22 mm. Dorsal lamina abruptly rounded to costa or stem; vaginant lamina extends one-half the length of the leaf, the free margin joins the lamina one-half the distance between costa and margin; costa ends in leaf apex. Only upper leaves or perichaetial leaves with border on vaginant laminae; margins regularly crenulate by projecting cell angles. Cells conic-papillose, thick-walled, rounded-hexagonal, 5–8 μ above, slightly larger adjacent to the costa and toward leaf base. Sporophytes terminal, erect, to 3 mm tall; urn 0.5–0.8 × 0.3–0.4 mm; operculum about 0.45 mm long. Peristome red, teeth to ca 200 μ long and densely spiculose-papillose near the base. Spores 15–18 μ, finely papillose.

ILLUSTRATIONS. Figure 16A–H.

TAHITI. Taiarapu Peninsula: Taravao, above experiment station, 800 m, on *Cyathea* trunk, *2161*, *2178*, *2179* (holotype, NY); on *Cyathea*, with *Leucomium aneurodictyon, Thyridium obtusifolium*, and *Spiridens balfourianus, 2145*; with *Calomnion schistostegiellum, Spiridens balfourianus*, and *Plagiochila, 2189*.

Distribution.—Society Islands (Tahiti), endemic.

Fissidens taiarapuensis is apparently autoicous, as axillary structures which seemed to be remnants of antheridia were observed on fruiting plants. The long spiculae at the base of the peristome are distinctive and unique. The crenate margins and conic papillae identify this species readily in the vegetative state.

8. *Fissidens mooreae* Whittier & Miller
   Bryologist 70(1): 85. 1967.

Plants about 6 × 2 mm; leaves in as many as 10–12 pairs in archegoniate plants, perichaetial leaves to 1.4 × 0.3 mm, normal leaves 1.2 × 0.3 mm, ovate to linear-lanceolate; costa ends 2–4 cells below an acute apex; margins crenulate. Vaginant laminae extend to one-half the length of the leaf, the free margin joined to the lamina one-half to two-thirds from the costa to the margin; lower lamina abruptly rounded to the stem or costa at insertion. Cells smooth, thin-walled, irregularly to regularly hexagonal, 8–(10–12)– 15 μ, gradually smaller toward the margins. Vaginant lamina occasionally with 1 or 2 marginal to submarginal rows of elongate cells, the cells 15–30 × 8–10 μ. Sporophytes unknown.

ILLUSTRATIONS. Figure 16I–P.

MOOREA. Papetoai–Paopao Bay trail: S of Mt. Rotui, 0–150 m, *3445* (holotype, NY).

Distribution.—Society Islands (Moorea), endemic.

The smooth laminal cells and crenulate margins, together with the marginal or submarginal border on the vaginant lamina of the leaves, serve to distinguish *Fissidens mooreae*.

9. *Fissidens aoraiensis* Whittier & Miller
   Bryologist 70(1): 87. 1967.

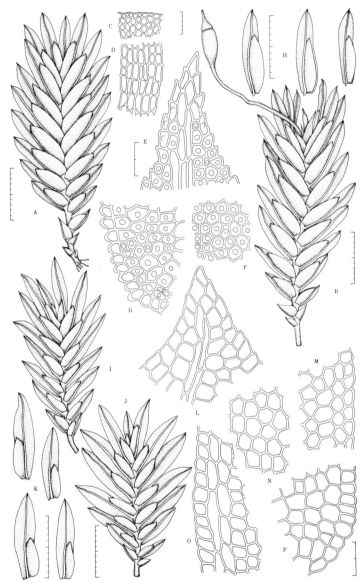

FIG. 16. A–H. *Fissidens taiarapuensis*. (*HOW 2179.*) A, B. Habits, vegetative and fruiting plants, scale 1 mm. C, D. Subannular and jacket cells, capsule, scale 50 μ. E. Leaf apex. F. Median cells, upper leaf. G. Lower lamina, leaf base. E–G, scale 20 μ. H. Leaves, scale 1 mm. I–P. *Fissidens mooreae*. (*HOW 3445.*) I, J. Habits, scale 1 mm. K. Leaves, scale 1 mm. L. Leaf apex. M. Margin, upper lamina. N. Median cells, upper lamina. O. Margin, vaginant lamina of an upper leaf. P. Lower lamina, leaf base. L–P, scale 20 μ. (Reproduced with permission of *The Bryologist.*)

Plants to 6 × 2 mm; leaves in 10–11 pairs, broadly linear-lanceolate, unbordered, 1–1.25 × 0.34 mm; costa ends 2–4 cells below the acute apex; margins finely crenulate-papillose to the apex. Cells of the lamina irregularly hexagonal, 5–(7–8)–10 μ, thin-walled, and pluripapillose. The free margin of the vaginant lamina ends about one-third the length of the leaf, joined to the lamina one-half to two-thirds from costa to margin; lower lamina abruptly rounded to stem at insertion of costa. Plants sterile.

ILLUSTRATIONS. Figure 17A–K.

TAHITI. Pirae District: Mt. Aorai, 1700 m, in stream bed of valley W of Chalet Fare Ata, associated with *Metzgeria, 2883* (holotype, NY); associated with *F. clarkii, Cyclodictyon blumeanum* var. *vescoanum,* and *Metzgeria, 2935.*

Distribution.—Society Islands (Tahiti), endemic.

Fissidens mooreae, although similar in stature, has smooth lamina cells and occasionally has marginal or submarginal borders on the vaginant laminae of upper leaves. A few plants with smaller, more erect leaves and somewhat larger cells with smaller papillae were found in the type locality, but they appear to merge into *F. aoraiensis;* the anomalous plants may comprise another taxon, but the limited material precludes final judgment.

10. *Fissidens raiatensis* Bartram
Bishop Mus. Occ. Pap. 9: 3. 1931.

Plants (fruiting) to 4 × 2 mm; leaves in 5–6 pairs (sterile plants described by Bartram as larger, having more pairs of leaves), linear-lanceolate, bordered to the apices or nearly so, 1.3–1.5 × 0.23 mm. Vaginant lamina extends nearly to midleaf, the free margin joined to the lamina from costa one-half the distance to the lamina margin. Leaves bordered, the border 1–2 cells thick and 3–4 cells wide below, the cells elongate below, shorter toward the leaf apex, and replaced in the apex by cells similar to those of the lamina. Margins irregularly crenulate at the leaf apices, entire below. Costa terminates in the apex or as much as 4–6 cells below. Cells of the lamina 6–(7–8)–10 μ, irregularly hexagonal, thin-walled, slightly mammillose or rounded-papillose, larger and more rectangular toward the leaf base. Sporophytes terminal, 3 mm tall; urn 0.7 × 0.23 mm; seta smooth. Peristome and spores not seen.

ILLUSTRATIONS. Figure 17L–P.

RAIATEA. Faaroa Valley: On wet rocks, on floor of *Inocarpus* (mapé) grove, *Moore 8* (Bartram, 1931, BISH; holotype, FH).

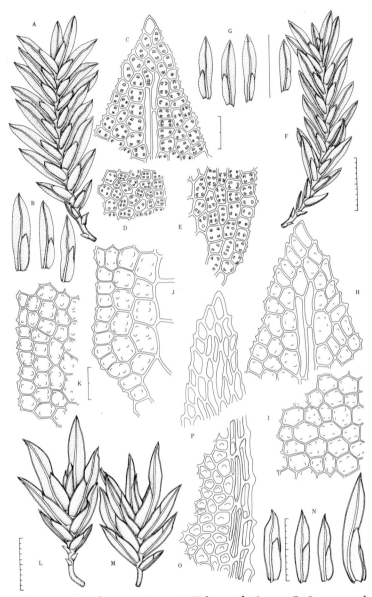

FIG. 17. A–K. *Fissidens aoraiensis*. A. Habit, scale 1 mm. B. Leaves, scale 1
mm. C. Leaf apex. D. Lamina cells. E. Dorsal lamina, leaf base. F. Habit of
variant, scale 1 mm (*HOW 2935*). G. Leaves, scale 1 mm. H. Leaf apex. I.
Median cells. J. Dorsal lamina, leaf base. K. Margin, upper lamina. H–K, scale
20 μ. L–P. *Fissidens raiatensis*. (*Moore 8*, type.) L, M. Habits, scale 1 mm.
N. Leaves, scale 1 mm. O. Margin and lamina cells. P. Leaf apex. O, P, scale
20 μ, as for H–K. (Reproduced with permission of *The Bryologist*.)

Distribution.—Society Islands (Raiatea), endemic.

Bartram (1931) compared this species to *F. rigidulus* Hook. f. & Wils., which is larger, and noted that the relatively inconspicuous border of *F. raiatensis* fades out entirely some distance below the apex of the leaf. Although Bartram illustrated the plant as pluripapillose, examination of the type indicates that the cells are typically rounded and only faintly unipapillose or mammillose, occasionally bipapillose.

11. *Fissidens zollingeri* Montagne
Ann. Sci. Nat. Bot. ser. 3, 4: 114. 1845.

> *Fissidens nanobryoides* Broth., *in* Fleischer, Musci Fl. Buitenzorg 1: 23. 1904. (*Lapsus? nom. nud.*, non *F. nanobryoides* Besch.)

Plants (fruiting) 2–6 mm tall; leaves in 3–10 pairs, broadly linear-lanceolate, to 1.6–1.8 × 0.36–0.46 mm, bordered to the apex or the border ending just below; costa percurrent, the vaginant lamina extends to midleaf, the free margin of the duplicate blade joined from costa to the margin of the lamina. Cells hexagonal, thin-walled, smooth, 7–(10)–16 μ above, rectangular to quadrate below, 10–30 × 10–15 μ. Border cells thick-walled, smooth, elongate, to 110–120 × 2–3 μ. Sporophytes terminal, 4–7 mm; capsules 0.4–0.5 × 0.2–0.3 mm, on a smooth seta; operculum conic-rostrate, 0.5 mm long. Spores green, smooth, 10–14 μ.

ILLUSTRATIONS. Figure 18.

TAHITI. Pirae District: Behind Papeete, ca 100 m, on roots, *295, 368, 369, 377*. Papenoo District: Papenoo Valley, W side, 180 m, *2456*; 180 m, on soil along road, with *Wilsoniella jardini* and *Trematodon puteensis, 2460*; 140 m, on roots, with *F. clarkii* and *Riccardia, 2462*. Taiarapu Peninsula: Pueu District, Haavini Valley, 120 m, on soil bank above first camp, with *F. nanobryoides* (!), *F. clarkii, Leucomium aneurodictyon, Vesicularia,* and *Anthoceros, 2528*; 130 m, on banks, with *F. clarkii, 2538*.

MOOREA. Trail from Papetoai Bay to Paopao Bay: S of Mt. Rotui, near sea level, *3420*. Paopao Bay: Haring Plantation, ca 5 m, on soil, with *Wilsoniella jardini, 2471*.

Distribution.—Society Islands (Tahiti, Moorea), Samoa (Upolu), Fiji, Tonga, New Zealand, Caroline Islands, Philippine Islands, Japan, southern China, Hongkong, Sumatra, Java, New Guinea, Andaman Islands.

This species is clearly distinguished from *F. nanobryoides* Besch.,

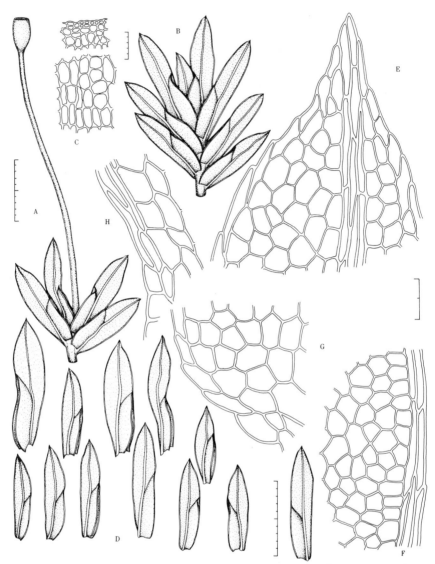

FIG. 18. *Fissidens zollingeri.* (*HOW 2456.*) A, B. Habit, scale 1 mm. C. Sub-annular and exothecial cells, scale 50 μ. D. Leaves, scale 1 mm. E. Leaf apex. F. Border and median cells, upper lamina. G, H. Lamina, leaf base. E–H, scale 20 μ. (Reproduced with permission of *The Bryologist.*)

which has linear leaves nearly 3 mm long, with rounded, abruptly acute apices. It is quite possible that some of the material distributed from the Bescherelle herbarium as *F. nanobryoides* was in fact *F. zollingeri*. Both species have been found together in a single collection (2528). Similar to *F. oahuensis*, specimens from Tahiti and Moorea have larger cells with thinner cell walls in the laminae, and their habit is larger. Since Fleischer's (1904) report, *F. zollingeri* Mont. has been listed from Tahiti, but this is the first confirmation of its presence in the Society Islands.

12. *Fissidens dixonianus* Bartram
  Bishop Mus. Occ. Pap. 19: 220. 1948.
  Fissidens diversiretis Dix., *in* Dixon and Greenwood, Proc. Linn. Soc. N. S. Wales 55: 270. 1930. (*hom. illeg.*)

Plants to 3 × 2 mm (fruiting); 3–4 pairs linear-lanceolate leaves, bordered from base to apex on margins of vaginant and upper laminae, 1.7–2.3 × 0.2 mm, forming an acute angle with the short stems; costa percurrent. Free margin of the duplicate blade joins margin of the upper lamina about midleaf. Borders in 1–3 rows of smooth, thick-walled, elongate cells, 70–140 × 2–3 μ. Cells of the lamina moderately thick-walled, large, smooth to rounded on free surfaces, approximately hexagonal above, 6–(7–8)–11 μ, uniform from costa to margin but more elongate in the leaf base. Lower lamina decurrent to the costa. Sporophytes with capsules 3.4–3.7 mm; setae smooth; capsules 0.6–0.7 × 0.3–0.4 mm. Only depauperate capsules seen.

ILLUSTRATIONS. Figure 19A–G.

TAHITI. Pirae District: Trail from Fare Rau Ape to Mt. Aorai, 800 m, on vertical volcanic rock, with *Cyathodium foetidissimum*, *Hürlimann T 1127* (Hürlimann, 1963, FH).

Distribution.—Society Islands (Tahiti), Fiji.

Guillemin (1837) reported *F. bryoides* for Tahiti, but on the basis of recent collections, it is possible that the specimen would now be placed with *F. dixonianus* or *F. zollingeri*. The only Tahitian material examined was collected by Hürlimann (1963) and determined by Bartram. It is smaller than *F. xiphoides* in both height and width; the very acute insertion of the leaves renders the plants narrower, although the leaves are longer than those described by Shin (1964) for *F. xiphoides*. In *F. zollingeri* there is a greater uniformity of cell size than in *F. dixonianus*, which has

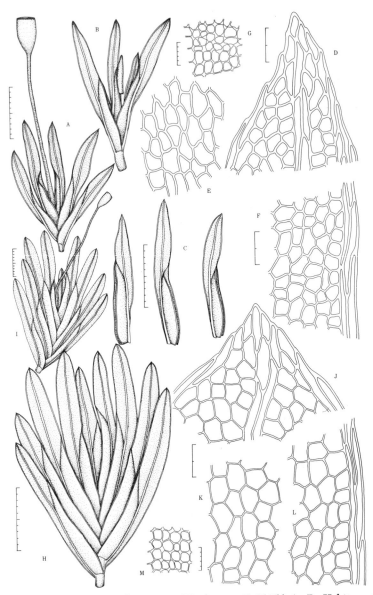

Fɪɢ. 19. A–G. *Fissidens dixonianus*. (*Hürlimann T 1127.*) A, B. Habit, scale 1 mm. C. Leaves, scale 1 mm. D. Leaf apex. E. Median cells, near lamina base. D, E, scale 20 μ. F. Margin and median cells, upper lamina, scale 20 μ. G. Exothecial cells, scale 50 μ. H–M. *Fissidens nanobryoides*. (*HOW 2559.*) H. Habit, scale 1 mm. I. Habit, scale 1 mm. J. Leaf apex. K. Median cells, upper lamina. L. Margin cells, upper lamina. J–L, scale 20 μ. M. Exothecial cells, scale 50 μ. (Reproduced with permission of *The Bryologist*.)

very elongate cells near the leaf insertion. A difficulty in reconciling Bartram's determination of Hürlimann's specimen lies in Dixon's original description of *F. diversiretis* as having "cellulae . . . obscurate, quaeque papilla singula alta coronata." We observed only smooth to rounded cells.

13. *Fissidens nanobryoides* Bescherelle
Bull. Soc. Bot. France 45: 58. 1898a.

Plants 5-7 × 3-4 mm; leaves oblong-linear, with rounded or rounded-acute apices, to 3.5 × 0.5 mm, leaves entirely bordered by 2–3 rows of elongate, thick-walled cells, to 100 × 2–3 μ, in 1–2 layers; costa percurrent. Duplicate blades long-decurrent on the ventral lamina, the free margins confluent with the laminar margin. Dorsal lamina decurrent to the stem, more rarely to the costa. Lamina cells large, thin-walled, approximately hexagonal, isodiametric or elongate in the upper lamina, 9–(13–15)–19 μ, slightly larger next to the costa than at the border, more elongate in the leaf base, 35 × 15 μ near the costa, quadrate, 15 × 15 μ toward the border. Sporophytes terminal, to 5 mm; seta smooth; urn 0.6 × 0.23 mm. Cells of the capsule jacket 17–18 μ, quadrate, thin-walled with the angles thickened. Spores not observed; the single peristome examined fragmentary.

ILLUSTRATIONS. Figure 19H–M.

TAHITI. Taiarapu Peninsula: Pueu District, Haavini Valley, 120 m, on bark, with *F. zollingeri*, *F. clarkii*, *Leucomium aneurodictyon*, and *Vesicularia, 2528*; 120 m, on rocks and soil, with *F. clarkii* and *Radula, 2559*.

Distribution.—Society Islands (Tahiti), endemic.

This distinctive species differs from *F. zollingeri* and *F. dixonianus* in the extremely long leaves, the broadly rounded leaf apex, and the very acute insertion of the leaves. In addition, the confluence of the vaginant lamina extends from the costa to the border in an exceptionally acute angle. Bescherelle's original description fits our plants so well that we have little hesitation in referring them here.

II. DICNEMONACEAE

Dicnemon Schwaegrichen
Spec. Musc. Suppl. 2(1): 126. 1824.
Dicnemon rugosum (Hooker) Schwaegrichen
Spec. Musc. Suppl. 2(1): 127. 1824.

Leucodon rugosus Hook., Musci Exotici 1: t. 20. 1818.
Eucnemis rugosa Brid., Bryol. Univ. 2: 217. 1827.
Dicnemon banksii C. Muell., Bot. Zeit. 16: 161. 1858.
Dicnemòs banksii (C. Muell.) Besch., Ann. Sci. Nat. Bot. ser. 7, 20: 18. 1895a.
Dicranum densifolium Web. & Mohr, Ann. Bot. 2: 546. 1806. *in* hb. Thunberg, *fide* C. Mueller, 1858.

Plants golden brown, forming tufts 4–5 (10) cm deep on bark and occasionally damp ground; leaves rigid, imbricated, appressed to erect-spreading, to 4–5 × 8–10 mm (those of the isotype from New Holland slightly wider; NY), perichaetial leaves longer, 11–12 mm. Mature normal leaves ovate-lanceolate, concave, the margins entire to slightly denticulate, hyaline and involuted in the upper blade; costa strong and percurrent. Cells of the lamina thick-walled, slightly pitted, elongate, 30–40 × 7–9 μ, longer toward the margins and more narrow, shorter and wider toward the costa and near the leaf base. Alar cells form a distinct dark brown or orange region at the angles of the leaf base. Seta sheathed in perichaetial leaves, 1.0–1.5 cm long; capsule about 3 mm. Stem and leaf bases surrounded by a dense felt of rhizoidal tomentum.

ILLUSTRATIONS. Hooker (1818, t. 20). Figure 20O–Q.

TAHITI. Without locality: "Ex insula Tahiti retulit Banks" (C. Mueller, 1858, as *D. banksii*; Bescherelle, 1895a, as *D. banksii*); *Wilkes sn*, United States Exploring Expedition, 1842 (Sullivant, 1859, as *D. banksii*); *Ribourt 161*, 1850, "très beaux exemplaires avec de nombreuses capsules operculées"; *Nadeaud 55*, "vallées sèches de la région N.O. de l'île, vers 800 mètres, au Pinai, sur les troncs du *Meryta lanceolata*" (Bescherelle, 1895a, as *D. banksii*). Pirae District: Fare Rau Ape–Mt. Aorai trail, *Quayle 155c, 697a, 699b*; *Whitney Expedition 704, 705* (Bartram, 1933a, BISH!); *Decker and Decker 1*; with *Macromitrium, Decker and Decker 7*; with *Masti-*

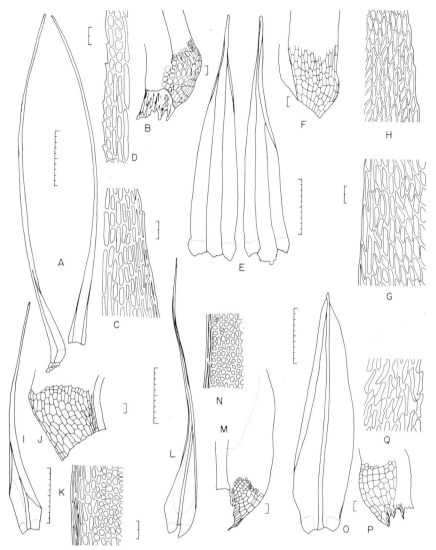

Fig. 20. A–D. *Campylopus obscurus.* (*HOW 2930.*) A. Leaves, scale 1 mm.
B. Leaf base and alar cells, scale 50 μ. C. Cells, leaf base shoulder, scale 20 μ.
D. Margin at midleaf, scale 20 μ. E–H. *Campylopus umbellatus.* (*HOW 2687.*)
E. Leaves, scale 1 mm. F. Leaf base, scale 50 μ. G. Cells, basal region. H.
Margin at midleaf. G, H, scale 20 μ. I–K. *Dicranoloma braunii.* (*HOW 3028.*)
I. Leaf, scale 1 mm. J. Leaf base and alar cells, scale 50 μ. K. Upper leaf cells
and margin, scale 20 μ. L–N. *Leucoloma molle.* (Java, *Junghuhn sn.*) L. Leaf,
scale 1 mm. M. Leaf base and alar cells, scale 50 μ. N. Upper leaf cells and
margin, scale 20 μ. O–Q. *Dicnemon rugosum.* (*del.* HAM.) O. Leaf, scale 1
mm. P. Leaf base and alar cells, scale 50 μ. Q. Upper leaf cells, median, scale
20 μ.

gophora, Decker and Decker 14; 27; with *Leucobryum* and *Pty-chomnion aciculare, Decker and Decker 46; 80; 114; 115; 124; 125; 140;* at altitudes over 1500 m, *Decker and Decker 144;* Mt. Orohena, S side, 1500 m, with fern, *MacDaniels 1478;* 1570 m, on ground, narrow mossy divide, *St. John and Fosberg 17135* (unreported, BISH!); Mt. Aorai, *249;* with *Ptychomnion aciculare, 2703;* with *Rhizogonium setosum, 2717;* 1400 m, *2472;* with *Mastigophora, Jamesoniella,* and *Frullania apiculata, 2753;* 1950 m, *2758;* on stunted trees and ground, with *Pleurozia, 2774; 2781;* on damp ground, with *Jamesoniella, 2785;* 1000 m, with *Acroporium* and *Plagiochila, 2845;* 1700 m, with *Herberta, 2879.* Hitiaa District: Above 100 m, with *Thyridium obtusifolium, 2172.*

Distribution.—Society Islands (Tahiti), Australia (Nova Hollandia, type locality).

Bescherelle (1895a) noted that the leaves of all Tahitian specimens exhibited the transverse wrinkles which characterize *Dicnemon rugosum* and that the specimen described by Mueller as *D. banksii* had leaves that were "*haud rugosa,*" or smooth and unwrinkled. This seems to be a variable feature, as are the margin teeth of Tahitian specimens, and the isotype of *D. rugosum* compares so well with collections from Tahiti that I have no hesitation in agreeing with Salmon (1902) that *D. banksii* is indeed a synonym.

III. DICRANACEAE

Represented by nine genera with seventeen species, the Dicranaceae is the largest single family in the Society Islands, as well as one of the most complex.

Plants are erect, ranging from a few millimeters to nearly 10 cm tall; the leaves are from less than 1 mm to over 1 cm long, all costate, with typically percurrent or excurrent costa. Cells of the lamina are quadrate to elongate, usually firm or thick-walled (*Wilsoniella* is an exception); in the leaf base the cells may be undifferentiated or inflated, colored or hyaline in the alar regions, sometimes giving the leaf base an auriculate appearance. Leaf margins are often incurved in the upper blade. The peristome is comprised of 16 usually reddish teeth, cleft about one-half the distance toward the base. The operculum is typically rostrate, the beak straight or curved. The calyptra is cucullate or mitriform, often entire at the base.

Most of the characters significant in distinguishing genera of the family Dicranaceae are to be found in the sporophyte. Even though these closely allied taxa are commonly found in fruit, their identification may pose problems even for an expert.

KEY TO GENERA OF THE DICRANACEAE

1. Leaves with a hyaline margin of elongate, thick-walled cells extending to, or above, midleaf..9. *Leucoloma*.
1. Leaves lacking a hyaline margin
    2. Areolation lax, cells often more than 100 × 18 μ............3. *Wilsoniella*.
    2. Lamina cells thick-walled, small, 25 μ or less
        3. Costa occupies one-half or more of the leaf base width, often ribbed on the back..7. *Campylopus*.
        3. Costa occupies less than one-half leaf base width, not ribbed on back.
            4. Plants robust, often over 5 cm tall, golden brown; leaves irregularly erect-spreading, to 1 cm long; stem densely clothed with rhizoidal filaments ....8. *Dicranoloma*.
            4. Plants considerably less than 5 cm tall; leaves much less than 1 cm long
                5. Sporophytes present
                    6. Seta curved downward at the top (cygneous) when moist, flexuose when dry............................4. *Campylopodium*.

6. Seta straight when moist
    7. Capsule with neck (apophysis) as long as urn................
    ....2. *Trematodon.*
    7. Capsule with neck shorter than urn or not developed
        8. Seta 1.5–2 cm, the urn 2–3 mm; spores 9–11 μ....
        ....6. *Holomitrium.*
        8. Seta less than 1 cm, urn less than 1.5 mm; spores
            over 15 μ
            9. Leaf apices obtuse; peristome teeth to 200 μ
            ....1. *Microdus.*
            9. Leaf apices acute; peristome teeth to 350 μ
            ....5. *Dicranella.*
5. Sporophytes absent
    6. Mature leaves usually under 1.5 mm long; obtuse............
    ....1. *Microdus.*
    6. Mature leaves over 2 mm long; acute
        7. Costa to 120 μ wide at leaf base............5. *Dicranella.*
        7. Costa 60–75 μ wide at leaf base
            8. Leaves 4–7 mm long................4. *Campylopodium.*
            8. Leaves less than 4 mm long
                9. Leaves under 2 mm long............6. *Holomitrium.*
                9. Leaves 2.5–3.5 mm long............2. *Trematodon.*

1. *Microdus picquenotii* Thériot & Corbière
   in Thériot, Dixon, and Buch, Ann. Bryol. 7: 157. 1934.

Plants terrestrial, yellow-green, with leaves to about 5 mm tall; leaves 0.9–1.5 × 0.1–0.2 mm, lanceolate-acuminate; costa stout, in lower leaves ending below the apex or percurrent, in upper leaves percurrent to short-excurrent, appressed below, straight to variably curved in the upper blade; perichaetial leaves longer, to 1.7 mm. Leaf margins plane to upturned, entire, rarely subentire, the cells similar to those of the lamina or slightly smaller, quadrate to elongate. Cells of the lamina smooth, thick-walled, quadrate to elongate, 3–4 times longer than broad in the base, 12–30 × 7–15 μ, becoming shorter toward the margins; upper lamina cells quadrate to 2 times longer than broad, 5–12 × 5–6 μ. Seta 4–7 mm, smooth; capsule 1.0–1.3 × 0.4 mm; no peristomes present in specimens examined; spores 15–18 μ, punctate-papillose.

ILLUSTRATIONS. Figure 21E–H.

TAHITI. Papeete: Hill near Ric Rouge, on soil, *Picquenot sn,* November, 1897 (Thériot, 1934). Fare Rau Ape: 500 m, on soil, *2032.*

Distribution.—Society Islands (Tahiti), endemic.

The extremely small size of the plants, the obtuse leaves, short seta, and the relatively large spores should set this genus and species

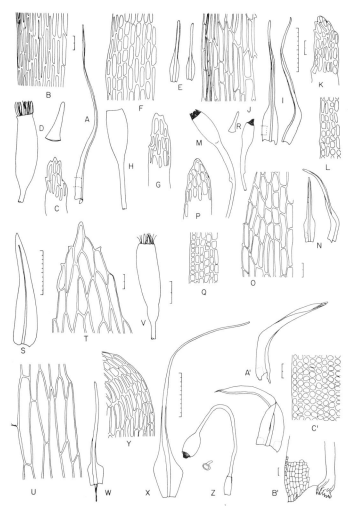

Fig. 21. A–D. *Dicranella hochreutineri.* (*HOW 2789.*) A. Leaf, scale 1 mm. B. Cells, basal region, scale 20 μ. C. Leaf tip, scale 20 μ. D. Capsule and operculum, scale 1 mm. E–H. *Microdus picquenotii.* (*HOW 2032.*) E. Leaves, scale 1 mm. F. Cells, basal region, scale 20 μ. G. Leaf tip, scale 20 μ. H. Old capsule, scale 1 mm. I–M. *Trematodon longicollis.* I. Leaves, scale 1 mm. J. Cells, basal region, scale 20 μ. K. Leaf tip, scale 20 μ. L. Upper leaf cells, scale 20 μ. M. Capsule, scale 1 mm. N–R. *Trematodon puteensis.* (*HOW 2380.*) N. Leaves, scale 1 mm. O. Median cells, basal region. P. Leaf tip. Q. Upper leaf cells. O–Q, scale 20 μ. R. Capsule and operculum, scale 1 mm. S–V. *Wilsoniella jardini.* (*HOW 3471.*) S. Leaf, scale 1 mm. T. Leaf tip. U. Median leaf cells and margin. T, U, scale 20 μ. V. Capsule, scale 1 mm. W–Z. *Campylopodium euphorocladum.* (*HOW 168.*) W. Lower leaf. X. Upper leaf. Y. Shoulder, leaf base, scale 20 μ. Z. Capsule and operculum, scale 1 mm. W, X, Z, scale 1 mm. A′–C′. *Holomitrium vaginatum.* (*HOW 3130.*) A′. Leaves, scale 1 mm. B′. Leaf base and alar cells, scale 50 μ. C′. Upper leaf cells and margin, scale 20 μ. (*del.* HAM.)

apart from other Dicranaceae found on Tahiti. *Wilsoniella*, the only other genus with similarly obtuse leaves, has extremely lax areolation and a comparatively weak costa. *Dicranella hochreutineri* has longer leaves (1.5–1.7 mm), the costa occupies less than one-quarter of the leaf base, and lamina cells are more elongate, 4–6 times longer than wide. The characteristics of my specimen match Bescherelle's description so closely that there is no question that it should be cited as *Microdus picquenotii* Besch.

2. *Trematodon* Michaux
Fl. Bor. Am. 2: 289. 1803.

Two species are recognized as part of the Society Islands bryoflora, *Trematodon puteensis* Besch. and *T. longicollis* Michx. A third species, *T. jardini*, is properly treated as *Wilsoniella jardini*. I have not seen authentic specimens of *T. puteensis* and the limited description provided by Bescherelle (1898a) offers little to separate *T. puteensis* from *T. longicollis*, but my own collections from the vicinity of the type locality are identical to specimens determined by Bartram and reported by Hürlimann (1961–1962) as *T. longicollis* with one exception (*2380*) in which the plants are about one-half the stature of that species.

KEY TO SPECIES OF *Trematodon*

1. Plants to 2 mm tall, leaves to 2.3 × 0.30 mm, lamina cells to 12.5 × 7.5 μ
   ....1. *T. puteensis*.
1. Plants to 4 mm tall, leaves to 3.5 mm, lamina cells to 18 × 5 μ................
   ....2. *T. longicollis*.

1. *Trematodon puteensis* Bescherelle
Bull. Soc. Bot. France 45: 54. 1898.

Plants similar in habit and coloration to *Trematodon longicollis*, but about one-half the stature, erect, to about 2 mm tall; leaves erect-spreading, twisted inward, 1.3–2.3 × 0.25–0.30 mm, ovate-acuminate from a sheathing base; costa percurrent, ending in a short, toothed, rounded apex with a single pointed terminal cell; leaf margins entire. Cells of the lamina smooth, quadrate to rectangular, 5.0–12.5 × 5.0–7.5 μ, elongate toward the costa, isodiametric toward the margins; basal cells rectangular, 25 × 12 μ, thick-walled, hyaline, more narrow toward the margins. Seta yellowish, smooth, 2–3 cm long; urn 1 mm; apophysis 1.5 mm long with a nodule (struma) often present on one side of the apophysis base; operculum conic-rostrate, about 1 mm long, beak straight (curved, according to Bescherelle's original description). Spores large, papillose, 20–23 μ. Peristome details not observed.

ILLUSTRATIONS. Figure 21N–R.

TAHITI. Puté: Teinarua Valley, *Nadeaud 203*, 1896 (Bescherelle, 1898a). Papeete: 17 km E, 30 m, on weathered rock in road cut, *2380*.

Distribution.—Society Islands (Tahiti), endemic.

The elongate apophysis, or neck, below the urn, together with the frequent appearance of a basal nodule, or struma, on the apophysis, immediately separates *Trematodon* from other Society Islands mosses. *Trematodon puteensis* should be readily distinguished from *T. longicollis* by its diminutive size.

2. *Trematodon longicollis* Michaux
Fl. Bor. Am. 2: 289. 1803.

Plants 3–4 mm tall, yellow-green, forming limited turfs on soil and rocks and common in road cuts; leaves erect-spreading, twisted, and curved inward, 2–3.5 mm long; costa percurrent or nearly so; leaf base broad and ovate, becoming constricted above so that the upper lamina is narrow and linear, canaliculate (channeled). Margins entire below, crenulate in the upper leaf. Cells of the lamina 8–18 × 4–5 μ in the upper blade, quadrate; in the lower blade 6–12 × 12–24 μ, quadrate to rectangular. Seta smooth, yellowish, 2–3 cm long; capsule inclined to horizontal; urn 2–3 mm; neck (apophysis) 3–5 mm long, often with a nodule (struma) at one side of the base. Stomata large and prominent on the lower part of the urn and neck. Peristome teeth reddish with a hyaline border, the colored portion with vertical striations and papillose, the teeth fragile and easily lost. Operculum conic-rostrate, about 1–2 mm; calyptra cucullate, entire at the base. Spores large, papillose, 19–22 μ.

ILLUSTRATIONS. Figure 21I–M.

TAHITI. Pirae District: Mt. Aorai trail between Fare Rau Ape and Fare Hamata, ca 800 m, on vertical lateritic slope, *Hürlimann T 1231* (Hürlimann, 1963); Fare Rau Ape–Mt. Aorai trail, 1200 m, *2736*. Papenoo District: Road along W side of Papenoo Valley, 180 m, on soil at side of road, with *Wilsoniella jardini* and *Fissidens zollingeri*, *2460*.

MOOREA. Paopao Bay: Near Haring's bungalow, ca 5 m, E side of bay near Hotel Eimeo, on ground, with *Wilsoniella jardini, 3471.*

Distribution.—Society Islands (Tahiti, Moorea), Philippine Islands (Luzon, Mindoro), Sri Lanka (Ceylon), Mexico, Cuba, eastern United States, Italy.

Bartram (1939) noted that spores may vary from 16 to 24 μ, that the apophysis might vary in length from 5 to 8 mm and appear with or without a basal nodule; the seta might vary from 1 to 3 cm. Bartram concluded that this interpretation would conceivably allow a number of other "species" to be brought into the *T. longicollis* taxon, but deferred judgment until types could be examined.

3. *Wilsoniella* C. Mueller
   Bot. Centralbl. 345. 1881.
Wilsoniella jardini Bescherelle
   Ann. Sci. Nat. Bot. ser. 7, 20: 14. 1895.
   Trematodon jardini Sch., nom. nud., in Jardin, Bull. Soc. Linn. Normandie
   ser. 2, 9: 264. 1875.

Plants pale to dark green, tufted (caespitose), turf-forming, about 1 cm tall; leaves to about 3 × 0.4 mm, ovate-lanceolate, costate; costa percurrent or nearly so, slender (about 25 μ wide in the leaf base); margins entire (smooth) except at the leaf apex where they become slightly denticulate. Cells of the lamina thin-walled, elongate-hexagonal (a distinctive feature), to about 140 × 18 μ in the upper blade, longer, to about 180 μ below. Seta 10–13 mm long; urn, together with its short neck, about 1.7 × 0.48 mm, with few stomata on the neck. Peristome teeth reddish, often lost with the operculum, papillose, with prominent ridges on the inner side (trabeculate), divided to the base, spirally striate, about 290–300 μ long. Capsule exothecial cells thick-walled, 40–60 × 16–19 μ. Spores papillose, 19–22 μ.

ILLUSTRATIONS. Figure 21S–V.

TAHITI. Papeete: On the ground, *Jardin sn,* 23 July 1852 (Bescherelle, 1898a). Papenoo District: Papenoo Valley, 180 m, W side, along road on soil bank, with *Trematodon longicollis* and *Fissidens zollingeri, 3471.*

MOOREA. Paopao Bay: E side, 5 m, Haring Plantation, near Hotel Eimeo, on recently exposed soil bank near bungalow, with *Trematodon longicollis, 3471.* A new record for Moorea!

Distribution.—Society Islands (Tahiti, type locality; Moorea), Samoa (Upolu).

Bescherelle (1898a) noted the similarity between *Wilsoniella jardini* and *W. pellucida* (Wils.) C. Muell., and separated the two on the basis of capsule size and shape, leaf denticulation, and sexuality. I have examined Philippine Islands specimens of *W. pellucida* determined by Bartram as var. *acutifolia* (Broth.) Dix. (no. *33393*, NY), and find that spores from these capsules may range to 24 μ, and that the capsule length and the length of the peristome (to about 290 μ), as well as the size of the capsule exothecial cells, provide no distinction. Leaf measurements are essentially the same. In another collection of Philippine *Wilsoniella* (*McGregor 20049*, originally as *W. squarrosa*, NY!) the sporophyte characters are not appreciably different, but the leaves are shorter and less acute; cells of the lamina and the costa width are not significantly different. I have not seen type material for these species, but conclude that *W. jardini* may come to be considered a synonym of *W. pellucida*, which has a distribution including Sri Lanka (Ceylon), Java, and Borneo. A single species, *W. karsteniana* C. Muell., is reported from Australia, but I have not seen specimens. *Wilsoniella flaccida* (Williams) Broth. is a Bolivian species distinguished primarily by being dioicous and smaller in habit. The peristome teeth show the same markings as *W. pellucida* and *W. jardini*, although Brotherus (1924b) reported them as key differences between subgenus *Euwilsoniella* and subgenus *Teretidens*.

4. *Campylopodium* (C. Mueller) Bescherelle
   Ann. Sci. Nat. Bot. ser. 5, 18: 189. 1873.
Campylopodium euphorocladum (C. Mueller) Bescherelle
   Ann. Sci. Nat. Bot. ser. 5, 18: 189. 1873.

   Aongstroemia euphoroclada C. Muell., Syn. 1: 429. 1849.
   Campylopodium tahitense Besch., Ann. Sci. Nat. Bot. ser. 7, 20: 15. 1895a.
   Aongstroemia microcampylopus C. Muell., Flora 82: 447. 1896. *fide* Bartram, 1933b.

Plants small, tufted, to 5 mm tall, yellow-green, forming turfs on soil and rocks in dry, exposed sites, the stems rarely branched; leaves to about 4 mm long, with an ovate base narrowing abruptly above to terminate in a bristle-like apex formed by the excurrent costa; costa about 75 μ wide near the base of the leaf. Cells of the lamina quadrate, thick-walled. Seta 5–10 mm long, smooth, cygneous when moist, flexuose when dry; capsule ovoid, furrowed when dry, the neck occasionally strumose, with a nodule to one side at the base (Bartram, 1933b); operculum shorter than the urn; ca-

lyptra entire, not laciniate, at the base. Spores papillose, 15–20 μ.
ILLUSTRATIONS. Bartram (1933b, p. 33, f. 18). Figure 21W–Z.

TAHITI. Pirae District: On exposed earth near Fort Fautaua, associated with *Pogonatum tahitense, Nadeaud 52* (Bescherelle, 1895b, as *C. tahitense*); Fare Rau Ape–Mt. Aorai trail, 750 m, on vertical lateritic face, *Hürlimann T 1225*! (Hürlimann, 1963, det. Bartram, FH); Fare Rau Ape, 500 m, in *Casuarina-Eucalyptus* zone, under *Dicranopteris* and *Lycopodium,* on soil bank with *Pogonatum tahitense* and *Notoscyphus paroicus, 2025;* with *Pogonatum tahitense, 2029, 2031;* 1016 m, with *Dicranella hochreutineri, 2698.* Vallée de Puaa: Au Pinai, 800–1000 m, *Nadeaud 204* (Bescherelle, 1898a, as *C. tahitense*). Taharaa: *Temarii Nadeaud sn* (Bescherelle, 1901, as *C. tahitense*).

RAIATEA. Highest mountain: W side, on wet rock, *Moore 41* (Bartram, 1931).

Distribution.—Society Islands (Tahiti, Raiatea), Hawaii (Oahu, Molokai, Maui, Hawaii), Samoa, Austral Islands (Rurutu, Rapa, Tubuai), New Zealand, Australia, Fiji, New Caledonia, New Guinea, Sumatra, Burma, Malaysia, Philippine Islands, East Africa.

Bartram (1933b) observed that in *Campylopodium euphorocladum* as it appears in Hawaii, the cygneous seta distinguishes the genus from *Dicranella* but allies it with *Campylopus,* from which it may readily be separated by the narrow costa. Barren plants are difficult to separate from *Dicranella,* and it is fortunate that both species fruit abundantly.

5. *Dicranella* (C. Mueller) Schimper
   Coroll. 13. 1856.
Dicranella hochreutineri Cardot
   Ann. Cons. Jard. Bot. Geneve 15–16: 158. f. 14. 1912.

Plants bright to yellowish-green, to about 1 cm tall, forming low turfs of varying density; leaves erect, secund, with a broadly ovate base which narrows abruptly to form a canaliculate (channeled) upper blade; costa excurrent. Seta to nearly 1 cm long; urn about 1.3 × 0.4–0.5 mm; peristome teeth split to about one-half their length, vertically striate, about 350 μ long, reddish toward the base, pale near the tips. Operculum long, conic-rostrate, oblique, about the same length as the urn. Annulus broad, composed of 2 rows of cells. Spores 20–24 μ (Bartram, 1933b; 18–20 μ in original description by Cardot, 1912).

ILLUSTRATIONS. Cardot (1912, p. 158, f. 14). Figure 21A–D.

TAHITI. Pirae District: Fare Rau Ape–Mt. Aorai trail, 750 m, on vertical lateritic face, *Hürlimann T 1224a* (Hürlimann, 1963, FH); above the old French Alpine Club, on soil, *256* (1960); ca 1000 m, along trail, with *Campylopodium euphorocladum, 2698*; 1040 m, on NW-facing bank, *2707*; 2065 m, summit of Mt. Aorai, on ground in front of shelter, with *Pogonatum tahitense, 2789*.

Distribution.—Society Islands (Tahiti), Hawaii (common to all the larger islands; type locality Kauai, Waimea, 1300 m).

Cardot (1912) recognized a similarity between this species and *Dicranella hawaiica*, which Bartram later (1933b) noted was distinct in extreme forms but related by intermediates. Cardot also observed that *D. hochreutineri* closely approached *D. coarctata* (C. Muell.) Bosch & Lac. (which has an Asian-Indomalayan distribution, the type locality Java), which differed in having a stronger costa, a shorter subula, the capsule formed by cells much smaller and shorter than in *D. hochreutineri*.

6. *Holomitrium* Bridel
Bryol. Univ. 1: 226. 1826.
Holomitrium vaginatum (Hooker) Bridel
Bryol. Univ. 1: 227. 1826.

Trichostomum vaginatum Hook., Musci Exotici t. 64. 1818.
Holomitrium tahitense C. Muell., Gen. Musc. Fr. 254. 1901. *nom. nud., fide* Thériot, Bull. Soc. Bot. Geneve ser. 2, 3: 246. 1911.

Plants yellow-green to golden brown, erect, branching, to 2 cm tall; leaves broadly lanceolate, 1.5–2 × 0.4 mm, margins incurved above the broadly sheathing base, the leaf apex recurved; costa strong and short excurrent. Perichaetial leaves ecostate, long-acuminate, to about twice the length of the stem leaves. Cells of the lamina thick-walled, irregularly rounded-quadrate above, about 10 μ in diameter, larger near the leaf base, inflated and colored at the alar regions, 30 × 15 μ, elongate near the costa, 50–70 × 10–15 μ. Sporophytes terminal or on short lateral branches, 1–1.5 cm tall; capsules erect, cylindrical, 2–3 mm long; operculum long-rostrate; beak straight or slightly curved, nearly as long as the capsule. Exothecial cells thick-walled, quadrate or nearly so, 50 × 40 μ. Spores 9–11 μ in diameter.

ILLUSTRATIONS. Hooker (1818, t. 64). Figure 22.

TAHITI. Without locality: *Menzies sn*, 1792, "In insula Otaheite, mare Pacifico" (Hooker, 1818, as *Trichostomum*; NY; Guillemin,

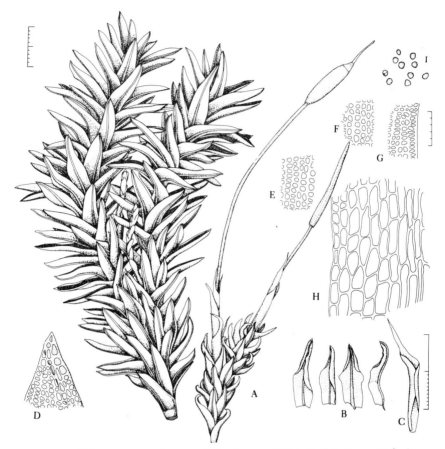

Fig. 22. *Holomitrium vaginatum.* (*Menzies sn,* "Otaheite," isotype, NY.) A. Habit, fruiting plant, scale 2 mm. B. Leaves, upper stem. C. Perichaetial leaf, ecostate. B, C, scale 2 mm. D. Leaf apex, side view. E, F. Median cells, upper and lower lamina. G. Margin lamina, cells. H. Leaf insertion cells. I. Spores. D–I, scale 50 μ.

1836); on rocks, lower valleys, *Nadeaud 60* (Nadeaud, 1873, as *Zygodon pusillus, fide* Bescherelle, 1895a); mountains near Marciati, Papenoo Valley, and Punarua Valley at the foot of Mt. Orohena, *Nadeaud 209*; mountains of Teoa, valley and district of Arue, to 1100 m, Pinai to 800 m, vicinity of Papeete, by Sainte-Amélie, *Nadeaud 210* (Bescherelle, 1898a). Pirae District: Fautaua Valley, *Temarii Nadeaud sn* (Bescherelle, 1901); 540 m, *3130*; Fare Rau Ape–Mt. Aorai trail, *Quayle 697k* (Bartram, 1933a, BISH); Fare Rau Ape, 500–1000 m, above Alpine Club buildings, *235*. Papeari District: Maara Valley, *Setchell and Parks 5321* (Brotherus, 1924a, NY).

MOOREA. Without locality: *Temarii Nadeaud sn* (Thériot, 1911).

Distribution.—Society Islands (Tahiti, Moorea), Java, Philippine Islands, New Caledonia (var. *brevifolium*), Cape of Good Hope, Malagasy Republic (Madagascar), Reunion, Mauritius.

Wijk, Margadant, and Florschutz (1959–1969) reported *Holomitrium vaginatum* to be a synonym of *H. cylindraceum*, apparently basing their decision on the priority of *H. cylindraceum* and C. Mueller's (1849) treatment of the two as synonyms. Thériot (1911) attempted to define *H. vaginatum* and its affinities, but although he was familiar with Mueller's (1849, 1901) work, he made no reference to *Cecalyphum* or to *Dicranum cylindraceum* which Mueller gave under *Holomitrium vaginatum*. I have examined what appears to be an authentic specimen (possibly an isotype, NY!) of *H. cylindraceum* (P. Beauv.) Wijk & Marg. (originally *Cecalyphum*, Isle de France). The leaves are 4–5 mm long, quite contorted when dry, long, lanceolate-acuminate, the cells of the upper lamina 12–15 μ, the margins of the lamina thickened, the costa much longer excurrent than in *H. vaginatum*.

The two taxa seem to represent distinct species and should be allowed to remain apart for the present. When specimens with a broad geographic range are examined, forms which could be considered to be intermediate appear, and I can only conclude that further study is needed.

7. *Campylopus* Bridel
   Mant. Musc. 4: 71. 1819.

Plants dark green to yellow-green, usually terrestrial, turf-forming, varying from less than 1 cm to as much as 10 cm tall, the stems often with a rhizoidal tomentum; leaves closely overlapping, erect to erect-spreading, the apices varying from rigid to flexuose; costa

broader than in any other Society Islands genus, percurrent to excurrent, often ridged on the lower (abaxial) side. Alar cells form
variable hyaline to colored auricles or lobes of inflated cell groups.
Upper cells are rhomboidal, thick-walled. Seta cygneous or arcuate
when moist; capsule ovoid, vertically furrowed when dry. Peristome
teeth are divided to the middle, vertically striate on the outer surface; operculum or lid is conic-rostrate; calyptra commonly cucullate and fringed at the base.

As numerous investigators have noted, *Campylopus* is a large and
difficult genus, comprised of polymorphic, intergrading forms. Over
500 species names are currently in use throughout the world; Hawaii
has 10 species recognized by Bartram (1933b) and I provisionally
accept 8 species for the Society Islands. Of these, 4 have been found
only on Tahiti, but I suspect that further study will show them to be
synonyms of more common, widely distributed taxa.

Key to Species of *Campylopus*

1. Costa markedly excurrent (over 100 μ) in a hyaline, toothed hairpoint;
   plants typically with a frosted appearance................1. *C. introflexus.*
1. Costa percurrent or short-excurrent (usually less than 100 μ), not commonly hyaline; plants lacking a frosted appearance
   2. Leaves to 6 mm or longer
      3. Leaves to 0.26 mm wide, costa to 0.14 mm wide........5. *C. obscurus.*
      3. Leaves to 0.84 mm wide, costa to 0.48 mm wide........4. *C. sulfureus.*
   2. Leaves usually less than 5 mm long
      3. Leaves less than 3 mm long, 1.8–2.5 × 0.29–0.36 mm, the costa
         0.12–0.14 mm wide at the base................7. *C. aoraiensis.*
      3. Leaves longer than 3 mm, larger in width and in costa width
         4. Upper lamina cells mostly parallel costa, short-rectangular
            5. Leaves 4.3–4.6 mm long, the costa 0.29–0.34 mm wide at
               base; basal cells 37–63 × 12–20 μ, upper lamina cells 10–20
               × 2.5–5 μ................3. *C. nudicaulis.*
            5. Leaves 4.0–4.3 mm long, the costa 0.22–0.24 mm wide at
               base; basal cells 15–30 × 15–25 μ, upper lamina cells 7–15 ×
               6–8 μ................2. *C. nadeaudianus.*
         4. Upper lamina cells with long axis mostly at an angle oblique to
            the costa, elongate rhomboidal
            5. Costa less than 0.25 mm wide at leaf base; leaves 3.5–4.9 ×
               0.50–0.74 mm................6. *C. vernieri.*
            5. Costa 0.29–0.34 mm wide at leaf base; leaves 3.6–4.6 ×
               0.68–0.84 mm................8. *C. umbellatus.*

1. *Campylopus introflexus* (Hedwig) Bridel
Mant. Musc. 72. 1819.

Plants forming turfs of densely tufted stems on rock and soil

(Sainsbury, 1955, reported stumps or logs as possible habitats for New Zealand plants), to 5 cm tall, green to yellow-green above, dark below; leaves erect-spreading to appressed, often in comose tufts, 3–6 mm long, lanceolate; costa excurrent in a hyaline (sometimes brownish, according to Dixon), reflexed, denticulate arista (Dixon, 1913, noted the hairpoint need not be reflexed). The back of the nerve typically deeply furrowed, with dorsal stereids only; costa to 300 μ wide at the base. Alar cells vary from indistinct and colored to inflated and hyaline. Seta 9–10 mm long; capsule about 1.5 mm long, horizontal to pendulous, often curved and furrowed (sulcate) when dry; operculum beaked, slightly curved, 7–8 mm long; calyptra cucullate and fringed at the base. Spores variable in size, 9–11 μ. Dixon (1913) observed that forms of *C. introflexus* may have the costa smooth on the lower side.

ILLUSTRATIONS. Figure 24A–D.

TAHITI. Pirae District: Fare Rau Ape–Mt. Aorai trail, 1950 m, near Chalet Fare Ata, on ground in disturbed, exposed area around cabin, *2750*; 2065 m, at summit of Mt. Aorai on exposed soil, *2790*; collected at 2050 m, *2792*.

Distribution.—Society Islands (Tahiti, a new record), New Zealand, New Caledonia, New Guinea, Galápagos Islands, Juan Fernández Island, Chile, Puerto Rico, West Indies, Mexico, Arizona, Texas, Europe.

Dixon (1913) observed that *Campylopus pudicus* (Hornsch.) Jaeg., which has a smooth-backed costa, was, at best, a subspecies of *C. introflexus*. Society Islands specimens collected by me in 1964 compare well with New Zealand specimens identified by Dixon as *C. introflexus*, but not with specimens from Hawaii, determined by Bartram as *C. introflexus*. A comparison of various descriptions together with the recognition of Dixon's (and others') broad interpretation of this species, has led me to conclude that the recent collections are indeed *C. introflexus* and apparently a new record for the Society Islands.

2. *Campylopus nadeaudianus* Bescherelle
  Ann. Sci. Nat. Bot. ser. 7, 20: 16. 1895.

Plants erect, yellow-green, dark green below, caespitose, the stems simple or branched at the base, to 1 cm tall; leaves erect in comal tufts, appressed below, 4.0–4.3 × 0.53–0.58 mm, linear-lanceolate from an ovate or slightly ovate base; upper margins inrolled, entire to denticulate just below the apex; costa percurrent, ending in a cluster of 3–4 teeth, 0.22–0.24 mm wide at the base. Lamina basal cells brownish to hyaline, slightly inflated or bulging, irregularly rhomboidal, 15–30 × 15–25 μ; those immediately above not bulging, rectangular to irregularly rhomboidal, 12–25 × 10–15 μ toward the costa, becoming narrower and hyaline toward the margins. Upper lamina cells parallel the leaf axis, irregularly rhomboidal, 7–15 × 6–8 μ; those of midleaf in 2 intermixed patterns, some with long axis at an angle oblique to the costa, others paralleling the costa. Sporophytes not found. (Based on 2760A.)

ILLUSTRATIONS. Figure 24I–L.

TAHITI. Mamono: On soil, ca 900 m, on burned spots between stems of *Pteris aurita*, *Nadeaud 58* (Bescherelle, 1895a). Mt. Aorai: Summit, *2760*.

Distribution.—Society Islands (Tahiti), endemic.

It should be interesting to compare *C. nadeaudianus* with *C. introflexus*, which seem to have something in common if Dixon's (1913) observations regarding *C. pudicus* are correct. Bescherelle, in his original description, called the costa of *C. nadeaudianus* percurrent, a feature which should at once separate this species from *C. introflexus*, which is characterized by an excurrent, hyaline costa.

3. *Campylopus nudicaulis* Bescherelle
Bull. Soc. Bot. France 45: 55. 1898.

Plants erect, irregularly branched, brownish below, green to yellow-green above, 5–6 cm tall; leaves slightly ovate at the base, lanceolate, erect to erect-spreading, forming terminal clusters or heads, appressed on the lower stem; lamina only 1 or 2 cells wide on either side of the costa toward the apex, serrulate above, entire below, 4.3–4.6 (–5.0) × 0.53–0.63 mm; costa 0.29–0.34 mm wide at the leaf base. Lamina basal cells hyaline to yellowish, irregularly rhomboidal to hexagonal, 37–63 × 12–20 μ, becoming narrower and slightly longer toward the margins, 50–75 × 5–8 μ; upper lamina cells irregularly rectangular, thick-walled (2–2.5 μ), 10–20 × 2.5–5 μ. The costa is percurrent or short-excurrent, slightly ribbed and toward the apex denticulate on the back. No sporophytes observed. (Based on 3221.)

ILLUSTRATIONS. Figure 24M–P.

TAHITI. Papara District: Temarua Valley (type locality), *Nadeaud 208* (Bescherelle, 1898a). Pirae District: Pirae–Mt. Aorai trail, *Quayle 697a* (Bartram, 1933a); Fare Rau Ape–Mt. Aorai trail, ca 1000 m, on the ground, *284; 268;* 1950 m, on bark of trees, *2761; 2762.* Hitiaa District: Ca 400 m, *3221.*

Distribution.—Society Islands (Tahiti), endemic.

Bescherelle (1898a) observed that this species differed from *Campylopus blumei* Dozy & Molk. (to which it was most closely related) in the green color of its tufts, in the narrower and more elongate leaves, and in the stronger denticulation of the leaf apices. Duplicates of a specimen determined by Bartram (1933a) as *C. nudicaulis* are deposited in the Bishop and the Farlow herbaria, but Bartram was himself unable to examine authentic material for comparison. He observed that the auriculate leaves, the clearly differentiated alar cells extending to the costa, and the different basal areolation could be used to separate his specimen from *C. sulfureus.* Bartram noted further that many of the plants have apical clusters of minute-leaved, flagellate branches similar to those produced by other dicranaceous genera, and concluded that they served in asexual reproduction. *Campylopus nudicaulis* as determined by Bartram differs from specimens he identified as *C. sulfureus* (in the Bishop herbarium) in the more regularly arranged, more closely appressed, more rigid leaves. In *C. sulfureus,* the leaves are all approximately the same size, but are not as uniformly distributed along the stem and are more flexuose.

4. *Campylopus sulfureus* Bescherelle
   Bull. Soc. Bot. France 45: 55. 1898a.

Plants 6–8 cm tall, yellow-green above, reddish-brown to dark green below; leaves erect, 5.2–6.7 × 0.70–0.84 mm; costa 0.44–0.48 mm wide at the base. Basal lamina cells not inflated, hyaline, rectangular to irregularly hexagonal and elongate, thin-walled, 20–35 × 7–25 μ; upper lamina cells parallel the costa, rectangular, angles rounded, 10–20 × 3–5 μ. Upper leaf margins remotely denticulate, incurved, apparently continuous to the costa apex in 1 or 2 cell rows on each side. The ovate, plane portion of the lower leaf occupies between 1.4 and 1.9 mm of the total leaf length. Sporophytes not observed. (Based on *2821, 2771.*)

ILLUSTRATIONS. Figure 24Q–T.

TAHITI. Hitiaa District: Plateau Talmaotira, ca 1214 m, fruiting, *Nadeaud 207* (Bescherelle, 1898a). Pirae District: Pirae–Mt. Aorai trail, *Quayle 697, 702* (Bartram, 1933a); Col de Hamata, ca 900 m, on trail from Fare Rau Ape to Aorai, on humose soil, *Hürlimann T 1258*; ca 1100 m, on decaying log, *Hürlimann T 1256*; 750 m, on vertical lateritic face, with *Pogonatum tahitense, Hürlimann T 1224* (Hürlimann, 1963); 1000 m, on log, *2696*; Mt. Aorai, 800 m, *2821*; 1950 m, *2771*. Mahina District: S side Mt. Orohena, on crest of ridge, *St. John and Fosberg 17090, 17136* (det. Bartram, BISH, unreported).

RAIATEA. Faaroa Bay: On moist red clay soil, 100 m, *Moore 70* (Bartram, 1931, BISH).

Distribution.—Society Islands (Tahiti, Raiatea), Austral Islands (Rapa).

Bartram (1933a) examined authentic material collected by Temarii Nadeaud (apparently unreported) and referred Quayle's collections to C. *sulfureus* on this basis, noting that the leaves are not at all auriculate and that the cells at the basal angles are scarcely differentiated from those of the leaf base. Quayle's specimens are only 1–3 cm tall even when fruiting, the leaves 3–4 mm long, slender, flexuose, not closely appressed to the stem in the upper portion of the plant.

5. *Campylopus obscurus* Aongstrom
Oefv. K. Svensk. Vet. Ak. Foerh. 30(5): 119. 1873.

Plants 6–8 cm tall, erect, yellow-green; leaves erect, tubular, upper margins inrolled, lanceolate-acuminate, 4.6–6.0 × 0.24–0.26 mm; costa 0.12–0.14 mm wide at the base, denticulate at the apex, percurrent to short-excurrent, toothed on the back. Lamina bases auriculate, basal cells brownish, quadrate to rectangular, slightly swollen, 20–50 × 12–25 μ; upper lamina cells quadrate to rhomboidal, 5–10 × 5 μ. Rhizoidal tomentum present on lower leaf bases. Sporophytes not observed. (Based on *2930*.)

ILLUSTRATIONS. Figure 20A–D.

TAHITI. Without locality: *Andersson sn*, 1852, *Eugenie* Expedition (Aongstrom, 1873). Mt. Aorai: Ca 1950 m, *2930*.

Distribution.—Society Islands (Tahiti), endemic.

Aongstrom (1873) described the plants as 4–6 cm tall, yellow-green, the stems covered by a brownish mat of rhizoidal filaments, slender and filiform beneath the fertile apices which form expanded heads. The lower stem leaves and those on sterile stems are erect-patent (forming an angle of about 45° with the stem), those of fertile branches within the terminal heads adpressed, lying tightly against the stem. Alar cells are brownish, enlarged, subquadrate to oval. Aongstrom compared this species to *Campylopus rosulatus* Hampe, which he noted has narrower, noncuspidate leaves, and with *C. involutus*, which has less involute leaves and different alar cells.

Bescherelle (1895a) considered the sterile specimen in his possession to be a young form of a species described by Duby (1875) as *Campylopus vernieri*, but noted that *if* the two became recognized as identical, this species would fall into synonymy with *C. obscurus*. Wijk, Margadant, and Florschutz (1959) gave *C. vernieri* as a synonym of *C. obscurus*, apparently on the strength of this observation, but it is obvious that Bescherelle intended to keep the two taxa separate pending further study.

6. *Campylopus vernieri* Duby
   Mem. Soc. Phys. Hist. Nat. Geneve 24: 372. 2 f. 5. 1875.

Plants 4–7 cm tall, dull yellow above, dark green or blackish below, erect, irregularly branched; upper leaves crowded in heads and erect-spreading on some stems, less crowded and more appressed on others, lanceolate-acuminate, 3.5–4.9 × 0.5–0.74 mm, sometimes auriculate; costa percurrent, 0.17–0.24 mm wide at the base, ribbed and denticulate on the back near the apex; leaf margins entire below, crenulate to serrulate toward the apex, inrolled in the upper one-half to three-quarters of the blade. Lamina basal cells brownish, irregularly rectangular to hexagonal, some bulging, 30–75 × 20–25 μ; upper cells rhomboidal, 10–25 × 4–5 μ, irregularly thick-walled, the walls to about 2 μ thick, some cells at an angle oblique to the costa, others paralleling the costa. Sporophytes cygneous, 4–5 mm long; capsules narrowly ovate, 0.9–1.2 × 0.45–0.5 mm; exothecial cells rectangular, 35–45 × 10–12 μ, thick-walled. Calyptra, operculum, peristome teeth, and spores not seen. (Based on Vernier's collection in the Boissier Herbarium, G!)

ILLUSTRATIONS. Figure 23, from the type.

TAHITI. Without locality: On the trunks of tree ferns, *Vernier sn* (Duby, 1875; Bescherelle, 1895a, G).

Distribution.—Society Islands (Tahiti), endemic.

Bescherelle (1895a) placed *Campylopus vernieri* near to *C. blumii* Dozy & Molk. (= *C. umbellatus*) and distinguished *C. vernieri* on the basis of longer stems, more narrow, larger, oval, innermost perichaetial leaves and on the more strongly denticulate stem

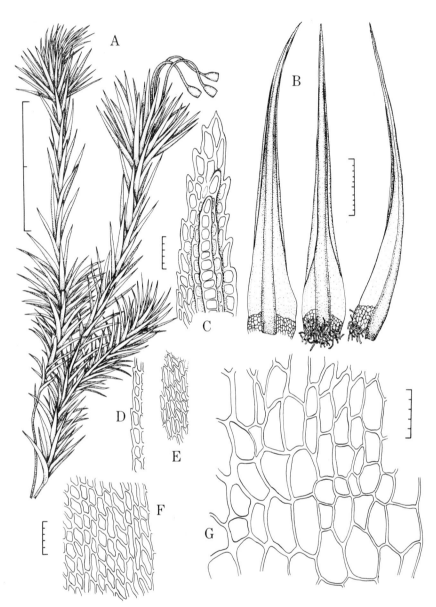

Fig. 23. *Campylopus vernieri.* (From the type collected by Vernier, *sn.*) A. Habit, scale 1 mm. B. Leaves, scale 1 mm. C. Leaf apex, dorsal surface. D. Leaf margin, upper. E. Lamina cells, upper median. F. Lamina cells, lower median. C–F, scale 50 μ. G. Lamina basal cells, scale 50 μ.

leaves. Further, he noted the capsule to be verrucose only at the base, the seta only at the summit (confirmed by my examination), the operculum to be shorter.

7. *Campylopus aoraiensis* sp. nov.

Habitu *C. nadeaudianus* Besch. similis, sed plantae et foliis staturae minoribus. Folia lanceolata, 1.8–2.5 × 0.29–0.36 mm, cellulis superiore incrassatis, 10–20 × 3–5 μ, ad basin decoloratis aut hyalinis, quadrato-ad elongato-ventricosis auriculata. Caetera ignota. Specimen typicum *2762A*, in hb. NY.

Plants about 1 cm tall, forming sparse turfs on soil; leaves lanceolate, 1.8–2.5 × 0.29–0.36; costa percurrent, 0.12–0.14 mm wide at the base; expanded basal portion of leaf occupies one-quarter to one-third the leaf length. Lamina upper cells irregularly thick-walled, rectangular, 10–20 × 3–5 μ; lower cells mostly hyaline, occasionally brownish, quadrate to short-rectangular, 20–30 × 20–25 μ; basal cells hyaline to brownish, slightly auriculate in some leaves. Upper margins inrolled, entire or nearly so, with 2–3 teeth at the leaf apex. Sporophytes not found.

ILLUSTRATIONS. Figure 24E–H.

TAHITI. Mt. Aorai: 1950 m, on tree trunk, *2762A*.

Distribution.—Society Islands (Tahiti), endemic.

Campylopus aoraiensis is the smallest of the Society Islands species and may be distinguished best on that basis.

8. *Campylopus umbellatus* (Walker-Arnott) Bartram
Bishop Mus. Bull. 101: 44. 1933b.

Campylopus blumii (Dozy & Molk.) Bosch & Lac., Bryol. Jav. 1: 81. t. 68. 1858. *fide* Dixon, J. Bot. 60: 289. 1922a.

Campylopus dozyanus (C. Muell.) Jaeg., Ber. S. Gall. Naturw. Ges. 1870–1871: 418. 1872. Adumbr. 1. 122. *fide* Wijk, Margadant, and Florschutz, 1959, *cf.* Dixon, J. Bot. 60: 287. 1922a. Also, Bescherelle, 1895a.

Dicranum flexifolium Nadeaud, 1873, *nec* Hornschuch. *fide* Bescherelle, 1895a.

Trichostomum blumii Dozy & Molk., Ann. Sci. Nat. 2: 385. 1844.

Thysanomitrium umbellatum Walker-Arnott, Disp. 34. 1826.

Campylopus geniculatus Aongstr., Oefv. K. Svensk. Vet. Ak. Foerh. 4: 18. 1872. *fide* Bartram, 1933b.

Thysanomitrium Hawaiicum C. Muell., Flora 82: 440. 1896. *fide* Bartram, 1933b, Dixon, 1922a.

Plants dark brown to black below, yellow-green above and glossy, turf-forming, the stems 8–10 cm tall, with reddish rhizoidal mats in the lower portions; leaves erect, crowded (especially at stem tips, where they form tufts), oblong-lanceolate, the base slightly

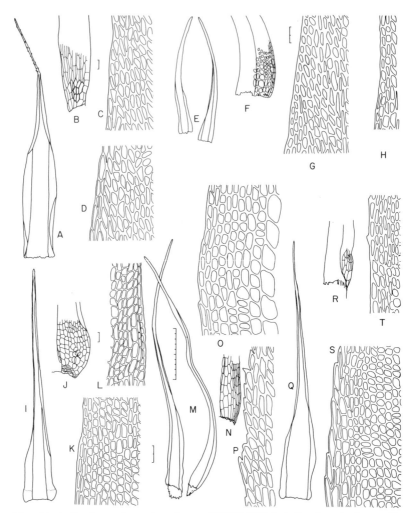

FIG. 24. A–D. *Campylopus introflexus*. (*HOW 2756*.) A. Leaf, scale 1 mm. B. Leaf base and alar cells, scale 50 μ. C. Lower leaf cells and margin, scale 20 μ. D. Upper leaf cells and margin. E–H. *Campylopus aoraiensis*. (*HOW 2762*.) E. Leaves, scale 1 mm. F. Leaf base and alar cells, scale 50 μ. G. Lower leaf cells and margin. H. Upper leaf cells and margin. G, H, scale 20 μ. I–L. *Campylopus nadeaudianus*. (*HOW 2760A*.) I. Leaf, scale 1 mm. J. Leaf base and alar cells, scale 50 μ. K. Lower leaf cells and margin. L. Upper leaf cells and margin. L, K, scale 20 μ. M–P. *Campylopus nudicaulis*. (*HOW 3221*.) M. Leaves, scale 1 mm. N. Leaf base and alar cells, scale 50 μ. O. Lower leaf cells and margin, scale 20 μ. P. Upper leaf cells and margin, scale 20 μ. Q–T. *Campylopus sulfureus*. (*HOW 2771*.) Q. Leaf, scale 1 mm. R. Leaf base and alar cells, scale 50 μ. S. Lower leaf and margin, scale 20 μ. T. Upper leaf cells and margin, scale 20 μ. (*del.* HAM.)

narrower than midleaf, auriculate, leaf apices short-acuminate to blunt, 4.5–5 mm long, about 1 mm wide, concave to nearly tubulose above, the margins incurved over the costa, margins entire in the lower blade, denticulate above. Costa to 300 μ wide, about one-half the width of the leaf base; stereid cells appear on both sides of the median row in leaf cross sections. Lamellae on the lower surface of the costa may be serrate. Alar cells brownish to hyaline, in 1 to 2 layers, extending from margins to costa. Cells of the lamina oval to short-linear, 20–25 μ long. Seta 5–6 mm long, smooth, cygneous to flexuose, papillose at the base of the capsule; capsule 1.5 mm long, ovoid-cylindric, the upper part furrowed when dry. Peristome teeth to 600 μ, brownish, pale at the tips, forked to about the middle, papillose above, vertically striate below. Operculum conic-rostrate, about one-half as long as the urn; calyptra cucullate, fringed at the base. Spores smooth, to 10 μ.

ILLUSTRATIONS. Bartram (1933b, p. 45, f. 27). Figure 20E–H.

TAHITI. Without locality: United States Exploring Expedition, *Wilkes sn* (Sullivant, 1859, as *Campylopus dozyanus*); *Vesco sn* (Bescherelle, 1895a, as *C. blumii*). Papenoo or Punarua valley: Near Mt. Orohena, on rocks in stream, *Nadeaud 206* (Bescherelle, 1898a, as *C. blumii*). Pirae District: Vicinity of Fort Fautaua, associated with *Dicranum arcuatum* (= ?) and *Pogonatum tahitense, Nadeaud sn* (Nadeaud, 1873, as *Dicranum flexifolium, fide* Bescherelle, 1895a, as *C. blumii*); Fautaua Valley, *Setchell and Parks 5428* (Brotherus, 1924b, as *Thysanomitrium blumii*); before first ford in stream above Fort Fautaua, on ground along trail, *3179*; with *Ectropothecium, 3159*; on branch, with orchid, *3174*; Fare Rau Ape–Mt. Aorai trail, *Quayle 208, 211b, 212c* (Bartram, 1933a, as *C. umbellatus,* BISH!); ca 1000 m, on ground, *2687, 2842.* Mahina District (?): Mt. Orohena, 1400 m, E side of S ridge, on rocks at base of waterfall, *St. John and Fosberg 17131* (unreported, BISH!). Mataiea District: Vaihiria Valley, ca 100 m, on branches, with *Garovaglia* and *Frullania, Whittier sn.* Taiarapu Peninsula: Pueu District, Haavini Valley, 250 m, on rocks, with *Ectropothecium* and *Bryum billardieri, 2589.*

RAIATEA. Mt. Temehani: Near the "hole," ca 450 m, on wet rocks, *Moore 22* (Bartram, 1931, as *Thysanomitrium umbellatum,* BISH!).

MOOREA. Without locality: *Wilkes sn* (Sullivant, 1859, as *Campylopus dozyanus*).

Distribution.—Society Islands (Tahiti, Moorea, Raiatea), Hawaii (all larger islands), Austral Islands, Mangareva, Samoa, Fiji, New Guinea, Malaya, Java, Borneo, Tonkin, Sunda Islands, Sri Lanka (Ceylon), south India, Japan, Ternate, Philippine Islands, Burma, Sumatra, Celebes, south China, Formosa, Sikkim, Ecuador, Peru, Chile, Mexico, Costa Rica, West Indies, Juan Fernández Island.

Dixon (1922) made an extensive review of the genus *Thysanomitrium* (= *Campylopus*), placing seven species in synonymy with *T. richardii,* including *Campylopus nigrescens, Dicranum dozyanum, Campylopus blumii, Thysanomitrium umbellatum, T. powellii,* and *T. hawaiicum.* Dixon further observed that *Thysanomitrium exasperatum* is linked by intermediate forms which might ultimately place it in synonymy with *T. richardii,* but he avoided making the reduction on the basis that there might possibly be some minor differences which would merit further consideration! Miller (personal communication, 1970) does not consider *Campylopus umbellatus* to be conspecific with *C. richardii,* a view with which I agree.

A brief review of collections in various herbaria is sufficient to demonstrate the taxonomic chaos which still exists within the genus *Campylopus.*

8. *Dicranoloma* (Renauld) Renauld
   Rev. Bryol. 28: 85. 1901.
Dicranoloma braunii (C. Mueller) Paris
   Ind. Bryol. ed. 2, 2: 25. 1904.
   Dicranum braunii C. Muell., in Dozy and Molkenboer, Bryol. Jav. 1: 69. t. 57. 1858.
   ?Dicranoloma graeffeanum (C. Muell.) Par., Ind. Bryol. ed. 2, 2: 27. 1904.
   ?Dicranum graeffeanum C. Muell., J. Mus. Godeffroy 3(6): 62. 1874.
   Dicranum dicarpon Dozy & Molk., in hb.

Plants erect, to about 10 cm tall, the stems flexuose, turf-forming, golden to greenish-brown; leaves erect-spreading, flexuose, about 1 cm long. Margins unbordered, coarsely toothed, teeth present also along the back of the costa, which is percurrent. Cells of the alar region inflated, irregularly quadrate, orange-brown. A dense tomentum of rhizoidal cells clothes the stem. (Based on *3028.*)

ILLUSTRATIONS. Dozy and Molkenboer (1858, t. 57). Figure 20I–K.

TAHITI. Pirae District: Mt. Aorai, above 1386 m, trail to summit, *Quayle 154b, 156c* (Bartram, 1933a, BISH, FH); near 2000 m, *Decker and Decker 50, 72;* about 1200 m, with *Trematodon, 2736;* 1040 m, associated with *Spiridens, 2708;* (1960) *278, 244a, 287;* Papenoo Valley, 400 m, on branches, *3028,* illustrated.

Distribution.—Society Islands (Tahiti), New Caledonia, Fiji, Samoa, New Hebrides, Louisades, d'Entrecasteaux, Philippine Islands, Moluccas, Celebes, Borneo, Java (type locality), Sumatra, New Guinea, Aneityum.

Bartram (1933a) wrote, "the distribution of the species is now fairly continuous from Sumatra to Tahiti. *D. Graeffeanum* (C. Mueller), of Samoa, is, as Mr. Dixon has remarked, probably the same thing and should be reduced to synonymy." Examination of the collections in the Bishop Museum and the New York Botanical Garden herbaria leads me to believe that the entire genus needs revision. Species as *D. robustum,* with a markedly similar appearance and broad distributions in the southern hemisphere, and *D. brevifolium* Bartram, known only from the nearby Marquesas, may belong to a single complex. *Dicranoloma subreflexifolium* (C. Muell.) Broth. differs in being smaller, the alar cell region more expanded, and is closer to *D. reflexum. Dicranoloma billardieri* has a differentiated margin and smaller teeth, and *D. pungens* lacks teeth altogether. *Dicranoloma plicatum* Bartram is related by Bartram (1933a) to *D. dicarpum* Hornsch., but differs in the plicate leaf base, areolation, and in the leaf margins.

9. *Leucoloma* Bridel
Bryol. Univ. 2: 218. 1827.

Plants erect, 3–4 cm tall, in lax to dense turfs, the stems branched, pale to silvery green; leaves crowded, falcate-secund, ovate-lanceolate; costa slender, excurrent in a long setaceous (bristle-like) point. Cells of the lamina small, papillose, the margin cells hyaline; alar cells form auriculate groups. Sporophytes typical of the family.

Leucoloma molle (C. Mueller) Mitten
J. Linn. Soc. Bot. Suppl. 1: 13. 1859.
Dicranum molle C. Muell., Syn. 1: 354. 1849.
Leucoloma hawaiiense Broth., Bishop Mus. Bull. 40: 9. 2 f. 6. 1927.
Leucoloma novae-guineae (C. Muell.) Par., Ind. Bryol. Suppl. 223. 1900. *nom. nud., fide* Fleischer, 1904.
Leucoloma limbatulum Besch., Bull. Soc. Bot. France 45: 54. 1898.

Plants densely tufted, stems to 3 cm long, pale green above, the upper leaves crowded, erect-spreading to secund, the apices long and flexuose, about 5×0.5 mm; costa long-excurrent, the point minutely denticulate. Lamina cells oval-oblong, minutely papillose, $5–7 \times 4–5$ μ; alar cells large, rhomboidal, brownish or hyaline.

ILLUSTRATIONS. Fleischer (1904, 1: 123), Bartram (1933b, p. 57, f. 36). Figure 20L–N.

TAHITI. Papenoo Valley: Foot of Mt. Orohena, on trees, *Nadeaud 205* (Bescherelle, 1898a, the type of *L. limbatulum*).

MOOREA. Vaianae: *Temarii Nadeaud sn* (Bescherelle, 1901, BISH, P).

RAIATEA. Temehani Range: S end, intermixed with liverworts on branches of shrubs, *Moore 47*; 500 m, on soil in shade of shrubs, *Moore 50* (Bartram, 1931, BISH, FH).

Distribution.—Society Islands (Tahiti, Moorea, Raiatea), New Guinea, Luzon, Formosa, Japan, Hongkong, Java (type locality).

The slender, falcate-secund leaves with hyaline borders are distinctive of the genus and readily serve to separate it from the genus *Campylopus* which it resembles. Specimens of *Leucoloma limbatulum* compare so closely with authentic material of *L. molle* (collected by Junghuhn on Java, NY!), that they must be recognized as conspecific. Bartram (1933b) recorded lamina cells of Hawaiian specimens referred to *L. molle* as 10–20 × 5 μ, but he was undoubtedly referring to cells near the leaf base, for cells in the upper lamina of Hawaiian collections compare well with those of the authentic Javan specimen. Sporophytes are apparently rare within the genus, but Fleischer (1904) reported that they appear along the major stem and that the seta is quite short (about 2–3 mm long).

IV. LEUCOBRYACEAE

The family Leucobryaceae is comprised of a complex of genera which may or may not be closely related. Brotherus' (1924b) treatment of the family includes four subfamily groups: Leucophanoideae, Leucobryoideae, Octoblepharoideae, and Arthrocormoideae, and Bartram (1933a, b, 1939) followed this approach. Fleischer (1904) recognized two basic groups or families, the Leucobryaceae and the Leucophanaceae, whereas Cardot (1900) maintained the family Leucobryaceae, subdividing it into the tribes recognized by Brotherus. A. L. Andrews (1947) recognized the Leucobryaceae as an artificial family and recommended that the genus *Leucobryum* be treated as a part of the family Dicranaceae on the basis of its dicranoid capsule, peristome, and calyptra. It is not my intention to review the construction of the family Leucobryaceae here, but it seems appropriate to observe that Andrews' suggestion the Leucobryaceae be eliminated together with Fleischer's Leucophanaceae is not necessarily the only resolution of the problem, despite the obvious similarities shared by members of these families. Taxa in the family Leucobryaceae are recognizable on the basis of vegetative characters alone (a fact far from insignificant). All are whitish to pale green, the leaves thick and stiff, unlike those of most other mosses in the differentiation of the lamina into enlarged hyaline cells and smaller chlorophyllose cells, the chlorophyllose cells usually appearing in a layer between 2 or more layers of hyaline cells. This pattern is approached only in the family Sphagnaceae, and then only in the presence of hyaline and chlorophyllose cells in a specific arrangement; there is no real similarity in the structure of these cells or in their distribution. Although hyaline and chlorophyllose cells are found in other families (especially the Calymperaceae), there is no integrated arrangement of these cells, and the hyaline cells are commonly restricted to the basal portion of the leaf blade, the chlorophyllose cells to the upper lamina. It seems fully as realistic to recognize Cardot's tribes (Brotherus' subfamilies) as distinct families: the Leucobryaceae, the Leucophanaceae, the Octoblepharaceae, and the Arthrocormaceae. These conceivably could be treated within their own order or within the Dicranales, the dicranoid affinities understood as indicative of a remote but common ancestry. However, I have followed Bartram's lead here as a matter of convenience, and consider the family in the older, broader sense.

Plants pale, whitish-green or white, forming low turfs or tufts, appearing as isolated plants or in dense, compact cushions which may be several centimeters thick at the center. Leaves are often densely imbricated, stiff, erect to erect-spreading, easily broken from the stem and characteristically more than 2 cell-layers thick throughout most of the blade. The thickened portion has been interpreted as an expanded costa, especially in *Leucobryum* and *Octoblepharum*, in which a layer of hyaline (leucocyst) cells appears on either side of a median row of chlorophyll-containing (chlorocyst) cells. There may be more than a single layer of leucocysts on the lower or dorsal side of the leaf, and the leucocysts are often porose. In the genus *Leucophanes* a strand of thick-walled elongate cells (stereid cells) is suggestive of a costa. In the interpretation of the leaf as being composed of expanded costa, the true lamina is present only as a single-layered marginal row of hyaline cells developed best near the base of the leaf. Sporophytes are not common in Pacific Islands Leucobryaceae; reproduction seems to be primarily vegetative, new plants arising from leaf fragments or from propagula (the latter in *Leucophanes*). Sporophytes are terminal, erect, solitary, the capsule erect and subcylindric or inclined, asymmetrical and strumose, according to Bartram (1933b). Peristome teeth 8 (*Octoblepharum*) or 16, entire or cleft above. The operculum is rostrate, the calyptra cucullate.

KEY TO GENERA OF THE LEUCOBRYACEAE

1. Stereid strand (costa or midrib) absent
  2. Leaves ligulate (strap-shaped), not tubulose or keeled above; markedly thickened with 1–3 layers of hyaline cells on either side of a single median layer of chlorophyllose cells................3. *Octoblepharum.*
  2. Leaves lanceolate, tubulose or keeled above; in cross section with a single layer of hyaline cells above the median chlorophyllose cells and 1–3 layers of hyaline cells below toward the base of the leaf..1. *Leucobryum.*
1. Stereid strand present
  2. Chlorophyllose cells in a single median row................2. *Leucophanes.*
  2. Chlorophyllose cells in 3 rows, a dorsal, a median, and a ventral series
    3. Leaves 3-ranked, approximately cylindrical and smooth above, with-

out suggestion of a blade-like lamina; in cross section the lower and upper rows of chlorophyllose cells covered by an outer layer of hyaline cells_____5. *Arthrocormus.*
3. Leaves not 3-ranked, not cylindrical above, spinose-papillose especially on the margins of a narrow lamina on either side of the central, thickened, costa-like region; the upper and lower series of chlorophyllose cells without external covering of hyaline cells when seen in cross section_____4. *Exodictyon.*

1. *Leucobryum* Hampe
Linnaea 13: 42. 1839.

Plants whitish to pale green, forming dense to loose cushions, 1 to several centimeters thick; leaves ovate-lanceolate, 3–5 mm long, formed mostly by a wide costa, in cross section formed by 2–5 layers of hyaline cells (leucocysts) and a single layer of widely separated chlorophyllose cells (chlorocysts) protected by 1 or 2 layers of leucocysts. No false costa (as is characteristic of the genus *Leucophanes*) is present.

Key to Species of *Leucobryum*

1. Leaves to 3.5 × 0.7 mm, falcate_____1. *L. scalare.*
1. Leaves to 5.0 × 0.7 mm, erect-spreading_____2. *L. tahitense.*

1. *Leucobryum scalare* C. Mueller *ex* Fleischer
Musci Fl. Buitenzorg 5(1): 143. 1904.

Plants 1–3 cm tall; leaves short, very rough on the back, to 3.5 × 0.7 mm, in cross section with 3–5 layers of leucocysts in the thickest part of the blade.

ILLUSTRATIONS. None.

TAHITI. Pirae District: Fautaua Valley, *Whitney Expedition sn;* above 1386 m, trail to summit Mt. Aorai, *Quayle 162, 165, 166* (Bartram, 1933a, FH).

MAKATEA. Interior: On log, *Whitney Expedition 874* (Bartram, 1933a).

Distribution.—Society Islands (Tahiti, Makatea), Nepal, Burma, Malacca, Thailand, Java, Sumatra, Borneo, Philippine Islands, Austral Islands (Rapa), Tuamotu Islands, Fiji.

Bartram (1933a) first reported this species from the Society Islands area from Makatea (Tuamotus). He noted that the specimens he examined were a slender form near Fleischer's variety *marschmeyeri,* but that they differed in having more erect, narrower leaves up to 3 mm long. Of the Tahitian plants, he wrote: "The leaves are erect and appressed with scarcely any evident falcate tendency, thus approaching Fleischer's variety more nearly than it does the typical form of the species." Later, Bartram (1940) noted: "These collections vary considerably but the differences seem to be slight and of little importance."

I am not at all convinced that there is a distinction between this species and *Leucobryum tahitense* Aongstr. Authentic specimens of *L. tahitense* fit Bartram's (1939) description for *L. scalare* characterized by the "short, crowded, slightly curved leaves, very rough on the back in the upper half so that in profile, the projections suggest a flight of steps in miniature, whence the specific name." Manuscript notes on herbarium sheets suggest that Mitten considered *L. tahitense* to be a synonym of *L. candidum* (P. Beauv.) Wils. *in* Hook. *f.*; Dixon considered it to be a synonym of *L. aduncum* Dozy & Molk. (see Fleischer, 1904, 1: 142, f. 18). A superficial examination of collections of *Leucobryum* species suggests that *L. aduncum* may eventually prove to be the name most properly applied to Society Islands species identified as *L. scalare* and *L. tahitense*. There seems to be a broad gradation in size and habit, and the most robust forms of Society Islands *Leucobryum* approach *L. sanctum* (Brid.) Hampe, which is still unreported for the archipelago although known widely in Indomalaya, Australia, and Samoa.

2. *Leucobryum tahitense* Aongstrom
   Oefv. K. Svensk. Vet. Ak. Foerh. 30(5): 118. 1873.

Plants erect, white, 2–3 cm tall, irregularly dichotomously branched; leaves uniformly crowded along stems, ovate-lanceolate, tubular above, 2.4–5.0 × 0.5–0.7 mm, ecostate, distinctively roughened, possessing forward pointing undulations on the dorsal surface below the apex, bordered by 2–3 rows of elongate cells, 100–250 × 4–7 μ, entire or nearly so; superficial "lamina" cells 25 × 12 μ, dorsally with distal ends projecting, irregularly rectangular; basal cells larger, smooth, 60–100 × 25–30 μ. (Based upon an isotype from Aongstrom's collection, NY!)

ILLUSTRATIONS. Figure 25A–C.

TAHITI. Without locality: *Andersson sn* (Aongstrom, 1873, 1875; Bescherelle, 1895a; isotype, NY!); toward 1100 m, frequent on all mountains of the interior, on ground and on trunks of old trees,

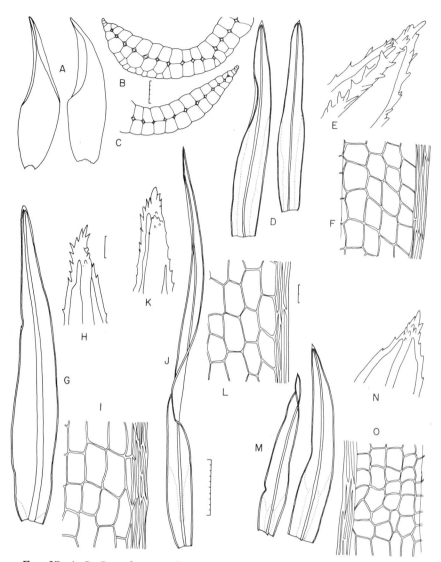

FIG. 25. A–C. *Leucobryum tahitense.* (Isotype.) A. Leaves, scale 1 mm. B. Leaf cross section near base. C. Midleaf cross section. B, C, scale 50 μ. D–F. *Leucophanes albescens.* (*Sachet 978.*) D. Leaves, scale 1 mm. E. Leaf tip, dorsal view, scale 50 μ. F. Cells and margin, lamina, scale 20 μ. G–I. *Leucophanes octoblepharoides.* (*HOW 2598.*) G. Leaf, scale 1 mm. H. Leaf tip, dorsal view, scale 50 μ. I. Cells and margin, lamina, scale 20 μ. J–L. *Leucophanes prasiophyllum.* (*HOW 256.*) J. Leaf, scale 1 mm. K. Leaf tip, dorsal view, scale 50 μ. L. Cells and margin, lamina, scale 20 μ. M–O. *Leucophanes tahiticum.* (*HOW 3460.*) M. Leaves, scale 1 mm. N. Leaf tip, dorsal view, scale 50 μ. O. Cells and margin, lamina, scale 20 μ. (*del.* HAM.)

Nadeaud 50; Vesco sn; Savatier sn (Bescherelle, 1895a); common in interior on ground and at higher elevations about 800–1000 m, *Nadeaud 211, 215* (Bescherelle, 1898a); Fautaua Valley, Rahi, 800 m; Miaa, 850 m, *Temarii Nadeaud sn* (Bescherelle, 1901). Pirae District: Mt. Aorai, above 1800 m, *Decker 37, 98*; above 500 m, *251, 255, 274* (1960); with *Dicranoloma braunii, 304*; Fare Rau Ape–Mt. Aorai trail, 700 m, with *Campylopus* and hepatics, *2659*; with *Pogonatum graeffeanum, Bryum billardieri,* and *Campylopus, 2660*; 1016 m, on bank, with *Thyridium obtusifolium, Pogonatum graeffeanum,* and *Dicranella hochreutineri, 2698*; 1030 m, with *Thyridium obtusifolium* and *Dicranoloma braunii, 2699; 2700*; with *Mastigophora, 2702*; 1120 m, *2722*; with *Pogonatum graeffeanum, Dicnemon rugosum, Mastigophora,* and *Jamesoniella, 2727*; 1800 m, on soil, with *Campylopus introflexus, 2749*; 1950 m, *2755*; 1300 m, *2821*; 1300 m, on bark of tree en route to One Tree Hill from Mt. Aorai, *2822*; 1200 m, on rotting stump on ridge, with *Bazzania, 2825*; on tree trunk, *2826*; 1700 m, *2869; 2918*; 1700 m, with *Schistochila* and *Distichophyllum, 2924*; Fautaua Valley, 540 m, overstory of *Hibiscus* and *Inocarpus, 3132*. Hitiaa District: Plateau region, 400 m, on bark of trees, with *Syrrhopodon ciliatus, Thyridium constrictum, Leucophanes,* and *Symphysodontella cylindracea, 3126*; 400 m, a very robust form, 5–7 cm tall, the leaves and stem not markedly different, *3219*; 400 m, with *Thyridium constrictum, 3224*; with *Macromitrium, 3225*; with *Acroporium, 3267*; with *Calomnion schistostegiellum* and *Trichosteleum hamatum, 3264*; with *Acroporium, 3226*; with *Thyridium constrictum, Hypnodendron samoanum,* and *Rhizogonium spiniforme, 3248*; with *Hypnodendron tahiticum, 3245*; with *Ectropothecium, 3246*; with *Thyridium constrictum, 3252; 3263*. Papenoo District: Papenoo Valley, 150 m, along stream banks and bed, to Vaihiria Valley, *3003*; on ridge between Papenoo and Vaihiria valleys, 840 m, with *Microlepidozia* and *Frullania, 3035*; 840 m, same locality, with *Porella, Plagiochila,* and *Microlepidozia, 3038*; W side, Papenoo Valley, to 180 m, on burned log, *2439*; on bark of tree, *2440*; on rotting log, *2445*. Mataiea District: Vaihiria Valley, 400 m, with *Callicostella papillata, Vesicularia, Rhynchostegium,* and *Trichocolea, 3048*; about 100 m, on dry places on banks, *3084*. Taiarapu Peninsula: Haavini Valley, 115 m, in *Inocarpus* and *Hibiscus* forest, *2506*; 260 m, on bark, with *Thyridium constrictum, Trichosteleum,* and *Acroporium, 2597*; Taravao, above experiment station, 800 m, with *Scapania* and *Frullania, 2136*; with *Rhizogonium spiniforme,*

2142, 2143; with *Syrrhopodon* (?) *banksii, 2147;* with *Acroporium, 2155;* 440–610 m, N slope above experiment station, in guava, *Miconia,* and *Cyathea* forest, with *Peperomia* and *Asplenium nidus* on ground, associated with *Cyathophorella tahitensis* (!), *Octoblepharum albidum, Racopilum,* and *Bazzania* at tree base, *2187;* 610 m, in mass of hepatics, with *Frullania, 2235;* forming thick cushion associated with *Rhizogonium, 2239;* W slope above experiment station, to 740 m, on rotten log, at 640 m, with *Ptychomnion aciculare* and *Lepidozia, 2275; 2285;* on rotten log, *2312.*

Moorea. Without locality: *Andersson sn, Eugenie* Expedition (Aongstrom, 1873, 1875).

Bora Bora: Pahia: W slope, 350 m, with *Inocarpus* and *Angiopteris, van Balgooy 1987A.*

Distribution.—Society Islands (Tahiti, Moorea; Bora Bora, a new record), endemic.

This species is doubtfully distinct from *Leucobryum scalare; Leucobryum tahitense* tends to have wider, more robust stems and broader leaves, the leaves 3–5 mm long.

2. *Leucophanes* Bridel
Bryol. Univ. 2: 763. 1826.

Three species of *Leucophanes* have been reported from the Society Islands: *L. octoblepharoides, L. prasiophyllum,* and *L. tahiticum.* The leaves are more delicate and more widely spreading than in species of the other genera of Leucobryaceae found in the archipelago, and the presence of a slender, costa-like strand is an immediately distinctive feature. Plants are small, less than 5–6 mm tall, and typically in Tahiti appear as scattered individuals rather than in cushions, and intermixed with other bryophytes, almost always on bark or rotting wood.

Key to Species of *Leucophanes*

1. Leaves keeled (carinate) for entire length................................4. *L. albescens.*
1. Leaves keeled or concave only in the upper blade
    2. Leaf central strand stereid cells covered by hyaline cells on the lower (dorsal) side as seen in section................................3. *L. tahiticum.*
    2. Leaf central strand stereid cells exposed, not covered by hyaline cells on the dorsal side as seen in section
        3. Leaves to 6 mm long, differentiated basal portion occupies as little as one-tenth the blade length................................1. *L. octoblepharoides.*
        3. Leaves to 9 mm long, differentiated basal portion occupies about one-fifth the blade length................................2. *L. prasiophyllum.*

1. *Leucophanes octoblepharoides* Bridel
   Bryol. Univ. 2: 763. 1826.
   Leucophanes minutum C. Muell., *in* Geheeb, Biblioth. Bot. 13: 2. 1889.
   Leucophanes korthalsii Dozy & Molk., Musci Fr. Ined. Archip. Indici 3: 65.
   f. 23. 1846. = var. *korthalsii* (Dozy & Molk.) Fleisch., Musci Fl. Buiten-
   zorg 1: 176. 1904.

Plants to 2 cm tall; leaves erect-spreading, 3–6 × 0.3–0.6 mm, lanceolate-acuminate, keeled above. At the leaf base there is a region of hyaline cells a single layer thick on either side of the thickened midsection, 6–10 rows of cells wide on each side. Fleischer (1904) described the seta as 6–8 mm long, reddish-yellow, the capsule ovoid-elongate, the mouth narrow. Peristome teeth 16, strongly papillose. Spores greenish, 12–16 μ, finely papillose.

ILLUSTRATIONS. Figure 25G–I.

TAHITI. Without locality: *Larminat sn* (Potier de la Varde, 1912).

Distribution.—Society Islands (Tahiti), Marquesas Islands, New Guinea, Java, Sumatra, Borneo, Banka, Moluccas (Amboina), Admiralty Islands, Philippine Islands, Nepal, Formosa, Caroline Islands (Yap).

Nadeaud (1873) first reported *L. octoblepharoides* from Tahiti but Bescherelle (1895a) examined the specimen and pronounced it to be *Leucobryum tahitense.* I have found nothing to support Fleischer's use of *L. octoblepharoides* var. *korthalsii* (Dozy & Molk.) Fleisch. as a record from the Society Islands.

2. *Leucophanes prasiophyllum* Bescherelle
   Bull. Soc. Bot. France 45: 56. 1898.

Plants 2–3 cm tall; leaves erect-spreading, lanceolate-acuminate, 5–9 × 0.3–0.5 mm, bordered by 3–4 rows elongate cells in 2–3 layers, flat below, concave to keeled just below the apex. Cells of the true lamina at the leaf base in 4–5 rows, 1–2:1, mostly quadrate, 20–46 × 16–25 μ. Costa smooth to slightly toothed below the apex. Sporophytes not found.

ILLUSTRATIONS. Figure 25J–L.

TAHITI. Arue District: Mountains near Teoa, 1100 m, *Nadeaud 216* (NY); Pinai, about 800 m, near Papeete, near Sainte-Amélie, *Nadeaud 217* (Bescherelle, 1898a). Haapape District: Rahi, 800 m, Miaa, 850 m, *Temarii Nadeaud sn* (Bescherelle, 1901). Mataiea District: Vaihiria Valley, on trunks of trees, *Eriksson 74* (Bartram, 1950b). Taiarapu Peninsula: Taravao, above experiment station,

500 m, near new dam, on detritus and tree fern, with *Trichosteleum hamatum, Hürlimann T 1186* (Hürlimann, 1963, det. Bartram).

RAIATEA. Faaroa Valley: 100 m, on decaying base of fern (nehe), *Moore 71* (Bartram, 1931, FH!).

Distribution.—Society Islands (Tahiti, Raiatea), endemic.

Bescherelle (1898a) distinguished *Leucophanes prasiophyllum* from *L. tahiticum* on the basis of a dorsal stereome, the median band of stereid cells exposed on the dorsal side of the leaf in the former, and a median stereome, the stereid cells covered by hyaline cells on the dorsal side in the latter.

3. *Leucophanes tahiticum* Bescherelle
   Bull. Soc. Bot. France 45: 57. 1898.

Plants erect, about 1 cm tall; leaves erect-spreading, lanceolate, 3–4 × 0.33–0.53 mm, bordered by 3–4 rows of elongate cells in 2–3 layers, flat below, concave or slightly keeled above. Cells of the true lamina at the leaf base in 4–5 rows, nearly isodiametric, irregularly quadrate to 6-sided, 12–25 × 17–25 μ. Costa and upper margins compactly toothed, the costa covered by hyaline cells on upper and lower surfaces. Sporophytes not found. (Based on *3460.*)

ILLUSTRATIONS. Figure 25M–O.

TAHITI. Papenoo District: Mountains near Marciati in the Punarua Valley at the foot of Mt. Orohena, *Nadeaud 218*; mountains of Pinai and Papeana, *Nadeaud 219* (Bescherelle, 1898a, NY). Haapape District: Miaa, 850 m, *Temarii Nadeaud sn* (Bescherelle, 1901, NY).

MOOREA. Papetoai Bay: 5 m, with *Thyridium, 3460.*

RAIATEA. Highest mountain: W side, 500 m, on wet branches of trees, *Moore 25.* Faaroa Bay: N side, 500 m, on top of mountain, *Moore 54* (Bartram, 1931, BISH!).

Distribution.—Society Islands (Tahiti, Raiatea), endemic.

The stereid strand, as previously noted, is entirely covered by hyaline cells on the lower side of the blade, a feature which serves to distinguish this species from *L. prasiophyllum.*

4. *Leucophanes albescens* C. Mueller
   Bot. Zeit. 22: 347. 1864.

Plants about 1 cm tall, erect; leaves lanceolate, acuminate, 3–4 × 0.5–0.6 mm, bordered to the apex, costate, spinose on the back of costa and margins below the apex. Leaf cross sections near the base show 2, occasionally 3, layers of hyalocysts below the median series of chlorocysts, 1 layer of hyalocysts above; the costa shows hyalocysts on both dorsal and ventral sides. Cells of the true lamina at the leaf base in 4–6 rows, irregularly 4–6-sided, nearly isodiametric, 12–20 × 12–25 μ. Sporophytes not found. (Based upon *Sachet 978*.)

ILLUSTRATIONS. Figure 25D–F.

MOPELIA. *Sachet 978.*

Distribution.—Society Islands (Mopelia), a new record. Celebes, Philippine Islands, New Guinea, Sunda Islands.

Leucophanes albescens is distinguished by the strongly keeled leaves and the prominent teeth extending down the back of the upper costa. Its closest counterpart in the Society Islands flora is *L. tahiticum* which has smaller lamina cells that occupy less than one-third the length of the blade in only 1 layer; those of *L. albescens* extend typically to one-half the length of the blade.

3. *Octoblepharum* Hedwig
Spec. Musc. 50. 1801.

This genus is easily recognized by the thickened, strap-shaped leaves each of which ends abruptly in an apiculus. The stout leaves, with nearly parallel margins, are not as brittle as those of *Arthrocormus* or *Exodictyon*, nor do they have the nearly cylindrical appearance of the leaves of those genera. The thick, opaque leaves of *Octoblepharum* serve to distinguish the genus from *Leucophanes*, which, in addition to having more translucent leaves, has a slender stereid strand. In cross section there is but a single layer of median, chlorophyllose cells, and in contrast with *Leucobryum* and *Leucophanes*, the thickest parts of leaves have 2 or more layers of hyaline cells above the median chlorophyllose cells as well as below them. As the generic name implies, there are 8 peristome teeth on the capsules.

Key to Species of *Octoblepharum*

1. Leaves to 5 mm, slightly recurved, strictly ligulate_____1. *O. albidum.*
1. Leaves to 8 mm, not recurved, slightly lanceolate_____2. *O. longifolium.*

1. *Octoblepharum albidum* Hedwig
Spec. Musc. 50. 1801.

This long-known species, nearly cosmopolitan, dates back at least to Linnaeus' *Species Plantarum* (1753), where it was reported as

Bryum albidum. Hedwig wrote: "trunco erecto ramoso, foliis e basi latiore lineari-lingulatis obtusis, capsulae erectae ovatae operculo conico-acuminato. . . . Folia extra partem amplexantem crassa, spongioso-vasculosa, e viridulo albidi coloris. Sporangium rectum, ovatum; operculum conico acuminatum, rectum."

Plants usually less than 1 cm tall, usually unbranched, and form loose cushions or turfs; leaves crowded, spreading, and recurved, 4–5 × 0.4 mm, the margins nearly parallel, entire to denticulate at the apex. The upper leaf is interpreted as being expanded costa, with 2–4 layers of hyaline cells above and below a median series of chlorophyllose cells. In the leaf base, near the stem, there is a marginal lamina of hyaline cells, 1 layer thick, which is interpreted as the true lamina. Seta about 5 mm long; capsule 1–1.5 mm long; operculum conic-rostrate, less than 1 mm long. Peristome teeth in 8 segments, widely spaced. Spores 18–22 μ, papillose.

ILLUSTRATIONS. Fleischer (1904, 1: 170, f. 22), Cardot (1900, pls. 12–15), Bartram (1933b, p. 58, f. 37). Figure 26A–C.

TAHITI. Without locality: *Lay and Collie sn* (Hooker and Walker-Arnott, 1831, 1832; Guillemin, 1836; Bescherelle, 1895a, as *O. ?longifolium*); *Wilkes sn,* United States Exploring Expedition (Sullivant, 1859). Pinai: 800 m, on trunks of trees, with *Syrrhopodon banksii, Nadeaud 223* (Bescherelle, 1898a).

Distribution.—Society Islands (Tahiti), Philippine Islands, New Guinea, Burma, Samoa, Fiji, Hawaii, Bahama Islands, Puerto Rico north to southern Florida, Africa, South America. Nearly cosmopolitan in tropical regions.

2. *Octoblepharum longifolium* Lindberg
Oefv. K. Svensk. Vet. Ak. Foerh. 21: 608. 1864.

Plants white, erect, irregularly, occasionally branched, 1–2 cm tall; leaves linear-ligulate, 5–8 × 0.4–0.5 mm, the expanded basal portion occupies less than one-sixth the length of the leaf. In cross section 4–5 layers of leucocysts appear above and below the median layer of chlorocysts. Sporophytes not found.

ILLUSTRATIONS. Figure 26D–F.

TAHITI. Without locality: *Pontén sn,* September, 1852 (Lindberg, 1865; Bescherelle, 1895a); *Savatier sn* (Bescherelle, 1895a); *Nadeaud 224* (Bescherelle, 1898a). Pirae District: Fautaua Valley, 540 m, with *Syrrhopodon banksii, 3129*; with *Fissidens mangarevensis, 3131*; 500 m, on branch with orchid, with *Campylopus umbellatus,*

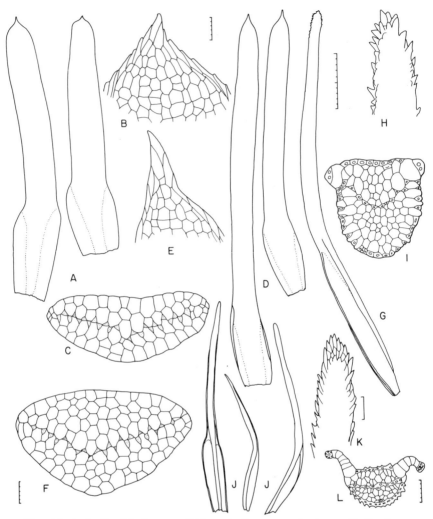

FIG. 26. A–C. *Octoblepharum albidum.* A. Leaves, scale 1 mm. B. Leaf tip,
scale 50 μ. C. Cross section, leaf, scale 50 μ. D–F. *Octoblepharum longifolium.*
(*HOW 2110.*) D. Leaves, scale 1 mm. E. Leaf tip, scale 50 μ. F. Cross section, midleaf, scale 50 μ. G–I. *Exodictyon dentatum.* (*Nadeaud 46.*) G. Leaf,
scale 1 mm. H. Leaf tip, scale 50 μ. I. Cross section, midleaf, scale 50 μ.
J–L. *Exodictyon nadeaudii.* (*Hürlimann T 1192.*) J. Leaves, scale 1 mm. K.
Leaf tip, scale 50 μ. L. Cross section, upper leaf base, scale 50 μ. (*del.* HAM.)

3174. Papeari District: Harrison Smith Botanical Garden, ca 10 m, on tree roots, *2110.*

MOOREA. Without locality: *Temarii Nadeaud sn* (Bescherelle, 1901).

RAIATEA. Uturoa: Third valley south, 50 m, on coconut palm, with *Leucophanes tahiticum, Moore 6a* (Bartram, 1931).

Distribution.—Society Islands (Tahiti, Moorea, Raiatea), endemic.

The few collections which I made on Tahiti can be divided into two groups: the first with leaves to about 5 mm, strictly ligulate and erect-spreading, slightly recurved; the second with leaves to 6–8 mm long, slightly lanceolate, and erect. The specimens of the second group I placed in *Octoblepharum longifolium*; those of the first group in *O. albidum*, recognizing that Bartram (1939) and van Zanten (1964) included forms with leaves to 8 mm long in *O. albidum*. I suspect the distinctions which can be used to separate *O. longifolium* may eventually prove to be insufficient and that all Society Islands *Octoblephara* will be placed under *O. albidum*, perhaps with varietal rank for forms such as *O. longifolium*.

4. *Exodictyon* Cardot
Rev. Bryol. 26: 6. 1899.

Two species have been reported: *Exodictyon dentatum* and *E. nadeaudii*. *Exodictyon dentatum* differs primarily in its larger size and more strongly toothed upper blade, a poor difference at best, when intermediate forms appear in collections. Considering extremes, however, the leaves of *E. dentatum* are almost 8 mm long, and are erect-spreading, recurved, the limited lamina portion on either side of the photosynthetic costa with an entire margin except near the apex and near the base where the lamina expands; in *E. nadeaudii,* the leaves are more slender and are shorter, to about 4 mm long, the upper lamina serrulate, the leaf shoulders spinose-serrate. I can find little to distinguish *E. nadeaudii* from *E. blumii* (C. Muell.) Fleisch. of Java, Borneo, and the Philippine Islands.

Key to Species of *Exodictyon*

1. Leaves to 4 mm, upper margins serrulate, leaf shoulders spinose-serrate....
....2. *E. nadeaudii.*
1. Leaves to nearly 8 mm, upper margins entire except at apex, leaf shoulders
   serrulate..1. *E. dentatum.*

1. *Exodictyon dentatum* (Mitten) Cardot
    Rev. Bryol. 26: 7. f. 13. 1899.
    Octoblepharum dentatum Mitt., J. Linn. Soc. Bot. 10: 178. 1868.
    Arthrocormus dentatus (Mitt.) Jaeg., Ber. S. Gall. Naturw. Ges. 1871–1872:
        320. 1873.
    Arthrocormus graeffii C. Muell., *in* Jaeger, Ber. S. Gall. Naturw. Ges. 1871–
        1872: 320. 1873. *nom. nud., cf.* Jaeger, Ber. S. Gall. Naturw. Ges. 1877–
        1878: 392. 1880.

Plants 2–3 cm tall, whitish; leaves erect-spreading, slightly re-curved, to 8 mm long, linear, the upper blade tubulose to cylindric. Chlorophyllose cells in 3 series, upper, median, and lower, the upper and lower series superficial, not covered by hyaline cells.

    ILLUSTRATIONS. Cardot (1900, pls. 15, 16). Figure 27.

    TAHITI. Without locality: Associated with *Symphyogyna, Lépine sn* (Bescherelle, 1895a, as *Arthrocormus*); abundant in the high mountains, sterile, *Nadeaud 46* (Nadeaud, 1873, as *Leucophanes octoblepharoides* in a mixed collection including *Leucobryum tahitense, fide* Bescherelle, 1895a, as *Arthrocormus*); sterile, *Nadeaud 222* (Bescherelle, 1898a, as *Arthrocormus*). Taiarapu Peninsula: Haavini Valley, 640 m, with *Plagiochila, 2274*. Papenoo–Vaihiria valleys: On roots of dead tree on ridge separating the valleys, 840 m, associated with *Leucobryum, Leucophanes, Rhizogonium, Microlepidozia, Plagiochila,* and *Exodictyon nadeaudii, 3038*; Vaihiria Valley, 200 m, with *Garovaglia, Hypnodendron tahiticum,* and *Thyridium obtusifolium, 3090*. Hitiaa District: Plateau, ca 400–500 m, with *Rhizogonium* and *Thyridium constrictum, 3243*; with *Leucobryum tahitense, 3250*.

    RAIATEA. Averaiti Valley: Upper end, 300 m, on dead branch of tree over stream bed, *Moore 76, 83a* (Bartram, 1931, BISH!).

    Distribution.—Society Islands (Tahiti, Raiatea), Samoa, New Hebrides, New Caledonia, Solomon Islands, Fiji.

2. *Exodictyon nadeaudii* (Bescherelle) Cardot
    Rev. Bryol. 26: 7. f. 13. 1899.
    Arthrocormus nadeaudii Besch., Bull. Soc. Bot. France 45: 51. 1898a.

Plants delicate, to 2 cm tall, about 5 mm wide; leaves fragile, to about 4 mm long.

    ILLUSTRATIONS. Cardot (1899, f. 13; 1900, pl. 17, f. 77). Figure 26J–L.

    TAHITI. Taiarapu Peninsula: Puaa Valley, to 800 m, associated with *Metzgeria* and *Leucomium aneurodictyon, Nadeaud 220* (NY!), *Nadeaud 221* (Bescherelle, 1898a, as *Arthrocormus*); Taravao, above

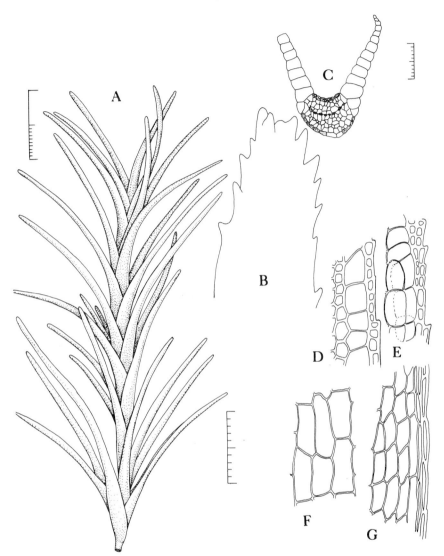

Fig. 27. *Exodictyon dentatum*. A. Habit, scale 2 mm. B. Leaf apex, outline to show denticulation. C. Cross section, leaf near base, scale 100 μ. D. Upper lamina cells. E. Leaf cells, lower one-third of lamina. F, G. Lamina cells, leaf base. D–G, scale 100 μ.

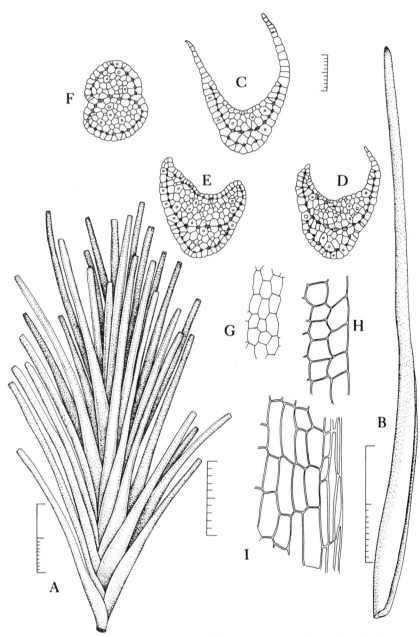

FIG. 28. *Arthrocormus schimperi.* A. Habit, scale 2 mm. B. Leaf, scale 2 mm.
C. Cross section, near leaf base. D, E. Cross section, lower one-third of leaf.
F. Cross section, upper one-third of leaf. C–F, scale 100 μ. G. Median surface
cells, upper leaf. H. Hyaline margin cells, lower one-third of leaf. I. Hyaline
margin cells, extreme leaf base. G–I, scale 100 μ.

experiment station, 400–500 m, near dam, *Hürlimann T 1192* (Hürlimann, 1963, FH!); 640 m, same locality, in *Cyathea* and *Aleurites* forest, on tree trunks, *2256*. Papenoo District: Papenoo Valley, 800 m, on tree trunk with ferns, *MacDaniels 1540a* (Bartram, 1933a); 840 m, on ridge between Papenoo and Vaihiria valleys, with *Exodictyon dentatum, Rhizogonium spiniforme,* and *Porella, 3038.*

MOOREA. Vaianae: *Temarii Nadeaud sn* (Bescherelle, 1901). Mt. Rotui: S side, between Papetoai and Paopao bays, with *Vesicularia, Trichosteleum,* and *Calomnion schistostegiellum, 3426.*

Distribution.—Society Islands (Tahiti, Moorea), endemic.

5. *Arthrocormus* Dozy & Molkenboer
Musci Fr. Ined. Archip. Indici 75. 1846.
Arthrocormus schimperi (Dozy & Molkenboer) Dozy & Molkenboer
Musci Fr. Ined. Archip. Indici 76. f. 27. 1846.
> *Mielichhoferia schimperi* Dozy & Molk., Ann. Sci. Nat. Bot. ser. 3, 2: 312. 1844.

The nearly cylindrical upper leaf section, the appearance of the chlorophyllose cells beneath an outer layer of hyaline cells, and the stiffly erect, nearly parallel leaves, their tips mostly broken off, serve to distinguish this genus and species.

ILLUSTRATIONS. Dozy and Molkenboer (1846, f. 27), Cardot (1900, pl. 14, f. 68). Figure 28.

TAHITI. Taiarapu Peninsula: Taravao, above experiment station, ca 800 m, with *Syrrhopodon, 2152;* Haavini Valley, 640 m, in sheltered spot among roots of tree, *2272;* about 1.5 m above the ground, on tree trunk, with *Fissidens nadeaudii, Rhizogonium,* and *Leucobryum, 2278;* in other collections, on logs and tree bases, associated with *Leucobryum tahitense, Cyathophorella tahitense, Racopilum, Octoblepharum,* and *Bazzania.* Hitiaa District: Plateau region, 400–500 m, with *Exodictyon dentatum* and *Rhizogonium, 3255.*

RAIATEA. Faaroa Bay: On dead *Hibiscus* branch, 200 m, *Moore 53* (Bartram, 1933a).

Distribution.—Society Islands (Tahiti, a new record; Raiatea), Fiji, Malaysia, Sri Lanka (Ceylon), Philippine Islands, Thailand, Java, Borneo, New Guinea, Queensland, d'Entrecasteaux, Amboina.

V. CALYMPERACEAE

The Calymperaceae is characterized by plants having leaves with a prominent region of rectangular or quadrate hyaline cells (the cancellineae) adjacent to each side of the costa at the base. In addition, most taxa bear clusters of spindle-shaped propagula on the costa at the leaf apex or along the upper side of the nerve toward the leaf tip. Leaf margins may be entire to serrate or ciliate, the cells in a single layer at the margins or in 2 or more layers to form a cylindrical border; some taxa are characterized by a marginal or submarginal series of elongate cells extending from the region of the cancellineae into the upper leaf or to the apex. Laminal cells are rounded to quadrate or hexagonal, and may be smooth or papillose. Perichaetial leaves are little differentiated. Capsules are erect, lack an annulus, and may have a single peristome or none. The operculum is conic-rostrate; the calyptra covers the entire capsule and may be cucullate or campanulate.

Plants are erect and branch sparingly to frequently, varying in height from less than 1 cm to nearly 10 cm, often appearing intermixed with other bryophytes and lichens as small solitary individuals, or in lax to dense turfs or pure tufts, or forming freely branching, tangled wefts. Members of the family Calymperaceae may be epilithic, on coral or basalt, or they may be corticolous, on branches, trunks, or roots of trees.

Three genera represent the family in the Society Islands: *Thyridium, Syrrhopodon,* and *Calymperes.* According to Herzog (1926, p. 33), 31 per cent of the two chief genera, *Syrrhopodon* and *Calymperes,* is African, and 35 per cent is Asian (including New Guinea). Australian and Polynesian taxa account for 10 per cent, and an important percentage (about 25 per cent) occurs in the Mediterranean-like regions of the Americas.

Calymperes species are seldom found above 600 m, but Herzog reported that *Syrrhopodon* taxa may be found at elevations approaching 2000 m. In the Society Islands and the central Pacific Islands, most taxa of the family Calymperaceae grow very close to sea level; *Thyridium* and *Calymperes* are seldom found much above 600 m, and *Syrrhopodon* seldom over 1000 m.

KEY TO GENERA OF THE CALYMPERACEAE

1. Leaves with simple margins (in some taxa with margins 2 cells thick but not elongated markedly), or with a submarginal row of elongated cells (teniolae)..3. *Calymperes.*
1. Leaves with a broad hyaline border of markedly elongated cells, or the border markedly thickened and cylindrical
   2. Stems erect, sparingly branched, often comose; seta terminal, leaves with a strongly thickened cylindrical border or comprised of a very narrow band of elongate cells (2–4 cells wide); cells of cancellineae typically not perforated ....1. *Syrrhopodon.*
   2. Stems creeping or suberect, freely branching; leaves uniformly distributed; setae borne terminally on branches; leaves with broad hyaline border (6–18 cells wide) of elongated cells, never more than 1 cell layer; cancellineae cells typically perforated............................2. *Thyridium.*

1. *Syrrhopodon* Schwaegrichen
   Spec. Musc. Suppl. 2(2): 110. 1824.

The genus *Syrrhopodon* is characterized by plants with leaves which have strongly thickened, cylindrical margins in which there may be a core of elongate cells, or the margins with a single layer of elongate cells 2–3 rows wide, and varying from entire (smooth) to denticulate or ciliate. Propagula, spindle-shaped bodies which serve in vegetative reproduction, are typically found along the upper surface of the costa in the upper leaf, but are not restricted to the leaf or costa tip as in the genus *Calymperes*. The capsules have 16 peristome teeth as in the genus *Thyridium*, a characteristic which separates *Syrrhopodon* from *Calymperes*, which has no peristome.

Key to Species of *Syrrhopodon*

1. Costa long-excurrent (by more than 100 μ).....................3. *S. subulatus.*
1. Costa percurrent or nearly so
   2. Cancellineae (enlarged hyaline cells) extend nearly to leaf apex
      3. Leaf margins involute.......................................8. *S. involutus.*
      3. Leaf margins plane or revolute
         4. Leaf margins plane...............................6. *S. banksii.*
         4. Leaf margins revolute...........................9. *S. rigescens.*
   2. Cancellineae restricted to lower half of leaf
      3. Leaf margins and costa with unicellular ciliate teeth to 90 μ long
         ....7. *S. ciliatus.*
      3. Leaf margins smooth to coarsely toothed, teeth unicellular to multicellular, usually less than 50 μ long
         4. Lamina cells smooth to rounded or conic-papillose
            5. Lamina cells smooth to rounded
               6. Leaf margins entire, lacking teeth even adjacent cancellineae and in leaf apex...........2. *S. aristifolius.*
               6. Leaf margins toothed.......................5. *S. moorei.*

5. Lamina cells conic-papillose
   6. Leaves 10–15 mm long; leaf borders characteristically separating from lamina near apex; papillae low_____1. S. apertus.
   6. Leaves 3–7 mm long; leaf borders intact; papillae high, forward pointing_____12. S. mamillatus.
4. Lamina cells pluripapillose
   5. Papillae forked or branched_____4. S. fissipapillatus.
   5. Papillae 1–2 per cell, simple, not forked or branched
      6. Leaves 4–6 mm long; lamina cells rounded-quadrate to rectangular with thickened angles; cancellineae cells porose on end or lateral walls_____11. S. tristichellus.
      6. Leaves 10–12 mm long; lamina cells 5–6-sided, their angles not thickened; cancellineae cells not porose_____10. S. nadeaudianus.

1. *Syrrhopodon apertus* Bescherelle
Bull. Soc. Bot. France 45: 60. 1898.

Plants 2–3 cm tall; leaves linear, trough-shaped, to 8–9 × 0.4 mm (the sheathing basal portion to 0.5 mm wide). Cancellineae extend along the costa as much as one-quarter the leaf length and consist of 12–15 series of hyaline, quadrate to rectangular cells, thin-walled, 35–60 × 20 μ (adjacent to the costa and in immediately subsequent series; smaller toward the margins). Lamina cells rounded, thick-walled, about 7 μ in diameter, free surfaces rounded to conic-papillose. Leaf margins bordered, the border thick, about 35 μ wide, strongly denticulate, the teeth in groups of 2–5 or individual, from the margin of the upper sheath to the leaf apex. The costa ends in the leaf apex, forming a small apiculus, or just below, with the border ending at about the same point; the upper surface of the costa is toothed near the leaf apex, the lower surface strongly papillose from the apex to the sheathing portion. Sporophytes not examined. Description from a collection by Temarii Nadeaud, 1901, from Taravao, Tahiti, determined by Bescherelle.

ILLUSTRATIONS. Figure 29.

TAHITI. Tamanu Valley: In the center of the island, *Nadeaud 245* (Bescherelle, 1898a). Isthmus de Taravao: *Temarii Nadeaud sn*, 1901 (det. Bescherelle, Bartram hb., FH).

Distribution.—Society Islands (Tahiti), endemic.

The heavy, cylindrical border, the pronounced teeth which appear from below the top of the sheathing portion and extend to the leaf apex, and the tendency of the border to separate from the upper lamina are distinctive and serve to separate *S. apertus* from S.

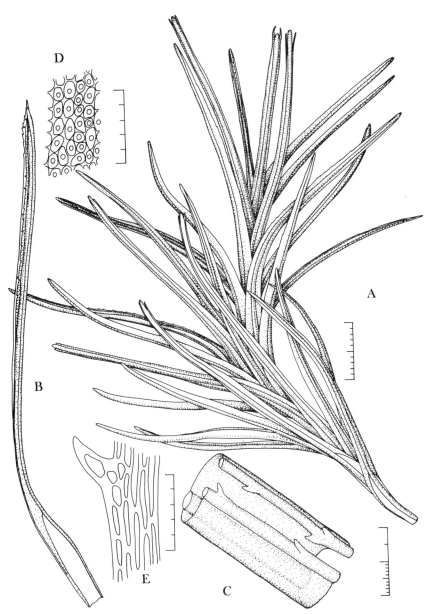

Fig. 29. *Syrrhopodon apertus.* (*Temarii Nadeaud sn,* 1901.) A. Habit. B. Leaf.
A, B, scale 1 mm. C. Leaf section, upper portion, showing inrolled margins
and denticulation, scale 200 μ. D. Lamina, upper median cells, scale 50 μ. E.
Upper lamina, border cells, scale 50 μ.

aristifolius, which has longer leaves (to 15 mm) with entire, bordered margins.

2. *Syrrhopodon aristifolius* Mitten
   J. Linn. Soc. Bot. 10: 176. 1868.

Plants comose, with numerous leaves arising from a stem 3–5 mm tall; leaves linear, flat, flexuose, 1–1.5 cm long and only 0.16 mm wide; margins variable, 1 cell thick or thickened and bordered, but entire. Cells of the upper lamina rounded-quadrate to rectangular, 5–12 × 4–7 μ, thick-walled. The costa percurrent. Sporophytes not examined. Description from Moore, no. 92, collected on Raiatea, determined by Bartram (FH!).

ILLUSTRATIONS. Figure 30A, B.

RAIATEA. Averaiti Valley: Upper end, 300 m, on dead branches of tree over stream bed, *Moore 76b*; on shrub, *Moore 92* (Bartram, 1931, FH!).

Distribution.—Society Islands (Raiatea), Samoa (Upolu, type locality).

The long, flexuose, narrowly linear leaves distinguish this species.

3. *Syrrhopodon subulatus* Lacoste
   Natuurk. Verh. K. Ak. Wet. Amsterdam 13: 5. 3 A. 1872.

Plants humicolous or corticolous, erect, yellow-green, caespitose, about 1.5 cm tall; leaves incurved when dry, erect-spreading when moist, 4–5 × 0.3–0.5 mm, linear-lanceolate, the upper margins merging with the costa from one-third the length of the leaf below the apex to within 0.1–0.3 mm below the apex; the leaf basal region about 0.3–0.5 mm long, the hyaline cells of the cancellineae about 8 rows wide on either side of the costa, merging gradually with the cells of the upper lamina; leaf margins irregularly thickened, from plane to cylindrical, to 2–3 cells thick and wide. Cells of the lamina 6–12 μ, irregularly rounded-quadrate, smooth, the walls 2–4 μ thick. Cells of the cancellineae 30–50 × 10–15 μ, intergrading with upper lamina cells rather than sharply demarked by them.

ILLUSTRATIONS. Figure 31E–G.

TAHITI. Hitiaa: 200–300 m, with *Syrrhopodon ciliatus, Thyridium constrictum, Leucobryum tahitense, Leucophanes,* and other mosses as isolated plants, *3216.*

Distribution.—Society Islands (Tahiti, a new record), Philippine Islands (Mindanao), Sumatra, Celebes, Borneo, New Guinea.

The subulate leaf apices formed by the leaf margins merging with

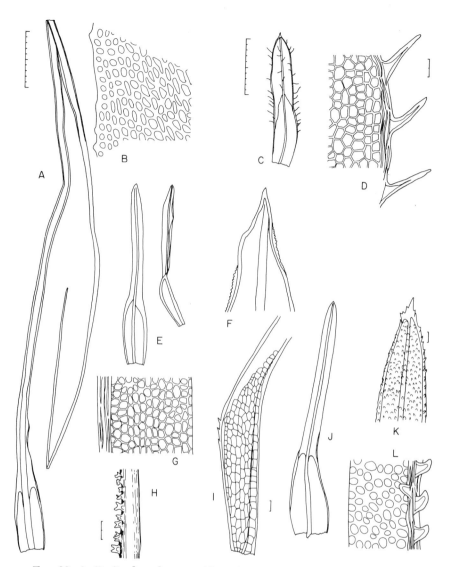

Fig. 30. A, B. *Syrrhopodon aristifolius.* (*Moore 92.*) A. Leaf, drawn folded, scale 1 mm. B. Cells, upper shoulder region, scale 20 μ. C, D. *Syrrhopodon ciliatus.* (*HOW 3213.*) C. Leaf, scale 1 mm. D. Upper leaf, cells and margin, scale 20 μ. E–I. *Syrrhopodon fissipapillatus.* (*HOW 24 sn.*) E. Leaves, scale 1 mm. F. Leaf tip, scale 100 μ. G. Upper leaf, cells and border, scale 20 μ. H. Papillae, back of leaf in profile, margin inrolled, scale 20 μ. I. Leaf base of folded leaf and cancellineae, scale 50 μ. J–L. *Syrrhopodon mamillatus.* (*Smith 975,* Fiji.) J. Leaf, scale 1 mm. K. Leaf tip, scale 50 μ. L. Upper leaf, cells and margin, scale 20 μ. (*del.* HAM.)

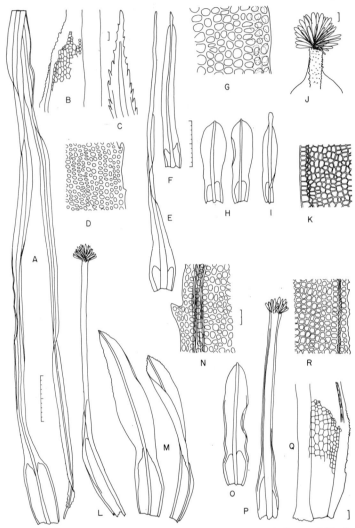

FIG. 31. A–D. *Syrrhopodon mooreae*. (*HOW 3093*.) A. Leaf, drawn folded, scale 1 mm. B. Leaf base and upper cancellineae. C. Leaf tip. B, C, scale 50 μ. D. Upper leaf, cells and margin, scale 20 μ. E–G. *Syrrhopodon subulatus*. (*HOW 3216*.) E. Subulate leaf. F. Normal leaf. E, F, scale 1 mm. G. Upper leaf, cells and margin, scale 20 μ. H–K. *Calymperes tenerum*. (*HOW 3373*.) H. Normal leaves, scale 1 mm. I. Propaguliferous leaf, scale 1 mm. J. Propaguliferous leaf tip, scale 50 μ. K. Upper leaf, cells and margin (rolled), scale 20 μ. L–N. *Calymperes porrectum*. (*HOW 2388*.) L. Propaguliferous leaf, scale 1 mm. M. Normal leaves, scale 1 mm. N. Upper leaf cells and margin, scale 20 μ. O–R. *Calymperes pseudopodianum*. (Isotype.) O. Normal leaf, scale 1 mm. P. Propaguliferous leaf, scale 1 mm. Q. Leaf base, scale 50 μ. R. Upper leaf cells and margin, scale 20 μ.

the costa well below the apex are distinctive of this species. The features of the Society Islands collections are essentially identical to those described for *S. subulatus* Lac. and I have no hesitation in referring them to this species.

4. *Syrrhopodon fissipapillatus* sp. nov.

Plantae caespitosi, dilute virides, humicola. Folia erecto-patentia, parum recurva et contorta ubi in sicco, 2.2–3.3 × 0.12–0.15 mm., lineari-lanceolata; costa ad apicem breviter excurrente; margine incrassato ad mucrone confluens; cancellineae hyalinis, quadratis vel rectangularis, vel 25–60 × 25–30 μ, ad costam 0.7–1.0 mm extenso; cellulae isodiametris, incrassatis, cum papillis altis, bifidis vel trifidis. Fructus nondum visa. Specimen typicum in via Papenoo-Vaihiria, in insulis Societatibus, Tahitensibus, legit *Whittier sn '24',* 1964 (specimen typicum in hb. NY conservatum).

Plants erect, pale or whitish-green, on humus; leaves erect-spreading, slightly recurved and contorted when dry, 2.2–3.3 × 0.12–0.15 mm, linear-lanceolate; costa ending in a short mucro, the borders thickened, merging with the costa in the apex. Cancellineae formed by 5–6 rows of quadrate to rectangular hyaline cells, 25–60 × 25–30 μ toward the costa, smaller and shorter toward the margins, and extending up along the costa for about 0.7–1.0 mm. Margins formed by a thickened cylindrical border of thick-walled, elongate cells, the lumina to about 75 × 2 μ, entire in the upper leaf, entire to serrulate or ciliate-denticulate in the region of the upper cancellineae, with a few irregular teeth just below the apex. Costa smooth, about 30 μ wide in midleaf, the border about 10 μ wide. Cells of the upper lamina mostly isodiametric, quadrate to hexagonal, thick-walled, the walls about 2.0–2.5 μ, the lumina 7–10 × 7 μ, nearly obscured by high (to about 7 μ), stalked papillae with 2–3 branches on both surfaces of the lamina. Sporophytes not found.

ILLUSTRATIONS. Figure 30E–I.

TAHITI. Papenoo–Vaihiria trail: *Whittier sn '24' typus!* (NY).

Distribution.—Society Islands (Tahiti), endemic.

No member of the Society Islands Calymperaceae possesses the strikingly branched papillae of *Syrrhopodon fissipapillatus.* The type specimen is deposited in the herbarium of the New York Botanical Garden.

5. *Syrrhopodon mooreae* (Bescherelle) Whittier *comb. nov.*
Calymperes mooreae Besch., Bull. Soc. Bot. France 48: 14. 1901.

Plants terrestrial or epilithic, loosely aggregated, in short tufts, the stems to about 5 mm tall; leaves loosely twisted when dry, erect-spreading when moist, linear, acuminate, 17–25 × 0.13–0.16 mm, bordered, the border 8–12 μ wide, 2–5 cells thick; costa smooth, about 50 μ thick in midleaf; the expanded leaf base about 0.6 × 0.3 mm. Cells of the lamina rounded, thick-walled, varying from isodiametric to elongate, some transversely elongate, the lumina from 2–4 μ, the cell walls 1.0–1.5 μ thick; cells of the leaf border as those of the lamina, surrounding a middle strand of elongate cells, the borders denticulate, the teeth distant, single to regularly paired, forward pointing, of 1, 2, or 3 cells except toward the leaf apex where they may be occasionally multicellular. The costa and thickened borders merge in the leaf apex. Cells of the lamina adjacent to the costa to twice as large as those of the lamina midway to the border. Cells of the cancellineae form 10–18 rows on either side of the costa; those of the leaf margins of the basal disc rhomboid, hyaline, oriented at an angle of approximately 45° to the main axis of the leaf, their lumina project beyond the leaf margin into the irregular denticulations. No sporophytes found.

ILLUSTRATIONS. Figure 31A–D.

TAHITI. Vaihiria Valley: On banks, ca 400 m, *3093*.

MOOREA. Without locality: *Temarii Nadeaud sn* (Bescherelle, 1901); *Welch sn.*

Calymperes mooreae appears similar to Fleischer's illustration of *C. cristatum* Hampe, from which it differs in having wider cancellineae (10–18 rows as opposed to 8 rows) and a narrower costa (occupying one-quarter to one-third the leaf base as opposed to almost one-half of the base). Bescherelle's species is readily distinguished from all other members of the Society Islands Calymperaceae by the extreme length of its linear leaves (25 mm). The thickened borders indicate that *C. mooreae* is better treated as *Syrrhopodon mooreae*.

6. *Syrrhopodon banksii* C. Mueller
Bot. Zeit. 16: 162. 1858.

Plants whitish-green, forming compact cushions (suggestive of the genus *Leucophanes*), the stems about 1 cm tall; leaves closely pressed against the stems, lanceolate or ovate-lanceolate; margins entire or nearly so, border 1–2 cell layers thick, 2–4 cells wide, comprised of elongate cells; costa percurrent. Chlorophyllose cells restricted to the upper one-quarter of the lamina, most of the blade occupied by hyaline cells of the cancellineae. In section, leaves flat to keeled or V-shaped, the margins neither incurved nor recurved. Sporophytes not examined.

ILLUSTRATIONS. Figure 32.

TAHITI. Without locality: *Banks sn* (Montagne, 1845, as *S. rigescens*; Mueller, 1858, type in hb. Thunberg); *Lépine sn* (Montagne, 1845, as *S. rigescens*; Bescherelle, 1895a); common on the trunks of trees in the island interior to the seashore in wet districts such as Hitiaa, *Picquenot sn* (in hb. Corbière); 800–1100 m, on windward side of Tahiti, *Nadeaud 240–242* (Bescherelle, 1898a). Papeiha: On trees, ca 900 m, *Nadeaud 47* (Nadeaud, 1873, as *Leucophanes fragile, fide* Bescherelle, 1895a). Miaa: 850 m, *Temarii Nadeaud sn,* 1899 (Bescherelle, 1901). Papeari District: Maara Valley, *Setchell and Parks 5301a; 5366* (Brotherus, 1924a, as *f. gracilis* Broth.). Hitiaa District: Along shore road, *Setchell and Parks sn* (Brotherus, 1924a). Taiarapu Peninsula: Taravao, above experiment station, 600 m, *Hürlimann T 1198* (Hürlimann, 1963).

MOOREA: Without locality: *Temarii Nadeaud sn* (Bescherelle, 1901).

RAIATEA. Tioo: On coconut palm near beach, 1 m, *Moore 51* (Bartram, 1931). Tetaro Islet: On tree trunk, 1 m, *St. John and Wight 17234*, October, 1934 (unreported, BISH!).

BORA BORA. Mt. Temanu: *Phillips sn* (Phillips, 1947).

Distribution.—Society Islands (Tahiti, type locality; Moorea, Raiatea, Bora Bora), Tuamotu Islands (Makatea), Austral Islands (Rapa, Tubuai, Rurutu, Rimatara), Solomon Islands, Fiji, Cook Islands, Santa Cruz (Vanikoro, Toukuoro), Caroline Islands (Yap).

7. *Syrrhopodon ciliatus* (Hooker) Schwaegrichen
Spec. Musc. Suppl. 2(1): 114. t. 130. 1823.
Weisia ciliata Hook., Musci Exotici t. 171. 1818.
Trachymitrium ciliatum Brid., Bryol. Univ. 1: 159. 1826.

Plants greenish, erect, about 2 cm tall, sparingly branched; leaves spreading when wet, ovate-acuminate; costa percurrent, margins bordered by a single layer of elongate, hyaline cells in 2–4 series, ciliate-dentate, the cilia to 90 μ long, appearing also on both sides of the costa. The cancellineae occupy less than one-half the length of the leaf and form 5–10 rows of cells on each side of the costa.

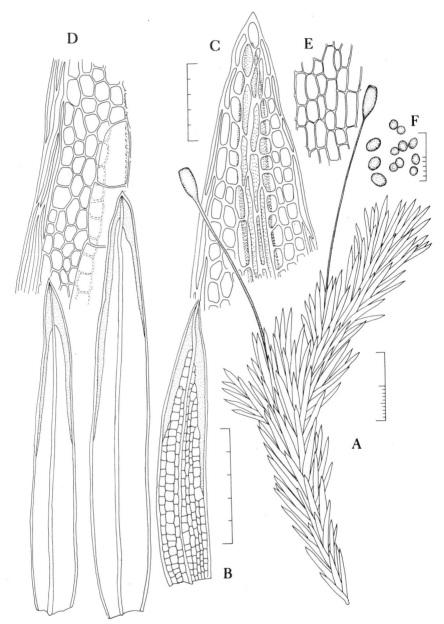

Fig. 32. *Syrrhopodon banksii.* (*HOW 2221.*) A. Habit, scale 2 mm. B. Leaves, scale 0.5 mm. C. Leaf apex. D. Upper margin and median cells with upper-most cells of the cancellineae. C, D, scale 50 μ. E. Capsule exothecial cells. F. Spores (from two different capsules on separate plants in tuft). E, F, scale 100 μ.

Fleischer (1904, 1: 210) described sporophytes with the seta to 5 mm long, the capsule ovoid-elongate. Peristome teeth 16. Spores 12–16 μ (for Javan specimens).

ILLUSTRATIONS. Hooker (1818, t. 171), Schwaegrichen (1826, t. 130), Whittier, *in* Miller, Whittier, and Bonner (1963, pl. 6). Figure 30C, D.

TAHITI. Hitiaa District: Plateau region, about 300 m, at margin of *Pandanus* and *Metrosideros* forest, *Whittier sn*.

RAIATEA. Faaroa Valley: On decaying base of fern, 100 m, mixed with *Leucophanes prasiophyllum* and *Syrrhopodon mamillatus, Moore 71b* (Bartram, 1931).

Distribution.—Society Islands (Tahiti, a new record; Raiatea), Caroline Islands (Ponape, Ant Atoll), New Guinea, Java, Sumatra, Borneo, Celebes, Amboina, Singapore, Admiralty Islands, Banca, Ternate.

The ciliate-dentate margins and costa serve to distinguish this species from all other Society Islands mosses.

8. *Syrrhopodon involutus* Schwaegrichen
   Spec. Musc. Suppl. 2(1): 117. t. 132. 1824.
   Syrrhopodon jardini Schimp., *in* Jardin, Bull. Soc. Linn. Normandie ser. 2, 9: 263, 264. 1875. *fide* Bescherelle, Ann. Sci. Nat. Bot. ser. 7, 20: 23. 1895.
   Cleistostoma involutum Brid., Bryol. Univ. 1: 157. 1826.
   Syrrhopodon glaucescens Schimp., in hb. Gaud. *fide* Bescherelle, 1895a.

Plants with the habit of *S. banksii*, differing primarily in the leaf margins which curve up and in toward the costa.

ILLUSTRATIONS. Schwaegrichen (1826, t. 132).

TAHITI. Pirae District: Fautaua Valley, near Papeete, *Jardin sn,* Schimper det. as *S. jardini* (Jardin, 1875; Bescherelle, 1895a).

Distribution.—Society Islands (Tahiti), Samoa, Rauwack, Banca, Moluccas.

9. *Syrrhopodon rigescens* Schwaegrichen
   Spec. Musc. Suppl. 2(2): 102. t. 181. 1827.

Essentially the same as *S. banksii* and *S. involutus,* this species is distinguished by the down-turned leaf margins, a poor criterion at best.

ILLUSTRATIONS. Schwaegrichen (1826, t. 181).

TAHITI. Without locality: In mountains, ca 800 m, *Lépine sn* (Montagne, 1848, coll. Mus. Par. Musci, no. 4).

Distribution.—Society Islands (Tahiti), endemic.

Further study is needed to determine the proper relationships of *Syrrhopodon banksii, S. involutus,* and *S. rigescens.* Bescherelle (1895a) recognized only *S. banksii* and *S. involutus* and gave *S. rigescens* in synonymy under *S. banksii.*

10. *Syrrhopodon nadeaudianus* Bescherelle
    Bull. Soc. Bot. France 45: 60. 1898.

Plants to about 2 cm tall; leaves stiff, linear-lanceolate, about 10–12 × 0.2–0.25 mm, abruptly acuminate, the margins thickened, about 25 μ wide; costa about 50 μ wide. Cells of the lamina 5–6-sided, thin-walled, the angles not rounded, 6–7 μ in diameter, with 1–2 large, rounded papillae over the lumina on both surfaces. The upper lamina margins denticulate just below the apex (about 0.3–0.6 mm of the upper margin toothed), in the apex, cells adjacent to the costa enlarged, rectangular, and hyaline in many leaves, about 12–20 × 7–10 μ. The cancellineae occupy less than one-fifth the length of the leaf and extend from 0.8 to 2.0 mm along the costa, at the widest point 6–8 rows of cells on either side of the costa, the largest cells about 70 × 25 μ, thin-walled and hyaline. A band of yellowish, elongate cells appears at the margins of the cancellineae, in a row 3–5 cells wide at the top of the sheath, the cells linear, 70–100 × 2–3 μ; the margins at the top of the cancellineae slightly serrulate. No sporophytes examined. Description from *Moore 53a,* Raiatea, determined by Bartram (FH!).

ILLUSTRATIONS. Figure 33.

TAHITI. Papenoo District: Mountains near Marciati, Papenoo Valley, *Nadeaud 244* (Bescherelle, 1898a).

RAIATEA. Faaroa Bay: On dead purau (*Hibiscus tiliaceus*) branch, 200 m, *Moore 53a.* Highest mountain: On tree branches, 800 m, *Moore 91* (Bartram, 1931).

Distribution.—Society Islands (Tahiti, type locality; Raiatea), endemic.

The untoothed, cylindrical borders, and once- to twice-papillose, irregularly hexagonal lamina cells are distinctive attributes of *S. nadeaudianus.* No other species of *Syrrhopodon* known from the Society Islands has the enlarged rectangular hyaline cells adjacent to the costa in the leaf apex, another characteristic of *S. nadeaudianus.*

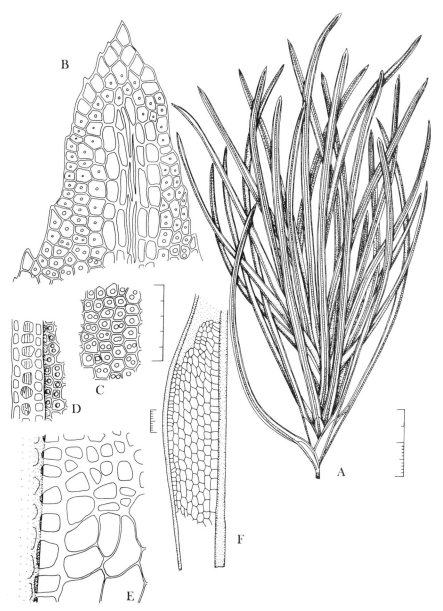

FIG. 33. *Syrrhopodon nadeaudianus.* (*Moore 53a.*) A. Habit, scale 2 mm. B. Leaf apex (note elongate, enlarged cells on either side of the costa). C. Lamina, upper median cells. D. Lamina, border cells. B–D, scale 50 μ. E. Lamina, cells adjacent to costa at top of cancellineae, scale 50 μ. F. Portion of leaf base, region of the cancellineae, scale 100 μ.

11. *Syrrhopodon tristichellus* Bescherelle
Bull. Soc. Bot. France 45: 60. 1898.

Plants 1–2 cm tall, erect, sparingly branched; leaves lanceolate, keeled, 4–6 × 0.2–0.23 mm, cancellineae 1.3–1.9 mm long, about 8 cells wide on each side of the costa, the cells rectangular, thin-walled, hyaline, 40–70 × 25 μ near the costa, porose on end or lateral walls. Cells of the lamina rounded-quadrate to rectangular, papillose, thick-walled, the angles thickened, 5–9 × 5–6 μ. Borders about 12 μ wide, thickened, denticulate above midleaf, the teeth most frequent in the upper one-quarter of the lamina, frequently in pairs or single. The costa is papillose on the lower surface near the base of the sheathing portion. Sporophytes not examined.

ILLUSTRATIONS. Figure 34.

TAHITI. Papara District: Temarua Valley, intermixed with other small mosses, *Nadeaud 243* (Bescherelle, 1898a).

RAIATEA. Highest mountain: W side, 400 m, on moist branches of trees, *Moore 36a* (Bartram, 1931, FH).

Distribution.—Society Islands (Tahiti, type locality; Raiatea), endemic.

Bescherelle (1898a) compared his new species *Syrrhopodon tristichellus* with *S. tristichus* Nees (cf. Fleischer, 1904, 1: 203, 205–7, f. 28, 29), and noted that the margins of his species are serrate from sheath to apex, that the cancellineae are narrow, long-ovate, and that at the margins the cells are in 2–3 series and chlorophyllose. From Fleischer's illustration (f. 29) it may also be seen that the structure of the margin teeth is different, that the cells are larger, the walls thinner in *S. tristichus*.

12. *Syrrhopodon mamillatus* C. Mueller
J. Mus. Godeffroy 3(6): 66. 1873.

This species is readily distinguished by the large, forward-pointing papillae which appear over the cell lumina.

ILLUSTRATIONS. Figure 30J–L.

RAIATEA. Faaroa Valley: On decaying base of nehe fern, 100 m, with *Syrrhopodon ciliatus* and *Leucophanes prasiophyllum, Moore 71a* (Bartram, 1931, FH).

Distribution.—Society Islands (Raiatea), Fiji (Ovalau, type locality), Samoa.

It is intriguing that Moore's new record for *Syrrhopodon mamillatus,* extending the range of that species from Samoa and Fiji,

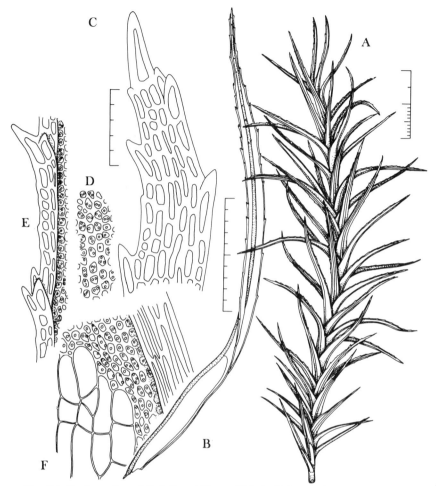

Fig. 34. *Syrrhopodon tristichellus*. (*Moore 36.*) A. Habit, scale 2 mm. B. Leaf, scale 1 mm. C. Leaf apex. D. Lamina, upper median cells. E. Lamina, border along upper margin. F. Lamina, upper portion of cancellineae and border. C–F, scale 50 μ.

should have appeared in the same collection with *S. ciliatus*, another new distribution record for a species previously known from Samoa and Indomalaya!

2. *Thyridium* Mitten
   J. Linn. Soc. Bot. 10: 188. 1868.

Two species are recorded from the Society Islands: *Thyridium constrictum* and *T. obtusifolium*. A third species, *T. glaucinum* (reported as *Syrrhopodon* by Bescherelle, 1901) is considered to be a synonym of *T. obtusifolium*.

Characteristic of the genus *Thyridium* is a broad marginal band of elongate, linear, hyaline cells, which distinguishes it from both *Calymperes* and *Syrrhopodon*.

Key to Species of *Thyridium*

1. Leaves with marked constriction below the expanded, flaired, or collar-shaped apex_____1. *T. constrictum.*
1. Leaves with rounded apex, the costa ending in an apiculus_____
   _____2. *T. obtusifolium.*

1. *Thyridium constrictum* (Sullivant) Mitten
   J. Linn. Soc. Bot. 10: 188. 1868.
   Calymperes constrictum Sull., U.S. Expl. Exped. Musci 6. 1859.
   Syrrhopodon (*Thyridium*) *constrictus* (Sull.) Mitt., *in* Seemann, Fl. Vit. 389. 1871.
   Syrrhopodon tubulosus Lac., Sp. Nov. vel ined. Arch. Ind. 7. 1872.

Plants yellow-green, stems erect or suberect, branched, 6–8 cm long; leaves erect-spreading when wet, without regular arrangement on the stem but uniformly distributed, ovate-lanceolate, constricted beneath a flaired, collar-shaped apex; propagula restricted to the apex of the costa. Margins entire, broadly bordered by a hyaline band of linear, thick-walled cells 10–20 rows wide. Sporophytes not seen.

ILLUSTRATIONS. Figure 35C–E.

TAHITI. Papenoo District: Mountains in vicinity of Marciati, Papenoo Valley, and in the Punarua Valley, foot of Mt. Orohena, *Nadeaud 237*; *Nadeaud 238, 239* are ascribed, respectively, to Hitiaa and Papara districts without specific localities (Bescherelle, 1898a, no. 239 as var. *tahiticum*); Papenoo Valley, W side, about 200 m, with *Calymperes* on exposed root, *2411*; 190 m, with *Thyridium obtusifolium, Syrrhopodon, Calymperes, Leucobryum*, and hepatics,

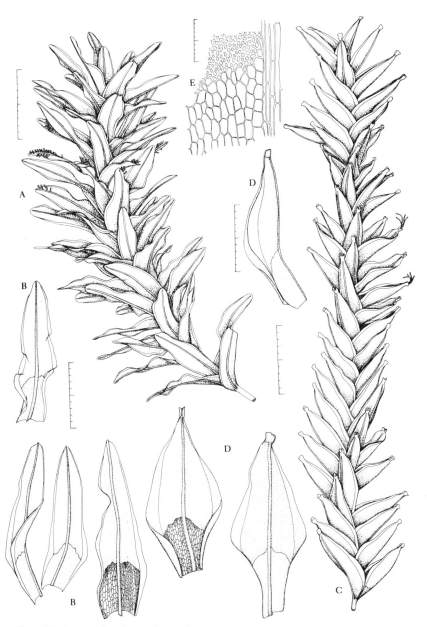

Fig. 35. A, B. *Thyridium obtusifolium*. A. Habit, portion of leafy stem, some leaves with propagula along upper part of costa, scale 2 mm. B. Leaves, scale 1 mm. C–E. *Thyridium constrictum*. C. Habit, portion of leafy stem, all leaves with constriction below a collar-shaped apex; propagula and rhizoid-like growths restricted to apex, scale 2 mm. D. Leaves, scale 1 mm. E. Cells of transition region between hyaline cancellineae and chlorophyllose upper lamina, adjacent to costa, scale 100 μ.

2440; 2441, 2443, 2472; with *Trichosteleum, Cyathophorella tahitensis*, and *Plagiochila, 2510*; Papenoo-Vaihiria cross-island expedition, 20–30 m, on bark, with *Frullania apiculata* and *Garovaglia, 2975*; 20–30 m, with *Plagiochila, 2978*; 60 m, with *Macromitrium, Ectropothecium*, and *Thyridium obtusifolium, 2982*; 60 m, with *Syrrhopodon banksii, Leucobryum*, and *Leucophanes, 2993*; 400 m, forming deep cushions on branches, *3062*. Hitiaa District: On base of coconut palm, *Hürlimann T 1134* (Hürlimann, 1963, FH!); 1–2 m, on base of coconut in plantation, *2372, 2374*; with *Calymperes tenerum* and *Syrrhopodon, 2377*; with *Syrrhopodon, 3200*; with *Calomnion schistostegiellum, 3201; 3205, 3211*; ca 300 m, with *Syrrhopodon ciliatus, Leucobryum, Trichosteleum, Bazzania*, and *Cephalozia, 3213*; with *Syrrhopodon ciliatus, Syrrhopodon*, and *Leucophanes, 3216*; ca 300 m, with *Acroporium* and *Herberta, 3223; 3224; 3229; 300 m*, with *Acroporium* and *Acromastigum, 3231*; 300 m, in *Pandanus, Metrosideros*, and *Coffea* forest, with *Ectropothecium, Trichosteleum, Bazzania, Lepidozia*, and *Herberta, 3238*; with *Calomnion schistostegiellum, 3241; 3243, 3249, 3251, 3252, 3260, 3262*; with *Hypnodendron samoanum, 3265*. Taiarapu Peninsula: Taravao, above experiment station, 440–610 m, on N slope, in *Miconia, Aleurites, Cyathea*, and guava forest, with *Leucobryum, Bazzania*, and *Lepidozia, 2197*; 450 m, with *Jamesoniella, 2217*; 450 m, with *Acroporium, Bazzania, Frullania apiculata, Drepanolejeunea*, and *Microlejeunea, 2219; 2220a*; 550 m, on *Aleurites* trunk with *Dendroceros* and *Bazzania, 2229*; 610 m, forming thick, loose cushions, with *Rhizogonium, Trichosteleum, Leucobryum*, and *Acroporium, 2239*; Haavini Valley, *Hibiscus–Inocarpus* forest, *2519*; with *Macromitrium, 2520*; with *Plagiochila, Drepanolejeunea*, and *Dendroceros, 2555*; 150 m, with *Frullania apiculata, 2561; 2562*; with *Acroporium* and *Leucobryum, 2598*; 60 m, with *Thyridium obtusifolium, 2657*; 90 m, on log near stream, with *Acroporium* and hepatics, *2632*. Papeari District: Harrison Smith Botanical Garden, 2 m, on coconut palm trunks with *Thyridium obtusifolium* and *Syrrhopodon banksii, 2101A; 2108*; on felled coconut palm, mostly near trunk base, *2103*; on coconut trunk intermixed with *Thyridium obtusifolium, Syrrhopodon banksii, Acroporium*, and *Bazzania, 2119*. Mataiea District: Vaihiria Valley, *3066*. Pirae District: Fautaua Valley, 200 m, with *Usnea, Leucophanes*, and *Ectropothecium, 2369*; 500 m, with *Ectropothecium, Trichosteleum*, and *Bazzania, Whittier sn.*

MOOREA. Mt. Rotui: Trail between Paopao and Papetoai bays, with *Calymperes tenerum* var. *edamense* and *Brachymenium indicum, 3376* (a new island record).

RAIATEA. Faaroa Bay: N side, 400 m, on wet branches of tree, *Moore 65*; Faaroa Valley, 100 m, on decaying wood in moist soil, *Moore 67* (Bartram, 1931, FH!).

Distribution.—Society Islands (Tahiti; Moorea, a new record; Raiatea), Hawaii (?), Sumatra, Borneo, Philippine Islands (Luzon), Java, Great Nantuna, Samoa, Caroline Islands (Palau, Ponape, Pingelap Atoll).

This common and easily identified moss is probably present on all the high islands of the Society archipelago. The flared leaf apices serve to distinguish this species from its nearest ally, *T. obtusifolium*, which also has its own characteristically 3-ranked leaves.

2. *Thyridium obtusifolium* (Lindberg) Fleischer
Musci Fl. Buitenzorg 1: 228. 1904.
Syrrhopodon obtusifolium Lindb. *fide* Fleischer, *loc. cit.*
Syrrhopodon glaucinus Besch., Bull. Soc. Bot. France 48: 14. 1901.

Plants to 10 cm long; leaves when moist, erect-spreading, distinctively 3-ranked, spiraled around the stem. Leaf apices rounded. Propagula appear along the upper side of the costa in the upper portion of the leaf, and are not restricted to the leaf apex.

ILLUSTRATIONS. Figure 35A, B.

TAHITI. Pirae District: Fautaua Valley, *3155a, 3168*; on tree branches, with *Papillaria, 3171*; Fare Rau Ape–Mt. Aorai trail, 1016 m, with *Papillaria, 2698*; 950 m, on ground, with *Mastigophora, Acroporium,* and *Rhizogonium, 2726*; 900 m, on orange tree roots, with *Leucobryum, 2829*; trail from Mt. Aorai to One Tree Hill, between 500 and 600 m, on soil under *Dicranopteris, 2835*; 900 m, on *Cyathea* stump, with *Leucobryum, Acroporium,* and *Leucophanes, 2830.* Papenoo District: 190 m, on burned log, with *Leucobyrum, 2438; 2439.* Hitiaa District: Plateau region, 100 m, on *Cocos* and *Hibiscus, 2172, 2173*; 300 m, in *Pandanus* forest, with *Ectropothecium sodale* and *Vesicularia, 3214.* Taiarapu Peninsula: Taravao, above experiment station, 800 m, with *Spiridens balfourianus, Leucophanes, Fissidens, Leucomium aneurodictyon* on *Cyathea* trunk, *2145; 2146*; 640 m, N side of peninsula, in *Miconia–Inocarpus–Cyathea–Pandanus* forest, with *Spiridens balfourianus, 2255.* Papeari District: Harrison Smith Botanical Garden, 1 m, on coconut trunks less than 2 m from ocean (no beach), associated with *Thyridium constrictum*, *Drepanolejeunea*, and *Usnea*, *Whittier sn*. Mataiea District: Vaihiria Valley, ca 400 m, with *Trichosteleum*, *Ectropothecium*, and hepatics on branches, *3068*; 100 m, with *Garovaglia*, *Exodictyon dentatum*, and *Hypnodendron samoanum*, *3090e*.

MOOREA. Vaianae Valley: *Nadeaud sn*, 1898 (Bescherelle, 1901, as *Syrrhopodon glaucinus*); between Paopao and Papetoai bays, growing on coconut palms and *Erythrina*, *3370*; on coconut palm trunk, with *Calymperes* and hepatics, *3374*. Mt. Rotui: 100–110 m, with *Calymperes*, on *Hibiscus tiliaceus*, *3447*; on roots of *Inocarpus edulis*, *3449*; on coconut trunk, *3460*. Mt. Matanui: Haring Plantation, opposite Hotel Eimeo, Paopao Bay, with *Syrrhopodon banksii*, *3474*.

RAIATEA. Averaiti Valley: Upper end, 300 m, on wet branch of tree, *Moore 78*, *83*, *86* (Bartram, 1931, FH!).

BORA BORA. Mt. Temanu: Vaihuna stream, S of Vaitape village, between sea level and 500 m, on tree base, *Phillips sn*, 1945 (Phillips, 1947, det. Bartram).

Distribution.—Society Islands (Tahiti, Moorea, Raiatea, Bora Bora), Austral Islands (Raivavae, Rurutu, Tubai), Mangareva, Pitcairn Island, Henderson, Marquesas Islands.

3. *Calymperes* Swartz
in Schwaegrichen, Spec. Musc. Suppl. 1(2): 333. 1816.

Plants erect, gregarious, frequently forming tufts or as isolated individuals on bark, less commonly on the ground; leaves costate, ligulate, from a usually expanded base, commonly involute and incurved when dry, erect-spreading and plane when wet. Cells on either side of the costa base enlarged, hyaline, characteristic of the family. Leaf margins 1 to several cells thick; isodiametric, with elongate cells (teniolae) present in a submarginal series or lacking; the margins entire (untoothed) to serrate. Sporophytes terminal but not common. The capsule lacks a peristome, separating *Calymperes* from *Thyridium* and *Syrrhopodon*. Propagula terminal on upper leaves. Calyptra cucullate or campanulate, smooth or roughened near the top. *Syrrhopodon* and *Thyridium* typically possess a cucullate (hood-shaped) calyptra, whereas *Calymperes* is characterized by a campanulate (bell-shaped) calyptra.

Key to Species of *Calymperes*

1. Leaf borders with teniolae (elongated submarginal cells)
    2. Leaf borders 1 cell thick
        3. Propaguliferous leaves ovate to obovate, the lamina many cells wide on either side of the costa and expanded slightly beneath the propagula _____5. *C. moorei.*
        3. Propaguliferous leaves linear, the lamina a few cells wide only, and not expanded below propagula_____1. *C. pseudopodianum.*
    2. Leaf borders more than 1 cell thick (in 2 cell layers)
        3. Leaf borders flattened, saw-toothed, the teeth formed by groups of cells_____ 2. *C. porrectum.*
        3. Leaf borders cylindrical, serrulate, teeth formed by projection of single cell_____3. *C. aongstroemii.*
1. Leaf borders lacking teniolae
    2. Propaguliferous leaves with costa excurrent
        3. Leaf borders cylindrical; leaves to 7 mm long_____8. *C. tahitense.*
        3. Leaf borders plane, not thickened; leaves less than 3 mm long _____
        _____ 9. *C. tenerum.*
    2. Propaguliferous leaves with costa percurrent or ending below apex
        3. Propaguliferous leaves less than 2 mm long; costa ends below apex____
        _____7. *C. quaylei.*
        3. Propaguliferous leaves longer than 2 mm; costa percurrent
            4. Cancellineae (hyaline cells of leaf base) obovate_____
            _____6. *C. nukuhivense.*
            4. Cancellineae scalariform (tapered toward costa at top)
            _____4. *C. tuamotuense.*

1. *Calymperes pseudopodianum* Bartram
Bishop Mus. Occ. Pap. 10(10): 7. 1933a.

Plants erect, yellow-green, to 3 cm tall; vegetative leaves erect, incurved, and crispate when dry, erect-spreading when moist, ovate-lanceolate, broader above than in the base; margins erect, slightly denticulate above, entire below, 1 cell-layer thick; elongate submarginal cells (teniolae) extend to above midleaf. Costa percurrent, strongly papillose on the back, papillose on the inner side in the upper leaf. Cells of the lamina rounded-hexagonal, 6–9 μ, mamillose on both surfaces; those of the hyaline basal portion form cancellineae in 6–8 rows on either side of the costa, typically arched above. Propaguliferous leaves linear, to 4 mm long, the lamina a few cells wide on either side of the costa. No sporophytes found.

ILLUSTRATIONS. Figures 31O–R, 36.

MAKATEA. *Emory sn*, 1930 (type); 100 m, on rotting log, *Jones 877* (Bartram, 1933a, FH!).

Distribution.—Makatea (endemic).

The unbordered leaves and extremely narrow lamina of propaguliferous leaves distinguish this species from others with teniolae.

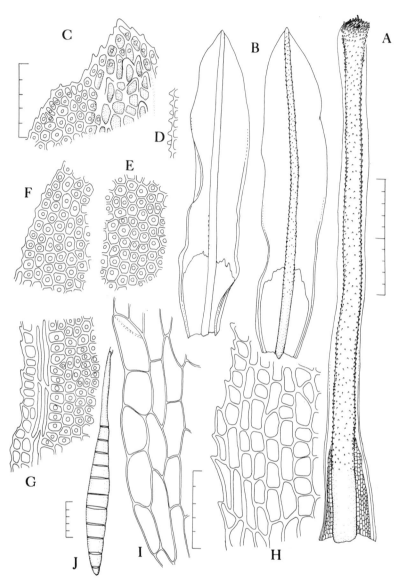

FIG. 36. *Calymperes pseudopodianum*. A. Propaguliferous leaf. B. Vegetative leaves. A, B, scale 1 mm. C. Leaf apex. D. Papillae on lower surface of leaf, side view, upper lamina. E. Lamina cells, upper median. F. Upper lamina, margin. G. Lower middle lamina, margin (note elongated submarginal cells [teniola]). H. Lower lamina near upper limit of hyaline cancellineae, margin. I. Leaf base, margin. C–I, scale 50 μ. J. Propagule of the type developed at apex of propaguliferous leaves (as in Fig. 36A); the elongated basal cell seems characteristic of this species, scale 50 μ.

2. Calymperes porrectum Mitten
J. Linn. Soc. Bot. 10: 172. 1868.

Calymperes aduncifolium Besch., Bull. Soc. Bot. France 45: 61. 1898. syn.
nov.
Calymperes salakense Besch., Ann. Sci. Nat. Bot. ser. 8, 1: 271, 302. 1895.

Plants erect, yellow-green, 1–2 cm tall; leaves broadly ovate-ligulate, sharply acute, vegetative leaves to 3.6 × 0.8–0.9 mm; costa percurrent, lamina basal portion slightly wider than midleaf; propaguliferous leaves to 8 mm long. Cancellineae occupy one-quarter to one-third the leaf base, in 10–12 rows, broadly rounded above. Teniolae present within thickened leaf margins, extend nearly to leaf apex. Leaf margins near base entire to slightly denticulate, the margins of the upper blade from 2 to several cells thick and several cells wide, the outer cells extending into coarse teeth, and similar to those of the lamina, irregularly quadrate to hexagonal, smooth, 6–10 μ in diameter. No sporophytes observed.

ILLUSTRATIONS. Figure 31L–N.

TAHITI. Hitiaa District: Mountains, on trees, Nadeaud 246 (Bescherelle, 1898a, as Calymperes aduncifolium). Papenoo District: About 12 km from Papeete, 30 m, on weathered rock cut, 2388.

Distribution.—Society Islands (Tahiti, a new distribution record), Caroline Islands (Ant), Samoa, New Guinea, Malakka, Java, Philippine Islands, Singapore.

The coarsely serrate upper margins and the submarginal teniolae serve to distinguish this species.

3. Calymperes aongstroemii Bescherelle
Ann. Sci. Nat. Bot. ser. 7, 20: 24. 1895a.

Calymperes tahitense Lindb., non Mitten. fide Bescherelle, 1895a.
Calymperes afzelii Mont., non Swartz, in hb. P. fide Bescherelle, 1895a.
Calymperes richardii Mont., non C. Mueller, in hb. P. fide Bescherelle, 1895a.
Calymperes moluccense Mont., non Schwaegrichen, in hb. P. fide Bescherelle, 1895a.

Plants erect, occasionally branched, to about 1 cm tall; leaves incurved when dry, erect-spreading when moist, ovate-ligulate; costa percurrent or vanishing just below the leaf apex, about 2.7 × 0.68 mm, widest at the sheathing base. Propaguliferous leaves longer, to about 4 mm long, the lamina very narrow on either side of the thick costa (72 μ), giving the leaf a linear-lanceolate appearance. Margins of vegetative and propaguliferous leaves curved up and over toward the costa, giving the leaves a nearly tubulose appearance. Cancellineae occupy up to one-third the length of the leaf in 6–9 rows on each side of the costa. Cells of the lamina quadrate to irregularly hexagonal, thick-walled, the angles thickened, 5–7 μ, rounded-papillose on the upper surfaces, conic-papillose on the lower sides; cells of the cancellineae quadrate to rectangular, 30–60 × 30 μ, thin-walled, hyaline. Margins of the sheathing portion formed by rectangular, hyaline cells 12–25 × 4–5 μ, and serrulate; in the upper one-third of the sheathing basal portion there is a transition from the elongate rectangular cells to a thick border, 2–4 cells wide, which contains some elongate cells and extends to within 0.1 mm of the leaf apex. The costa papillose on the lower surface from leaf apex to the base. Sporophytes not seen. Description from *Lépine 10* (Tahiti, Mitten hb., NY).

ILLUSTRATIONS. Figure 37.

TAHITI. Without locality: On bank, *Lépine 10* (Montagne, 1848, as *Calymperes afzelii*, P); *Andersson sn, Eugenie* Expedition (Aongtrom, 1872, as *C. tahitense*); *Vesco sn* (Bescherelle, 1895a). Papeiha: *Nadeaud sn* (Nadeaud, 1873, as *Leucophanes blumii*; Bescherelle, 1895a). Puaa Valley and Mountain in Pinai: 800–1000 m, *Nadeaud 247*. Seashore at Hitiaa and mountains: Also at Faaiti, at the foot of Mt. Aorai, and in the Tipaeaui Valley, *Nadeaud 248* (Bescherelle, 1898a). Papenoo District: *Tilden 71c* (Brotherus, 1924b).

MOOREA. Without locality: *Andersson sn, Eugenie* Expedition (Aongstrom, 1872); *Nadeaud sn* (Bescherelle, 1895a, 1901).

RAIATEA. Faaroa Valley: On base of *Inocarpus edulis* tree (mapé), 150 m, *Moore 9*. Tioo: On bark of *Inocarpus* in shade, *Moore 84* (Bartram, 1931).

BORA BORA. Mt. Temanu: *Phillips sn* (Phillips, 1947).

Distribution.—Society Islands (Tahiti, Moorea, Raiatea, Bora Bora), Marquesas Islands (Nuku Hiva), Mangareva, Caroline Islands (Kayangle, Puluwat), New Hebrides.

Bescherelle (1895a) distinguished *Calymperes aongstroemii* from *C. moluccense* Schwaegrichen, from Rauwak, which has more narrow leaves, the margins broadly involuted and serrulate, the cancellineae rounded-oval, with chlorophyllose cells extending along the margins to the leaf base, and more strongly papillose lamina cells.

4. *Calymperes tuamotuense* Bartram
   Bishop Mus. Occ. Pap. 10(10): 6. 1933a.

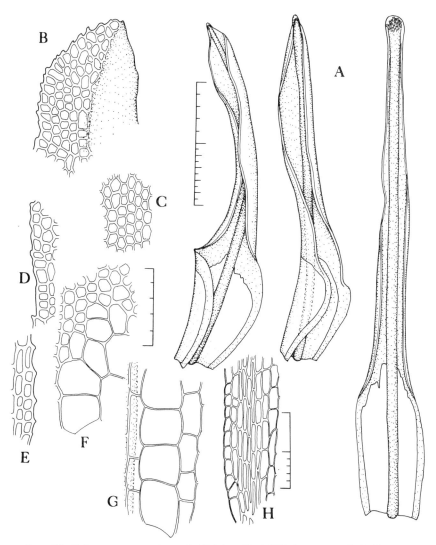

Fig. 37. *Calymperes aongstroemii.* (*Lépine 10,* 1895, isotype, NY.) A. Leaves. Right: a propaguliferous leaf. Left: two normal vegetative leaves, scale 1 mm. B. Leaf apex, side view. C. Lamina, upper median cells. D. Lamina, margin cells. E. Lamina, margin cells near top of cancellineae. F. Uppermost cells of cancellineae and cells of chlorophyllose lamina. B–F, scale 50 μ. G. Cells of cancellineae adjacent to costa. H. Cells of leaf base (note elongate submarginal cells continuous with thickened borders which extend nearly to the leaf apex). G, H, scale 100 μ.

Plants erect, yellow-green, 3 cm tall; leaves ligulate, 2.8 × 0.5 mm, base slightly expanded; costa ends in leaf apex or 1 to several cells below apex in both normal and propaguliferous leaves; propaguliferous leaves larger, to 4.0 × 0.6 mm, the costa thicker, the lamina narrower than in normal leaves. Cancellineae are broad and scalariform above, in 2 cell layers adjacent to the base of the costa, in 6–(8)–10 rows of rectangular cells which become quadrate toward the margins. Teniolae not present, although some slightly elongated cells are to be found. Lamina margin denticulate in the base, the upper margins involute, denticulate, 2–4 cells thick; median leaf cells rounded-papillose on both surfaces, 5–10 μ in diameter, quadrate. No sporophytes observed.

ILLUSTRATIONS. Bartram (1933a, p. 7, f. 2).

MOPELIA ATOLL. Main islet: S tip, 1–3 m, common on some tree trunks and on ground in coconut plantation, *Sachet 977.*

Distribution.—Tuamotu Islands (Makatea), Caroline Islands (Puluwat), Marshall Islands (Lae), a new record for the Society Islands.

Calymperes tuamotuense is distinguished from *C. nukuhivense* by the presence of scalariform cancellineae and rectangular cells. *Calymperes aongstroemii* belongs to the same complex but has more broadly rounded leaf apices and the border is not so regularly thickened.

5. *Calymperes moorei* Bartram
Bishop Mus. Occ. Pap. 9(16): 6. 1931.

Plants yellow-green, about 0.5 cm tall; leaves erect-spreading when moist, oblong-ovate, obtuse, slightly contracted above an expanded base, 1.5 × 0.5 mm, costate; the costa percurrent or ending within a few cells of the apex, smooth; margins plane, entire. Cells of the lamina slightly rounded, thick-walled, isodiametric, 7–12 μ; cancellineae rounded above, higher near the margins than toward the costa. Teniolae (elongate cells near the leaf margin) extend a short distance above the shoulders of the leaf base, usually not more than one-third the length of the leaf. Propagula-bearing leaves constricted just below the rounded apex, producing numerous septate, spindle-shaped propagula on the inner (upper) side of the flared throat. Sporophytes not found. (Based on *Moore 85,* FH!)

ILLUSTRATIONS. Bartram (1931, p. 7, f. 2). Figures 38, 39.

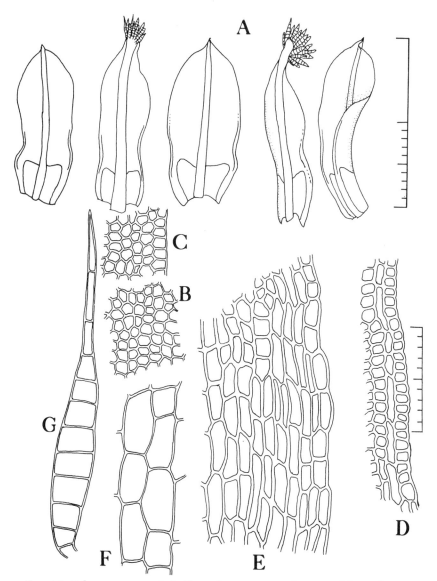

Fig. 38. *Calymperes moorei.* A. Normal vegetative and propaguliferous leaves, scale 2 mm. B. Lamina, upper median cells. C. Lamina, upper margin cells. D. Lamina, margin cells about midleaf (note submarginal elongate cells). E. Lamina, leaf base cells. F. Cancellineae, hyaline cells. G. Propagule. B–G, scale 100 μ.

RAIATEA. S of Fatuna, 1 km: On bark of coconut palm, 1 m, *Moore 85* (Bartram, 1931, type, FH).

MOOREA. Papetoai Bay: E side, ca 10 m, across road from Kellum home, on coconut palm, *3370b.* A new record for Moorea.

Distribution.—Society Islands (Raiatea, type locality; Moorea; probably on all the high islands), Caroline Islands (Ifaluk, Puluwat).

Bartram (1931) compared *Calymperes moorei* with *C. chamaeleontum* C. Mueller, and distinguished *C. moorei* by its broader leaves, entire margins, and smooth lamina cells. The flared apex of propaguliferous leaves separates this species from all Society Islands taxa in the genus *Calymperes.*

6. *Calymperes nukuhivense* Bescherelle
   Ann. Sci. Nat. Bot. ser. 8, 1: 269, 295. 1895.

Plants similar to *Calymperes aongstroemii,* the dry leaves rigidly circinate, the margins inrolled forming a cylinder; leaf apices broadly rounded. Lamina cells chlorophyllose, the quadrate hyaline cells forming obovate cancellineae, not scalariform. Teniolae absent (Bescherelle, 1895b). Capsule with immersed seta, the calyptra ribbed, the apex hairy (Bescherelle, 1898a).

ILLUSTRATIONS. None.

TAHITI. Hitiaa District: On trees near sea level, *Nadeaud 249* (Bescherelle, 1898a).

Distribution.—Society Islands (Tahiti), Marquesas Islands, (Nuku Hiva, type locality).

I have not yet examined authentic specimens of *Calymperes nukuhivense,* presently known from a single locality and collection from Tahiti, and from the type locality from the original collection made by Jardin on Nuku Hiva. Bescherelle (1896) distinguished this species from *Calymperes aongstroemii* by the features noted in the description above.

7. *Calymperes quaylei* Bartram
   Bishop Mus. Occ. Pap. 10(10): 18. 1933a.

Plants erect, to about 1.5 cm tall, usually unbranched, forming dense yellow-green tufts; leaves erect-spreading when moist, with incurved points when dry, 1.2–1.5 × 0.4–0.6 mm, oblong-ovate, apices obtuse, margins erect, crenulate-papillose. Costa strong, ending below apex, papillose on back, about 60 μ wide at the base.

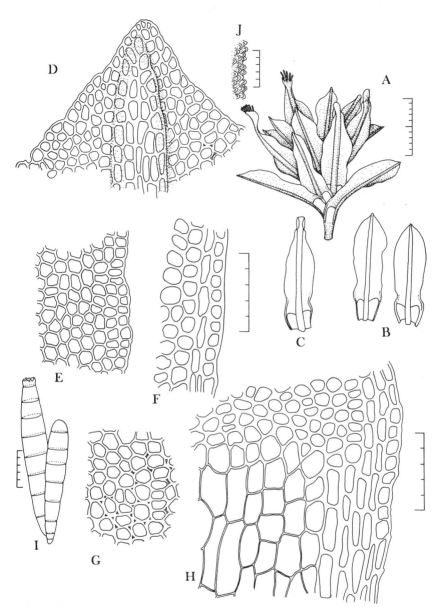

Fɪɢ. 39. *Calymperes moorei.* (*Moore 85*, type, ꜰʜ.) A. Habit, scale 1 mm. B. Normal vegetative leaves. C. Propaguliferous leaf (without propagula). A–C, scale 1 mm. D. Leaf apex (normal vegetative leaf), scale 50 μ. E. Lamina upper margin cells. F. Lamina, margin above basal sheathing portion (note elongate submarginal cells). G. Lamina, upper median cells. H. Leaf, sheathing basal portion margin at top of sheath. I. Propagula, scale 50 μ. J. Oblique surface view of cells on back of propaguliferous leaf apex, scale 50 μ.

Lamina cells papillose on both sides, 4- to 6-sided, rounded, isodiametric, 10–15 μ. Teniolae absent. Cancellineae formed by about 5 rows of rectangular to quadrate hyaline cells on each side of the costa in the leaf base, rounded or arched above. Propagula-bearing leaves abruptly contracted at the apex to form a wide, broadly rounded, flattened tip, the margins toothed. Sporophytes not found. (Based on *Quayle 227*, FH!)

ILLUSTRATIONS. Bartram (1933a, p. 18, f. 8). Figure 40.

SCILLY. *Quayle 227* (Bartram, 1933a, type, FH!).

Distribution.—Society Islands (Scilly), Austral Islands (Raivavae, Tubuai).

Bartram (1933a) wrote: "The much larger leaf cells and the costa ending below the apex separate this species from *Calymperes tenerum*. It is apparently closer to *Calymperes Motleyi* Mitten, but the relatively broader and shorter leaves and especially the larger, papillose leaf cells will distinguish it at once from this species."

8. *Calymperes tahitense* (Sullivant) Mitten
J. Linn. Soc. Bot. 10: 172. 1868.
   Syrrhopodon taitense Sull., U.S. Expl. Exped. Musci 6. t. 4. 1859.

Plants dark green, erect, 2–4 cm tall; leaves stiffly erect, canaliculate, linear-lanceolate, 6–7 × 0.6–0.8 mm, widest in the sheathing basal portion; costa excurrent, usually propaguliferous at the tip; the cancellineae about one-quarter the length of the leaf, tapering up to the costa and extending in 15–20 rows on either side of the costa. Cells of the cancellineae hyaline, thin-walled, quadrate to rectangular, 30–70 × 25–35 μ; cells of the upper lamina pluripapillose, quadrate to irregularly hexagonal, 3–5 μ, the angles thickened. The margin thickly bordered, the borders 35 μ wide, the costa about 80 μ, upper borders dentate, the teeth widely spaced, comprised of cells similar to those of the lamina and not enlarged, about 15 μ tall. In abnormal (propaguliferous) leaves, the uppermost part is almost entirely costa, the lamina tapered along the costa and reduced to a few cells on each side. Sporophytes not seen.

ILLUSTRATIONS. Sullivant (1859, t. 4, as *Syrrhopodon*). Figure 41.

TAHITI. Without locality: *Wilkes sn* (Sullivant, 1859, as *Syrrhopodon*), *Vernier sn* (Bescherelle, 1895a, as *Syrrhopodon*); numerous localities in the wetter regions of Tahiti, 800–1100 m, *Nadeaud 250–253* (Bescherelle, 1898a, as *Calymperes*). Pueu: On rocks with ferns, 250 m, *L. H. MacDaniels 1577* (Bartram, 1933a). Taiarapu

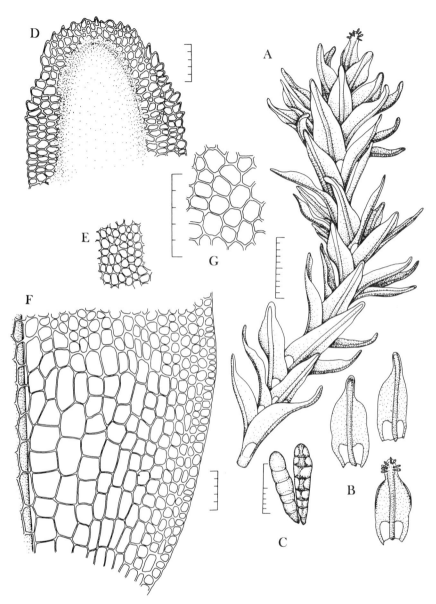

FIG. 40. *Calymperes quaylei*. (*Quayle 227*, type.) A. Habit. B. Leaves (one
with propagula). A, B, scale 1 mm. C. Propagula, scale 100 μ. D. Leaf apex.
E. Lamina, upper median cells. F. Leaf base, cancellineae and margin. D–F,
scale 50 μ. G. Lamina, upper median cells, scale 50 μ.

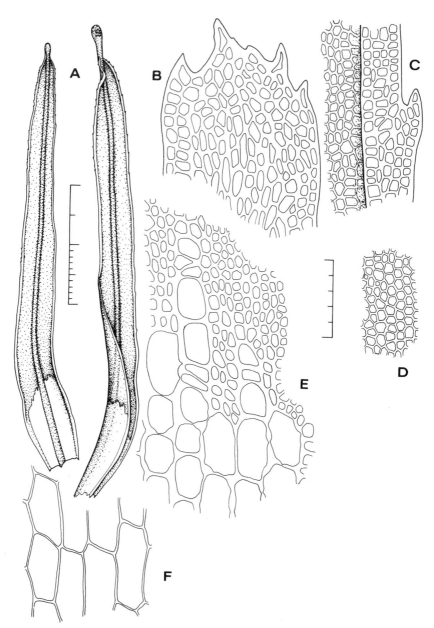

FIG. 41. *Calymperes tahitense.* A. Leaves, scale 2 mm. B. Leaf apex. C. Upper
leaf margin. D. Upper lamina cells. E. Cells, upper cancellineae and lower
lamina. F. Cells, middle cancellineae. B–F, scale 50 μ.

Peninsula: Experiment station, 400–500 m, on liana stem, *Hürli-mann T 1161* (Hürlimann, 1963). Papenoo: Papenoo River, 20–30 m, *2975*.

MOOREA. Trail from Papetoai to Paopao Bay: S of Mt. Rotui, *3430, 3451*. Haring Plantation: Opposite Hotel Eimeo, lower slope Mt. Matanui, usually on rocks, occasionally on bark, with *Homa-liodendron exiguum* and *Fissidens mangarevensis, 3418, 3434, 3437–3439*.

RAIATEA. Mt. Temehani: On bare wet rocks, 400 m, *Moore 19*. Averaiti Valley: On rotten log along stream, 300 m, *Moore 73* (Bartram, 1931).

BORA BORA. Mt. Temanu: *Phillips sn,* 1945 (Phillips, 1947).

Distribution.—Society Islands (Tahiti, type locality; Moorea, a new record; Raiatea, Bora Bora), Marquesas Islands (Nuku Hiva), Fiji (Viti Levu, Vanua Levu, Ovalau), Samoa (Tutuila), Gambier Archipelago, New Hebrides, Java, Borneo, Solomon Islands, Philippine Islands, New Guinea, Formosa, Mariana Islands.

Sullivant (1859) described the plants as 2.5–4 inches high, and the vegetative characters he gave supported his placement of this species in the genus *Syrrhopodon.* Fruiting plants examined by Mitten demonstrated peristome development of a rudimentary form in which teeth were absent, a character which places this species in the genus *Calymperes. Calymperes tahitense* is one of a number of species which show what might be considered "transitional" characters, the gametophytic structure of *Syrrhopodon,* the sporophyte of *Calymperes.* The distinction is somewhat artificial, but certainly it emphasizes that the two genera are closely related.

Dixon and Greenwood (1930) found *Calymperes orientale* Mitt. and *C. denticulatum* C. Muell. to be identical to *C. tahitense.* Paris (1904, 1: 286) gave *Calymperes daemelii* Hampe (mss. name) as a synonym. Wijk, Margadant, and Florschutz (1959) made *Calymperes denticulatum* a variety of *C. tahitense,* but offered no reason for doing so.

9. *Calymperes tenerum* C. Mueller
Linnaea 37: 174. 1872.

Plants dark green, erect, to 1.5 cm tall; leaves elongate-obovate, 2.3–2.6 × 0.5–0.6 mm, the basal sheathing portion slightly narrower than the upper lamina; costa percurrent. Propaguliferous leaves longer, 2.6–2.8 mm, the costa excurrent, characteristically with clusters of spindle-shaped propagula at the tip. Cancellineae rounded at the top, ending below the top of the leaf base, cells in 5–8 rows on each side of the costa, largest adjacent to the costa, quadrate to rectangular. No teniolae. Cells of the upper lamina irregularly quadrate to hexagonal, 5–7 μ in diameter, rounded-papillose, thick-walled. Margins involuted in the upper lamina, plane below, entire throughout, usually 1 cell thick but in some forms occasionally 2 cells thick. All specimens examined have been sterile.

ILLUSTRATIONS. Miller, Whittier, and Bonner (1963, pl. 8). Figure 31H–K.

TAHITI. Tipiare: On volcanic rock, *Hürlimann T 1133* (Hürlimann, 1963, det. Bartram, FH!). Arue District: 2 km W of Papeete, on bark of trees lining highway, *3485*.

MOOREA. N side of island: 8 km W of Club Méditerranée, with hepatics on rocks along highway, *3461*; on bark, same locality, *3462*; on *Erythrina* sp., *3373*; on *Artocarpus* (breadfruit) bark, near road between Paopao and Papetoai bays, *3379*. Apparently new records for the island of Moorea.

RAIATEA. Nao Nao Island: On lichens and bark of tree, 1 m, *Moore 88* (Bartram, 1931, BISH!).

BORA BORA. Mt. Temanu: *Phillips sn*, 1945 (Phillips, 1947).

MAKATEA. On coconut trunk, 200 ft, *G. P. Wilder 108*; interior jungle, 100 m, *W. B. Jones 862* (det. Bartram, BISH!).

Distribution.—Society Islands (Tahiti, Raiatea, Bora Bora; Moorea, a new record), Tuamotu Islands (Mangareva, Tikei, Ahii, Makatea), Austral Islands (Tubuai), Pitcairn Island, Hawaii (Oahu, Maui, Hawaii, Kauai), Palmyra, Australia (North Queensland), Malaya, New Guinea, Java, Philippine Islands, New Caledonia, Sumatra, India, Borneo, Vietnam, Marshall Islands (Rongerik, Rongelap, Bikini, Eniwetok, Arno, Utirik, Ailuk, Likiep, Wotho, Ujae, Lae, Ujelang Majuro, Kwajalein), Caroline Islands (Kapingamarangi, Mokil, Pakin, Truk, Namonuito, Puluwat, Ifaluk, Sorol, Pulo Anna). Common throughout the Pacific and Indomalaya, *Calymperes tenerum* is typically found on the trunks of coconut palms and on coconut husks as a low turf composed of erect plants with strongly incurved leaves, the propaguliferous leaves with distinct, spherical clusters of club-shaped propagula on the tips of excurrent costae.

VI. GRIMMIACEAE

Rhacomitrium Bridel
  Mant. Musc. 78. 1819.
Rhacomitrium papeetense Bescherelle
  Ann. Sci. Nat. Bot. ser. 7, 20: 25. 1895.

Plants yellow-green or yellow-brown above, black below, irregularly branched, to about 2 cm tall; leaves incurved to erect, contorted when dry, erect to erect-spreading when moist, ovate-lanceolate, blunt-pointed, 2.5–3.0 × 0.6–0.8 mm, margins entire, erect to recurved, the blade longitudinally wrinkled; costa stout, ending in the upper one-quarter to one-third of the blade. Cells linear, sinuose, irregularly thick-walled, pitted, in the upper lamina 20–30 × 6–8 μ, in the lower blade 40–50 × 8–10 μ, smaller toward the margins, 10–15 × 4–6 μ; in the basal angles smooth-walled, more nearly isodiametric, 10–20 μ. Reproductive structures were not observed, but Bescherelle (1895a) described capsules as elliptic-ovate, on a seta of 4 mm.

ILLUSTRATIONS. Figure 42S–Z.

TAHITI. Papeete: Without locality, *Jardin sn*, 1872 (Bescherelle, 1895a, P!).

Distribution.—Society Islands (Tahiti), endemic.

Bescherelle (1895a) compared this species with *Rhacomitrium fasciculare* (Hedw.) Brid., which he thought had a similar habit, and with *R. ericoides* (Hedw.) Brid., which had a similar branching pattern, and noted that *R. papeetense* differed in its regularly muticous (blunt) leaf apices from the latter species, and from the former in having leaves pressed close to the stem when dry, diverging when wet.

147

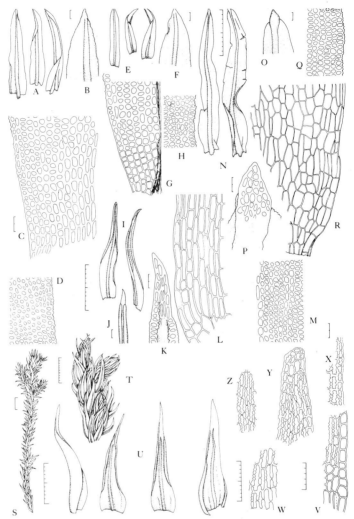

Fɪɢ. 42. A–D. *Anoectangium euchloron.* (*HOW 290.*) A. Leaves, scale 1 mm.
B. Leaf tip, scale 50 μ. C. Leaf base, scale 20 μ. D. Upper leaf cells and
margin, scale 20 μ. E–H. *Anoectangium tapes.* (Isotype.) E. Leaves, scale 1
mm. F. Leaf tip, scale 50 μ. G. Leaf base, scale 20 μ. H. Upper leaf cells and
margin, scale 20 μ. I–M. *Weisia controversa.* (*HOW 2663.*) I. Leaves, scale
1 mm. J. Leaf tip, scale 50 μ. K. Leaf tip, scale 20 μ. L. Leaf base, scale 20 μ.
M. Upper leaf cells, scale 20 μ. N–R. *Trichostomum clavinervis.* (*HOW 3160.*)
N. Leaves, scale 1 mm. O. Leaf tip, scale 50 μ. P. Leaf tip, scale 20 μ. Q.
Upper leaf cells and margin, scale 20 μ. R. Leaf base, scale 20 μ. (*del.* HAM.)
S–Z. *Rhacomitrium papeetense* Besch. (*Jardin sn,* 1872.) S. Habit, wet, scale
1 mm. T. Habit, dry, scale 1 mm. U. Leaves, scale 1 mm. V. Leaf base, margin. W. Leaf base, median cells. X. Leaf, upper margin. Y. Leaf apex. Z. Leaf,
median cells. V–Z, scale 50 μ.

VII. POTTIACEAE

Four genera are now known in the Society Islands: *Anoectangium, Weisia, Trichostomum,* and *Hyophila.* Plants small, yellow-green to green, about 5 mm tall, erect, branched, crowded on soil, rocks, or bark. Leaves often spirally arranged on stems, crispate when dry, erect-spreading when moist, the margins plane to involute; costate, the costa ending below the apex or short-excurrent. Cells of the lamina smooth below, smooth to papillose or pluripapillose above; lower cells elongate, yellowish to hyaline, upper cells small, irregularly isodiametric, chlorophyllose. Sporophytes erect, seta smooth, capsule erect-symmetrical, cylindric or ovoid-cylindric, operculum conic-rostrate. Peristomes absent in *Anoectangium* and *Hyophila,* of 16 teeth in *Weisia* and *Trichostomum.*

KEY TO GENERA OF THE POTTIACEAE

1. Upper lamina cells smooth..4. *Hyophila beruensis.*
1. Upper lamina cells papillose
    2. Terminal cell of costa enlarged; peristome absent........1. *Anoectangium.*
    2. Terminal cell of costa not enlarged; peristome present
        3. Costa apex bulbous, at least on some leaves..................................
        ....3. *Trichostomum clavinervis.*
        3. Costa apex not bulbous on any leaves..........2. *Weisia controversa.*

1. *Anoectangium* Schwaegrichen
Spec. Musc. Suppl. 1(1): 33. 1811. *nom. cons.*

Plants small, forming dense turfs; leaves ligulate-lanceolate, spirally twisted about the stem and contorted when dry, erect-spreading when moist; costa ending in the apex in a single enlarged cell. Sporophytes lateral, peristome absent.

Key to Species of *Anoectangium*

1. Leaves 1.5–1.8 × 0.3–0.35 mm; basal cells thick-walled, 7–25 × 5–8 μ, becoming markedly smaller, rounded-quadrate toward margins, larger, rectangular toward the costa.......................................1. *A. euchloron.*
1. Leaves 1.0–1.4 × 0.2–0.3 mm; basal cells thin-walled, 7–18 × 7–10 μ, not markedly reduced in size toward margins but more quadrate than toward the costa ....2. *A. tapes.*

149

1. *Anoectangium euchloron* (Schwaegrichen) Mitten
   J. Linn. Soc. Bot. 12: 176. 1869.
   Gymnostomum euchloron Schwaegr., Spec. Musc. Suppl. 2(2): 83. f. 177.
   1827.

Plants erect, 5–6 mm tall, yellow-green, forming crowded colonies on soil or rocks; leaves spirally twisted about the stems when dry, erect-spreading when moist, plane to carinate above, 1.5–1.8 × 0.30–0.35 mm, lingulate-lanceolate; costa ends in the apex; leaf base formed by thin-walled, quadrate to rectangular cells, hyaline to yellowish. Margins plane to erect, entire below, crenulate papillose. Cells of the lamina pluripapillose, 4–6 μ, isodiametric, and thick-walled, the walls 2–2.5 μ in the upper blade; basal cells thick-walled, 7–25 × 5–8 μ. The costa is papillose in the upper blade, smooth below. Sporophytes not observed in local collections, but Bartram (1939) described them as lateral, the seta yellowish, 6 mm long, the capsule erect, oblong-cylindric, the urn 0.8 mm, peristome absent, annulus absent, operculum subulate-rostrate as long as the urn, oblique, the calyptra cucullate, spores papillose, 10–12 μ.

ILLUSTRATIONS. Figure 42A–D.

TAHITI. Mt. Aorai: On soil along trail to summit, ca 1000 m, *290*.

Distribution.—Society Islands (Tahiti, a new record); tropical America, Java, Philippine Islands, Africa.

Miller (personal communication, 1970) studied the Society Islands collection and suggested that it is *Anoectangium euchloron*. It differs from *A. tapes* which has shorter leaves and thin-walled basal cells.

2. *Anoectangium tapes* Bescherelle
   Bull. Soc. Bot. France 45: 53. 1898.

Plants erect, 5–6 mm tall, yellow-green, forming turfs on rocks or bark; leaves spirally twisted about the stems when dry, erect-spreading when moist, ligulate-lanceolate, 1.0–1.4 × 0.2–0.3 mm, broadly acuminate at the apex, a single prominent cell forming an apiculus at the end of the costa. Margins plane, entire below, slightly crenulate from the large papillae present on both surfaces of the lamina. Cells of the lamina near the leaf base smooth, thin-walled, quadrate to rectangular, the angles not rounded, 7–18 × 7–10 μ, in the upper lamina obscure, pluripapillose, irregularly quadrate, about 3–5 μ inside diameter. The single sporophyte examined (isotype, NY!) is deoperculate; seta 5.4 mm long (to 9 mm long, Bescherelle, 1898a). Spores 9–(12)–15 μ, finely papillose, light green. The urn lacked a peristome and was about 1.0 × 0.4 mm. Exothecial cells rectangular to irregularly elongate-hexagonal, 50–60 × 15–25 μ. Operculum 1 mm long, rostrate; calyptra minute, cucullate (Bescherelle, 1898a).

ILLUSTRATIONS. Figure 42E–H.

TAHITI. Marciate: Floor of the Papenoo Valley, and Punaruu Valley at the foot of Mt. Orohena, *Nadeaud 202* (Bescherelle, 1898a, isotype, NY!). Without locality: *Moseley sn, Challenger* Expedition (in hb. Mitten, NY! as *Anoectangium oceanicum* Mitt., mss. name, apparently unreported).

Distribution.—Society Islands (Tahiti), endemic.

2. *Weisia* Hedwig
Spec. Musc. 64. 1801.
Weisia controversa Hedwig
Spec. Musc. 67. 1801.
Weisia viridula (Linn.) Hedw., Fund. Musc. 2: 90. 1781.

Plants erect, about 5 mm tall, forming low turfs on bark or rocks; leaves erect-spreading when moist, linear-lanceolate, up to 2.0 × 0.4–0.5 mm, the margins strongly involuted, the leaf base plane; costa strong, ending in a short apiculus or mucro, the terminal cell not markedly enlarged or prominent. Cells of the upper lamina rounded-quadrate, 6–8 μ, pluripapillose; cells near the leaf base smooth, hyaline, elongate. Sporophytes to 4–8 mm long; capsule ovoid, about 0.8 mm long; peristome teeth 16, from 160 to 200 μ long. Spores 14–17 μ, brownish, papillose. Description from Fleischer, Musc. Archip. Ind. Exsicc. no. *159*, 1901, from West Java, as *Weisia viridula*, NY!

ILLUSTRATIONS. Figure 42I–M.

TAHITI. Without locality: *Andersson sn*, 1852 (Aongstrom, 1873, "exacte cum forma e California allata congruit"; Bescherelle, 1895, *fide* Aongstrom). Fort Fautaua: On damp, clayey soil, *Nadeaud 59* (Nadeaud, 1873; Bescherelle, 1895a, 1898a). Hitiaa District: Mountain and seashore collections, and at Faaiti, at the foot of Mt. Aorai, and at Tipaeaui, *Nadeaud 20* (Bescherelle, 1898a, as *Weisia viridula*). Pic Rouge: At the base, *Temarii Nadeaud sn* (Bescherelle, 1901, as *W. viridula*). Taiarapu Peninsula: Haavini Valley, 165 m, on ground, *2469*. Mt. Aorai: On rotting roots on trail, 1800 m, *2848*.

Distribution.—Society Islands (Tahiti), Mangareva, Rapa, New

Zealand, Hawaii (Oahu, Kauai, Hawaii), Java, Sri Lanka (Ceylon), Africa, Asia, Europe, North America, South America, Tasmania.

Weisia controversa is characterized by reflexed leaves having whitish, laxly areolate bases and strongly inrolled upper margins which give them a linear appearance. Leaf apices are acuminate, the costa pale yellowish, short-excurrent, its point formed by 6–9 only slightly enlarged, elongate cells. Basal cells of the lamina are long-rectangular, the larger cells 30–50 × 6–10 μ, becoming shorter, more thin-walled, and hyaline toward the margins. *Trichostomum clavinervis* differs in the club-shaped costa apex, the leaf bases not markedly distinct from the upper blade, the leaf margins variably upturned, plane, or even curved down, but not strongly inrolled; basal cells are short-rectangular.

3. *Trichostomum* Bruch
   Flora 2: 295. 1829. *nom. cons.*
Trichostomum clavinervis (Cardot & de la Varde) Whittier, *comb. nov.*
   Weisia clavinervis Card. & P. de la Varde, Rev. Bryol. 39: 20. 1912.

Plants erect, green, gregarious on soil or decaying wood, to 5 mm tall; leaves irregularly crispate when dry, erect to recurved when moist, linear, 2.5–3.8 × 0.4–0.5 mm; costate, the costa short-excurrent, expanded at the apex. Leaf margins plane to upturned, slightly inrolled or even downturned, crenulate-papillose. Cells of the upper lamina isodiametric, irregularly hexagonal, the angles not rounded, 5–8 μ inside diameter, the walls 1–2 μ thick, pluripapillose on both surfaces; lower lamina cells smooth, yellowish to hyaline, mostly short-rectangular, to 40 × 15 μ near the costa, shorter, more nearly quadrate toward the margins, 10–12 × 8–10 μ. Sporophytes not observed.

ILLUSTRATIONS. Figure 42N–R.

TAHITI. Without locality: *Larminat sn* (Potier de la Varde, 1912). Mt. Aorai: On soil, 918 m, associated with *Weisia controversa, 2663.* Fautaua Valley: 590 m, *3160.*

Distribution.—Society Islands (Tahiti), endemic.

4. *Hyophila beruensis* Dixon
   J. Bot. Brit. For. 65: 255. 1927.

Plants terrestrial, yellow-green, erect; leaves incurved and inrolled when dry, erect-spreading when moist, variably ovate to ligulate,

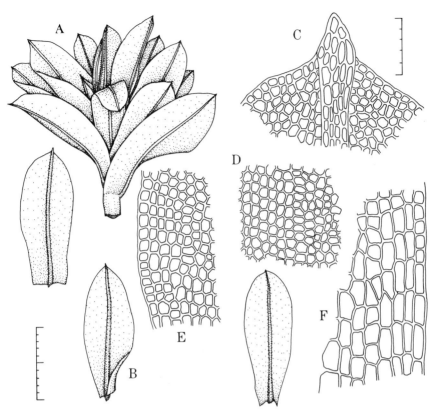

Fɪɢ. 43. *Hyophila beruensis.* A. Habit, scale 1 mm. B. Leaves, scale 1 mm. C. Leaf apex. D. Lamina, upper median cells. E. Lamina, margin cells. F. Lamina, base and margin cells, scale 50 μ.

most commonly obovate, 1.3–2.2 × 0.5–0.8 mm, the apex broadly rounded, abruptly mucronate; costa ending 2–3 cells below the apex in lower leaves, in upper leaves short-excurrent, smooth to slightly papillose, about 80 μ thick at the base. Leaf margins plane to erect, entire to faintly crenulate. Cells of the lamina smooth to rounded, irregularly quadrate to hexagonal, largest adjacent to the costa, to about 60 × 15 μ, shorter and more narrow toward the margins, 25 × 7–10 μ. Sporophytes not found. Propagula common, stellate, in axillary clusters.

ILLUSTRATIONS. Figure 43.

TAHITI. Papeete: Above Gendarmire, ca 200 m, on rocks along trail, *371a*.

Distribution.—Society Islands (Tahiti, a new record), Caroline Islands (Kayangle, Pulo Anna, Sorol, Ifaluk, Ant), Gilbert Islands (Onotoa; Beru, the type locality), New Caledonia (Noumea, *Welch 20432*, a new record).

Hyophila beruensis compares in stature and construction closely with the genus *Calymperes,* but differs in having the enlarged basal cells less strongly differentiated than the cancellineae of *Calymperes.* Further, the propagula are borne in axillary clusters and are typically stellate; those of *Calymperes* are terminal on propaguliferous leaves.

VIII. SPLACHNACEAE

Splachnobryum C. Mueller
  Verhz. Zool. Bot. Ges. Wien 19: 503. 1869.
Splachnobryum indicum C. Mueller
  Linnaea 37: 174. 1872.

Plants scattered, erect, in loose, low tufts, the stems unbranched, 0.5–1.0 cm tall; upper leaves erect-spreading, obovate to spathulate, to 1.2 × 0.54 mm; costa ends 2–5 cells below the broadly rounded to bluntly acute apex. Margins irregularly crenulate, usually plane. Cells of the lamina smooth, thin-walled, in the median upper blade 4–6-sided, elongate, 45–70 × 9–12 μ, at the leaf apex 20–30 μ long, and toward the leaf base elongate-rectangular to 6-sided, 70–120 × 15–18 μ, decurrent at the basal angles. Cells of the leaf margins with outer walls thinner than those adjacent to the inner lamina cells. Costa 45–50 μ wide at the leaf base. All plants examined sterile.

ILLUSTRATIONS. Figure 44.

TAHITI. Route des Maraichiers: On soil under shower installed since 1960 near view point overlooking Papeete, ca 250 m, general vegetation of area *Dicranopteris, Casuarina,* and *Eucalyptus, 2097.*

Distribution.—Society Islands (Tahiti, a new record for the genus and the family in the archipelago), Marshall Islands (Arno, Wotho), Java, Philippine Islands (Cebu), India.

Breen (personal communication, 1962) and Breen and Pursell (1959) emphasize the variable nature of species in the genus *Splachnobryum,* which differ vegetatively in response to age and to growth conditions, especially to moisture. The species described here compares well with specimens collected in the Marshall Islands determined by Miller, Whittier, and Bonner (1963) as *S. indicum.* The genus has been reported from Tonga (Hürlimann, 1965), but it appears to be absent from New Zealand and Hawaii, although present in both Old and New World tropics and temperate regions. The family Splachnaceae has not been reported previously from the Society Islands, and I believe the genus *Splachnobryum* to be of recent introduction on Tahiti. Within its normal range, the genus is not uncommon and may be abundant near human habitations. The single record of its collection and the peculiarity of its habitat support the belief in its newness in the Society Islands.

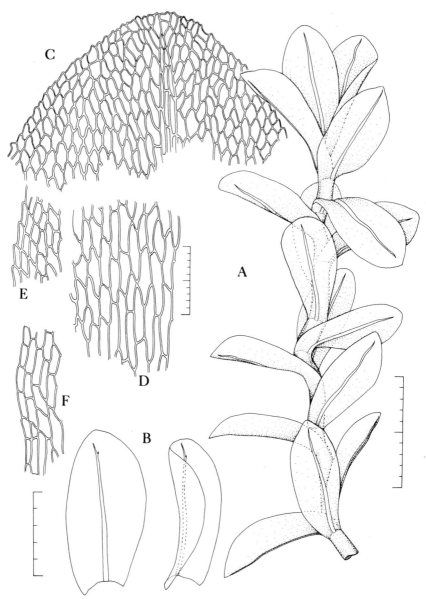

Fig. 44. *Splachnobryum indicum.* (*HOW 2097.*) A. Habit, scale 1 mm. B. Upper leaves, scale 0.5 mm. C. Leaf apex cells. D. Lamina, upper median cells. E. Lamina margin, cells of upper blade. F. Lamina margin, cells of blade base. C–F, scale 100 μ.

IX. BRYACEAE

The family Bryaceae is represented in the Society Islands by the genera *Bryum* and *Brachymenium,* both comprised of species which are small, tufted plants forming turfs on rock or soil, occasionally on bark. Stems are erect, usually less than 1 cm tall, occasionally branched, leaves appressed when dry, erect-spreading when moist, ovate to obovate-lanceolate, the costa ending in the upper leaf, percurrent or excurrent. Leaf margins unbordered or bordered, entire to denticulate. The setae are long, yellow to reddish, capsules erect (*Brachymenium*) or inclined to pendulous (*Bryum*), peristome double, exostome of 16 papillose teeth, endostome of 16 keeled segments which may alternate with exostome teeth. Cilia present between endostome segments (*Bryum*), or absent (*Brachymenium*). Vegetatively the two genera are quite alike, the distinctions more subjective: in *Bryum* the costa terminates in the upper lamina, percurrent or short-excurrent (Bescherelle's [1898a] *Bryum bigibbosum* has a long-excurrent, denticulate costa, but the capsules are pendulous); in *Brachymenium indicum* the costa is long-excurrent.

KEY TO GENERA OF THE BRYACEAE

1. Capsules erect, cilia absent between endostome segments; costa excurrent to 3 mm ....1. *Brachymenium.*
1. Capsules inclined, cilia present between endostome teeth; costa terminates in upper lamina or to about 2.5 mm excurrent................2. *Bryum.*

1. *Brachymenium* Schwaegrichen
   Spec. Musc. Suppl. 2(1): 131. 1824.
Brachymenium indicum (Dozy & Molkenboer) Bosch & Lacoste
   Bryol. Jav. 1: 141. 1860.
   Bryum indicum Dozy & Molk., Musci Fr. Ined. Archip. Indici 1: 22. f. 11. 1845.
   Brachymenium melanothecium (C. Muell.) Jaeg., Ber. S. Gall. Naturw. Ges. 1873–1874: 114. 1875.

Plants erect, branched, to 1 cm tall, green to dark green, the stems reddish-brown, in compact turfs; leaves appressed when dry, erect-spreading when moist, ovate-lanceolate to 2.3 × 0.7 mm, the

157

blade to about 2 mm long; costa long-excurrent and prominent. Cells of the upper lamina linear-rhomboidal, 7–8:1, 70–90 × 10–12 μ, short-rectangular or rhomboidal in the base, 14–25 × 14–18 μ. Margins entire below, entire to serrulate in the upper leaf, cells elongate, to 115 × 10 μ. Sporophytes not present in collections examined.

ILLUSTRATIONS. Miller, Whittier, and Bonner (1963, pl. 11). Figure 45A, B.

TAHITI. Without locality: *Wilkes sn*, 1838 (Sullivant, 1859, as *Bryum*); *Harvey sn*; *Jardin sn*; *Vernier sn* (Bescherelle, 1895a, as *Brachymenium melanothecium*); Tahiti nui, general localities on N side, *Nadeaud 274, 275* (Bescherelle, 1898a, as *B. melanothecium*). Pirae District: Fautaua Valley, on rocks near Fort Fautaua, specimen with an incomplete peristome, *Nadeaud sn* (Nadeaud, 1873, as *Bryum australe*; Bescherelle, 1895a).

Distribution.—Society Islands (Tahiti), Hawaii (?), Samoa, Tonga, Gambier Archipelago (Mangareva), Austral Islands (Raivavae, Tubuai), Tuamotu Islands (Hao, Marutea), Pitcairn Island, Gilbert Islands (Beru, Onotoa, Tarawa, Abemama, Little Makin), Caroline Islands (Puluwat, Kapingamarangi), Marshall Islands (Likiep, Ailuk), Java, Amboina, New Caledonia, Fiji, Timoe Island.

Bartram (personal correspondence, 1961) wrote concerning the identity of *Brachymenium melanothecium*: "I came to the conclusion some years ago that *B. melanothecium* (C. Muell.) Jaeg. was inseparable from *B. indicum* (Dozy & Molk.) Bry. Jav. As Mueller's type was probably destroyed in Berlin-Dahlem during the last war, no comparison is possible, but there is certainly nothing in the description that suggests a valid distinction." Further attempts to locate the type or authentic specimens have been unsuccessful. An Hawaiian species, *Brachymenium exile* (Dozy & Molk.) Bosch & Lac., originally reported from Indomalaya and Sri Lanka (Ceylon), is to some extent allied to *B. indicum* but differs in the very small leaves (0.6 × 0.35 mm; Bartram, 1933a) and shorter lamina cells.

Excluded species

Brachymenium bryoides Hooker *ex* Schwaegrichen
Spec. Musc. Suppl. 2(1): 134. f. 135. 1824.

I have not seen any specimens so identified from Tahiti, but this southeast Asian species has been reported from the Society Islands

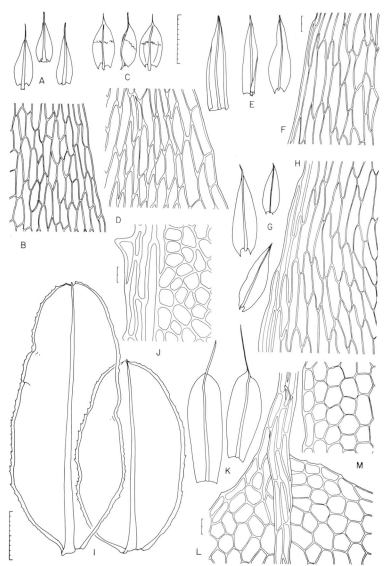

FIG. 45. A, B. *Brachymenium indicum*. A. Leaves, scale 1 mm. B. Upper leaf cells and margin, scale 20 μ. C, D. *Bryum argenteum* var. *lanatum*. (Oahu, *del.* HAM. 1431.) C. Leaves, scale 1 mm. D. Upper leaf cells and margin, scale 20 μ. E, F. *Bryum bigibbosum*. (*HOW 297, 298.*) E. Leaves, scale 1 mm. F. Upper leaf cells and margin, scale 20 μ. G, H. *Bryum weberaceum*. (*Hürlimann T 1142.*) G. Leaves, scale 1 mm. H. Upper leaf cells and margin, scale 20 μ. I, J. *Plagiomnium rostratum*. (Oahu, *HAM 2629.*) I. Leaves, scale 1 mm. J. Upper leaf cells and margin, scale 20 μ. K–M. *Leptostomum miller-ianum*. (*HOW 2808.*) K. Leaves, scale 1 mm. L. Apical region. M. Upper leaf cells and margin. L, M, scale 20 μ. (*del.* HAM.)

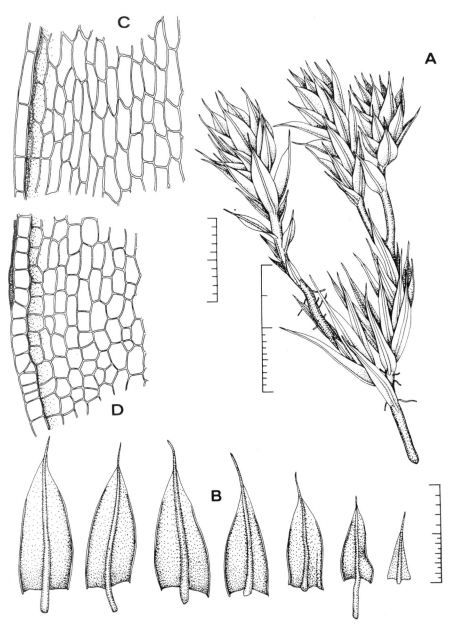

Fig. 46. *Brachymenium indicum.* A. Habit, scale 2 mm. B. Leaves, the longest uppermost in tufts, the shortest lower on stems, scale 2 mm. C. Upper median and margin cells. D. Basal median and margin cells. C, D, scale 100 μ.

by Guillemin (1860, p. 242, Mem. Soc. Sci. Cherbourg, France). For the moment, I include this record with *B. indicum.*

2. *Bryum* Hedwig
Spec. Musc. 178. 1801.

Characteristics of the genus *Bryum* are discussed in the description of the family Bryaceae. Four species are separated by the following key, and a fifth species, *Bryum larminati* Cardot & Potier de la Varde, reported from the Society Islands, and indistinguishable from *Bryum bigibbosum* Bescherelle, is reduced to synonymy with that species.

Key to Species of *Bryum*

1. Leaf apices whitish or hyaline, at least on some leaves, costa ending below apex in most leaves_____1. *B. argenteum.*
1. Leaf apices green, costa percurrent to excurrent
    2. Leaves bordered by 2–3 rows elongate, thick-walled cells, strongly dentate above, 2.0 × 0.5 mm _____3. *B. billardieri.*
    2. Leaves not bordered; cells of margins elongate but not thick-walled, margins entire or only slightly denticulate
        3. Leaves to 2.0 × 0.46 mm; sporophytes 1.0–1.5 cm__2. *B. bigibbosum.*
        3. Leaves to 1.5 × 0.3 mm; sporophytes 2–2.5 cm___4. *B. weberaceum.*

1. *Bryum argenteum* Hedwig
Spec. Musc. 181. 1801.

I have not seen collections of this cosmopolitan species from Tahiti or the other Society Islands.

Plants pale green to silvery-white, erect, the stems branching, to 5–6 mm tall, forming compacted turfs on banks, rocks, and soil; leaves pressed against the stems when dry, spreading when moist, about 1.0 × 0.5 mm, ovate to ovate-lanceolate; costa usually two-thirds the length of the leaf, the leaves crowded, appressed, the apices whitish, the lower lamina chlorophyllose and sometimes red-tinged. Cells of the lamina elongate-rhomboidal to hexagonal, 80–100 × 10–12 μ in the upper blade. Seta red, to 2 cm long, curved at the tip; capsule to 1.5 × 0.5 mm, red, horizontal to pendulous, oblong, with a short, distinct neck. Operculum convex, apiculate. Cilia of the inner peristome with short, transverse appendages.

ILLUSTRATIONS. Bartram (1933a, p. 124, f. 90). Figure 45C, D.

TAHITI. Without locality: *Jelinek sn,* 1857–1858, *Novara* Expedition (Reichardt, 1870; Bescherelle, 1895a).

Distribution.—Society Islands (Tahiti, apparently from this single record), Austral Islands (Rapa, Raivavae), Pitcairn Island, Hawaii (Kauai, Hawaii), bipolar.

Bartram (1933a, b; 1940) provided some notes on ecology: collections from Rapa were from grooves in rock at 7 m; those from the Austral Islands were on dry soil at 400 m, and on basalt ledges on a mountain summit at 304 m. In Hawaii, collections were made on a stone wall near Hilo, in lava pockets in the vicinity of Kilauea crater, and near Kealakekua; on Maui, near the rest house at Haleakala, and along the Honokohau ditch trail. These collections were all placed in the variety *lanatum* (P. Beauv.) B. S. G., which is distinguished primarily on the basis of longer, more acuminate leaves, the costa extending well into the apex or percurrent (to excurrent, Bartram, 1933b); this variety was considered by Bartram to represent a xerophytic form of *B. argenteum*. The hyaline or whitish leaf tips are a convenient diagnostic feature.

2. *Bryum bigibbosum* Bescherelle
  Bull. Soc. Bot. France 45: 65. 1898.
    ?*Bryum larminati* Card. & P. de la V., *in* Potier de la Varde, Rev. Bryol. 39: 20. 1912.

Plants forming turfs on sandy soil, green, 0.5–1.0 cm tall, irregularly branched, with reddish rhizoidal tomentum toward stem base. Small plantlets, apparently serving in asexual reproduction, form in the axils of upper leaves. Leaves press against the stem when dry, spreading only slightly when moist, lanceolate to ovate-lanceolate, 1–2 × 0.3–0.46 mm, margins entire, unbordered, reflexed above; costa green to reddish, prominent on the lower surface of the leaf, the base about 70 μ wide, the apex percurrent to excurrent as much as 100 μ and denticulate. Lamina basal cells rhomboidal, 35–60 × 12–15 μ, median cells rhomboidal to irregularly hexagonal, smooth, 35–65 × 7.5–12.5 μ. Sporophytes 1–1.5 cm tall; seta yellow to brownish, smooth; capsule pendulous, ovate, about 1.0 × 0.3 mm; operculum conic, about 0.3 mm long; exothecial cells irregularly rhomboidal, 35–50 × 20–25 μ, thick-walled.

ILLUSTRATIONS. Figure 45E, F.

TAHITI. Tarutu (Mamano) Valley: Teapiri, to 900 m, between Papeava and Puaa, to 1000 m, *Nadeaud 276*. Hitiaa: Seashore and mountains of Faaiti at the foot of Mt. Aorai, and in the Tipaeaui Valley, *Nadeaud 277* (Bescherelle, 1898a). Fare Rau Ape–Mt. Aorai trail: *297*.

Distribution.—Society Islands (Tahiti), endemic.

Bescherelle recognized this species as belonging to the section *Doliolidium.* The group in which Brotherus (1924b) placed this species is quite large and the allied species are widespread. No satisfactory distinctions exist to distinguish between *B. larminatii* and *B. bigibbosum.*

3. *Bryum billardieri* Schwaegrichen
   Spec. Musc. Suppl. 1(2): 115. f. 76. 1816.
   Bryum truncorum (Brid.) Brid., Mant. Musc. 119. 1819.
   Mnium truncorum Brid., Spec. Musc. 3: 50. 1817.
   Bryum leptothecium Tayl., Phytologist 1: 1094. 1844. *fide* Dixon, S. African
        J. Sci. 18: 321. 1922.

Plants erect, green to yellow-green, 2–3 cm tall, the lower stems brownish, green above, commonly on soil in rock crevices in deep valleys or at low elevations under *Dicranopteris.* Leaves erect to adpressed, crisped when dry, erect-spreading when moist, clustered at or near the tip of the stem, broadly obovate, to about 5.0×2.0 mm; costa about 75 μ wide near the leaf base, and short-excurrent. Margins bordered by 2–3 rows of elongate, thick-walled cells, 150–250 $\times$ 3–8 μ, the margins of the upper blade dentate, the teeth formed by protruding cell ends. Cells of the lamina elongate-hexagonal, thin-walled (the walls less than 3 μ thick), 60–90 $\times$ 9–12 μ (in *Quayle 212*, margin border cells appear in a submarginal position, 4–6 cells from the edge in the lower half of the blade, the cells of the lamina 40–60 $\times$ 10–17 μ). Sporophytes not found.

ILLUSTRATIONS. Brotherus (1924b, 1: 399, f. E–H, as *B. leptothecium*). Figure 47.

TAHITI. Without locality: *Bidwill sn* (in hb. Hooker; Mitten, 1871, as *B. leptothecium*); *Nadeaud 49* (Nadeaud, 1873, as *Mnium rostratum, fide* Bescherelle, 1895a); numerous but unspecified localities, *Nadeaud 268–273* (Bescherelle, 1898a, as *B. leptothecium*); *Quayle sn*, 1922 (Bartram, 1933a, as *B. leptothecium*). Pirae: Fare Rau Ape–Mt. Aorai trail, 600 m, on volcanic rock, *Hürlimann T 1212* (Hürlimann, 1963, det. Bartram); 500 m, old Alpine Club grounds at beginning of trail, on banks, *200, 220;* ca 700 m, on soil, with *Pogonatum graeffeanum, Leucobryum tahitense, Campylopus,* and *Trichosteleum, Whittier sn;* 1700 m, with *Campylopus, Macromitrium, Dicranella, Mastigophora, Jamesoniella, Microlepidozia,* and *Bazzania, 2970;* Fautaua Valley, *Fosberg and St. John 14142,* unreported (BISH!); 312 m, on coconut palm, with *Pinnatella keuhliana,*

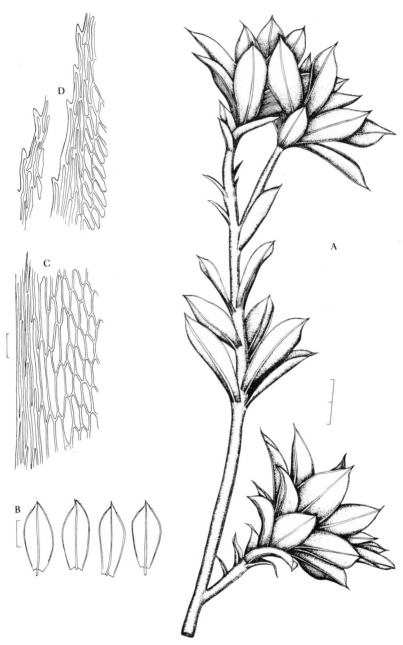

FIG. 47. *Bryum billardieri*. A. Habit, scale 2 mm. B. Leaf outlines, scale 2 mm. C. Cells, leaf margins and median lamina. D. Cells, margin of upper leaf. C, D, scale 50 μ.

2350; 490 m, on rock and adjacent tree trunk, with *Fissidens mangarevensis, Pinnatella keuhliana, Hypopterygium, Calyptothecium, Trichosteleum, Ectropothecium,* and *Bazzania, 3121*; 480–530 m, on tree branch, with orchid, *Calyptothecium, Hypopterygium,* and *Anthoceros, 3137*; Mt. Aorai–One Tree Hill trail, common between 300 and 500 m, on soil, under *Gleichenia* (*Dicranopteris*), *2834*; 180 m, on trunk of *Mangifera indica, 2837*.

RAIATEA. Temehani Range: S end, 500 m, among other mosses on branches of shrubs, *Moore 46e* (Bartram, 1931, as *B. leptothecium,* BISH!).

Distribution.—Society Islands (Tahiti, Raiatea), Austral Islands (Raivavae, Rapa), New Zealand, Australia, Tasmania, Campbell Island, Norfolk Island, New Guinea, Mascarene Islands, Inaccessible Islands, Tristan d'Acunha, West Indies, South America, Hawaii (?), Fiji.

My collections have been distributed mostly as *Bryum truncorum.*

4. *Bryum weberaceum* Bescherelle
Bull. Soc. Bot. France ser. 3, 45: 65–66. 1898.

Plants turf-forming on rocks, erect, irregularly branched, green, stems reddish, to about 1 cm tall. Leaves press against stem when dry, erect-spreading when moist, ovate-lanceolate, to 1.8 × 0.48 mm, the upper margins slightly denticulate, slightly involute. Costa green to reddish, slender, about 40 μ wide at the base, percurrent to short-excurrent by as much as 50 μ, denticulate in the excurrent portion. Lamina basal cells rhomboidal to irregularly elongate-hexagonal, 35–70 × 12.5–17.5 μ toward the costa, narrower and more elongate, to 120 × 7.5 μ at the margins; upper median cells irregularly elongate-hexagonal, thin-walled (about 2–2.5 μ), 50–85 × 10–12.5 μ, becoming narrower and more elongate at the margins, 140–150 × 3.5–5 μ. Sporophytes 2–2.5 cm tall; seta smooth, yellowish; capsules horizontal to inclined, short-cylindric, 2.4 × 1.2 mm; operculum and calyptra not seen. Exothecial cells irregularly rhomboidal to hexagonal, 25–45 × 12.5–25 μ. (Based on *Hürlimann T 1142, T 1243,* FH!).

ILLUSTRATIONS. Brotherus (1924b, 1: 395, f. 343). Figure 45G, H.

TAHITI. Pute: Temarua Valley: On rocks in stream, *Nadeaud 278* (Bescherelle, 1898a). Miaa: 850 m, *Temarii Nadeaud sn* (Bescherelle, 1901). Hitiaa District: On old wall, *Hürlimann T 1142.* Pirae District: Fare Rau Ape–Mt. Aorai trail, *Hürlimann T 1243* (Hürlimann, 1963, det. Bartram, FH!).

RAIATEA. Tioo: On soil in coconut grove, 1 m, *Moore 90* (Bartram, 1931, BISH!).

Distribution.—Society Islands (Tahiti, Raiatea), endemic.

Bartram (1931) noted that Moore's collection was sterile, and that the costa was excurrent in a point longer than typical in plants from Tahiti, and that it might prove to be a new species. In Moore's specimen, the plants are to 8 mm tall, the costa short-excurrent, leaves to 1.5 × 0.3 mm, cells irregularly rhomboidal to hexagonal, 40–50 × 8–11 μ, the costa about 34 μ wide near the base of the leaf, excurrent by 30–100 μ; margins serrulate above.

Dubious species

Bryum larminati Cardot & de la Varde

in Potier de la Varde, Rev. Bryol. 39: 20. f. 1. 1912.

This species is known only from the original collection, the type in the Paris herbarium. The original description follows:

> Dioicum (?). Caespites densi sed laxe cohaerentes, superne virides, inferne brunnei et radiculosi. Caulis erectus (10–20 mm. altus), paulum flexuosus, superne innovans, ramulis elongato-ovoideis, acuminate attenuatis desinentibus. Folia inferiora sicca ad caulem arcte adpressa, madida erecta, superiora latiora, sicca arcte imbricata, madida erecto-patentia, concava, lanceolato-acuminata, marginibus 3/4 longitudine revolutis, integris, apicem versus subdenticulatis. Costa rufescente in foliis vetustis, viridi in junioribus, in aristam brevem denticulatam excurrente; cellulis inferioribus subquadratis, deinde rectangulis, superioribus hexagono-rhomboideis (40–50 × 10–15 μ), ad margines angustioribus, in foliis junioribus copiose chlorophyllosis.
>
> Bracteae perichaetii exteriores foliis superioribus sat similes, tamen majores, marginibus planioribus, costa minus excurrente vel etiam in apice dissoluta, mediae angustiores acuminato-lanceolatae subintegrae, intimae minimae acute lineales vel breviter lanceolatae, enerviae. Archegonia circiter 10–15, paraphysibus haud multis parum coloratis.
>
> Caetera inquirenda.
>
> *Bryo bigibboso* Besch. proximum, a quo habitu altiore, foliis brevioribus latioribusque, superioribus validius revolutis, costa brevius excurrente, cellulis copiosius chlorophyllosis, reti laxiore, distinguitur.

ILLUSTRATIONS. Potier de la Varde (1912, p. 22).

TAHITI. Without locality: *Larminat sn* (Potier de la Varde, 1912).

Distribution.—Society Islands (Tahiti), endemic.

Potier de la Varde observed small, ovoid plantlets in the axils of upper leaves. No truly useful character separates this species from *Bryum bigibbosum* Besch.

X. MNIACEAE

Plagiomnium Koponen
　Ann. Bot. Fennici 5(2): 117–51. 1968.
Plagiomnium rostratum (Schrader) Koponen
　Ann. Bot. Fennici 5(2): 147. 1968.
　　Mnium rostratum (Schrad.) Schrad., Bot. Zeit. Regensburg 1: 79. 1802.
　　Mnium longirostrum Brid., Musc. Recent. 2: 106. 1803.

Plants erect or suberect to prostrate, forming tufts 2 cm or more deep, commonly on wet, shaded earth, rocks, or logs. A variable species, fertile stems (described by Sainsbury, 1955) are erect and short, with leaves in comal, rosulate tufts. Barren branches are semiprostrate and straggling, the leaves distant and complanate. Leaves 6–7 mm long, oblong or obovate, rounded at the apex and apiculate, crispate when dry, plane when moist, distinctly bordered by 3–4 rows of elongate, thick-walled cells, the borders variably entire to denticulate above, entire toward the leaf base. Costa broad at the base, percurrent. Cells of the lamina rounded-hexagonal, the angles thick-walled (collenchymatous), 25–30 μ. Seta typically about 2 cm long; sometimes in aggregates of 2–4. Capsule 3–3.5 mm long, horizontal to pendulous, broadly ovate or oblong, pale, the mouth wide and red-rimmed; operculum conic, with a long, curved beak; peristome orange-yellow, the teeth finely striate at the tips and unbordered, papillose on the backs. Spores to 32 μ in diameter. After Sainsbury (1955) and Bartram (1933b).

ILLUSTRATIONS. Bartram (1933b, p. 127, f. 92). Figure 45I, J.

TAHITI. Without locality: *Wilkes sn* (Sullivant, 1859, as *Mnium*).

Distribution.—Society Islands (Tahiti), Hawaii (Oahu, Maui, Hawaii, Kauai), Java, Borneo, Sumatra, Burma, Philippine Islands, Africa, South America, Australia, New Zealand, Europe.

That *Plagiomnium rostratum* should appear in the Society Islands is no surprise, for the species has a broad range in both Old and New World tropics, and occurs in Australia, New Zealand, and Hawaii. Experience based upon my field work in Hawaii suggests that the species might easily be overlooked if its abundance in the

Society Islands were comparable to its presence on Oahu. An early report of *P. rostratum,* made by Nadeaud (1873), was corrected by Bescherelle (1898a), who indicated the specimen to be *Bryum leptothecium* Tayl. (= *Bryum billardieri*). Bescherelle made no comment regarding Sullivant's (1859) report.

XI. LEPTOSTOMACEAE

Leptostomum R. Brown
   Trans. Linn. Soc. London 10: 130. 1811. *nom. cons.*
Leptostomum millerianum sp. nov.

Leptostomum macrocarpum (Hedw.) R. Br. aemulans, differt apicis foliorum integris; cellulis laminarum apicem versus plus minusve incrassatis et marginem versus elongatis vel rectangulatis. Specimen typicum *2808* in hb. NY.

Plants erect, turf-forming, to about 1 cm tall; leaves crisped when dry, appressed to the stem, erect-spreading when moist, oblong, the upper leaves rounded at the apex; costa variably excurrent ending in a fine hairpoint. Lamina 1.2–1.6 × 0.6–0.7 mm, the excurrent portion as much as an additional 0.6 mm long but frequently broken and shorter; margins entire and unbordered. Lamina cells smooth, thin-walled, isodiametric to about 2 times longer than wide, those of the base quadrate to irregularly rhomboidal or hexagonal, slightly longer toward the costa than toward the margins, 15–30–(50) × 15–30 μ, those of the upper lamina not markedly different, but slightly smaller, more often isodiametric. Sporophytes not found.

ILLUSTRATIONS. Figure 45K–M.

TAHITI. Mt. Aorai: Trail to One Tree Hill, 1890 m, forming cushions, *2801*; 1450 m, *2807*; 1500 m, associated with *Symphysodontella cylindracea*, *2808* (type!).

Distribution.—Society Islands (Tahiti), endemic.

A long-standing record of the genus *Leptostomum* for the Society Islands dates to the collection of Banks and Solander made in 1769 and reported by Hedwig in 1792 and 1801 as *Bryum macrocarpum, without locality.* A subsequent citation of this collection by Bridel in 1826 states, "praesertim in Otaheiti." Later authors also refer to this collection as Tahitian (Mueller, 1849; Mitten, 1871; Jaeger and Sauerbeck, 1875), but the only other possible collection for the Society Islands seems to be that of the Forsters made in 1773 and reported by Guillemin in 1836, without locality. *Leptostomum millerianum* is smaller and lacks the branched excurrent costa characteristic of *L. macrocarpum.* Mitten's (1871) note referring to the Banks and Solander collection ascribes it to Tahiti, and a second collection by Cunningham from Norfolk Island, characterizes both as containing specimens smaller than those from New Zealand, but provides no additional insight. *Leptostomum macrocarpum* seems to be an uncertain member of the Society Islands moss flora.

Dubious species

Leptostomum macrocarpum (Hedwig) Pylaie
J. Bot. ser. 2, 3: 15. 1814.
Bryum macrocarpum Hedw., Spec. Musc. 178. 1801.

I have not examined authentic specimens from the Society Islands, if any exist. This species is well-known from Norfolk Island and New Zealand, and it is upon Sainsbury's (1955, p. 282) description that the following is based.

Plants erect, 1–2 cm tall, yellow-green above with dense reddish tomentum below, common on bark as a low turf; leaves densely imbricated on the upper stem, 2–3 mm long, ovate, the margins revolute and entire, erect and twisted about the stem when dry, erect-spreading when moist; costa strong, long-excurrent, frequently branched near the tip in upper stem leaves. Cells of the lamina thin-walled, hexagonal to irregularly quadrate, smooth, 20–30 × 10–15 μ, the chloroplasts clustered in the center of the cell lumen. Seta 1–1.5 cm long (to 4.5 cm), yellow to orange; capsule 3–4.5 mm, erect, ovate; operculum conic. Peristome rudimentary, consisting of inner peristome in form of low papillose membrane about 150 μ high, the margin erose. Spores 16–24 μ, finely papillose.

ILLUSTRATIONS. Brotherus (1924b, 1: 406), Sainsbury (1955, p. 283).

?TAHITI. Without locality: *Banks and Solander sn*, 1769 (Hedwig, 1801, "in insulis australibus, praesertim in Otaheiti, probabiliter in locis turfosis habitat," as *Bryum macrocarpum*; Bridel, 1826; C. Mueller, 1849; Mitten, 1871; Jaeger and Sauerbeck, 1875; Bescherelle, 1895a, citing Mitten); *Forster sn*, 1773 (Guillemin, 1836).

Distribution.—Society Islands (?), Norfolk Island, New Zealand, Rapa.

Bartram (1940) observed that Dixon and Brotherus cite only New Zealand or Norfolk Island for the distribution of this species, overlooking or ignoring the "important" Tahitian record, which I feel might be questioned on the basis of my collections. The interesting Southern Hemisphere distribution of the genus includes New Zealand, Australia, Tasmania, Norfolk Island, New Caledonia, Java, Rapa, Tahiti, and the western and southern tips of South America.

XII. RHIZOGONIACEAE

Rhizogonium Bridel
Bryol. Univ. 2: 644. 1827.

Plants robust, often forming deep tufts, reddish-brown to green; leaves erect-spreading when moist, linear-lanceolate, the margins bordered by 2–3 rows of cells in 2 layers, spinose; lamina cells thick-walled, rounded-quadrate above, rectangular at the base. Sporophytes terminal, arising from a short, lateral basal branch, 6–7 cm tall, capsules inclined; peristome formed by an endostome and an exostome.

Key to Species of *Rhizogonium*

1. Leaves to 7 mm long, incurved when dry; lamina margin teeth cells 35–40 μ long _____1. *R. spiniforme.*
1. Leaves to 9.5 mm or longer, erect-spreading when dry; lamina margin teeth cells singular, 28–30 μ long_____2. *R. setosum.*

1. *Rhizogonium spiniforme* (Hedwig) Bruch
in Krauss, Flora 29. 1846.

Hypnum spiniforme Linn. *ex* Hedw., Spec. Musc. 236. 1801.
Mnium spiniforme (Hedw.) C. Muell., Syn. 1: 175. 1849.
Pyrrhobryum spiniforme (Hedw.) Mitt., J. Linn. Soc. Bot. 10: 174. 1868.
Rhynchostegium latifolium Aongstr., Oefv. K. Svensk. Vet. Ak. Foerh. 29: 18. 1873. *fide* Fleischer, Musci Fl. Buitenzorg 2: 593. 1904.

Plants green to reddish-brown, to 4 cm tall, forming loose turfs on rocks or bark; leaves incurved and slightly contorted when dry, erect-spreading when moist, 6–7 × 0.48–0.54 mm, linear-lanceolate; costa strong, percurrent, the margins with a strong border 2–3 cells thick, denticulate, the teeth single or in pairs in the upper three-quarters of the leaf, the back of the costa also denticulate in the upper half of the leaf, with a series of cells extending in a ridge from each tooth toward the leaf base. Cells of the lamina rounded-quadrate, thick-walled, smooth, 9–12 μ; the cells of the margin teeth 35–40 μ long, the tips of the teeth as much as 25 μ from the leaf border; from one-third to two-thirds the length of the cell may project. Sporophytes 4–6 cm long; seta from a short, basal, lateral branch; urn about 3.0 × 1.2 mm, curved, asymmetrical, inclined to horizontal; exothecial cells irregularly thickened; upper subannular cells smaller, quadrate; cells of the apophysis thick-walled, with stomata occasionally present. Operculum short, conic, apiculate. Peristome teeth to 540 μ, transversely striate, faintly papillose, the endostome also faintly papillose. Spores 16–20 μ, smooth to faintly papillose, greenish. Description from 2970.

ILLUSTRATIONS. Bartram (1933b, p. 131, f. 95), Brotherus (1924b, 1: 427, f. 377d, e). Figure 48.

TAHITI: Without locality: 700–800 m, Lépine sn (Montagne, 1848); Vesco sn, Lequerré sn (hb. Camus); on wet ridges on ground and on trunks of trees, Nadeaud 53 (Bescherelle, 1895a). Puaa Valley: Nadeaud 287 (Bescherelle, 1898a). Taiarapu Peninsula: Taravao, above experiment station, Hürlimann sn (Hürlimann, 1963, as var. samoanum Mitt., det. Bartram, FH); 600–700 m, with Metzgeria, Riccardia, Leucomium aneurodictyon, Floribundaria aeruginosa, and Ptychomnion aciculare, 2316a. Haavini Valley: Near Pueu, 130 m, with Exodictyon dentatum, Leucobryum, and Bazzania, 2536. Mt. Orohena: S side, 1100 m, on tree trunk, with Ophioglossum pendulum, MacDaniels 1533 (unreported, BISH). Pirae District: Fare Rau Ape–Mt. Aorai trail, 263; 1800 m, with Trichosteleum, Bazzania, Ptychomnion aciculare, and Plagiochila, Decker and Decker 35; with Ptychomnion and Floribundaria aeruginosa, Decker and Decker 108; with Acroporium, Leucobryum, and Ectropothecium, 2700; 1040 m, with Dicranella hochreutineri, Leucobryum, and Bazzania, 2707; 1100 m, ridge from Aorai to One Tree Hill, with Thyridium obtusifolium and Trichosteleum, 2799; 1700–1800 m, Mt. Aorai, near summit, with Plagiochila, Frullania, and Bazzania, 2876; Mt. Aorai, summit, on soil, with Dicranella hochreutineri and Pogonatum tahitense, 2889; below 1500 m, with Bryum, Campylopus, Macromitrium, Bazzania, Jamesoniella, Microlepidozia, and Garovaglia, 2790.

Distribution.—Society Islands (Tahiti), Fiji (Vanua Levu, Kandavu, Koro, Moala), Samoa (Tutuila, Upolu), Hawaii (Kauai, Oahu, Molokai, Maui, Lanai, Hawaii), Austral Islands, Cook Islands (Rarotonga), New Caledonia, Australia, Tasmania, Kermadec Islands, New Zealand (excluded by Sainsbury, 1955), Malaya, China, India, Africa, Malagasy Republic (Madagascar), Central America, North America (Florida, Alabama, Louisiana), Antilles Islands, Puerto Rico.

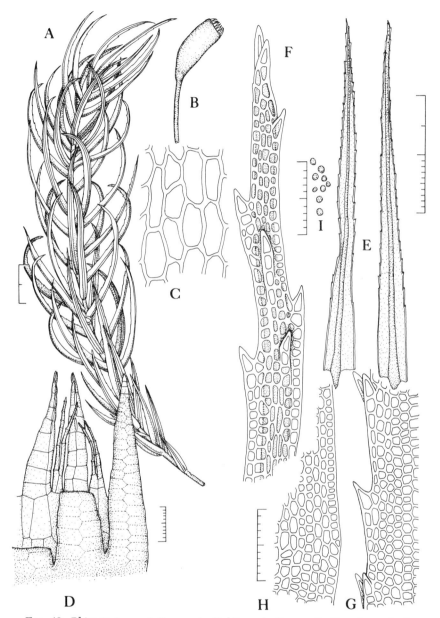

Fig. 48. *Rhizogonium spiniforme*. A. Habit, scale 2 mm. B. Capsule, scale 2 mm. C. Exothecial cells, scale 100 μ. D. Peristome, detail of segment, scale 100 μ. E. Leaves, scale 2 mm. F. Leaf apex. G. Leaf upper margin, cells. H. Leaf base, cells. F–H, scale 100 μ. I. Spores, scale 100 μ.

Monographic revision of the genus *Rhizogonium* will be needed to give the true distribution of *Rhizogonium spiniforme,* which seems to be represented by considerable variation throughout its range. Bescherelle identified Nadeaud's collection no. 69, from the Puaa Valley of Tahiti, as *R. paramattense* (C. Muell.) Reichdt., but did not publish this name in 1898 with the other collections Nadeaud sent him. It appears to be identical to Mitten's *R. spiniforme* var. *samoanum* (NY!), a small-leaved form with more slender leaves suggestive of a reduced *Rhizogonium setosum.* Other specimens in the Mitten herbarium, identified as *R. paramattense* from Tasmania and New South Wales, are certainly only minor variations of *R. spiniforme.*

2. *Rhizogonium setosum* (Mitten) Mitten
   in Seemann, Fl. Vit. 384. 1871.

   Pyrrhobryum setosum Mitt., J. Linn. Soc. Bot. 10: 174. 1868.

Plants erect, on bark or rotting wood, rarely on the ground; leaves erect-spreading (even when dry), 8–9.5 × 0.4–0.5 mm, linear-lanceolate, long-acuminate, the margins bordered, 2–3 cells thick, denticulate, the teeth formed by a single cell 28–30 μ long, the tips of the teeth 20–25 μ from the border; the costa occupies most or all of the upper lamina, where it is denticulate on the lower surface, the teeth with a very short series (2–4) of cells extending toward the leaf base. Cells of the upper lamina thick-walled, smooth, rounded-quadrate, 7–10 μ. No sporophytes were seen in Tahitian material, but in authentic specimens of *R. setosum* from Samoa, incomplete sporophytes 6–7 cm tall were seen, the capsule inclined to horizontal, about 3 mm long; exothecial cells irregularly rectangular to elongate-hexagonal, thick-walled, 60–85 × 25–30 μ. Spores 14–18 μ, smooth to finely papillose, greenish.

ILLUSTRATIONS. Brotherus (1924b, 1: 429, f. 378f, g). Figure 49.

TAHITI. Without locality: *Vesco sn; Lépine sn* (Bescherelle, 1895a). Puaa: On old tree trunks, *Nadeaud sn,* 1896 (Bescherelle, 1898a; NY). Pirae District: Fare Rau Ape–Mt. Aorai trail, above old French Alpine Club buildings, *231* (1960); 1030 m, with *Rhizogonium spiniforme, Leucobryum tahitense, Dicranoloma braunii,* and *Acroporium, 2700;* with *Ptychomnion aciculare, Leucobryum,* and *Dicnemon rugosum, 2703;* on *Cyathea* trunk, with *Spiridens balfourianus* and *Ptychomnion aciculare, 2713;* 1120 m, on tree, with *Acroporium* and *Thyridium obtusifolium, 2720;* 1200 m, with fern,

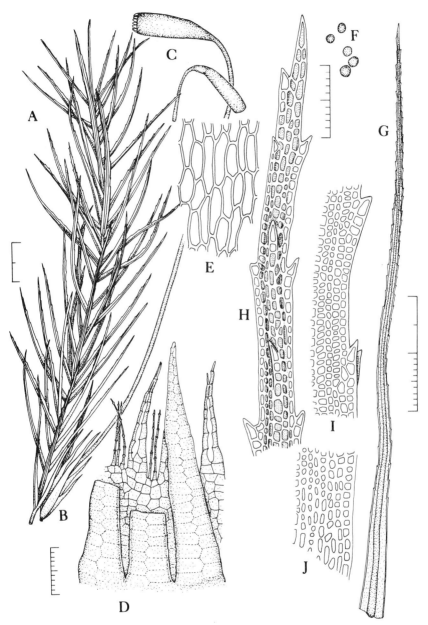

Fig. 49. *Rhizogonium setosum*. A. Habit. B. Perichaetial leaves. C. Capsules. A–C, scale 2 mm. D. Peristome. E. Exothecial cells. F. Spores. D–F, scale 100 µ. G. Leaf, scale 2 mm. H. Leaf apex, margin and cells. I. Leaf upper margin and median cells. J. Leaf base cells. H–J, scale 100 µ.

on tree trunk, *2737*; 1930 m, *2797*; 1700 m, with *Trachyloma tahitense, 2875*; 1700 m, *2904*. Papenoo–Vaihiria valleys: 310–400 m, with *Trichomanes* (fern) and *Trichocolea, 3022*; 700 m, N side of ridge between Papenoo and Vaihiria valleys, on tree trunk and stump, with *Fissidens* and *Schistochila, 3033*; 840 m, on crest of ridge between valleys, *3037*. Hitiaa District: Plateau region, ca 200 m, with *Thyridium constrictum, Acroporium lepinei,* and *Bazzania, 3222*; with *T. constrictum, Acroporium, Arthrocormus schimperi,* and *Herberta, 3223*. Taiarapu Peninsula: Taravao, above experiment station, in *Miconia* forest, *2239*.

MOOREA. Without locality: *Temarii Nadeaud sn*, 1899 (Bescherelle, 1901).

Distribution.—Society Islands (Tahiti, Moorea), Samoa (Upolu, type locality; Tutuila), Fiji (Viti Levu, Ovalau, Ngau), New Guinea, New Hebrides, Aneityum, Australia (Sydney).

Mitten (1868) wrote: "Size, mode of growth, and colour of the foliage as in *P. spiniforme,* Linn. (*Hypnum*), but with leaves scarcely half as wide, more bristle-like and rigid; the teeth toward the apex of the leaf are evidently a continuation of the margin, so that the nerve is not terete and excurrent as is stated to be the case in *P. pungens,* Sull. Amer. Expl. Exp. (*Rhizogonium*), which appears also to be a much larger species in all its parts." Both *R. pungens* and *R. setosum* are reported to be dioicous. Leaves of the Samoan *R. setosum* may be as long as 12 mm; the costa 135 μ wide at the leaf base, and it may occupy the entire width of the upper leaf, where, with the exception of the few cells below the teeth, the lamina is absent. Confusion arises when less robust specimens of the Hawaiian *R. pungens* are examined; the general characters seem to be quite similar to those of the Samoan species *R. setosum!* In typical *R. pungens,* however, the expanded leaf base narrows abruptly to the costa about 3 mm from the leaf base, and the upper 10–14 mm of the leaf are essentially composed of the denticulate costa. The teeth of the margins are composed of several cells, especially near the leaf base. These characters combine to suggest that *R. pungens* is a distinct species, but that it must be considered strongly related to the Samoan *R. setosum.*

XIII. CALOMNIACEAE

Calomnion Hooker f. & Wilson
Fl. Nov. Zel. 2: 97. 1854.
Calomnion schistostegiellum (Bescherelle) Wijk & Margadant
Taxon 8: 72. 1959.
Nadeaudia schistostegiella Besch., Rev. Bryol. 25: 11. 1898.
Calomnion nadeaudii Besch., Rev. Bryol. 25: 42. 1898.
Calomnion denticulatum Herz., *non* Mitten, *in* Herzog, Geographie der Moose 357. 1926.

Plants dioicous, orange-brown or greenish-orange, apparently restricted to fern rhizomes or to *Cyathea* trunks, primary stems prostrate, weak, and ephemeral, the secondary stems forming loose turfs, about 1.0–1.5 cm tall; leaves arranged in 3 rows, lateral leaves ovate-apiculate, slightly asymmetric, about 1.0 × 0.27 mm, ventral leaves (or amphigastria) more nearly symmetrical, roughly orbicular with an apiculus, about 0.65 × 0.36 mm; perichaetial leaves long, ligulate, to about 1.5 × 0.21 mm. Costa strong, percurrent or slightly excurrent, typically surrounded by lamina cells nearly to the apex. Margins entire to irregularly serrulate. Cells of the lamina quadrate to hexagonal, thick-walled, 4–7 μ in diameter in the upper blade, more elongate toward the leaf base, slightly rounded on free surfaces.

ILLUSTRATIONS. Figure 50.

TAHITI. Taiarapu Peninsula (type locality): On the rhizomes of ferns, *Nadeaud sn*, 1896 (Bescherelle, 1898a, c, d, as *Nadeaudia*; 1901, as *Calomnion nadeaudii*). Arue District: *Nadeaud sn* (Bescherelle, 1901). Hitiaa District: Lower plateau region, 395–400 m, on *Cyathea* trunks, associated with *Thyridium constrictum, Plagiochila pulchra* (det. Inoue, 1968), *Bazzania,* and *Trichocolea, 3201;* with *Acroporium, Thyridium,* and *Bazzania, 3241;* with *Thyridium* and *Syrrhopodon, 3251.*

MOOREA. Without locality: *Temarii Nadeaud sn* (Bescherelle, 1901). S of Mt. Rotui: Between Papetoai and Paopao bays, with *Arthrocormus schimperi, 3426.*

Distribution.—Society Islands (Tahiti, Moorea), Austral Islands (Rurutu).

179

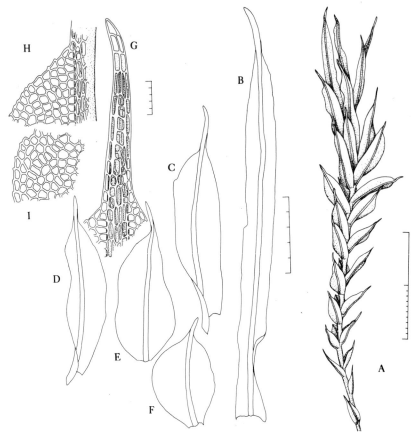

FIG. 50. *Calomnion schistostegiellum.* (*HOW 3241.*) A. Habit, archegoniate plant, scale 2 mm. B. Perichaetial leaf. C, D. Lateral leaves. E, F. Amphigastrial leaves. B–F, scale 0.5 mm. G. Leaf apex, cells. H. Lamina, upper cells. I. Margin cells and cells of upper lamina. G–I, scale 50 μ.

Apparently derived from the Rhizogoniaceae, this Austral-Oceanic family is comprised of only three species: *Calomnion complanatum* (*C. laetum*) from North and South Islands, New Zealand, and Tasmania; *Calomnion denticulatum* from Upolu, Samoa; and *Calomnion schistostegiellum* from Tahiti and Moorea, Society Islands. Herzog (1926, p. 357) gives the presence of *C. denticulatum* in the Society Islands in error, as only *C. schisto-stegiellum* has been recorded from the archipelago.

Sainsbury (1955) followed Jaeger, Fleischer, and Brotherus, in treating the family as allied to the Mitteniaceae, Mniaceae, and the Rhizogoniaceae, but although he noted that in his *Classification of Mosses,* Dixon placed the family near the Georgiaceae, in his *Studies in the Bryology of New Zealand* (4: 333. 1926) Dixon later placed the family Calomniaceae following the Bartramiaceae. The terminal position of the sporophyte in *Calomnion* is not far removed, in a phylogenetic sense, from a terminal position on a short basal or lateral branch as in the genus *Rhizogonium*. Certain taxa of *Rhizogonium* demonstrate a leaf arrangement and areolation similar to that of the species of *Calomnion*. *Rhizogonium* is a widely distributed genus with species throughout the tropics of the Old World and the New World, and it does not seem difficult to imagine the derivation of the gymnostomous Calomniaceae from Austral *Rhizogonium*-like ancestors.

XIV. HYPNODENDRACEAE

This family is represented in the Society Islands by the genus *Hypnodendron,* but includes one other genus, *Braithwaitea,* which is essentially Austral, appearing in New Caledonia, Australia, Lord Howe Island, and New Zealand. *Hypnodendron* (including *Mniodendron,* following Touw's 1971 taxonomic revision of the Hypnodendraceae) is Asian and Indomalayan in origin, extending widely into the South Pacific, Australia, Tasmania, New Zealand, and South America.

Two species of *Hypnodendron* are present in the flora: *H. samoanum* Mitten and *H.* (*Mniodendron*) *tahiticum* (Besch.) Touw. Both are dendroid, with prominent secondary stems arising from a prostrate primary rhizomatous stem. Branches of secondary stems are restricted to the upper ends to suggest the form of a minute tree. In *H. tahiticum* the secondary stem is covered with a dense, brown tomentum, and plants are usually less than 4–5 cm tall. *Hypnodendron samoanum* possesses shiny, black, erect secondary stems, lacking profuse brown tomentum, and is usually 6–10 cm tall. In both, the seta is 3–5 cm long, reddish, the capsule markedly ridged, the operculum conic-rostrate.

Both species are common in middle and upper valleys in shaded places where moisture levels are constantly high, on decomposing wood, rich organic debris, and even on rocks and tree trunks.

Hypnodendron (C. Mueller) Lindberg *ex* Mitten
   Musci. Fl. Vit. 401. 1871.

Key to Species of *Hypnodendron*

1. Erect secondary stems more than 6 cm tall, lacking brown tomentum, but characteristically shiny black..1. *H. samoanum.*
1. Erect secondary stems less than 5 cm tall, covered with dense brown tomentum, not shiny black..2. *H. tahiticum.*

1. *Hypnodendron samoanum* Mitten *ex* Mitten
   Musci. Fl. Vit. 401. 1871.
      Hypnodendron samoanum Mitt., J. Linn. Soc. Bot. 10: 192. 1868. *comb. inval. fide* Touw, 1971.

Hypnodendron vescoanum Besch., Ann. Sci. Nat. Bot. ser. 7, 20: 55. 1895. *fide* Touw, 1971.
Hypnum junghuhnii non C. Muell. Nadeaud, 1873. Enumeration, p. 16. *fide* Bescherelle, 1895a.
Hypnum spininervium non (Hook.) Reich. Sullivant, 1859. *fide* Bescherelle, 1895a.
Hypnum reinwardtii non Schwaegr. Montagne, 1848, p. 107. *fide* Touw, 1971.

Plants arborescent, to 10 cm tall; tertiary branch leaves ovate-lanceolate, 1.7–2.2 × 0.6–0.75 mm; costa percurrent, denticulate on upper and lower surfaces; leaf margins strongly denticulate in the upper lamina, serrulate near the base. Cells of the upper median lamina elongate, 35 × 5–9 μ, not porose or pitted, thick-walled and papillose, the papillae formed over cell walls; cells of the leaf base thick-walled (as thick as 9 μ), orange-brown in alar regions, quadrate to rectangular, 15–35 μ. Secondary stems erect, black, stiff, smooth, the leaves distant, squarrose-spreading. Sporophytes (*Decker 103*) 3–4 cm long; capsules ridged, about 4 × 1.2 mm, cylindrical; peristome teeth 480–540 μ long; exothecial cells thick-walled, 48–72 × 17–24 μ; endostome finely papillose, the segments keeled, with 2–3 ciliate processes between the endostome teeth. Spores 12–17 μ, smooth, greenish-brown. Based on *2910*.

ILLUSTRATIONS. Figure 51A–D.

TAHITI. Without locality: In mountains, 700 m, with *Ptychomnion aciculare*, *Lépine sn* (Montagne, 1848, as *Hypnodendron reinwardtii*); *Vesco sn*; *Wilkes sn* (Sullivant, 1859, as *H. spininervium*); *Vieillard and Pancher sn*. Marau: Mt. Rereaoa, 1100 m, humid ravines, *Nadeaud 91*, 1859 (Nadeaud, 1873, as *H. junghuhnii*; Bescherelle, 1895a). Puaa: 800–1000 m, *Nadeaud 431, 432* (Bescherelle, 1898a). Haapape District: Miaa, 850 m, *Temarii Nadeaud sn*, 1899; Rahi, 800 m, *Temarii Nadeaud sn* (Bescherelle, 1901). Pirae District: Fautaua Valley, 820 m, second falls, on moist rock in bed of stream, *Quayle 212*; Mt. Aorai, 1230 m, shoulder ridge SE of NW ridge, on rocks in bed of ravine, *Quayle 96* (Bartram, 1933a, BISH!); Fare Rau Ape–Mt. Aorai trail, *Decker and Decker 87, 89*; *93*; 1500 m, on soil, *Decker and Decker 93*; fruiting, *Decker and Decker 103*; 1800 m, *Decker and Decker 163*; 1000 m, with *Rhizogonium spiniforme* and *Ptychomnion aciculare*, *2683*; with *Vesicularia inflectens* and *Cyclodictyon blumeanum*, *2693*; on rotting *Cyathea*, *2695*; 1700 m, in ravine N of Chalet Fare Ata, with *Spiridens* on *Cyathea* trunks, *2910*; with *Distichophyllum, Fissidens nadeaudii, Ptychom-*

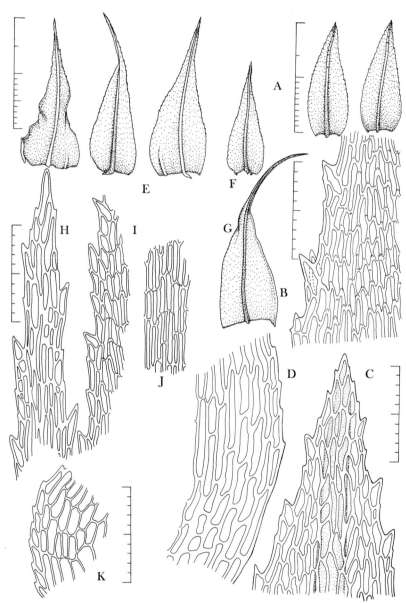

Fig. 51. A–D. *Hypnodendron samoanum.* A. Leaves from erect stem, scale 2 mm. B. Lamina, upper margin and median cells, scale 100 μ. C. Leaf apex, cells. D. Leaf base, margin cells. C, D, scale 100 μ. E–K. *Hypnodendron tahiticum.* (*HOW 2909.*) E. Leaves (3) from erect stem. F. Branch leaf. G. Perichaetial leaf. E–G, scale 2 mm. H. Leaf apex, cells. I. Leaf, upper margin cells. J. Leaf, upper lamina median cells. K. Leaf base, margin cells. H–K, scale 100 μ.

nion, and *Metzgeria, 2938;* 1700 m, same locality, *2943;* a juvenile form, *2963.* Mataiea District: Vaihiria Valley, on tree trunk, *Eriksson 74* (Bartram, 1950b). Papenoo District: Papenoo Valley, 150 m, with *Neckeropsis lepineana, 3007;* 400 m, with *Rhizogonium setosum, 3022;* 840 m, ridge between Papenoo and Vaihiria valleys, with *Rhizogonium, Ptychomnion,* and *Acroporium, 3036.* Taiarapu Peninsula: Taravao, above experiment station, 650 m, in *Miconia* and *Cyathea* forest, *2231;* same locality, with *Rhizogonium, Leucomium aneurodictyon, Isopterygium albescens, Trichosteleum hamatum, Riccardia,* and *Metzgeria, 2316; 2293;* Haavini Valley, 90 m, on rotting log, with *Vesicularia* and *Ectropothecium, Whittier sn.* Hitiaa District: Plateau region, 200 m, on organic debris, *3218; 3244.*

MOOREA. Without locality: *Wilkes sn* (Touw, 1971, BM, US).

RAIATEA. Averaiti Valley: Upper end, 300 m, on *Pandanus, Moore 74* (Bartram, 1931; Touw, 1971, FH!).

Distribution.—Society Islands (Tahiti, Moorea, Raiatea), Samoa (Tutuila), Marquesas Islands (Nuku Hiva).

2. *Hypnodendron tahiticum* (Besch.) Touw
Blumea 19: 332. 1971.

Mniodendron tahiticum Besch., Ann. Sci. Nat. Bot. ser. 7, 20: 55. 1895.
Hypnum comosum non Labill. Nadeaud, 1873. Enumeration, p. 16. *fide* Touw, 1971.
Hypnum divaricatum non Reinwardt & Hornschuch. Sullivant, p. 13, 1859.

Plants dendroid, erect secondary stems (stipes) to 4 cm tall; tertiary branches atop stipes sparingly branched, usually less than 1 cm long; leaves ovate-lanceolate, costate; costa percurrent to short-excurrent, dentate on the back in upper leaf. Stipe leaves 2.7–3.0 × 0.8–1.1 mm, tertiary branch leaves shorter, 1.6–2.2 × 0.60–0.75 mm, perichaetial leaves to 3.8 × 1.1 mm. Margins of stem and branch leaves denticulate, perichaetial leaf margins entire or nearly so. Cells of the upper lamina of stem leaves pitted, elongate-rectangular, 36–48 × 3.5–5 μ, slightly shorter in branch leaves, and papillose in both, the papillae small, conic, located over cell walls. Sporophytes are borne in groups on short branches at the top of the erect stipe, 3–4 cm tall; urn 3–3.5 × 1 mm, cylindrical, ridged; operculum long, conic-rostrate, about 3 mm.

ILLUSTRATIONS. Touw (1971, p. 324, f. 38l–x). Figure 51E–K.

TAHITI. Without locality: *Lépine 3* (Touw, 1971). Arue to Marau: To 1100 m, *Nadeaud 90* (Nadeaud, 1873, as *H. comosum*; Bescherelle, 1895a); *Nadeaud 427–430* (Bescherelle, 1895a). Miaa:

850 m, *Temarii Nadeaud sn*, 1899 (Bescherelle, 1901). Pirae District: Mt. Aorai (?), *Whitney Expedition 703d*, 1922 (Bartram, 1933a); unreported, *Whitney 701b, 706* (BISH); *Quayle 697* (Bartram, 1933a); 1100 m, *2811*; *2825*; with *Dicnemon rugosum*, *2879*; with *Rhizogonium*, *Callicostella*, *Plagiochila*, and *Trachyloma*, *2875*; fruiting, *2882*; with *Spiridens balfourianus*, *2894, 2909*; 1700 m, in ravine N of Chalet Fare Ata, with *Ptychomnion*, *Schistochila*, and *Riccardia*, *2925*. Mt. Orohena: E side of S ridge, 1150 m, wet tree fern forest on mossy tree trunks, *St. John and Fosberg 17056, 17151*. Mataiea District: Along road to Vaihiria, 1000–1500 m (feet?), on ground, *Eriksson 75* (Bartram, 1950b); with *Garovaglia*, *Trichosteleum*, *Exodictyon*, and *Thyridium obtusifolium*, *3090*; *3100*. Papenoo District: Ridge between Papenoo and Vaihiria valleys, 700 m, on N side, on stump and base of adjacent tree trunk, with *Rhizogonium setosum*, *Schistochila*, and *Fissidens*, *3033*; 840 m, at crest of ridge, on branches, fruiting, with *Ptychomnion*, *Microlepidozia*, and *Metzgeria*, *3039*; on *Cyathea* trunks, with *Schistochila*, *Herberta*, *Frullania*, *Acroporium*, and *Trichosteleum*, *3040*; *3052*. Hitiaa District: Elevated plateau region, *3220*; with *Leucobryum tahitense* and *Thyridium constrictum*, *3224*; *3227*; 200–400 m, *3257*. Taiarapu Peninsula: N side, Haavini Valley, 100 m, *2581*.

RAIATEA. Highest mountain: W side, 800 m, on wet branches of trees, *Moore 45*. Temehani Range: S end, 500 m, among other mosses on branches of shrubs, *Moore 46a*. Averaiti Valley: Upper end, 400 m, on wet branches of trees in deep shade, *Moore 57*; 300 m, on dead branch of tree over stream bed, *Moore 77*. Faaroa Bay: N side, 400 m, on wet branches of trees in deep shade, *Moore 61, 62* (Bartram, 1931).

Distribution.—Society Islands (Tahiti, Raiatea), Samoa, Marquesas Islands (Uapou).

Touw (1971) observed an upper limit of 1500 m reported for the specimens he studied, which fits my own records well. The maximum altitude for my collections was 1700 m, in a small valley near Fare Ata on Mt. Aorai. The minimum altitude was 100 m, in the Haavini Valley on the Taiarapu Peninsula.

There is no question that Touw (1971) is correct in relating *H. tahiticum* and *H. dendroides*.

Bartram (1948) wrote: "At first I thought this [Eriksson's no. 75, from Vaihiria] was an undescribed species. The stems only a few centimeters high with small, dense capitate heads less than 1 centimeter in diameter are quite distinctive. Examination of herbarium material showed similar plants mixed with the typical ones. They are apparently antheridial plants with the antheridia occurring on very short, densely crowded branches forming conspicuous capitate clusters."

The dense, reddish tomentum on the erect stems, coupled with the smaller stature, more compact construction, and the more erect leaves of *H. tahiticum* serve to distinguish this species from *H. samoanum* which has sparing tomentum to shiny black erect stems, the leaves of tertiary branches more closely pressed against the branch stems.

XV. BARTRAMIACEAE

Plants erect, varying from less than 1 cm tall (*Philonotis*) to several centimeters in height (*Breutelia*). Leaves are lanceolate, acuminate, the margins denticulate, the costa percurrent or short-excurrent, the cells papillose, alar cells differentiated (*Breutelia*) or undifferentiated (*Philonotis*). The seta is terminal, elongate, the capsule globose, erect to inclined, furrowed, the peristome double, the operculum conic and apiculate.

Key to Genera of the Bartramiaceae

1. Leaves longitudinally furrowed, alar cells differentiated............1. *Breutelia.*
1. Leaves not longitudinally furrowed, alar cells undifferentiated....2. *Philonotis.*

1. *Breutelia* (Bruch, Schimper, & Guembel) Schimper
   Coroll. 85. 1856.
Breutelia eugeniae Aongstrom
   Oefv. K. Svensk. Vet. Ak. Foerh. 30(5): 120. 1873.
> *B. intermedia* Aongstr., Oefv. K. Svensk. Vet. Ak. Foerh. 30(5): 120. 1873.
> *nom. inval. in synon., fide* Aongstr., 1873.

Plants pale green, erect, forming turfs on organic debris and rocks in wet humid places, 4–6 cm tall, irregularly branched, stems clothed in dense reddish tomentum; leaves squarrose, contorted, 2.7–3.0 × 0.75–0.80 mm, lanceolate-acuminate; costa short-excurrent, extending about 0.55–0.70 mm beyond the lamina; margins of the lamina denticulate to the apex. Cells of the lamina elongate-rectangular, 7–12 × 4–5 μ, unipapillose, the papilla apparently formed on the end of the cell nearest the leaf base, on the lower surface of the lamina; cells of the leaf base adjacent to the costa slightly longer, to about 40 μ, smooth or nearly so; alar cells quadrate to rectangular, slightly inflated, to about 40 × 20 μ, extending about 3–5 cells toward the leaf apex along the margins of the lamina. All specimens examined were sterile.

ILLUSTRATIONS. Figure 52A–C.

TAHITI. Without locality: *Andersson sn*, 1852 (Aongstrom, 1873); *Vesco sn*, 1847; on rocks, valleys of the interior, associated with

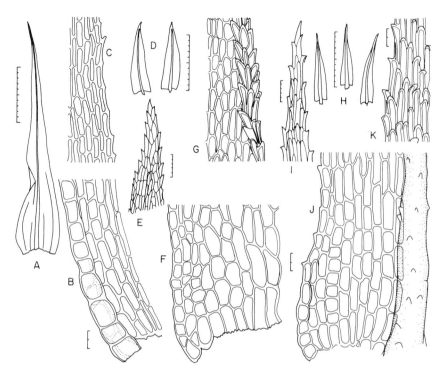

FIG. 52. A–C. *Breutelia eugeniae*. (*Andersson sn.*) A. Leaf, scale 1 mm. B. Leaf base. C. Upper leaf cells and margin. B, C, scale 20 μ. D–G. *Philonotis hastata*. (*Nadeaud 284*, as *Philonotula jardini*.) D. Leaves, scale 1 mm. E. Leaf tip, scale 50 μ. F. Leaf base, scale 20 μ. G. Upper leaf cells and margin (reflexed), scale 20 μ. H–K. *Philonotis runcinata*. (*HOW 3471*.) H. Leaves, scale 1 mm. I. Leaf tip, scale 50 μ. J. Leaf base with costa, scale 20 μ. K. Upper leaf cells and margin, scale 20 μ. (*del.* HAM.)

Holomitrium vaginatum, Nadeaud sn (Bescherelle, 1895a). Pute: Tamarua Valley, on rocks in stream, *Nadeaud 285, 286* (Bescherelle, 1898a). Pirae District: Mt. Aorai trail, *Quayle 697e, 698* (Bartram, 1933a); unreported, *Quayle 697d, h; Quayle 701, 704d* (BISH); 1200 m, with *Philonotis vescoana, Dicranella hochreutineri,* and *Plagiochila, 2736;* 1000 m, in stream bed, in valley N of Chalet Fare Ata, *2914;* 1950 m, on ground, *2754.* Taiarapu Peninsula: N side, Haavini Valley, 255 m, on ground, associated with *Leucophanes, Ectropothecium, Callicostella, Campylopus,* and *Porella, 2589.*

Distribution.—Society Islands (Tahiti), endemic.

Aongstrom (1873) compared *Breutelia eugeniae* with the American and European *B. arcuata* (Sw.) Schimp. (= *B. chrysocoma* [Hedw.] Lindb.) and with *B. gigantea* (Brid.) Bosch & Lac. (= *B. arundinifolia* [Duby] Fleisch.), the latter known from Java, Sumatra, the Celebes, and Hawaii, and markedly larger, the leaves 6–7 mm long, the cells of the lamina 40–60 × 4–5 μ. A collection made at 1950 m on Mt. Aorai (*2754*) has longer than average leaves, typically about 3.5 mm, more prominent papillae, and slightly larger lamina cells, some as long as 25 μ, with the alar cells more highly developed than in specimens from lower elevations. There is no doubt in my mind that Aongstrom was correct in relating his species to *B. gigantea,* but it certainly should be considered distinct. Aongstrom (1873) in his original description indicated the plants are dioicous, 3–12 cm tall, the stems tomentose, the leaves 8 × 0.76 mm, but the length he reported for the leaves must be in error, for isotypes (Uggla and Möller herbaria, NY!) have stem leaves which at their longest are no more than 4.1 mm, and my own collections agree exactly with the isotypes.

No Society Islands species of *Philonotis* approaches *Breutelia eugeniae* in stature, and there are no other species with which it might be confused.

2. *Philonotis* Bridel
Bryol. Univ. 2: 15. 1827.

Plants small, slender, usually less than 3–4 cm tall, with whorls of branches near the tops of the erect, primary stems, growing on wet rocks or soil, forming tufts or limited turfs; leaves rigid, erectspreading to appressed, ovate-lanceolate, acuminate, the margins serrate, the teeth often doubled in the upper lamina; costa ends below the apex or is percurrent. Cells irregularly rectangular, thin-walled, papillose in the upper lamina, the papilla formed by the projecting cell end wall; the costa may be papillose on the lower surface in the upper lamina. Sporophytes terminal; capsule globose, furrowed; operculum conic and apiculate.

The absence of differentiated alar cells and plicate leaves (which characterize *Breutelia*) serves to identify *Philonotis*.

Key to Species of *Philonotis*

1. Leaf margins with teeth single; costa percurrent............2. *P. runcinata*.
1. Leaf margins with teeth doubled; costa ends below apex in most leaves
    2. Leaves to 0.33 mm wide..............................1. *P. hastata*.
    2. Leaves to 0.21 mm wide..............................3. *P. vescoana*.

1. *Philonotis hastata* (Duby) Wijk & Margadant
Taxon 8: 74. 1959.

Hypnum hastatum Duby, in Moritzi, Syst. Verz. Zoll. Pfl. Java. 132. 1846.
Bartramia laxissima C. Muell., Syn. 1: 480. 1849. *nom. illeg. incl. spec. prior* (*Hypnum hastatum* Dub.).
Bartramia wallisi C. Muell., Linnaea 38: 554. 1874. *fide* Bartram, 1939.
Philonotis laxissima (C. Muell.) Mitt., J. Linn. Soc. Bot. Suppl. 1: 61. 1859.
Philonotis laxissima (C. Muell.) Bosch & Lac., Bryol. Jav. 1: 154. t. 124. 1861.
Philonotis curvifolia Besch., Ann. Sci. Nat. Bot. ser. 6, 10: 245. 1880. *fide* Dixon, Trans. R. Soc. S. Afr, 8: 205. 1920.
Philonotis imbricatula Mitt., J. Linn. Soc. Bot. Suppl. 1: 61. 1859. *fide* Index Muscorum 4: 38. 1967.
Philonotis tenuicaulis Jaeg., Ber. S. Gall. Naturw. Ges. 1874–1875: 79. 1875. *nom. illeg. incl. spec. prior* (*Bartramia tenuicula* Hamp., 1874), *fide* Index Muscorum 4: 48. 1967.
Philonotis tenuicula (Hamp.) Besch., Ann. Sci. Nat. Bot. ser. 6, 10: 245. 1880.
Philonotis jardini (Besch.) Paris, Ind. Bryol. 923. 1897.
Philonotula jardini Besch., Ann. Sci. Nat. Bot. ser. 7, 20: 29. 1895.

Plants pale green, to about 3 cm tall, 2–3 mm wide with leaves, with subterminal whorls of 5–7 branches, each about 1 cm long; leaves erect-spreading to appressed, ovate, lanceolate-acuminate, 1.2–1.3 × 0.33 mm, the margins doubly serrate above, variably serrate to serrulate or entire toward the leaf base, costate; costa vanishing in the leaf apex or a few cells below the apex. Cells of the lamina variable in size and papillosity, 19–50 × 4–10 μ; cells near the leaf base larger, more regularly quadrate in the alar regions, to rectangular adjacent to the costa; upper cells markedly unipapillose by the projection of cell end walls, lower cells slightly papillose to smooth. All specimens examined were sterile.

ILLUSTRATIONS. Dozy and Molkenboer (1861, t. 124), Bartram (1933b, p. 138, f. 101; 1939, pl. 12, f. 199). Figure 52D–G.

TAHITI. Without locality: *Jardin sn* (Bescherelle, 1895a, as *Philonotula jardini*). Floor of the Tipaearui and Tamarua valleys: *Nadeaud 282* (NY); *Nadeaud 283*; *Nadeaud 284* (NY). Pirae District: Fautaua Valley, *Setchell and Parks sn* (Brotherus, 1924a, as *Philonotis jardini*).

RAIATEA. Averaiti Valley: Upper end, 300 m, on rock of small waterfall, *Moore 75* (Bartram, 1931, as *P. laxissima*, BISH).

Distribution.—Society Islands (Tahiti, Raiatea), Marquesas Islands (Nuku Hiva), Hawaii (Oahu, Maui, Hawaii), New Guinea, Java, Philippine Islands, Malagasy Republic (Madagascar), Assam, Banka, Borneo, Celebes, Amboina, Japan.

Bartram (1931) found little in the description of *Philonotula jardini* to distinguish it from *P. laxissima*, and although authentic material of *P. jardini* from Nadeaud's collections (NY) does not exhibit the obtuse leaves described by Bescherelle (1895a) and figured by Bartram (1933b) for *P. laxissima*, it does provide characters which fit within the ranges of leaf size and shape recorded over the entire range of *Philonotis hastata*. As Mueller's *Philonotis laxissima* was originally based on *P. hastata*, an older name, it must be placed in synonymy. *Bartramia (Philonotis) tahitensis* C. Muell. (Bot. Zeit. 17: 220. 1859) probably belongs here.

2. *Philonotis runcinata* C. Mueller *ex* Aongstrom

Oefv. K. Svensk. Vet. Ak. Foerh. 33(4): 52. 1876.

?*Philonotis tahitensis* (C. Muell.) *sensu* Aongstr., p. 120, 1873, *non* C. Mueller, 1859.

Bartramia runcinatula C. Muell., Gen. Musc. Fr. 339. 1901. *nom. nud. fide* Index Muscorum 1: 179. 1959.

Philonotula runcinata (C. Muell.) Besch., Ann. Sci. Nat. Bot. ser. 7, 20: 28. 1895.

Plants erect, yellow-green, 1–3 cm tall; leaves erect to erect-spreading, 1.1–1.3 × 0.22 mm, lanceolate; costa 40–70 μ wide at the base, percurrent; leaf margins entire to serrulate in the leaf base, singly serrate to the apex. Lamina basal cells quadrate to irregularly rectangular, 12–30 × 12–15 μ, some papillose with a single papilla at the upper end of the cell; median cells also unipapillose, elongate-rectangular, 35–40 × 4–6 μ. No sporophytes examined. (Description based upon *3471* from Moorea.)

ILLUSTRATIONS. Figure 52H–K.

TAHITI. Without locality: *Andersson sn* (Aongstrom, 1873, as *P. tahitensis*, 1876; Bescherelle, 1895a, as *Philonotula*).
MOOREA. Paopao Bay: Haring Plantation, 5 m, on soil, *3471*.
Distribution.—Society Islands (Tahiti, Moorea), endemic.

Bescherelle (1895a) examined the collection made by Andersson, but provided no additional information and simply reproduced Aongstrom's description without change.

3. *Philonotis vescoana* (Bescherelle) Paris
Ind. Bryol. 931. 1897.
Philonotula vescoana Besch., Ann. Sci. Nat. Bot. ser. 7, 20: 29. 1895a.

Plants pale to yellow-green, to 4 cm tall and 2 mm wide; leaves erect-spreading, ovate-lanceolate, 1.1–1.2 × 0.21 mm; margins doubly denticulate in the upper lamina, entire or nearly so in the leaf base; cells unipapillose, the papilla formed by the projecting upper cell end on the lower surface in the upper leaf, percurrent or ending just below the leaf apex. Cells of the lamina firm, smooth-walled, 30–60 × 7–10 μ.
ILLUSTRATIONS. Figure 53.
TAHITI. Without locality: *Vesco sn* (Bescherelle, 1895a, as *Philonotula*). Papara District: Pute, Temarua Valley floor, *Nadeaud 280, 281*, 1896 (Bescherelle, 1898a, as *Philonotula*, NY).
Distribution.—Society Islands (Tahiti), Austral Islands (Rapa, Raivavae), Samoa (Upolu).

Bescherelle (1895a) described the plants as dioicous, as are the other Society Islands taxa of *Philonotis*. Small plants, either males or juveniles, were examined, the largest leaves 0.4 mm long, the stems only one-sixth as wide as in the larger plants. Sporophytes were described by Bescherelle from Nadeaud's collections, the seta 25–35 mm long, the capsule inclined to horizontal, large, globose, the mouth small, the endostome teeth yellowish, and he compared this species with *Philonotis asperifolia* Mitt., from Samoa, which has smaller, more triangulate leaves 0.7–0.9 × 0.26–0.30 mm, the cells (where the leaf is 250 μ wide), 19–40 × 7–9 μ (NY).

Dubious species

I am not satisfied with the disposition of species of *Philonotis* recorded from the Society Islands. Monographic revision of the genus, with a re-evaluation and redefinition of specific characters, is sorely

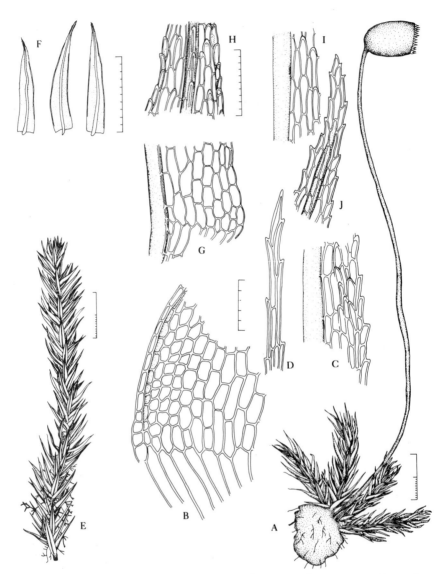

Fig. 53. *Philonotis vescoana*. A, E. Habit sketches, scale 2 mm. B. Alar and basal cells. C. Upper leaf, margin and median cells. D. Leaf apex. B–D, scale 50 μ. F. Leaves, scale 1 mm. G. Leaf base, cells. H. Upper leaf, margin and median cells. I. Upper leaf, cells adjacent costa. J. Leaf apex, cells. G–J, scale 50 μ.

needed. The following species, *P. tahitensis,* has not been studied and cannot now be excluded from the Society Islands flora. Apparently no one but Mueller and Aongstrom has ever seen the original collection from the van den Bosch Herbarium. To be consistent, I have included Mueller's original description, which follows.

Philonotis tahitensis (C. Mueller) Aongstrom
  Oefv. K. Svensk. Vet. Ak. Foerh. 30(5): 120. 1873.
  Bartramia tahitensis C. Muell., Bot. Zeit. 17: 220. 1859.

"Dioica, late et laxe caespitosa, laxe cohaerens radiculosa viridissima; caulis humilis gracillimus plumulose foliosus pallescens (haud rufus), apice minus uncinatus; folia caulina laxe disposita plumoso-erecta, haud subsecunda, brevia, lato-lanceolata, stricta vel parum curvata flaccidiora, e cellulis laxioribus amplioribus pellucidis hexagonis utriculo primordiali tenerrimo viridissimo instructis reticulata, papillis as parietes cellularum obscuris praedita, margine e basi fere usque ad apicem duplicato-serrulata, nervo crasso carinato viridissimo ante apicem dissoluto."

ILLUSTRATIONS. None.

TAHITI. Without details, hb. van den Bosch, C. Mueller (1859).

Distribution.—Society Islands (Tahiti), endemic.

Mueller (1859) compared this species with *Bartramia* (*Philonotis*) *laxissima.* Bescherelle (1895a) simply reproduced Mueller's original description but introduced (intentionally?) an error in the quotation, by comparing *B. tahitensis* with '*B. javanicus*' instead of with *B. laxissima.* With the recognition of the broad distribution of *Philonotis hastata,* now including a number of synonyms, has come the acceptance of a wider range of variability for the species, and eventually it may be shown that Mueller's *Bartramia tahitensis* is conspecific with *Philonotis hastata.*

XVI. SPIRIDENTACEAE

Spiridens Nees
    Nova Acta Ac. Leop.-Carol. 11(1): 143. 1823.

Large, usually golden-brown or golden-green plants, forming horizontal or slightly pendulous tufts, with irregular branching from a major stem, the branches usually shorter than the prominent main axis, the plants dioicous, male plants short, 6–10 cm long, archegoniate plants to 20–30 cm long. Leaves are erect-spreading from a sheathing base, lanceolate, acuminate, costate, the costa vanishes near the leaf insertion onto the stem and at the apex of the leaf is percurrent or short-excurrent, the broad, thickened leaf borders confluent with the costa in the leaf apex. Leaf margins are variably denticulate, even on different leaves of the same plant. Cells of the upper lamina are irregularly rounded-quadrate to elongate; lower lamina cells are thin-walled, pitted, and rectangular. Sporophytes are lateral, the seta shorter than the capsule, the capsule ovate-cylindric, the operculum conic-rostrate, the beak curved to one side; the peristome double, the exostome teeth inrolled, the endostome teeth erect, without cilia.

Spiridens balfourianus Greville
    Ann. Mag. Nat. Hist. ser. 2, 1: 326. f. 18. 1848.
    Neckera balfouriana C. Muell., Syn. 2: 121. 1851.

Greville described this species: "Foliis anguste marginatis, remote dentatis; capsulis ovato-cylindraceis." He compared the new species with *S. reinwardtii*, and wrote: "The new species is a smaller and more slender plant, six to nine inches long or more, the leaves scarcely half the size, the capsules more cylindrical and the subulate termination of the operculum considerably longer and finer. It is under the microscope, however, that the most characteristic features are perceived to exist in the leaves; the margin of which in *S. reinwardtii* is distinguished by a broad, flat border closely and sharply toothed: in the new species by a very narrow, thickened border remotely toothed." Leaves from the type (*Sibbald*, Tahiti, isotype fragments, NY) are about 10 × 1.6 mm, costate; costa vanishes in the leaf base above the insertion of the leaf onto the stem, and in the leaf apex the costa is slightly excurrent, the thickened leaf borders confluent with the costa below the leaf apex. In the upper leaf (measured where the blade is about 250 μ wide) the border is about 50 μ wide and several cell layers thick; the costa also is about 50 μ wide at this point, and the leaves have a tricostate appearance. Cells of the upper lamina 7–19 $\times$ 5–8 μ, irregularly quadrate to rectangular, rounded, irregularly thick-walled, smooth-walled, or pitted, and occasionally to frequently in 2 layers (especially in archegoniate plants); cells of the sheathing basal portion much more elongate, irregularly rectangular, 35–85 $\times$ 5–8 μ, the walls thinner and pitted, but in the extreme base, the cells shorter, 12–35 μ long, and pitted. Border cells (measured where the leaf is about 250 μ wide) elongate, 19–25 $\times$ 2–4 μ, and 2–3 times longer than the shortest lamina cells. Leaf margins denticulate, the teeth variable in size and orientation, and formed by a single cell or by a group of cells, several cell layers thick at the base of the tooth. Toward the leaf base the teeth may appear close together, 100–150 μ apart, but in the middle third of the lamina they become more widely spaced, 300–350 μ apart, and in the upper third, somewhat closer again, about 250 μ apart, in branch leaves; in stem leaves the spacing is slightly closer, about 200 μ. The teeth stand nearly erect, forming a 45° angle to the margin, but the majority form a more acute angle with the margin. The largest teeth are about 40 μ long, but most are less than 25 μ, and consist of only 3–4 cells. The terminal cell is 20–35 μ long and about 12 μ wide (outside measurement). Schimper's (1865, t. 3) illustration of leaf margins suggests an extreme development, apparently supported by one of my Tahitian collections (2925), in young leaves, but only barely represented in the largest teeth in Greville's type. Mitten (1871) noted, "Schimper . . . figures the leaf of S. *Balfourianus* with large and leafy teeth, a character in opposition to that given by Greville, who figures it narrower than in S. *Reinwardtii*." I suspect that Greville selected his illustration to provide as much contrast to S. *reinwardtii* as possible, but the fact that the teeth of S. *balfourianus* may appear as close together as those of S. *reinwardtii* does not make it a less valid species. The teeth of S. *reinwardtii* tend to be larger and more divergent, and the areolation of the upper lamina is much more regularly developed, the cells rounded-quadrate or rectangular, the walls more evenly thickened, the cells usually in only 1 layer except at the costa and the borders; cells of the borders are similar to those of the lamina and only slightly elongate in *S. reinwardtii.* Capsules of *S. balfourianus* are 5 × 1.6 mm, cylindrical; operculum conic-rostrate; beak curved to one side, about 3 mm long. Spores may possibly be dimorphic, 12–19 μ, brownish, finely papillose.

ILLUSTRATIONS. Greville (1848, pl. 18; 1850, pl. 3), Schimper (1865, t. 3). Figure 54.

TAHITI. Without locality: *Sibbald sn,* 1847 (Greville, 1848; isotype, NY; Mueller, 1851, as *Neckera;* Mitten, 1871); *Vesco sn; Vieillard sn* (Bescherelle, 1895a). Mamano and Touhi: Very frequent on trunks of tree ferns, about 800 m, *Nadeaud 76* (Nadeaud, 1873, as *Neckera;* Bescherelle, 1895a); *Bidwill sn* (Mitten, 1871, NY); *Mosely sn, Challenger* Expedition (in hb. Mitten, NY, as *S. reinwardtii*). Puaa Valley: 1000–1100 m, and interior of the island, above 800 m, on trunks of *Cyathea* and arborescent ferns, *Nadeaud 293–295,* 1896. Ternatii: *Temarii Nadeaud sn* (Bescherelle, 1901). Pirae District: Mt. Aorai (?), *Quayle 62, 197, 201* (Bartram, 1933a, BISH); Fare Rau Ape–Mt. Aorai trail, 900 m, with rock and organic debris on ground, *2682;* 1000 m, on *Cyathea, 2688;* with *Ptychomnion, 2696;* 1060 m, E side of ridge to Mt. Aorai, on *Cyathea, 2712;* 1065 m, *2713;* 1700 m, in valley below Chalet Fare Ata, on *Cyathea,* individual plants to 25–30 cm tall, *2751;* 1960 m, *2780; 2899; 2900;* with *Mniodendron, 2909;* with *Hypnodendron, 2910;* male plants, *2925;* 1865 m, on branches, *Decker and Decker 24, 29; 101, 105;* 900 m, *109; 110, 112;* 1500 m, *158;* without elevation, *289, 309* (1960); Fautaua Valley, 600 m, male plants, on *Cyathea* with *Leucophanes* and *Asplenium, 3165.* Mt. Orohena: S side, 1300 m, *MacDaniels 1547, 1549;* S side of ridge, 1500 m, *St. John and Fosberg 17128,* unreported (BISH). Papenoo District: Upper river valley, 800 m, on tree trunk with ferns, *MacDaniels 1540;* Papenoo River Valley, 300 m, first observation, *3029.* Mataiea District: Vaihiria Valley, 400 m, *3043.* Taiarapu Peninsula: Taravao, above experiment station, on *Cyathea* trunk, *2149;* 615 m, the lowest elevation recorded for this locality, with *Hymenophyllum, Bazzania,* and *Plagiochila, 2242;* 640 m, on NW-facing slope above experiment station, *2254;* 640 m, with *Peperomia* and *Plagiochila* on tree bark in *Miconia* and *Inocarpus* forest, *2273; Hürlimann T 1195, T 1200* (Hürlimann, 1963, det. Bartram as *S. aristifolius,* FH).

MOOREA. Mountain: 400 m, *Lépine sn* (Montagne, 1845, as *S. reinwardtii;* Bescherelle, 1895a; Sherrin, 1938).

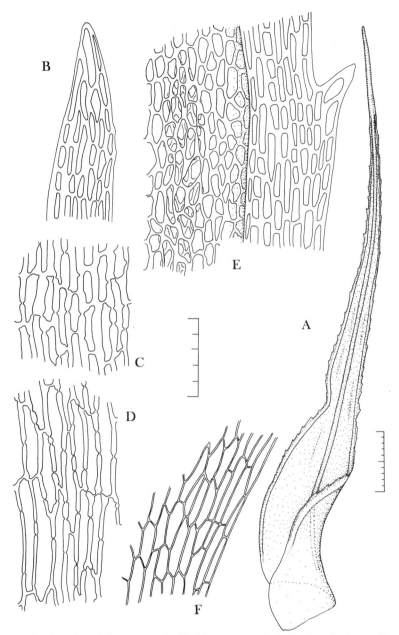

FIG. 54. *Spiridens balfourianus.* (*Sibbald sn,* isotype.) A. Leaf, scale 1 mm. B.
Leaf apex. C. Lamina cells, about midleaf. D. Lamina cells, top of basal
sheathing portion. E. Lamina cells, upper half of leaf (note region of lamina
which is two cells thick and the irregular areolation) and border. F. Lamina,
basal angle cells (from hyaline sheathing portion). B–F, scale 50 μ.

RAIATEA. Mt. Temehani: 250 m, on wet branches of *Pandanus, Moore 18* (Bartram, 1931, BISH, FH).

Distribution.—Society Islands (Tahiti, Moorea, Raiatea), endemic.

Sullivant's (1859) report of *S. reinwardtii* in collections from the United States Exploring Expedition may be based on specimens from Samoa, rather than from the Society Islands, if the vague data on herbarium labels (NY) are correct. Montagne's (1845) report, based on a collection by Lépine, seems to be the result of a superficial examination. *Spiridens balfourianus* seems best distinguished from *S. reinwardtii* by the irregular areolation of upper lamina cells and their frequent appearance in two layers, as well as by the more elongate border cells; *S. reinwardtii* characteristically has larger, more spreading teeth along the leaf margins.

XVII. ORTHOTRICHACEAE

This family is represented by *Macromitrium* and *Zygodon*, which both form turfs or cushions on trees and occasionally on rocks or humus. Erect secondary stems characteristically arise from creeping, rhizomatous primary stems, the leaves oblong-lanceolate, crowded, crisped, often incurved when dry, erect-spreading when moist. Cells of the lamina are rounded-quadrate, papillose in the upper portion of the leaf, elongate and smooth near the leaf base. Leaf margins of *Macromitrium* species and *Zygodon intermedius* are entire or only slightly crenulate in the upper part; those of *Zygodon reinwardtii* are characteristically and distinctively serrate near the leaf apex. The calyptra of *Zygodon* species is cucullate whereas the calyptra of *Macromitrium* is campanulate; in *Zygodon* the calyptra is smooth, whereas in *Macromitrium* the calyptra may be smooth or hairy. The peristome of *Zygodon reinwardtii* is single, of 16 paired teeth forming 8 pairs; *M. intermedius* has an inner peristome of 8 rudimentary hyaline processes, the exostome rudimentary in 8 pairs, but both may be absent. The peristome of *Macromitrium* may be single, double, or absent. Spores of both genera are papillose, but those of *Zygodon* are less than 25 μ in diameter, those of *Macromitrium* usually larger in those species from which they have been measured.

KEY TO GENERA OF THE ORTHOTRICHACEAE

1. Calyptra cucullate, smooth; spores less than 25 μ_____1. *Zygodon*.
1. Calyptra campanulate, smooth to hairy; spores usually more than 25 μ_____
_____2. *Macromitrium*.

1. *Zygodon* Hooker & Taylor
Musc. Brit. 70. 1818.

Key to Species of *Zygodon*

1. Leaf margins serrulate near apex_____1. *Z. reinwardtii.*
1. Leaf margins entire or only slightly irregular_____2. *Z. intermedius.*

1. *Zygodon reinwardtii* (Hornschuch) A. Braun
Bry. Eur. 4: 9. 1838.

201

Syrrhopodon reinwardtii Hornsch., Nova Acta Ac. Leop.-Carol. 14(2): 700. f. 39. 1829. Schwaegrichen, Spec. Musc. Suppl. 4. t. 312. 1842.

Plants to 2 cm tall, erect, reddish-tomentose; leaves to 1.5 mm, yellow-green on the upper stem, brown below, lingulate-lanceolate; costa percurrent or ending just below the leaf apex. Upper leaf margins irregularly serrate, the leaves carinate. Cells rounded-quadrate, 8–10 μ, papillose, in the upper lamina, toward the leaf base more elongate and smooth. Seta to 1 cm tall; capsule erect to inclined, pyriform, 8-striate; peristome single, of 16 teeth, rudimentary, pale. Spores 20–25 μ, papillose.

ILLUSTRATIONS. Reinwardt and Hornschuch (1829, f. 39), Schwaegrichen (1842, t. 312), Bartram (1933b, p. 145, f. 106).

TAHITI. Pirae District: Pirae–Mt. Aorai trail, *Quayle 697, 699* (Bartram, 1933a, det. confirmed by Malta as var. *subintegrifolius* Malta).

Distribution.—Society Islands (Tahiti), Hawaii (Maui: Haleakala, on tree trunks, 8,000 ft), Java, East Africa, India, Alaska, Mexico, South America.

2. *Zygodon intermedius* Bruch, Schimper & Guembel

Bry. Eur. 3: 41. 1838 (fasc. 4 Mon. 9).

Plants erect, in compact tufts on humus, 1–2 cm tall, frequently and irregularly branched, yellow-green; leaves 1.5–2.0 × 0.3–0.4 mm, ovate-acuminate, the apices incurved, the margins inrolled when dry, when moist, recurved to squarrose; apices abruptly acuminate, leaf bases long-decurrent onto the stem; costa ends 4–6 cells below the cuspidate apex. Leaf margins entire, less commonly subentire or slightly irregular. Cells of the lamina pluripapillose, the papillae obscuring the lumina and walls, the walls thick, 1–3 μ, the lumina 5–8 μ in the upper blade, irregularly rounded-quadrate; lower lamina cells yellowish, thick-walled, quadrate to rectangular. Seta smooth, yellow-brown, 1.3–2.0 cm long; capsule cylindric, 2.0 × 0.55 mm, with longitudinal grooves; exothecial cells thick-walled, 25–50 × 12–25 μ, the walls 2–4 μ. Spores brown, finely papillose, 20–23 μ.

ILLUSTRATIONS. Sainsbury (1955, p. 203, pl. 33). Figure 57O–R.

TAHITI. Mt. Aorai trail: Common on tree branches, 1950 m, *2771.*

Distribution.—Society Islands (Tahiti, a new record), Africa (monsoon regions), South America, Juan Fernández Island, Australia, Tasmania, New Zealand.

The features of the recent collection are those of *Zygodon intermedius*, characterized by the entire leaf margins, the costa ending several cells below the leaf apex; in *Z. reinwardtii* the upper leaf margins are denticulate and the costa is percurrent.

2. *Macromitrium* Bridel
Mant. Musc. 132. 1819.

Key to Species of *Macromitrium*

1. Lamina cells strongly conic-papillose on both surfaces; seta papillose, less than 3 mm long_____1. *M. ruginosum.*
1. Upper lamina cells not strongly conic-papillose; seta smooth, longer than 3 mm
   2. Leaves with portions of upper lamina variably 1–3 cells thick in section _____2. *M. bescherellei.*
   2. Leaves with upper lamina uniformly 1 cell layer thick
      3. Basal cells strongly pitted, crescent-shaped; conic papillae centered over cell lumina; leaves 3–4 mm long_____3. *M. menziesii.*
      3. Basal cells smooth or only faintly pitted, straight to only slightly S-shaped or C-shaped; leaves less than 2.5 mm long
         4. Basal cell area long-rectangular, to one-half length of leaf; basal cells straight, rectangular
            5. Leaves to 1.4 × 0.35 mm; seta to 9 mm, lamina basal cells hyaline, not colored_____4. *M. savatieri.*
            5. Leaves 1.5–2.0 × 0.55 mm; lamina basal cells brownish; seta 10–20 mm long_____5. *M. reinwardtii.*
         4. Basal cell region short, one-quarter to one-third length of leaf; basal cells short-quadrate to rectangular, S- or C-shaped
            5. Basal cells hyaline, short-rectangular to quadrate_____6. *M. paridis.*
            5. Basal cells orange at insertion, S- or C-shaped
               6. Leaves to 1.8 × 0.5 mm; costa percurrent to 100 μ excurrent; seta 5–7 mm, urn to 1.8 mm_____7. *M. eurymitrium.*
               6. Leaves to 2.0–2.3 × 0.4–0.5 mm; costa percurrent to short-excurrent; seta 3–5 mm, urn to 1.3 mm_____8. *M. incurvifolium.*

1. *Macromitrium ruginosum* Bescherelle
Bull. Soc. Bot. France 45: 63. 1898a.

Erect stems frequently branched, 1–2 cm tall, golden brown; leaves contorted and incurved when dry, erect-spreading when moist, ovate-lanceolate, 1.0–1.2 × 0.27 mm; costa percurrent or excurrent in a very short point, by a single cell. Cells of the lamina rounded-quadrate, strongly conic-papillose on exposed surfaces, 4.5–7 μ in the upper blade, rectangular, 20–25 × 3–5 μ, and smooth near the insertion of the leaf onto the stem. Margins of the upper lamina crenulate. Seta reddish, papillose, short, 1.5–2.5 mm; capsule short-ovoid or globose, about 1.3 × 0.7 mm, the outer wall cells thin-walled, rectangular or irregularly hexagonal, averaging 35 × 15 μ. Peristome not found. Operculum conic-rostrate; calyptra pilose, the hairs denticulate, cellular, arising near the base of the calyptra as in *M. piliferum*. Spores not found. Stomata numerous at the base of the capsule.

ILLUSTRATIONS. Figure 55.

TAHITI. Puaa Valley: *Nadeaud 254* (Bescherelle, 1898a, isotype, NY!). Pirae District: Pirae–Mt. Aorai trail, above 1386 m, to summit Mt. Aorai, *Quayle 148d* (Bartram, 1933a, BISH!, FH!). Taiarapu Peninsula: Taravao, at experiment station, 500 m, on *Freycinetia* stem, *Hürlimann T 1194* (Hürlimann, 1963, FH!).

Distribution.—Society Islands (Tahiti), endemic.

This species is allied to *Macromitrium intricatum* C. Muell., from Hawaii (Maui, Oahu), but differs in the smaller size of its sporophyte, the rough seta, and the nearly globose capsule. Both have a similar branching habit, a very rudimentary peristome, similar leaves and areolation, and a pilose calyptra.

2. *Macromitrium bescherellei* Whittier *nom. nov.*
Dasymitrium nadeaudii Besch., Bull. Soc. Bot. France 45: 65. 1898a.
Macromitrium tahitense Broth., E. & P. Nat. Pfl. 1(3): 486. 1905. *hom. illeg. non* Nadeaud, 1873.

Plants yellow-green, with prostrate primary stems, secondary stems erect, 5–10 mm tall; leaves 1.2–1.4 × 0.25–0.30 mm, spirally incurved about the stem when dry; margins incurled to reflexed, keeled, entire to crenulate, lingulate, broadly rounded at the apex; costa terminating in an abrupt mucro or an apiculus. Cells of the upper one-half to one-third of the lamina irregularly in 1, 2, occasionally 3, layers, the dorsal and ventral cells free, isolated or in irregular patches, rounded, pluripapillose; cell walls 1–2 μ thick; lumina 4–7 μ, often slightly larger than the pluripapillose median cells. Lamina cells of midleaf in 1 layer, irregularly rounded-quadrate to hexagonal, smooth to rounded-papillose, approximately the same size as upper lamina cells, appearing at the margins of the upper lamina as well. Lamina cells of the base quadrate to short-rectangular; lumina 8–12 × 2–3 μ, straight to curved; walls 2–3 μ thick, with single, large papillae 3–5 μ high over the walls or lumina on both surfaces. Cells of the lower and middle lamina appear in distinct seriate rows. Sporophytes 6–8 mm tall; seta smooth, twisted,

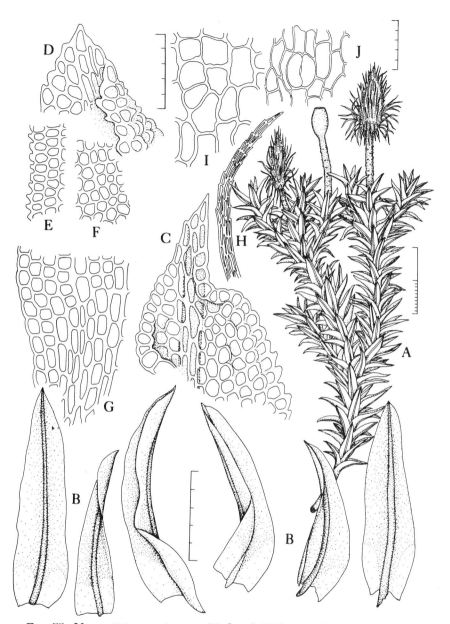

Fig. 55. *Macromitrium ruginosum.* (*Nadeaud 254.*) A. Habit, fruiting, erect secondary stems, scale 2 mm. Note scabrous seta and pilose calyptra; peristome is rudimentary or gymnostomous. B. Leaves, scale 0.5 mm. C. Leaf apex, cells. D. Leaf apex, cells. E. Upper lamina, margin cells. F. Upper lamina, median cells. G. Lamina, basal cells. C–G, scale 50 μ. H. Calyptra scale. I, J. Exothecial cells, capsule jacket. H–J, scale 50 μ. (I. Upper capsule, J. Lower capsule, region of apophysis.)

4–5 mm long; capsule 2.5 mm long; urn 1.6–1.8 × 0.5–0.6 mm, cylindric, constricted at the mouth; operculum conic-rostrate; beak erect, 0.9 mm long. Peristome fragmentary, of 16 teeth, brown, finely papillose, transversely striolate, to about 150 μ long. Exothecial cells irregularly quadrate to rectangular, 20–30 × 5–8 (20) μ, the walls 2–3 μ thick. Calyptra (1, immature, examined) cucullate, sparingly pilose. Stomata present on the capsule apophysis. Spores brown, finely papillose, apparently dimorphic, the smaller around 20 μ, the larger 30 μ or more in diameter.

ILLUSTRATIONS. Figure 56.

TAHITI. Without locality: On dry ridges on branches, 800–900 m, *Nadeaud sn*, 1896 (Bescherelle, 1898a, as *Dasymitrium nadeaudii*).

Distribution.—Society Islands (Tahiti), endemic.

Although Bescherelle described *Dasymitrium nadeaudii* as a new species, Brotherus (1905) later recognized it as belonging to the genus *Macromitrium*. As the specific epithet *M. nadeaudii* had already been used by Bescherelle, Brotherus provided the new name *M. tahitensis,* unaware that Nadeaud (1873) had already used it (=*M. incurvifolium*). I therefore propose the new name *Macromitrium bescherellei* for this unique and distinctive species, to honor the distinguished French bryologist who contributed so much to our present knowledge of the Polynesian moss flora.

Bescherelle (1898a) recognized this species as distinctive, but did not note its most unique feature, that of the irregularly 2–3-cell-layered organization of the upper lamina. As noted in the description, the dorsal and ventral cells appear isolated or in irregular patches, and are free from each other. These cells are easily dislodged and might function as unicellular propagules. Both gametophyte and sporophyte are typical of the genus *Macromitrium*. *Macromitrium bescherellei* should be compared with *M. anomodictyon* Card. from Tananarive (Cardot, 1916, p. 4), which has secondary stems of approximately the same size, but which possesses considerably larger leaves (2.25–2.75 × 0.5–0.6 mm). The seta is erect, 5–6 mm long, the capsule 1.5 × 0.6–0.7 mm. The biological and geographical affinities are interesting and suggest the appropriateness of further study.

3. *Macromitrium menziesii* C. Mueller
    Bot. Zeit. 20: 361. 1862.

Plants yellow-green, primary stems prostrate on bark of branches,

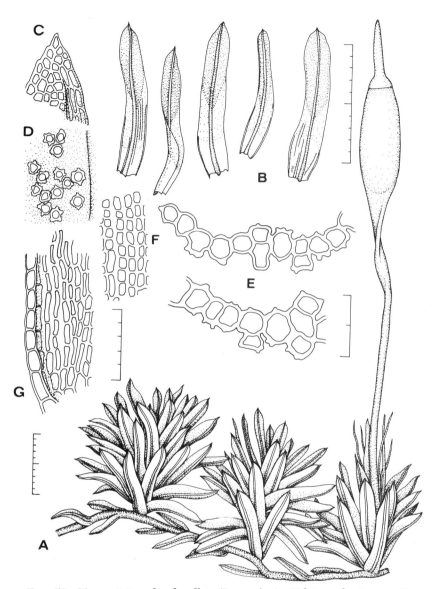

FIG. 56. *Macromitrium bescherellei.* (Isotype.) A. Habit, scale 1 mm. B.
Leaves, scale 1 mm. C. Leaf apex, side view. D. Leaf surface, showing isolated
projecting cells. E. Lamina, cross section, scale 20 μ. F. Lamina, median cells
in transition region about midleaf. G. Lamina, basal cells. C, D, F, G, scale
50 μ.

secondary stems 1–2 cm tall, irregularly branched, the branches to about 5 mm long; leaves keeled, not distinctly spirally arranged on stems, variably incurved and twisted when dry, the margins in-rolled, 3–4 × 0.6–0.9 mm; when moist, erect-spreading to recurved, the upper leaf margins erect, plane to reflexed, the lamina often with longitudinal folds; costa smooth, ending beneath the apex or forming an apiculus or a short mucro. Leaf margins crenulate-papillose above, distantly serrulate in the leaf base. Cells of the upper lamina conic-papillose on both surfaces, rounded-quadrate to hexagonal; walls 1.5–2.5 μ thick; lumina 5–10 μ. Cells of the lower middle lamina less strongly papillose, rectangular, 10–18 × 5–8 μ, pitted; those of the lower one-quarter to one-third of the lamina thick-walled; walls 3–5 μ, strongly pitted, 30–50 × 5–10 μ, strongly conic-papillose; papillae centered over the lumina, erect to forward pointing, to 5 μ tall. Sporophytes about 5 mm tall; seta smooth, 2.7 mm; urn 1.7 mm. No peristome. No operculum or calyptra examined. Spores 20–38 μ, in two size ranges.

ILLUSTRATIONS. Figure 57A–E.

TAHITI. Without locality: "Ex insula Otaheiti, ubi Menzies legit, specimina manca Swartziana in Hb. Mohrii sub nom 'Orthotr. crispi? ex Otaheiti: *Menzies* in Hb. Swartziano' inveni" (C. Mueller, 1862). Mt. Aorai: 1030 m, on tree branches, with *Leucobryum tahitense* and *Mastigophora, 2702*; 1940 m, on branches, with *Ectropothecium* and *Papillaria, 2769*.

Distribution.—Society Islands (Tahiti), endemic.

This species was described by C. Mueller on the basis of a single collection by Menzies, cited in Mohr's herbarium as *Orthotrichum crispum*, but placed in the genus *Macromitrium* section *Orthophyllaria* by Mueller. Although I have not yet examined authentic material, the recent collections cited above compare so well with the original description that there is no doubt about their identification as *Macromitrium menziesii*. The strongly pitted, conic-papillose basal cells are distinctive features of this species.

4. *Macromitrium savatieri* Bescherelle
  Ann. Sci. Nat. Bot. ser. 7, 20: 25. 1895.

Plants with primary stem prostrate on branches, the secondary stems erect, 5–10 mm tall; leaves longitudinally folded, keeled, incurved, and contorted, margins recurved, 1.2–1.4 × 0.30–0.35 mm, ovate-lanceolate; costa smooth, ending 2–6 cells below the acute

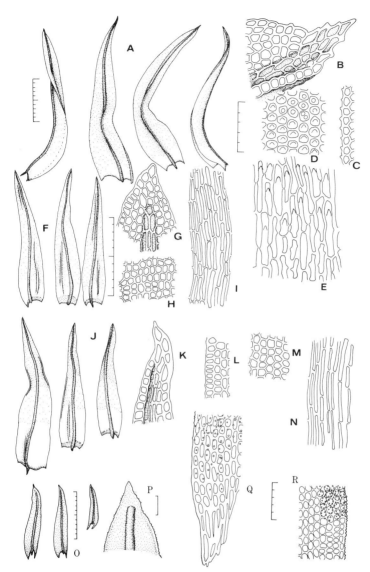

Fig. 57. A–E. *Macromitrium menziesii.* (*HOW 2702.*) A. Leaves, scale 1 mm.
B. Leaf apex. C. Upper lamina, margin. D. Median cells. E. Basal cells. B–E,
scale 50 μ. F–I. *Macromitrium savatieri.* (*HOW 2742.*) F. Leaves, scale 1 mm.
G. Leaf apex. H. Median cells. I. Basal cells. G–I, scale 50 μ. J–N. *Macromitrium reinwardtii.* J. Leaves, scale 1 mm. K. Leaf apex. L. Upper lamina,
margin. M. Median cells. N. Basal cells. K–N, scale 50 μ. O–R. *Zygodon
intermedius.* (*HOW 2771.*) O. Leaves, scale 1 mm. P. Leaf apex, scale 50 μ.
Q. Leaf base, cells. R. Median and marginal cells, some with papillae shown.
Q, R, scale 50 μ.

apex. Cells of the upper lamina thick-walled; walls 2–3 μ; lumina rounded, irregularly quadrate to hexagonal, rectangular to transversely elongate, mostly isodiametric, 3.5–7.5 μ, more elongate adjacent to the costa, to 30 × 5 μ, smooth. Cells of the lamina base brownish at insertion, elongate, straight to slightly S-shaped, thick-walled; walls 3–5 μ; lumina 25–50 × 2–3 μ just above insertion. Capsule 2.3 × 0.9 mm; seta 8–9 mm, smooth, twisted. Exothecial cells irregularly thick-walled; walls about 2–2.5 μ; lumina irregularly rectangular, 25–40 × 12–15 μ. Peristome teeth brown, finely papillose. Operculum, calyptra, and spores not found.

ILLUSTRATIONS. Figure 57F–I.

TAHITI. Papeete: Reine Valley, on trunks of old trees, *Savatier 741* (Bescherelle, 1895a). Mt. Aorai: 1400 m, on branches, with *Dicnemon rugosum, 2742.*

Distribution.—Society Islands (Tahiti), endemic.

I have not yet examined Bescherelle's authentic material, but my collection compares well with the original description in most respects. Bescherelle described the seta as 3 mm long and observed that *M. savatieri* differed from *M. subtile* (= *M. incurvifolium*) in having striations beneath the peristome mouth, and larger rhomboidal laminal cells, the cells of the leaf base only slightly curved and more often rectangular. In *M. subtile*, Bescherelle (1895a) noted the capsule to be globose, whereas in *M. savatieri* the capsule was supposed to be ovoid-elongate. Specimens identified by Aongstrom and by Mitten as *M. subtile* which I examined, from the *Eugenie* Expedition and collected on Moorea (Eimeo), show no appreciable differences: the capsules may be ovoid-cylindric and there may be striations beneath the peristome. I can only conclude that examination of Bescherelle's type specimen of *M. savatieri* may prove it to be a synonym for *M. incurvifolium.*

5. *Macromitrium reinwardtii* Schwaegrichen
   Spec. Musc. Suppl. 2(2): 69. t. 173. 1826.
   Macromitrium owahiense C. Muell., Bot. Zeit. 22: 359. 1864.

Plants yellow-green to yellow-brown, autoicous, forming turfs on bark, the male buds on short, separate branches. Primary stems to 6 cm long, creeping; secondary stems short, about 8–10 mm, unbranched or with short tertiary branches. Leaves erect, apices incurved when dry, the margins inrolled, arranged in a spiral about the stem, flexuose and erect-spreading when moist, ovate-lanceolate, acuminate, carinate, 1.5–2.0 × 0.45–0.55 mm, the margins entire, erect, usually recurved on one side near the leaf base. Costa percurrent to ending 2–5 cells below the apex, yellow, smooth. Cells of the lamina smooth, thick-walled, rounded-quadrate to ellipsoidal, sometimes transversely elongate, 5–8 μ, walls 2–5 μ thick; basal cells very thick-walled, walls 5–6 μ, thick, lumina 20–50 × 2–3 μ, straight to slightly curved. Perichaetial leaves to 3.5 × 0.75 mm. Seta 1–2 cm long, reddish, smooth; capsule erect, ovoid-cylindric, 1.5–2.3 × 0.8 mm, puckered around the mouth when dry. Peristome single, inner peristome absent, teeth brownish opaque, papillose, inserted beneath the rim, ephemeral; operculum erect or slightly inclined, conic-rostrate, about 0.7–0.9 mm long; calyptra hairless. Spores greenish, finely papillose, 50–55 μ.

ILLUSTRATIONS. Noguchi (1967, p. 225, f. 10), Bartram (1933b, p. 155, f. 115), Brotherus (1924b, 2: 32, f. 449), Schwaegrichen (1826, p. 69, t. 173). Figure 57J–N.

TAHITI. Without locality: *Wilkes sn,* 1838 (Sullivant, 1859). Pirae District: Pirae–Mt. Aorai trail to summit, above 1386 m, *Quayle 697c, 699; 152a, 153b, 154, 165; Whitney Expedition 698, 699c, 704b* (Bartram, 1933a, BISH!); 2050 m, on ground, with *Campylopus, 2752.*

Distribution.—Society Islands (Tahiti), Hawaii (Oahu, Kauai, Maui, Hawaii), Java, Borneo, Celebes, Tasmania, Japan, Philippine Islands, Taiwan.

Originally described from Javan material, this species was first reported from Tahiti by Sullivant (1859), with numerous citation records (Mitten, 1871; Jaeger and Sauerbeck, 1875; Fleischer, 1904; Bartram, 1939) based on this record. Bescherelle (1895a) cited the Wilkes collection as *Macromitrium owahiense.* I can find no significant difference between this species and *M. reinwardtii* and believe that Sullivant was correct in selecting *M. reinwardtii* as the name for his Tahitian material.

6. *Macromitrium paridis* Bescherelle
Rev. Bryol. 25(6): 90. 1898e.
Macromitrium cacuminicola Besch., Bull. Soc. Bot. France 45: 63. 1898a. *hom. illeg.*

Plants yellow-green, on branches of trees, with erect secondary branches 2–3 cm tall, irregularly branched; leaves spirally arranged, incurved and contorted when dry, keeled, 2.2 × 0.6 mm, when moist, erect-spreading to recurved, the margins erect to reflexed, entire; costa smooth, percurrent or ending in a short, straight to recurved apiculus. Cells of the upper lamina rounded, smooth, isodiametric to (often) transversely elongate, 5–8 μ, the walls irregularly thickened, 1–3 μ, thicker between lateral series of cells than between cells within a series. Basal cells above the insertion thick-walled, faintly pitted; lateral walls 3–5 μ thick, the angles rounded, rectangular to rhomboidal; lumina 30–60 $\times$ 10–12 μ toward the costa, quadrate to short-rectangular at the margins, 10–25 $\times$ 10–12 μ; at insertion, cells irregularly quadrate, hyaline, thin-walled (about 1–2 μ), lumina 25–30 μ. No sporophytes found.

ILLUSTRATIONS. Figure 58A–E.

TAHITI. Without locality: Ridges to 900 m, on trees, *Nadeaud 260* (Bescherelle, 1898a, as *Macromitrium cacuminicola*; 1898e). Haapape District: Rahi, 800 m, *Temarii Nadeaud sn* (Bescherelle, 1901). Taiarapu Peninsula: Haavini Valley, 115 m, with *Thyridium constrictum, 2520.*

Distribution.—Society Islands (Tahiti), endemic.

I have not yet examined authentic material of this species, known only from the collections cited above, but my own collection seems to fit Bescherelle's original description very closely. Bescherelle described the seta as 5 mm long, the capsule spherical, small, microstomous, plicate beneath the mouth; the calyptra was reported as short, mitriform, smooth, laciniate at the base, the apex brownish and scabrous. Bescherelle renamed this species in honor of General Paris, who had directed his attention to the fact that the specific epithet for *Macromitrium cacuminicola* was already occupied. Bescherelle considered this species to be close to *M. owahiense* C. Muell., and noted that it differed primarily in its shorter seta (to 5 mm, as opposed to 14–18 mm), in the gymnostomous capsule, and in the more obtuse leaves. The costa ends beneath the leaf apex as Bescherelle described, in lower leaves, but in upper leaves of my collection the costa terminates in an apiculus.

7. *Macromitrium eurymitrium* Bescherelle
   Bull. Soc. Bot. France 45: 64. 1898.

Plants sordid yellow-green, with prostrate primary stems on bark, secondary stems unbranched to branched, from 5 mm to 2–3 cm tall; leaves 1.5–1.8 $\times$ 0.2–0.5 mm, incurved and twisted, keeled when dry, erect-spreading to squarrose when moist, ovate-lanceolate, acuminate; costa ends below the apex or percurrent in lower leaves,

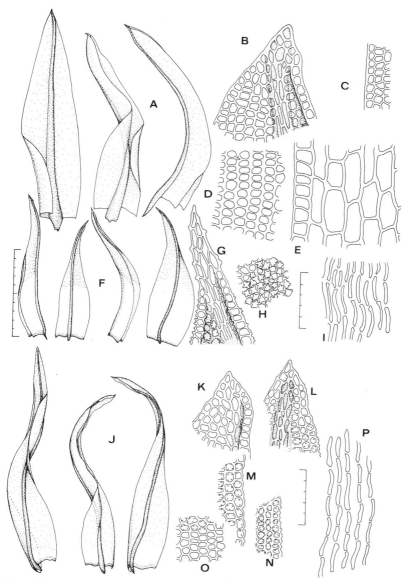

FIG. 58. A–E. *Macromitrium paridis*. (*HOW 2520*.) A. Leaves, scale 1 mm. B. Leaf apex. C. Lamina, upper margin. D. Median cells. E. Basal cells. B–E, scale 50 μ. F–I. *Macromitrium eurymitrium*. (*HOW 2535*.) F. Leaves, scale 1 mm. G. Leaf apex. H. Median cells. I. Basal cells. G–I, scale 50 μ. J–P. *Macromitrium incurvifolium*. (Isotype.) J. Leaves, scale 1 mm. K, L. Leaf apices. M. Midleaf, margin. N. Upper leaf, margin. O. Median cells. P. Basal cells. K–P, scale 50 μ.

excurrent, ending in a mucro about 100 μ long in upper leaves. Upper leaf margins reflexed, entire. Cells of the upper lamina obscure (even after clearing), finely pluripapillose, irregularly rounded-quadrate to hexagonal, 4–5 μ; those of the leaf base irregularly thick-walled, the walls 3–5 μ wide, the lumina 25–35 × 2–3 μ, rectangular, straight to more commonly C-shaped, smooth, not pitted. The hyaline basal region extends about one-half the length of the leaf. Cells at leaf insertion yellow-brown. Seta 5–6 mm, smooth; capsule ovoid-cylindric, about 1.8 mm long. No peristomes found; the original description cited 16 lanceolate, yellowish, granulose teeth. No spores found.

ILLUSTRATIONS. Figure 58F–I.

TAHITI. Pinai Mountains: Puaa Valley, to 1000 m, *Nadeaud 262*. Marciati: Papenoo and Punarua valleys at the foot of Mt. Orohena, *Nadeaud 263*. Hitiaa District (?): *Nadeaud 264*. Mountains of Pinai and Papeana: *Nadeaud 265*. Pirae District: Fautaua Valley, *Whitney Expedition sn* (Bartram, 1933a); Mt. Aorai Trail, 700 m, *2660, 2972*. Papenoo District: Papenoo Valley, 180 m, on *Hibiscus* branches, *2413*. Taiarapu Peninsula: Haavini Valley, 125 m, with *Rhizogonium spiniforme* and *Ectropothecium, 2535, 2536*; 100 m, on *Hibiscus, 2621, 2625, 2630*. Mataiea District: Vaihiria Valley, 100 m, on branches, with *Bryum truncorum, Ectropothecium sodale, Garovaglia,* and *Anoectangium, 3081*; on organic debris on ground, with *Racopilum pacificum, Hypopterygium, Eurrhynchium,* and *Vesicularia, 3088*.

Distribution.—Society Islands (Tahiti), endemic.

The obscure, pluripapillose cells of the upper lamina and the relatively (for Society Islands *Macromitrium* species) long excurrent costa have apparently led to the confusion of *M. eurymitrium* with *M. piliferum* Schwaegr., which has the costa much longer-excurrent, and knob-like papillae over the lumina of lower lamina cells; the lower lamina cells of *M. eurymitrium* are smooth. The collection made by Lay and Collie on Tahiti and cited by Guillemin (1836) may prove to be best placed here under *M. eurymitrium*; no Tahitian material I have examined compares well with authentic Hawaiian material collected by Menzies and identified by Schwaegrichen deposited in the herbarium of the New York Botanical Garden. The large hyaline region, occupying up to one-half the lower leaf, the C-shaped basal cells, and the pluripapillose upper cells, distinguish this species from all other Society Islands *Macromitria*.

8. *Macromitrium incurvifolium* (Hooker & Greville) Schwaegrichen Spec. Musc. Suppl. 2(2): 144. 1827.

Orthotrichum incurvifolium Hook. & Grev., Edinburgh J. Sci. 1: 177. f. 4. 1824.
Macromitrium subtile Schwaegr., Spec. Musc. Suppl. 2(2): 140. 1827.
Macromitrium tahitense Nad., Enum. Pl. Indig. Tahiti 13. 1873. fide Bescherelle 1895a = M. subtile.
Macromitrium nadeaudii Besch., Bull. Soc. Bot. France 45: 64. 1898. fide Fleischer, Musci Fl. Buitenzorg 2: 440. 1904.
Macromitrium beecheyanum Mitt., J. Linn. Soc. Bot. 10: 167. 1868.
Macromitrium cumingi C. Muell., Flora 82: 452. 1896. fide Bartram, 1933b.
Macromitrium subsemipellucidum Broth., Bishop Mus. Bull. 40: 64. 1898. fide Bartram 1933b = M. subtile.

Plants irregularly branched, primary stems suberect to erect, secondary branches 5–10 mm long; leaves erect-spreading, apices twisted and inrolled when dry, slightly incurved from the erect-spreading lower portions when wet, ovate-lanceolate, acuminate, 2.0–2.3 × 0.4–0.5 mm; costa ends in the apex or slightly excurrent, about 35–38 μ wide near the leaf base. Cells of the lamina 5–7 μ, rounded-quadrate, obscure in the upper lamina, thick-walled, in regular rows, punctate-papillose to mammillose or rounded-papillose; cells of the lower lamina more rectangular, smooth, pellucid, thick-walled, 10–30 × 5–8 μ, and orange at insertion of leaf onto stem. Margins of the upper leaf are slightly crenulate from projecting papillae; in the lower leaf the margins entire. Sporophyte lateral, 3–5 mm long; capsule 1.3 × 0.73 mm (deoperculate capsules only, in original collection); operculum conic-rostrate, 0.7–0.9 mm; capsule gymnostomous (no suggestion a peristome was ever present), ovoid, varying from nearly spherical to short, ovoid-cylindric. Exothecial cells irregularly rectangular, 30–40 × 7–12 μ. Calyptra pilose. Spores 19–25 μ, greenish, papillose.

ILLUSTRATIONS. Hooker and Greville (1824, p. 177, f. 4). Figure 58J–P.

TAHITI. Without locality: *Menzies sn* (Schwaegrichen, 1827, as *Macromitrium subtile*, isotype, NY); with *Papillaria helictophylla*, *Jacquinot sn*, 1838 (Montagne, 1845; 1848, as *M. subtile*); *Wilkes sn* (Sullivant, 1859, as *M. subtile*); *Barclay sn* (in hb. Mitten, *ex* BM, unreported); *Jelinek sn, Novara* Expedition, "near Papeete" (Reichardt, 1870, as *M. subtile*); *Andersson sn*, 1852 (Aongstrom, 1872, as *M. subtile*, NY); on rocks and trees in the interior, *Nadeaud 62*, 1856–1859 (1873, as *M. tahitense*; Bescherelle, 1895a, as *M. subtile*); *Lépine sn; Vesco sn; Vernier sn* (Bescherelle, 1895a);

Nadeaud sn, 1896 (Bescherelle, 1898a, as *M. subtile*). Puaa Valley: *Nadeaud 261,* 1896 (Bescherelle, 1898a, as *M. nadeaudii,* isotype, NY). Miaa: 850 m, *Temarii Nadeaud sn,* 1899 (Bescherelle, 1901, as *M. nadeaudii*). Paea District: Orofere Valley, *Setchell and Parks 5301;* purau (*Hibiscus tiliaceus*) swamp about 34 km stone, beyond Maraa Caves, *Setchell and Parks 5390, 5392.* Papenoo District: Roadside beyond Papenoo River, *Setchell and Parks 5353.* Punaauia District: Punaruu Valley, *Setchell and Parks 5374* (Brotherus, 1924a, as *M. subtile*). Pirae District: Pirae–Mt. Aorai trail, *Quayle sn* (Bartram, 1933a, as *M. subtile*). Taiarapu Peninsula: Taravao, near experiment station, 400–500 m, on dead wood, *Hürlimann T 1191* (Hürlimann, 1963, det. Bartram, as *M. subtile*).

MOOREA. Without locality: *Andersson sn,* 1852 (Aongstrom, 1872); *Temarii Nadeaud sn,* 1899 (Bescherelle, 1901).

RAIATEA. Faaroa Valley: On ridge, 100 m, on branches of *Hibiscus, Moore 17.* Mt. Temehani: On ridge E of mountain, 250 m, on dry branches of shrubs, *Moore 20.* Tioo: 1 m, on coconut palm, *Moore 52.* Faaroa Bay: N side, on ridge of mountain, 150 m, on branch of tree, *Moore 89* (Bartram, 1931, as *M. subtile*).

Distribution.—Society Islands (Tahiti, Moorea, Raiatea), King George's Sound and Ternate Island (type locality), Hawaii (Kauai, Oahu, Maui, Hawaii), Samoa, New Hebrides, Fiji, Tuamotu Islands, Austral Islands (Tubuai, Raivavae, Rurutu), Pitcairn Island (Beechey!), Java, Amboina, New Zealand, Australia.

A comparison of authentic specimens indicates there is no significant difference between *Macromitrium subtile* and *M. incurvifolium,* a fact long ago recognized by Mitten in a note accompanying his authentic specimens (isotypes) of *M. incurvifolium.* Bescherelle (1895a) noted that *M. tahitense* Nadeaud is a synonym of *M. subtile,* and there is no reason it should not be treated in synonymy with *M. incurvifolium.* Fleischer (1904) considered *M. nadeaudii* Besch. (isotype, NY!) as a probable synonym of *M. subtile,* and examination of authentic material supports its placement in synonymy with *M. incurvifolium.* Examination of the type specimen of *M. beecheyanum* Mitt. (NY!) from Samoa, shows no major differences from *M. incurvifolium,* and I consider them to be identical. Bartram (1933b) examined type specimens of *M. cumingi* and *M. subsemipellucidum* and found little or nothing to distinguish either one from *M. subtile.* In all probability the synonymy is much more extensive than the records would indicate.

XVIII. RACOPILACEAE

Racopilum P. de Beauvois
Prodr. 36. 1805.

Three species of the genus *Racopilum* are provisionally recognized from the Society Islands: *R. cuspidigerum, R. spectabile,* and *R. pacificum.* The genus *Racopilum* is readily identified by its prostrate habit, irregular branching, the leaves in 3 ranks and dimorphous, the 2 series of lateral leaves large, slightly asymmetrical, costate, the costa excurrent in an arista which may be up to almost one-half the length of the entire leaf, the upper series of leaves smaller and symmetrical, with an excurrent costa. Reddish-brown rhizoids appear in tufts at irregular intervals along the lower surface of the stems. The Society Islands species are dioicous, and male plants are reported to appear as reduced stems among the rhizoids of the archegoniate plants. The genus *Racopilum* is commonly found on bark and decomposing organic material or on wet rocks in cool, humid localities.

Key to Species of *Racopilum*

1. Cells adjacent to the costa in the leaf base quadrate; margins of the upper lamina entire to crenulate but not serrulate or denticulate..1. *R. cuspidigerum.*
1. Cells adjacent to the costa in the leaf base rectangular; margins of the upper lamina serrulate to denticulate
   2. Leaves to over 2.5 mm long; margins of the lamina strongly denticulate to near the leaf base; upper lamina median cells hexagonal, 14–24 × 9–20 μ, the cell walls thin and regular; lamina basal cells elongate throughout the leaf base..3. *R. spectabile.*
   2. Leaves less than 2.5 mm; margins of the upper lamina with small teeth, formed by portions of single cells, entire or crenulate in the lower two-thirds of the leaf; cells of the upper lamina irregularly hexagonal, 7–17 × 7–10 μ, the walls regularly to irregularly thickened; basal cells rectangular next to the costa, short-rectangular to quadrate at the margins...2. *R. pacificum.*

1. *Racopilum cuspidigerum* (Schwaegrichen) Aongstrom
Oefv. K. Svensk. Vet. Ak. Foerh. 29(4): 10. 1872.

Hypnum cuspidigerum Schwaegr., *in* Gaud. *in* Freycinet, Voy. Sut. Monde
Uranie Phys. Bot. 229. 1828.
Hookeria tomentosa var. *subintegrifolia* Arnott, 1827. *fide* Paris, Ind. Bryol.
587. 1897.
Racopilum demissum Bosch & Lac., Bryol. Jav. 2: 18. t. 146. 1861. var.
demissum (Bosch & Lac.) Fleisch., Musci Fl. Buitenzorg 4: 1625. 1923.

Lateral leaves 0.95–1.2 × 0.4–0.54 mm; upper leaves to about 1.0
× 0.3–0.4 mm; leaf upper margins crenulate to entire. Cells of the
upper median lamina smooth or minutely pluripapillose, isodiametric to slightly elongate, irregularly hexagonal, the walls irregularly thickened, the angles rounded, about 7–12 μ, relatively uniform in size, but slightly larger and quadrate toward the leaf base
and smaller, with thicker, more irregular walls toward the apex. The
costa prominent and excurrent by one-quarter to one-half the
length of the entire leaf; in the isotype (Gaudichaud, Hawaii, NY),
it is usually excurrent by less than one-third the overall length.

Bartram (1933a) described the sporophytes: "Seta 1.5–2.2 cm
long, reddish below, paler above; capsule inclined, oblong-cylindric,
brown, strongly sulcate when dry, contracted below the oblique
mouth, urn 2 mm long; peristome teeth yellowish, finely transversely
striate on the outer plates, inner peristome pale, basal membrane
about half the height of the teeth, segments widely split along the
median line, cilia two or three, slightly appendiculate; lid with a
short oblique beak from a conic base, 0.9 mm long; calyptra cucullate, with numerous long, spreading, crispate hairs similar to those
of the vaginula; spores yellowish, smooth, up to 17 μ in diameter."

ILLUSTRATIONS. Fleischer (1923, 4: 1623, f. 256), Bartram (1933b,
p. 158, f. 117). Figure 59.

TAHITI. Without locality: *Andersson sn*, 1852, *Eugenie* Expedition
(Aongstrom, 1873, as *R. demissum*); *Quayle sn* (Bartram, 1933a).
Pirae District: Mt. Aorai, 1700 m, in valley W of Chalet Fare Ata,
on bark, associated with *Distichophyllum, Hypopterygium, Ptychomnion, Riccardia,* and *Anthoceros, 2931;* Fautaua Valley, 480 m,
with *Leucomium aneurodictyon, Ectropothecium sodale,* and *Porella, 3144.* Taiarapu Peninsula: N side, Haavini Valley, on bark
with *Callicostella, Ectropothecium,* and *Metzgeria, 2480.*

MOOREA. Cooks Bay: Lower slopes Mt. Matanui, 50 m, Haring
Plantation, with *Hypopterygium* and *Fissidens mangarevensis, 3411.*

Distribution.—Society Islands (Tahiti; Moorea, a new record),
Samoa, Fiji, Hawaii, New Caledonia, Guam, Java, Bali, Celebes,
Ceram, Norfolk Island, Mangareva, Henderson Island.

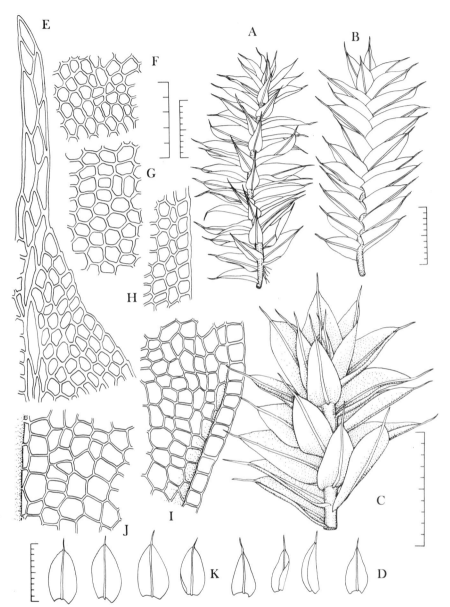

FIG. 59. *Racopilum cuspidigerum*. (*Gaudichaud sn,* 1828, Sandwich Islands [Hawaii].) A. Habit, upper side of stem, scale 1 mm. B. Habit, lower side of stem, scale 1 mm. C. Habit, upper side of stem, scale 1 mm. D. Leaves (4), upper series, scale 1 mm. E. Costa and lamina apex. F. Lamina, upper median cells. G. Lamina, lower median cells. H. Lamina, upper margin cells. I. Lamina, basal angle cells. J. Lamina, basal cells adjacent to the costa. E–J, scale 50 μ. K. Leaves (4), lateral series, scale 1 mm.

2. *Racopilum pacificum* Bescherelle

J. Bot. Morot 12: 42. 1898b.

Lateral leaves ovate-lanceolate, 1.6–2.5 × 0.75–0.8–(1.2) mm; costa excurrent by 0.32–0.38 mm; leaf margins irregularly serrulate in the upper lamina, the teeth formed by single cells projecting for part of their length beyond the margin. Upper leaves 1.2–1.4 × 0.5–0.68 mm, cordate, lanceolate, the costa excurrent by up to 0.46 mm. Cells of the upper lamina of lateral leaves 12–22 × 7–12 μ, irregularly hexagonal, elongate, the walls regularly to irregularly thickened, with slight pit formation toward midleaf and the leaf base; cells of the leaf base elongate, rectangular, to 67 × 14 μ adjacent to the costa; cells near the leaf apex smooth to rounded-papillose on the lower surface. Seta 2–3 cm long; capsule cylindric, curved, slightly asymmetric, about 3 × 0.8 mm; operculum conic-rostrate, 1.2 mm long, about 0.6 mm formed by the beak. Calyptra not seen, but described by Bescherelle (1898b) as cucullate and slightly pilose. Spores yellow-green to golden, smooth, 12–15 μ in diameter.

ILLUSTRATIONS. Bescherelle (1898b, p. 45, f. 2c, d). Figure 60.

TAHITI. On organic debris in humid localities in the interior of the island, *Nadeaud sn,* 1859 (Nadeaud, 1873, as *Hypopterygium spectabile* C. Muell.; Bescherelle, 1895). Without locality: *Vesco sn*; *Mercier sn* (Bescherelle, 1895a, as *Racopilum convolutaceum*); numerous collections, very common in humid ravines, to about 1000 m, *Nadeaud sn,* 1896 (Bescherelle, 1898b, as var. *tahitense,* nos. 442–448). Miaa: 850 m, *Temarii Nadeaud sn,* 1899; Haapape District, Rahi, 800 m, *Temarii Nadeaud sn* (Bescherelle, 1901). Pirae District: Mt. Aorai, 1700 m, with *Hypnodendron vescoanum, Plagiochila, Herberta,* and *Leiocolea,* 2897. Taiarapu Peninsula: Haavini Valley, 130 m, on organic debris, 2534; Taravao, above experiment station, 650 m, on bark with *Callicostella, Ectropothecium,* and *Frullania,* 2284. Mataiea District: Vaihiria Valley, on branches of trees, with *Hypopterygium, Homaliodendron exiguum, Fissidens mangarevensis,* and *Plagiochila,* 3061.

Distribution.—Society Islands (Tahiti), Fiji, Samoa, New Caledonia, New Hebrides, Loyalty Islands, Java, Celebes, Ceram.

Bescherelle (1898b) described *R. pacificum* without citing a type specimen, although at the time he was engaged primarily in the study of Society Islands mosses and did refer to Tahitian collections made by Nadeaud, which he placed in a variety *tahitense.*

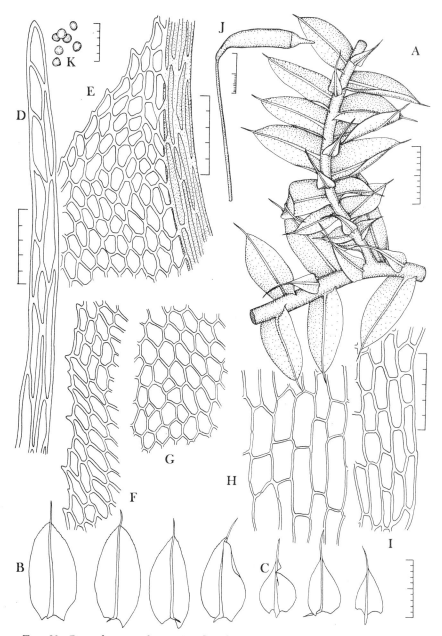

FIG. 60. *Racopilum pacificum.* (*Nadeaud sn.*) A. Habit, upper side of stem, scale 1 mm. B. Leaves (4), lateral series. C. Leaves (3), upper series. B, C, scale 1 mm. D. Costa apex, scale 50 μ. E. Lamina apex, cells, scale 50 μ. F. Lamina, upper margin, cells. G. Lamina, upper median cells. H. Lamina, leaf base cells. I. Lamina, basal angle cells. F–I, scale 50 μ. J. Capsule and operculum, scale 2 mm. K. Spores, scale 50 μ.

At the same time, he described varieties *samoanum,* from Samoa, and *gracilescens* for New Caledonian specimens, with the observation that the Tahitian variety was most robust, the New Caledonian variety most slender, and the Samoan variety intermediate. Both the Samoan and New Caledonian varieties were previously treated by Mitten and by Bescherelle, respectively, as *R. cuspidigerum.* Mueller (1873) apparently did not recognize Mitten's (1871) application of the name *R. cuspidigerum* to the Samoan specimen which Mitten earlier (1868) cited as *R. convolutaceum* C. Muell. (*Powell 39,* NY).

Bescherelle followed the currently accepted procedure in designating vars. *tahitense, samoanum,* and *gracilescens,* but he made no provision for the typical variety, which could only be var. *pacificum.* As no type specimen was designated, a lectotype must be selected, and I propose that it be chosen from among Nadeaud's collections on Tahiti, numbered 442–448 in Bescherelle's herbarium (P). Since only a single unnumbered specimen from this series is conserved in the New York Botanical Garden Herbarium, it seems best to defer a final decision until all of these collections can be examined and the most representative selected. In keeping with the international rules of nomenclature, *Racopilum pacificum* var. *pacificum* must be officially recognized, with *R. pacificum* var. *tahitense* cited in synonymy.

3. *Racopilum spectabile* Reinwardt & Hornschuch
   Nova Acta Ac. Leop.-Carol. 14(2): 721. f. 40c. 1829.

   Hypnum moritzi Duby, *in* Moritz, Syst. Verz. Zoll. Pfl. 231. 1846. *fide* C. Mueller, Syn. 2: 13. 1850.

   Racopilum caudatum C. Muell., Flora 82: 455. 1896. *fide* Geheeb, Biblioth. Bot. 44: 15. 1898.

   Racopilum nova-guinense Fleisch., Hedwigia 50: 285. 1911.

Plants large, robust, to 5 mm wide; leaves ovate-lanceolate, to 2.7 × 0.95 mm; costa excurrent by about 0.33 mm; upper series leaves shorter, to 2.0 × 0.8 mm. Leaf margins irregularly and strongly denticulate; teeth frequently formed by several cells and occasionally with smaller, flanking teeth; margins may be denticulate almost to the leaf base for both lateral and upper leaves. Cells of the upper median lamina of lateral leaves smooth to minutely pluripapillose, hexagonal, thin-walled, 14–24 × 9–20 μ, rectangular toward the leaf base, 40–80 × 8–15 μ across the leaf base from costa to margin, slightly shorter at the margin, and next to the costa the elongate cells continue to midleaf in some specimens. Seta yellowish, 3–4 cm long; capsule inclined to horizontal, 3.5 × 1.2 mm. Spores yellow-green, minutely papillose, 14–17 μ in diameter.

ILLUSTRATIONS. Dozy and Molkenboer (1861, 2: t. 144, 145), Reinwardt and Hornschuch (1829, t. 40c). Figure 61.

TAHITI. Faaiti Valley: Foot of Mt. Aorai, rarely in fruit, *Nadeaud 100*, 1896 (Bescherelle, 1898a, as var. *spinosum* Besch.). Taiarapu Peninsula: Haavini Valley, 125 m, on soil with *Riccardia*, *2542*; with *Cyclodictyon* and *Philonotis*, specimen markedly denticulate, *2557*.

Distribution.—Society Islands (Tahiti), New Caledonia, Sumatra, Java, Borneo, Celebes, Philippine Islands, Moluccas, Bismark Archipelago, d'Entrecasteaux, Solomon Islands, New Hebrides, Fiji, Samoa (Upolu).

Racopilum spectabile is distinguished by the large, robust plants, strongly denticulate leaves, to 2.7 mm long, and large, nearly isodiametric upper lamina cells. Of the other Society Islands species, *R. cuspidigerum* has quadrate basal cells and small, irregularly thick-walled, rounded upper lamina cells, the margins entire or nearly so. *Racopilum pacificum* has smaller leaves, the teeth small, formed by single cells; upper lamina cells tend to be elongate, rather than isodiametric.

Bartram (1933b) agreed with Dixon and Greenwood (1930), who felt that *R. pacificum* is probably not distinct from *R. cuspidigerum*. Dixon and Greenwood, however, cited Fleischer's Musci Fr. Arch. Ind. et Polyn. no. 477 as representative of *R. cuspidigerum*, and noted that in this specimen the cells are quite distinctly elongate-hexagonal, to disagree with Bescherelle's (1898b) observation that the cells are rounded. Bartram himself described the cells as "smooth, rounded-hexagonal, up to 10 μ wide and 10–14 μ long, more lax and short-rectangular toward the base." In Gaudichaud's isotype (Mitten hb., NY!) the cells are dorsally minutely pluripapillose, but the cell dimensions are essentially correct; the basal cells are predominantly quadrate. Concerning *R. pacificum*, *R. cuspidigerum*, and *R. convolutaceum*, Dixon wrote: "The distinguishing characters as given by Bescherelle differ very considerably from those given by Fleischer (1923), and the most probable con-

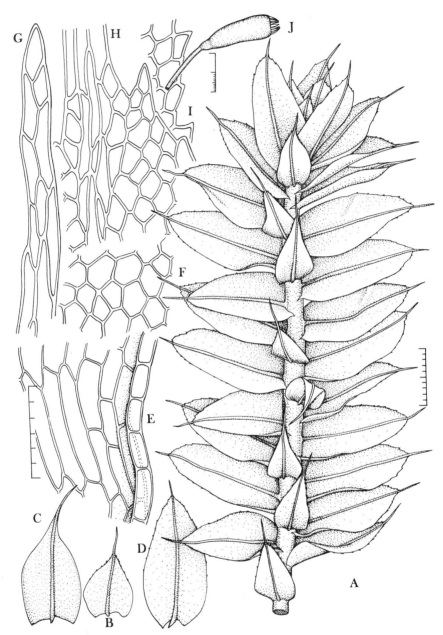

Fig. 61. *Racopilum spectabile*. A. Habit, upper side of stem. B. Leaf, upper side of stem. C. Leaf, upper side of stem. D. Leaf, lateral series. A–D, scale 1 mm. E. Lamina, basal angle cells. F. Lamina, upper median cells. G. Costa apex. H. Lamina apex, cells. I. Lamina, upper margin cells. E–I, scale 60 μ. J. Capsule, deoperculate, scale 2 mm.

clusion to be drawn is that the supposed specific characters do not hold, and that we have to deal with a widespread and rather variable species." It seems quite possible that Dixon's insight will prove to be correct, but only thorough monographic revision will resolve the issue. The results will, in any event, prove to be very interesting.

XIX. CRYPHAEACEAE

Cryphaea Mohr *in* Weber
Tab. Syn. Musc. 1814.

Cryphaea tenella (Schwaegrichen) Hornschuch *ex* C. Mueller
Linnaea 18: 679. 1844.

Neckera tenella Schwaegr., Spec. Musc. Suppl. 2(2): 163. f. 198. 1827.
Cryphaea tenella Hornsch., mss. name, *in* Schwaegrichen, 1827.
Cryphaea consimilis Mont., Ann. Sci. Nat. Bot. ser. 3, 4: 100. 1845. *fide*
   Dixon, New Zealand Inst. Bull. 3(5): 243. 1927.
Cryphaea parvula Mitt., in Hooker f., Handb. New Zealand Fl. 460. 1867.
   fide Dixon, 1927. (Isotype, NY!)
Cryphaea acuminata Hook. f. & Wils., Fl. Nov. Zel. 2: 102. 88 f. 4. 1854.
   fide Dixon, 1927. (Isotype, NY!)
Cryphaea pusilla C. Muell., Hedwigia 41: 130. 1902. *fide* Dixon, 1927.
Cryphaea brevidens C. Muell., Hedwigia 41: 130. 1902. *fide* Fleischer,
   Hedwigia 55: 284. 1914.
Cryphaea tahitica Besch., Bull. Soc. Bot. France 45: 116. 1898a. = C.
   tenella var. *tahitica* (Besch.) Fleisch., Hedwigia 55: 284. 1914.
Cryphaea tahitensis Besch. *ex* Paris, Ind. Bryol. Suppl. 105. 1900. *err. pro*
   C. *tahitica* Besch.

Plants monoicous, common on bark, erect, 2–5 cm tall, irregularly
branched; leaves imbricated, erect-spreading when wet, slightly
concave, ovate-lanceolate, acuminate, $0.7–1.0 \times 0.3–0.4$ mm; costa
ends in midleaf, below the apex, or extends into the acumen; leaf
margins entire to slightly crenulate. Cells of the lamina ovate,
irregularly thick-walled, $5–14 \times 4–7$ μ. Perichaetial leaves to 2.0–2.2
$\times$ 0.4–0.6 mm, the leaf base oblong, hyaline, sheathing, forming
about one-half to three-quarters the length of the entire leaf, abruptly constricted above to form a thickened, acuminate apex;
costa ends in the acumen, below the apex. Cells of the sheathing
base short, rhomboidal near the margins, linear toward the costa,
to 60×5 μ; cells of the leaf apex more nearly like those of vegetative leaves. Sporophytes immersed but visible through the tips of
perichaetial leaves; seta less than 1 mm long; urn 1.35×0.4 mm;
operculum conic-rostrate, 0.4 mm long. Peristome 300–400 μ high,
variably papillose, nearly smooth in some specimens, densely so in
others (Dixon, 1927). Exothecial cells thin-walled, quadrate to
rectangular, $20–50 \times 20$ μ. Spores brown, finely papillose, 20–24 μ
in diameter.

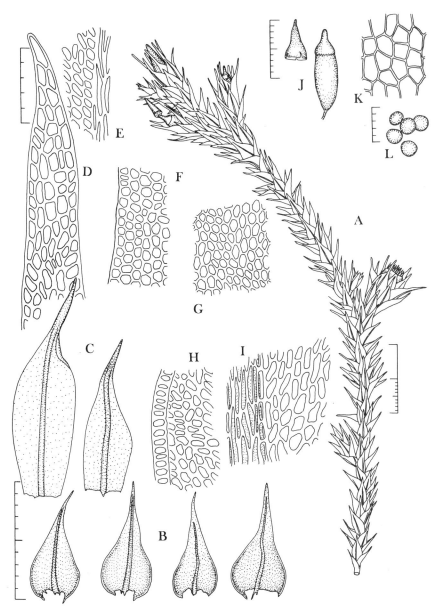

FIG. 62. *Cryphaea tenella*. (*Travers sn*, 1880, New Zealand.) A. Habit, scale 2 mm. B. Vegetative leaves. C. Perichaetial leaves. B, C, scale 1 mm. D. Leaf apex. E. Lamina, upper cells near costa. F. Upper cells and margins. G. Upper lamina cells. H. Basal angle cells. I. Basal cells, adjacent costa. D–I, scale 50 μ. J. Calyptra and capsule, scale 1 mm. K. Capsule exothecial cells. L. Spores. K, L, scale 50 μ.

ILLUSTRATIONS. Schwaegrichen (1827, pl. 198), Sainsbury (1955, p. 330, f. 1). Figure 62.

TAHITI. Punaruu Valley: On trees, rare, *Nadeaud 292*, 1896 (Bescherelle, 1898a, as *C. tahitica*).

Distribution.—Society Islands (Tahiti), Australia, Tasmania, New Zealand.

It seems reasonable to accept Fleischer's (1914) treatment of *C. tahitica* as a variety of *C. tenella* in light of Dixon's (1927) further studies on the variability of that species. Bescherelle (1898a) recognized the similarity between *C. tahitica* and *C. tenella*, and noted that the former had stem leaves which were narrower at the base, longer-acuminate, with rounded oval cells in the upper leaf margins. Although Bescherelle described the outer peristome as smooth, Dixon observed that "the peristome teeth may be sparsely papillose so as to be almost translucent, or densely papillose and opaque." My technical description is based on a New Zealand collection made by Travers in 1880, determined by G. O. K. Sainsbury, and conserved in the New York Botanical Garden Herbarium. Bescherelle's original specimen is to be found in the Paris Museum Herbarium.

XX. PTYCHOMNIACEAE

Ptychomnion Mitten
J. Linn. Soc. Bot. 12: 536. 1868.
Ptychomnion aciculare (Bridel) Mitten
J. Linn. Soc. Bot. 12: 536. 1868.
Hypnum aciculare Brid., Musc. Rec. 2(2): 158. 1801.
Bryum cucullifolium Pal. Beauv., Prodr. 62. 1805. *fide* Paris, 1906.
Stereodon (*Achyrophyllum*) *acicularis* (Brid.) Mitt., J. Linn. Soc. Bot. 4: 89. 1859.

Plants pale green, often tinged with brown, with reddish stems, forming tufts or intricate wefts on trunks and branches of trees at upper elevations; leaves erect-spreading, squarrose, 4–4.5 × 2–3 mm, ovate, abruptly acuminate, the upper margins serrulate to denticulate, entire below; costa absent or short and double, faint. Cells of lamina smooth to pitted, 30–50 × 5–8 μ, elongate-oval, in the lamina base longer, rectangular, more strongly pitted. Sporophytes lateral on the stem, seta 3–4 cm long, dark; capsule 2.5–3.5 × 0.9 mm, furrowed when dry, angled when moist, horizontal to inclined; operculum conic-rostrate, long-beaked, 1–2 mm. Capsule exothecial cells with uniformly thickened walls, quadrate to irregularly hexagonal, 25–35 μ. Spores 9–12 μ, greenish, smooth. From *2692*.
ILLUSTRATIONS. Brotherus (1924b, 2: 108, f. 514). Figure 63.
TAHITI. Without locality: *Lépine 107* (Montagne, 1845, as *Hypnum*); *Lépine 8, 12*; *Vesco sn*; *Nadeaud 89* (Bescherelle, 1895a); 800–1000 m, *Nadeaud sn*, 1896 (Bescherelle, 1898a). Miaa: 850 m, *Temarii Nadeaud sn* (Bescherelle, 1901). Pirae District: Fautaua, *Temarii Nadeaud sn*, 1899 (Bescherelle, 1901); Mt. Aorai trail, *Quayle 77, 151, 152, 148, 150, 160* (Bartram, 1933a); *Hürlimann sn* (Hürlimann, 1963); with *Leucobryum, 2674*; 1000 m, with *Spiridens, 2696*; 1065 m, on *Cyathea* trunk, with *Spiridens, 2713*; 1360 m, with *Porella* and *Ectropothecium, 2741*; with *Jamesoniella, 2779*; with *Distichophyllum, 2783*; with *Plagiochila, 2851*; 1800 m, below Chalet Fare Ata, *2859*; *2863*; 1700 m, pendent from tree branches, with *Papillaria, 2866*; with *Ectropothecium, 2867*; *2870*; with *Bazzania, 2877*; with *Dendroceros javanicus, 2934*; on dead *Cyathea* frond, *2945*; with *Plagiochila, 2947*; *2966*. Papenoo District: On ridge, 840

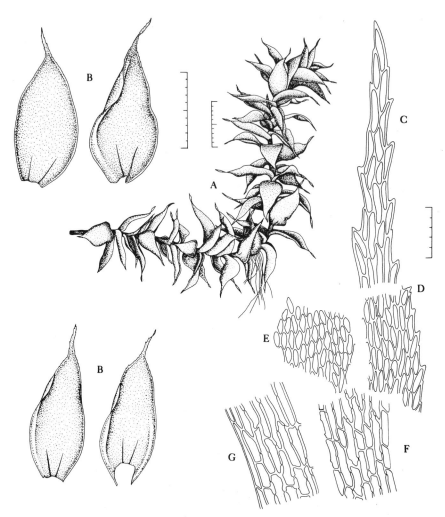

FIG. 63. *Ptychomnion aciculare*. A. Habit, portion of plant, scale 2 mm. B. Leaves, scale 1 mm. C. Leaf apex, cells. D. Leaf, upper margin cells. E. Leaf, upper median cells. F. Leaf base, median cells. G. Leaf base, margin cells. C–G, scale 50 μ.

m, between Papenoo and Vaihiria valleys, with *Spiridens, Ectropothecium,* and *Porella, 3036;* with *Trichocolea, 3037;* on tree branches, with *Microlepidozia* and *Metzgeria, 3039.* Mataiea District: Vaihiria Valley, 400 m, with *Dumortiera, 3059;* 200 m, on branches, with *Exodictyon, Acroporium,* and *Plagiochila, 3090.* Taiarapu Peninsula: Taravao, above experiment station, *Hürlimann sn* (Hürlimann, 1963); Haavini Valley, 640 m, on log, with *Leucobryum tahitense, 2275;* 670 m, with *Exodictyon* and *Garovaglia, 2304;* with *Leucomium aneurodictyon, Leucobryum,* and *Dendroceros, 2647.* Mt. Orohena: S side, 1200–1500 m, *MacDaniels 1482; 1454, 1531* (Bartram, 1933a, BISH).

MOOREA. Without locality: *Temarii Nadeaud sn,* 1899 (Bescherelle, 1901, NY).

RAIATEA. Mt. Temehani: In valley E of mountain, 300 m, on wet *Pandanus* branches, *Moore 24.* Highest mountain: W side, 700 m, on branches of shrubs in shade, *Moore 56;* 500 m, on branch of shrub, *Moore 59* (Bartram, 1931, BISH); 700 m, on branches of shrubs in shade, *Moore 42* (unreported, BISH).

Distribution.—Society Islands (Tahiti, Raiatea, Moorea), Marquesas Islands (Hiva Oa, Uapou), Hawaii (now excluded, personal communication, H. A. Miller, 1967, 1968), Samoa, Fiji, Lord Howe Island, Austral Islands (Rapa), New Caledonia, Australia, Tasmania, New Zealand, Auckland, and Campbell Islands, Juan Fernández Island, South America (Chile, Patagonia, Magellan Land).

Robinson (1968, personal communication) considers the South American taxa in the genus *Ptychomnion* to be distinct from *Ptychomnion aciculare.* My examination of South American collections conserved in the herbarium of the New York Botanical Garden indicates he is probably correct.

XXI. PTEROBRYACEAE

In this treatment, the Society Islands are represented by the genera *Trachyloma, Garovaglia, Symphysodontella,* and *Calyptothecium,* the last genus placed in the family Pterobryaceae following Noguchi's (1965) concept of the family.

The genera found in the Society Islands are typically found on trunks and tree branches, either as tufts (*Garovaglia*) or as frondose, flattened, dendroid forms. Leaves ovate-acuminate, the margins entire to denticulate, alar regions undeveloped to rounded or auriculate, the leaves with costa absent, single, or double. Cells of the lamina smooth, the walls smooth to pitted, elongate. Sporophytes rare, the seta short, the capsule hidden by perichaetial leaves or extending beyond them, the peristome double with the endostome rudimentary, the operculum with a short beak, the calyptra small, hairless.

KEY TO GENERA OF THE PTEROBRYACEAE

1. Plants forming tufts, stems rarely branched, leaves with strong longitudinal folds or creases (plicate), arranged uniformly around the stem⸺ ⸺2. *Garovaglia.*
1. Plants frondose, the branch pattern in one plane
   2. Branches with numerous axillary clusters of septate, thread-like propagula, leaves, especially at branch tips, white and papery in patches⸺ ⸺1. *Trachyloma.*
   2. Propagula absent; branch tip leaves not whitish
      3. Costa short and double or unequally forked, with one segment extending nearly to midleaf; leaves strongly concave, abruptly short-acuminate, basal angles not auriculate⸺3. *Symphysodontella.*
      3. Costa single, ending in midleaf; leaves plane or only slightly concave, short-acuminate, but not abruptly so, leaf basal angles broadly rounded to auriculate⸺4. *Calyptothecium.*

1. *Trachyloma* Bridel
Bryol. Univ. 2: 227. 1827.

Trachyloma indicum Mitten
J. Linn. Soc. Suppl. 1: 91. 1859.

Trachyloma papillosum Broth., Philippine J. Sci. 31: 288. 1926.
Trachyloma hawaiiense Broth., Bull. Soc. Bot. Ital., p. 24, 1904.
Trachyloma tahitense Besch., Bull. Soc. Bot. France 45: 118. 1898.
Trachyloma novae-guineae C. Muell., *in* Paris, Ind. Bryol. 5: 1302. 1894.

Plants erect, frondose, yellow-green, 5–6 cm tall, the erect secondary stems stiff, with lower branches sparingly branched, longer than the branches above. Tips of branches with axillary clusters of brown, septate, thread-like propagula, the leaves at branch tips often whitish and papery. Stem leaves squarrose-spreading, ovate-acuminate, 3.5–4 × 2.0–2.2 mm; margins plane, serrulate in the upper blade, entire toward the base. Costa faint, single or forked, ending near midleaf. Cells of the lamina linear, 60–90 × 8–12 μ, smooth, thin-walled above, the walls thicker and pitted in the leaf base, orange-brown at the leaf insertion. Branch leaves complanate, more closely pressed against the stem, smaller, the costa absent or very faint. Sporophytes not found. Based on *2950*.

ILLUSTRATIONS. Fleischer (1908, 3: 717, f. 134), Bartram (1933b, p. 166, f. 123, as *T. tahitense*). Figure 64.

TAHITI. Valley de Puaa: 800–1000 m, *Nadeaud sn*, 1896 (Bescherelle, 1898a, as *T. tahitense*). Pirae District: Fare Rau Ape–Mt. Aorai trail, 1700 m, associated with *Metzgeria* and *Trichomanes*, *2950*.

Distribution.—Society Islands (Tahiti), Hawaii (Maui), New Caledonia, Sri Lanka (Ceylon), Java, New Guinea, Celebes, Borneo, Sumatra, Malaysia, Vietnam, Formosa, Lombok, Ceram, Philippine Islands (Luzon, Mindanao), Annam.

I have examined the type specimen of *Trachyloma indicum* as well as other collections in the New York Botanical Garden Herbarium and can only conclude that *Trachyloma tahitense* is at the most a varietal form of *T. indicum*. Sainsbury (1955) suggested that *T. planifolium* and *T. tahitense* might be members of the same variable species, an observation worthy of serious consideration. My present opinion is that the New Zealand species is sufficiently distinct to exclude it from consideration here, but that it is definitely allied to *T. indicum*. The more broadly ovate and more complanate leaves give the plants of *T. planifolium* a distinctive appearance. The range of *T. planifolium* is restricted to Australia, Tasmania, and New Zealand.

2. *Garovaglia* Endlicher
Gen. Pl. 57. 1836.

One species of *Garovaglia*, *G. plicata*, is recognized from Tahiti. Examination of the collections and the notes made by Dixon, Mitten, Potier de la Varde, Bescherelle, and Bartram indicates the genus to be complex and variable. *Garovaglia tahitensis* and *G. powellii*

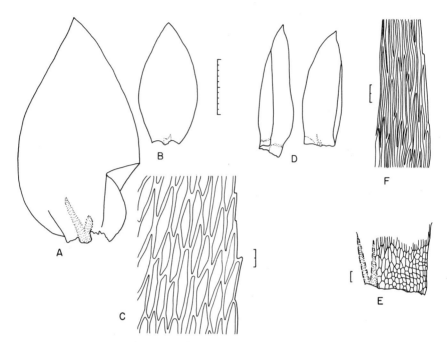

Fɪɢ. 64. A–C. *Trachyloma indicum.* (Type.) **A.** Leaf. **B.** Branch leaf. A, B, scale 1 mm. **C.** Leaf, upper margin and median cells, scale 20 μ. D–F, *Symphysodontella cylindracea.* (*HOW 2663.*) **D.** Leaves, scale 1 mm. **E.** Leaf, basal and alar cells, scale 50 μ. **F.** Leaf, upper margin and median cells, scale 20 μ. (*del.* HAM.)

(the former material identified by Bescherelle, the latter the type designated by Mitten, both NY!), are conspecific. Both are merely forms of G. plicata, which has been reported only once from Tahiti, from the United States Exploring Expedition collections by Wilkes and identified by Sullivant as *Endotrichum densum.*

Plants corticolous, typically found in the cloud forest on the trunks of trees and tree ferns, and not extremely common. Species of *Garovaglia* form tufts of 6 or 8 curved, semi-erect plants, the leaves arranged regularly about the stems, ovate-acuminate, markedly plicate, ecostate.

Garovaglia plicata (Bridel) Bosch & Lacoste
Bryol. Jav. 2: 79. 1863.

  Esenbeckia plicata Brid., Bryol. Univ. 2: 754. 1827.
  Endotrichum densum Dozy & Molk., Ann. Sci. Nat. Bot. ser. 3, 2: 303. 1844.
  Neckera plicata Schwaegr., Spec. Musc. Suppl. 3(2): t. 268. 1829.
  Pilotrichum plicatum C. Muell., Syn. 2: 158. 1851.
  Meteorium plicatum Mitt., J. Linn. Soc. Bot. 4: 84. 1859.
  Endotrichum plicatum Jaeg., Adumbr. 2: 135. 1871–1875.
  Garovaglia tahitensis Besch., Ann. Sci. Nat. Bot. ser. 7, 20: 34. 1895.
  Cyrtopus tahitensis Schimp., *nom. nud.*
  Garovaglia powellii Mitt., J. Linn. Soc. Bot. 10: 169. 1868.

Erect stems 3–6 cm long, golden brown to greenish, forming tufts on trunks and branches of trees and tree ferns; leaves arranged regularly around the stem, appressed, ovate-lanceolate, acuminate, to 4×2.0 mm, plicate, ecostate. Margins serrate in the upper lamina. Cells of the lamina $30–50 \times 10–15$ μ, elongate, smooth, walls irregularly thickened to pitted in the upper lamina; cells of the leaf base larger, $70–90 \times 15–20$ μ, the walls porose toward the middle of the base; smaller, quadrate to rectangular, $15–30 \times 15$ μ at the basal angles. Outermost perichaetial leaves nearly orbicular, abruptly acuminate. Sporophytes immersed, nearly hidden by perichaetial leaves; seta 0.2 mm long; capsule about 1.5×0.3 mm, operculum conic-rostrate; beak about 0.2 mm long. Spores (Fleischer, 1908, 3: 705), 15–25 μ, individuals to 45 μ, ovoid, papillose, yellow-green.

ILLUSTRATIONS. Bartram (1939, pl. 15, f. 256). Figure 65.

TAHITI. Without locality: *Wilkes sn* (Sullivant, 1859, as *Endotrichum densum*); below 1000 m, on branches of trees on ridges, *Nadeaud 67*; *Lequerré sn* (in hb. F. Camus); as *Cyrtopus tahitensis* Schimper, *Vieillard sn*; *Vesco sn* (Bescherelle, 1895a, as *Garovaglia tahitensis*); common in mountains toward 800 m and below, *Na-*

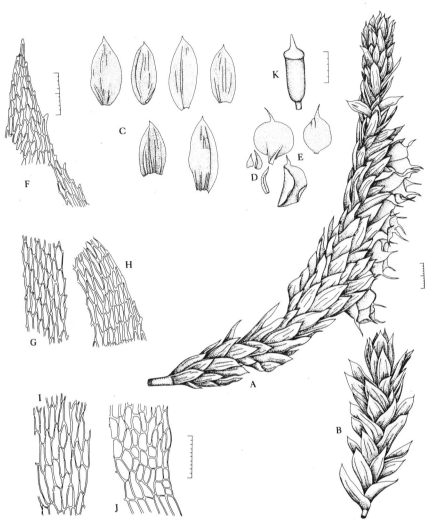

Fig. 65. *Garovaglia plicata*. A. Leafy stem, upper portion with inflorescences. B. Leafy stem segment. A, B, scale 1 mm. C. Leaves. D. Inner perichaetial leaves. E. Outer perichaetial leaves. C–E, scale 1 mm. F. Leaf apex cells. G. Leaf, upper median cells. H. Leaf, upper margin cells. F–H, scale 100 μ. I. Leaf base, median cells. J. Leaf base, margin cells. H, J, scale 100 μ. K. Capsule and operculum, scale 1 mm.

deaud 297; 800–1100 m, numerous other localities, *Nadeaud 298–303* (Bescherelle, 1898a, as *G. tahitensis*). Haapape District: Rahi, 800 m, *Temarii Nadeaud sn* (Bescherelle, 1901, as *G. tahitensis*). Pirae District: Mt. Aorai trail, with *Bryum, Macromitrium, Bazzania, Solenostoma, Microlepidozia,* and *Jamesoniella, 2970;* Fautaua Valley, above 400 m, *3122; Quayle 697n* (Bartram, 1933a, as *G. tahitensis*). Papenoo District: Papenoo River Valley, 20–38 m, on bark, with *Calymperes, Neckeropsis lepineana,* and *Porella, 2975;* with *Ectropothecium sodale, 2981.* Taiarapu Peninsula: Taravao, experiment station aqueduct, 400–500 m, on small tree, *Hürlimann T 1165;* on twig of *Psidium guajava,* with *Taxithelium mundulum, Hürlimann T 1181* (Hürlimann, 1963, det. Bartram as *G. tahitensis*); 610 m, N slope above experiment station, *2243;* 640 m, on trail into cloud forest, on tree trunk, *2261, 2267;* 660 m, *2295;* 670 m, *2304;* Haavini Valley, 115 m, N side peninsula, *2530;* 130 m, *2544;* 180 m, with *Bryum billardieri, Floribundaria aeruginosa,* and hepatics on *Hibiscus tiliaceus* branches, *2610.* Mataiea District: Vaihiria Valley, 400 m, on tree branches, *3064, 3077.*

RAIATEA. Highest mountain: Small valley W side, 600 m, in shade of trees on branches, *Moore 27* (type of *G. tahitensis* var. *brevicuspidata* Bartram); 800 m, *Moore 44.* Temehani Range: S end, 500 m, among other mosses on branches of shrubs, *Moore 46* (Bartram, 1931).

Distribution.—Society Islands (Tahiti, Raiatea), Samoa, Tubuai, Java .

Fleischer (1908) considered *Garovaglia tahitensis* to be so near *G. plicata* that it might be considered a subspecies, but I find no justification to separate the two even at the level of subspecies.

3. *Symphysodontella* Fleischer
Musci Fl. Buitenzorg 3: 688. 1908.
Symphysodontella cylindracea (Montagne) Fleischer
Musci Fl. Buitenzorg 3: 692. f. 129. 1908.
    Neckera cylindracea Mont., Ann. Sci. Nat. Bot. ser. 3, 10: 109. 1848.
    Pilotrichum cylindraceum C. Muell., Syn. 2: 182. 1851.
    Pterobryum cylindraceum Bosch & Lac., Bryol. Jav. 2: 78. 1863.
    Pterobryum dextrum Schimp., *in* Jardin, Bull. Linn. Soc. Normandie ser. 2, 9: 266. 1875. *nom. nud.*
    Pterobryum subcylindraceum Broth., mss.
    Symphysodon cylindraceus Broth., E. & P. Nat. Pfl. 799. 1906.

Plants erect from creeping rhizomatous, leafless primary stem, the secondary stems branched in one plane to form a frondose habit, 4–6 cm tall. Leaves somewhat compressed above and below; lateral leaves erect-spreading, ovate-lanceolate, abruptly acuminate, concave; branch leaves 0.8–1.5 × 0.2–0.4 mm; stem leaves larger, to 2.75 × 0.75 mm; costa short and double, faint, or forked unequally, with one fork extending nearly to midleaf. Cells linear, thin-walled, smooth, pitted, 30–60 × 3–5 μ in branch leaves, to 100 μ long in stem leaves, rectangular to quadrate at the leaf basal angles, 10–20 × 10–15 μ. Sporophytes not examined, but described by Fleischer (1908): seta 0.6 mm long; urn 3 mm; exostome teeth to 300 μ long; endostome rudimentary; operculum conic-rostrate; beak at an angle; calyptra cucullate, small, hairless. Spores round, green, papillose, 25–35 μ.

ILLUSTRATIONS. Fleischer (1908, 3: 693, f. 129), Bartram (1939, pl. 16, f. 268). Figure 64D–F.

TAHITI. Without locality: *Lépine sn*; "sur les arbres des vallées sèches de la région N.-O," fruiting, *Nadeaud 82*; "sur les sommets les plus élevés de l'ile," *Jardin 3* (Bescherelle, 1895a); as *Neckera filicina, Beechey sn* (in hb. Mitten, NY). Haapape District: Rahi, 800 m, *Temarii Nadeaud sn* (Bescherelle, 1901, as *Pterobryum*). Pirae District: Fare Rau Ape–Mt. Aorai trail, 800 m, on dead twig, with *Calyptothecium urvilleanum, Hürlimann T 1230* (Hürlimann, 1963, FH); above 1386 m, *Quayle 156b* (Bartram, 1933a); on bark with *Papillaria, Calyptothecium, Thuidium, Hypopterygium, Plagiochila, Frullania apiculata,* and *Porella, 2664*; 1000 m, about 100 m beyond first rest house, with *Neckeropsis lepineana, Papillaria, Metzgeria, Lopholejeunea,* and *Lejeunea, 2840*; 1700–1800 m, on bark, *2878*. Papenoo District: Papenoo Valley, W side, about 150 m, 2 km from highway on tree trunks at edge of Chinese garden, *2403*; 190 m, on tree trunks, *2447*. Taiarapu Peninsula: Taravao, above experiment station, 450 m, on tree trunks, *2214*.

MOOREA. Without locality: *Temarii Nadeaud sn* (Bescherelle, 1901, as *Pterobryum*).

Distribution.—Society Islands (Tahiti, Moorea), Cook Islands (Rarotonga), Samoa, Fiji, New Caledonia, New Hebrides, Java, Philippine Islands (Mindoro, Mindanao), Sumatra, New Guinea, Aneityum.

The frondose habit, abruptly acuminate leaves, and the pale green, lustrous appearance are characteristic of *Symphysodontella cylindracea*.

4. Calyptothecium Mitten
J. Linn. Soc. Bot. 10: 190. 1868.

Prominent, corticolous, frondose plants characterize the genus *Calyptothecium*, presently recognized as having two species in the Society Islands: *C. crispulum*, a small, compact form, and *C. urvilleanum*, a larger, more irregularly branched, sprawling type. The former seldom is taller than 5 cm, the leaves not transversely wrinkled; the latter characteristically larger, more robust, the leaves transversely wrinkled, the leaf bases auriculate. In both taxa, branching is in one plane, the leaves complanate, with a single costa which extends to midleaf.

Key to Species of Calyptothecium

1. Plants with secondary stems less than 5 cm tall, regularly and compactly branched, lowermost branches longest, uppermost branches shortest; stem leaves to 2.5 × 1.0 mm, not auriculate_____1. *C. crispulum.*
1. Plants with secondary stems 10–15 cm tall, irregularly branched and outlined; stem leaves 3–4 × 1.0–1.5 mm, auriculate_____2. *C. urvilleanum.*

1. *Calyptothecium crispulum* (Bosch & Lacoste) Brotherus
E. & P. Nat. Pfl. 1(3): 839. 1906.
Neckera crispulum Bosch & Lac., Bryol. Jav. 2: 66. 1863.

Erect secondary stems to about 5 cm tall, the branches closely pinnate, longest toward the stem base to give the plants a frondose habit. Stem leaves lingulate, broadly to rounded-acuminate, to 2.5 × 1.0 mm; the costa ending from one-third to one-half the length of the leaf. Upper margins denticulate, entire below. Cells of the lamina 30–60 × 8–10 μ, smooth, pitted, shorter toward the leaf base, rectangular to quadrate in the basal angles. Sporophytes not found in Society Islands collections examined.

ILLUSTRATIONS. Bartram (1939, pl. 17, f. 290). Figure 66.

TAHITI. Pirae District: Fautaua Valley, 50 m, on volcanic rock in forest, *Hürlimann T 1126* (Hürlimann, 1963, FH); 310 m, on rocks, *2349*; 290 m, with *Fissidens mangarevensis, 2354; 2358*; common above 150 m, on rocks and tree trunks, with *Porella, 2364*; Fare Rau Ape–Mt. Aorai trail, on tree trunks, associated with *Papillaria, Hypopterygium, Frullania*, and *Porella, 2664*. Mataiea District: Vaihiria Valley, 400 m, on bark with *Spiridens balfourianus, Plagiochila*, and other bryophytes, *3043; 3044; 3076*; with *Symphysodontella cylindracea, 3086*.

Distribution.—Society Islands (Tahiti), Nepal, Sumatra, Java.

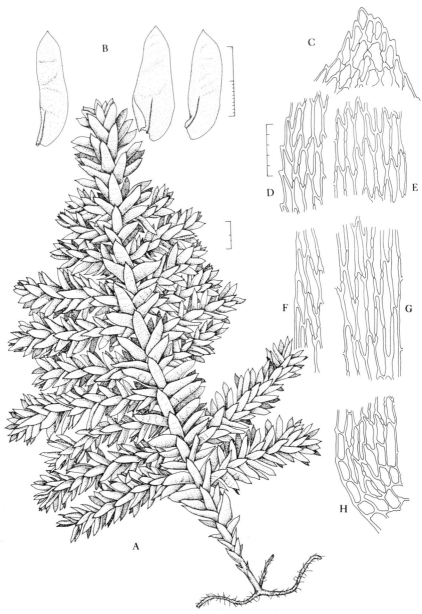

FIG. 66. *Calyptothecium crispulum.* (*Hürlimann T 1126.*) A. Habit, scale 2 mm.
B. Leaves, scale 2 mm. C. Leaf, apex cells. D. Leaf, upper margin cells. E.
Leaf, upper median cells. F. Leaf base, margin cells. G. Leaf base, median
cells. H. Leaf base, alar cells. C–H, scale 50 μ.

2. *Calyptothecium urvilleanum* (C. Mueller) Brotherus
E. & P. Nat. Pfl. 1(3): 839. 1906.

Neckera urvilleanum C. Muell., Syn. 2: 52. 1851.
Calyptothecium philippinense Broth., *in* Warburg, Monsunia 1: 48. 1899.
  fide Dixon, J. Bot. 75: 122. 1937. *fide* Bartram, 1939.
Calyptothecium tumidum (Dicks.) Fleisch., Musci Archip. Ind. Exs. ser. 5,
  p. 222. 1902. *p. p. non typ. fide* Index Muscorum 1: 416. 1959.
Calyptothecium praelongum Mitt., J. Linn. Soc. Bot. 10: 190. 1868. *fide*
  Dixon, 1937; Bartram, 1939.
Calyptothecium japonicum Thér., Le Monde des Plantes 9: 22. 1907. *fide*
  Noguchi, Bot. Mag. Tokyo 78: 63. 1965.
Calyptothecium densirameum Broth., Rev. Bryol. 56: 9. 1929. *fide* Noguchi,
  1965b.
Calyptothecium taitensis (Schimp.) Paris, Ind. Bryol. ed. 2, 1: 289. 1904.
  nom. illeg. incl. spec. prior, Index Muscorum 1: 416. 1959.
Neckera taitensis Schimp., *in* Hb. Mus. Paris, 1850. *fide* Paris, Index, p. 860.
  1896.
Neckera eugeniae Lindb., *in* Reichardt, Voy. Novara. 1870.
Neckera pennata sensu Guillemin, Ann. Sci. Nat. Bot. ser. 2, 6: 297. 1836.

Secondary stems erect, to about 10–15 cm tall (to 40 cm long in
the Philippine Islands forms described by Bartram, 1939, p. 235),
irregularly branched; leaves slightly compressed against the stem
on upper and lower surfaces (in the plane of branching), spreading to the sides, ovate-lingulate, broadly acuminate; margins denticulate in the upper lamina, serrulate to entire below; costa extending to about one-half the length of the blade, leaf base with the
angles broadly rounded, auriculate, the leaves transversely wrinkled
to 3–4 × 1.0–1.5 mm. Cells of the upper lamina 30–60 × 5–10 μ
wide, smooth, the walls thick, pitted, basal cells with thicker walls,
more strongly pitted or porose, cells of the basal angles short-
rectangular, 20–30 × 10 μ. Sporophytes not found in Society Islands
collections examined.

ILLUSTRATIONS. Bartram (1939, pl. 17, f. 292), Fleischer (1908, 3:
862, f. 152, *Calyptothecium tumidum*). Figure 67.

TAHITI. Without locality: *Menzies sn; Jacquinot and Hombron sn;
Du Petit-Thouars sn; Jelinek sn; Andersson sn; Quayle 98a* (Bartram, 1933a). Papeete: "Vallée de la Reine," *Savatier 740, 1037;
Nadeaud 81* (Bescherelle, 1895a, as *C. praelongum*); *Nadeaud 321–
325,* 1896 (Bescherelle, 1898a, as *C. praelongum*). Paea District:
Maara Valley, *Setchell and Parks 5313.* Pirae District: Fautaua Valley, *Setchell and Parks 5424* (Brotherus, 1924a, as *C. praelongum*);
490 m, *3126; 3162;* 590 m, *3168;* within the forest, *Vesco sn* (Aongstrom, 1873); fruiting, *Vieillard sn;* Fare Rau Ape–Mt. Aorai trail,

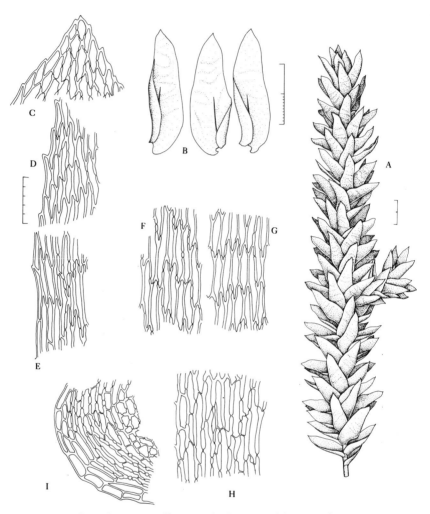

Fɪɢ. 67. *Calyptothecium urvilleanum.* (*HOW 3162A.*) A. Leafy stem, uppermost portion, scale 1 mm. The whole plant has the aspect of a large but more irregularly branched *C. crispulum.* B. Stem leaves, scale 2 mm. C. Leaf apex, cells. D. Leaf, upper margin cells. E. Midleaf margin. F. Leaf, upper median cells. G. Midleaf, median cells. H. Leaf base, median cells. I. Leaf base, auriculate region cells. C–I, scale 50 μ.

800 m, on dead twig, with *Symphysodontella cylindracea, Hürli-mann sn* (Hürlimann, 1963, det. Bartram, FH); same locality, 1000 m, on tree trunks with *Symphysodontella, Porella,* and *Metzgeria, 314;* with *Leucomium aneurodictyon* and *Lejeunea, 354;* same locality, with fruit, *2669;* same locality, with *Neckeropsis lepineana, Symphysodontella, Papillaria, Thuidium, Metzgeria,* and *Frullania, 2675.* Mataiea District: Vicinity of Lake Vaihiria, about 400 m, associated with *Calymperes* and *Syrrhopodon,* on rocks, *3051.* Hitiaa District: On plateau, about 500 m, associated with *Syrrhopodon ciliatus, Thyridium constrictum, Fissidens mangarevensis,* and *Leucophanes, 3216.*

Distribution.—Society Islands (Tahiti), Fiji, Samoa, Caroline Islands, Philippine Islands (Luzon, Mindanao, Palawan, Negros), Rapa, Malaysia, India, Burma, New Guinea, China, Sri Lanka (Ceylon), d'Entrecasteaux, New Caledonia, New Hebrides, Borneo, Java, Japan (Yuwandake), Formosa.

The taxonomic organization of the genus *Calyptothecium* is much in need of revision. As has already been noted, the larger, more irregular habit, together with leaves having distinct auriculate basal angles, separate *Calyptothecium urvilleanum* from *C. crispulum,* which has a more compact, more regularly branched habit, the leaves with rounded but not auriculate basal angles.

XXII. METEORIACEAE

Plants slender to robust, forming pendent masses on tree trunks and branches, common in upper valleys and on the higher ridges. Primary stems rhizomatous, poorly developed; secondary stems of indefinite length, irregularly branched, the branches variable in length. Leaves ovate-lanceolate, acuminate; costa single, ending in midleaf or below the apex. Cells of the lamina usually papillose, the alar cells undifferentiated. Sporophytes rare. Peristome double; operculum short, conic; calyptra cucullate.

KEY TO GENERA OF THE METEORIACEAE

1. Leaves rigid, pressed against the stem, closely overlapping (imbricated) ....
   ....1. *Papillaria.*
1. Leaves spreading, not rigid, not closely imbricated
   2. Leaves to 2 mm long, lamina cells seriate-papillose........3. *Floribundaria.*
   2. Leaves 2–4 mm long, lamina cells singly papillose........2. *Aerobryopsis.*

1. *Papillaria* (C. Mueller) C. Mueller
Oefv. K. Svensk. Vet. Ak. Foerh. 33(4): 34. 1876.

Plants yellow to yellow-green with blackened strands, forming tangled masses on tree trunks and branches; leaves typically imbricated, appressed against the stems when dry, spreading when moist; costa extends to midleaf or vanishes in the acuminate apex, the leaf base auriculate. Cells of the lamina thick-walled, ovate-elongate, seriate-papillose. Sporophytes rare; capsule extends beyond the perichaetial leaves, erect; peristome double; calyptra small, hairy.

Key to Species of *Papillaria*

1. Stems less than 2 mm wide; leaves 1.5–1.6 × 0.8 mm, the upper blade lanceolate to short-acuminate, costa ending in upper one-third of the blade
   ....1. *P. aongstroemii.*
1. Stems more than 2 mm wide; leaves to 2.0 × 0.9–1.2 mm, the upper blade long-acuminate, costa ending at midleaf or just above....2. *P. helictophylla.*

1. *Papillaria aongstroemii* C. Mueller *ex* Aongstrom
Oefv. K. Svensk. Vet. Ak. Foerh. 33(4): 53. 1876.

Cryphaea helictophylla Aongstr., 1873, *non* Montagne. *fide* Aongstrom, 1876.
Cryphaea nigrescens Mont., 1845, *non* Hedwig. *fide* Bescherelle, 1895a.

Secondary stems to 10 cm long, irregularly branched, the branches short, slender; leaves closely imbricated, pressed to the stem when dry, spreading when moist, ovate-acuminate or cordate, the basal angles strongly auriculate, to 1.5 × 0.8 mm; costa vanishes in the upper blade. Cells of the lamina thick-walled, pluripapillose, slightly pitted, 6–9 × 3–4 μ, more elongate toward the leaf base and smooth. Sporophytes not examined in Society Islands collections. Fleischer (1908, 3: 770–71, *P. cuspidifera*) described sporophytes with seta to 3 mm long, the capsule ovoid. The capsule about 1 mm long (Bescherelle, 1895a, p. 37). Spores yellow-brown, 12–15 μ, papillose (Fleischer, 1908).

ILLUSTRATIONS. Fleischer (1908, 3: 769, f. 140. *P. cuspidifera*). Figure 68A–D.

TAHITI. Without locality: Pendent from branches of trees, *Hombron sn* (Montagne, 1845, as *Cryphaea nigrescens*); on trees, fruiting, *Vesco sn*; *Thiébault 531*, 1865 (Bescherelle, 1895a); *Andersson sn* (Aongstrom, 1873, as *Cryphaea helictophylla*; 1876); common on branches of trees, rarely fruiting, *Nadeaud 305–308* (Bescherelle, 1898a). Teahupa: Maire Valley, 200 m, *MacDaniels 1638* (Bartram, 1933a). Pirae District: Fautaua Valley, *Quayle 661a*; 50 m, on volcanic rock in forest, *Hürlimann T 1126* (Hürlimann, 1963, FH); Rahi, 800 m, *Temarii Nadeaud sn* (Bescherelle, 1901). Mt. Aorai, over 1386 m, *Quayle 153a, 155, 157a, 159, 161, 697*; *Brown and Brown sn*; on rocks, *Whitney Expedition sn*, 1922; *Quayle 698, 700* (Bartram, 1933a). Paea District: Orofere Valley, *Setchell and Parks 5302*. Papeari District: Maara Valley, *Setchell and Parks 5315* (Brotherus, 1924a, NY).

MOOREA. Without locality: *Andersson sn*, 1851–1853 (Aongstrom, 1873, as *Cryphaea helictophylla*; 1876, NY); *Temarii Nadeaud sn*, 1899 (Bescherelle, 1901, NY).

Distribution.—Society Islands (Tahiti, Moorea), Rapa, Mangareva, Tubuai, Marquesas Islands.

This very common species is typical on tree branches in upper valleys on Tahiti and Moorea. Fleischer (1908, p. 770) reported that *Papillaria aongstromii* (*P. aongstromiana*) and *P. cuspidifera* (Tayl.) Jaeg. were vegetatively so similar that in the absence of sporophyte characters, *P. aongstroemii* might be considered a sub-

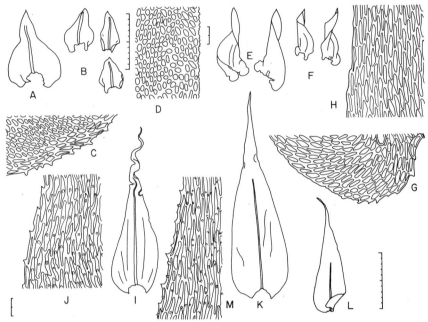

FIG. 68. A–D. *Papillaria aongstroemii.* (*Picquenot sn,* Tahiti.) A. Leaf. B.
Branch leaves. A, B, scale 1 mm. C. Leaf base, cells. D. Leaf, upper margin
cells. C, D, scale 20 μ. E–H. *Papillaria helictophylla.* (*Picquenot sn,* Tahiti.)
E. Leaves of stem. F. Branch leaves. E, F, scale 1 mm. G. Leaf base, cells.
H. Leaf, upper margin and median cells. G, H, scale 20 μ. I, J. *Aerobryopsis
longissima.* (*Miller 2160,* Hawaii.) I. Leaf, scale 1 mm. J. Leaf, upper margin
and median cells, scale 20 μ. K–M. *Floribundaria aeruginosa.* (*HOW 343.*)
K. Stem leaf. L. Branch leaf. K, L, scale 1 mm. M. Leaf, upper margin and
median cells, scale 20 μ. (*del.* HAM.)

species or variety of *P. cuspidifera*. Dixon (1927, p. 259) treated *P. cuspidifera* as a synonym of *P. crocea* (Hampe) Jaeg.

Although *Papillaria aongstroemii* stands provisionally, it may be synonymous with *P. crocea*, and the range of this Society Islands species would be expanded to include Indomalaya, Southeastern Asia, Australia, and New Zealand. *Papillaria crocea* has not been reported previously from the Society Islands.

2. *Papillaria helictophylla* (Montagne) Brotherus
   E. & P. Nat. Pfl. 1(3): 815. f. 608. 1906.
   Cryphaea helictophylla Mont., Ann. Sci. Nat. Bot. ser. 3, 4: 99. 1845.
   Pilotrichum helictophyllum (Mont.) C. Muell., Syn. 2: 174. 1851.
   Papillaria tahitensis Aongstr., Oefv. K. Svensk. Vet. Ak. Foerh. 30(5): 124. 1873.
   Meteorium helictophyllum (Mont.) Sull., U.S. Expl. Exped. Wilkes Musci, p. 22. 1859.
   Dendropogon helictophyllus (Mont.) Jaeg., Ber. S. Gall. Naturw. Ges. 1874–1875: 186. 1876.

Plants appear as tangled, pendent masses; leaves imbricated, pressed to the stem when dry, spreading when moist, with a cordate base, ovate-lanceolate, the apex long-acuminate, to 2.0 × 0.9–1.2 mm; costa ends about midleaf or a short distance above midleaf. Cells thick-walled, ovate-elongate, pluripapillose in the upper lamina, larger near the costa and toward the leaf base, smooth at the insertion. Sporophytes not found.

ILLUSTRATIONS. Fleischer (1908, 3: 758, f. 139, *P. fuscescens*), Brotherus (1924a, 2: 162, f. 554), Bartram (1939, p. 218, pl. 16, f. 269). Figure 68E–H.

TAHITI. Venus Point: *Lesson sn*, 1825. Without locality: Fruiting, *Hombron and Jacquinot sn*, 1837–1840 (Montagne, 1845, original description of *Cryphaea helictophylla*; Jardin, 1860, as *Cryphaea*; Jaeger and Sauerbeck, 1875, as *Dendropogonella*); *Du Petit-Thouars sn*, 1837–1839; *Vesco sn*; *Lépine sn*; frequent on trees on the summits of the island interior, *Jardin sn*, 1852–1855; *Vernier sn*; *Andersson sn*, 1851–1853 (Aongstrom, 1873, as *Papillaria tahitensis sp. nov.*; 1876, as *Cryphaea helictophylla*; Bescherelle, 1895a, as *Meteorium helictophyllum*); *Nadeaud sn*, 1896 (Bescherelle, 1898a, as *Meteorium*); *Larminat sn* (Potier de la Varde, 1912, as *Meteorium*). Papenoo District: Roadside beyond Papenoo River, *Setchell and Parks 5355* (Brotherus, 1924a); Papenoo Valley, 50 m, on tree trunks, *MacDaniels 1511* (Bartram, 1933a). Paea District: *Purau (Hibiscus)* swamp at about the 34 km stone, beyond the Maraa

Caves, *Setchell and Parks 5389*. Pirae District: Fautaua Valley, *Setchell and Parks 5427, 5430* (Brotherus, 1924a); *Quayle 76* (Bartram, 1933a), *Quayle 96*, unreported (BISH). Tautira: Vaita Valley, 250 m, on trunk with ferns, *MacDaniels 1656*, unreported (BISH).

MOOREA. Without locality: *Temarii Nadeaud sn*, 1898 (Bescherelle, 1901, as *Meteorium*); *Andersson sn*, 1851–1853 (Aongstrom, 1873, as *Papillaria tahitensis*; 1876, as *Cryphaea helictophylla*, NY).

RAIATEA. Highest mountain: W side, 800 m, on branch of tree in shade, *Moore 43*. Temehani Range: S end, 500 m, among other mosses on branches of shrubs, *Moore 46f* (Bartram, 1931).

Distribution.—Society Islands (Tahiti, Moorea, Raiatea), Marquesas Islands, New Caledonia, Futuna.

Fleischer (1908, 3: 761) treated *Papillaria helictophylla* as a species very closely related to *P. fuscescens*, differing from that species in its shorter and broader capsule exothecial cells and in other minor features. Further study may demonstrate that *P. helictophylla* is synonymous with *P. fuscescens*, extending considerably the range of this Society Islands species to include Indomalaya and Southeastern Asia.

Doubtful and excluded species

Papillaria intricata (Mitten) C. Mueller & Brotherus
  Abh. Naturw. Ver. Bremen 16: 505. 1900.
  Meteorium intricatum Mitt., J. Linn. Soc. Bot. 10: 171. f. 5A. 1868.

Paris (1905, 3: 228–29) noted that *Meteorium helictophyllum* cited in the Wilke's Expedition report (Sullivant, 1859) was a misdetermination by Sullivant for *M. intricatum*, but indicated by the use of a question mark (p. 229) an element of uncertainty. There are no other records for *Papillaria intricata* from the Society Islands, but its presence in Fiji and Samoa suggests the possibility that it may indeed be found there. Fleischer (1908, 3: 762) allied this species to *Papillaria semitorta* (C. Muell.) Jaeg., from Southeastern Asia and Indomalaya, which has leaves 1–2 mm long, lamina cells 18–32 × 3–4 μ, spores 25–30 μ, greenish, papillose.

Papillaria nigrescens (Hedwig) Jaeger
  Ber. S. Gall. Naturw. Ges. 1875–1876: 265. 1877.
  Hypnum nigrescens Sw. *ex* Hedw., Spec. Musc. 250. 65 f. 1–4. 1801.

Cryphaea nigrescens (Hedw.) Mont., Voy. Pole Sud Astrolabe et Zelee
Bot. 1: 324. 1845.
Pterogonium nigrescens (Hedw.) Sw.
Pterigynandrum nigrescens (Hedw.) Sw.

Bescherelle (1895a, p. 5) expressed the opinion that Montagne's
(1845) Cryphaea nigrescens was Papillaria andersoni, undoubtedly
a lapsus for P. aongstroemii under which he later (loc. cit. p. 36)
cites the specimens apparently seen by Montagne. Jardin (1860, p.
242) also reported Cryphaea nigrescens from collections by Pancher, Vieillard, and Deplanche, following Montagne's report. On
the basis of Bescherelle's observations of actual specimens, I exclude
P. nigrescens from the Society Islands moss flora. Since the distribution of this species includes both Old World and New World
tropics, further study might well show that the range of P. nigrescens does include the Society Islands.

2. Aerobryopsis Fleischer
Hedwigia 44: 304. 1905.

Aerobryopsis longissima (Dozy & Molkenboer) Fleischer
Hedwigia 44: 304. 1905.

Neckera longissima Dozy & Molk., Ann. Sci. Nat. Bot. ser. 3, 2: 313. 1844.
Meteorium longissimum (Dozy & Molk.) Dozy & Molk., Musci Fr. Ined.
Archip. Indici 6: 159. f. 48. 1848.
Meteorium lanosum Mitt., J. Linn. Soc. Bot. Suppl. 1: 90. 1859. fide
Fleischer, Hedwigia 44: 305. 1905.
Aerobryopsis vitiana (Sull.) Fleisch., Hedwigia 44: 306. 1905.
Aerobryum vitianum Sull., Proc. Am. Acad. Arts Sci. 3: 73. 1857. fide Jaeger,
Adumbr. 252. 1877.
Meteorium vitianum (Sull.) Sull., U.S. Expl. Exped. Wilkes Musci p. 22, f.
21A. 1859.

A large species, growing in loose and extensive masses. Stems
flexuose, pendulous, 6–8 in. (15–20 cm) long, variously divided;
branches distant, 1–3 in. (2.5–7.6 cm) long, simple or sparingly
ramulose. Leaves horizontal, loose, bifarious, from a broad cordate-
ovate base, lanceolate, filiformly attenuated, seriate from the base
to the apex; costa reaching halfway; texture thin and firm, composed
of minute, linear-fusiform cellules, each having a single central
papilla (Sullivant, 1859). No sporophytes are reported.

ILLUSTRATIONS. Brotherus (1924a, 2: 166, f. 557), Fleischer (1908,
3: 781, f. 142). Figure 68I, J.

TAHITI. Without locality: Vesco sn (Bescherelle, 1895a); "Vallée
de Puaa à Tearapau, sur les arbres vers 1100 mètres d'altitude, 309,
stérile," Nadeaud, 1896 (Bescherelle, 1898a, as Aerobryum vitia-

num). Mt. Orohena: 1400 m, on trees with *Lycopodium, Mac-Daniels 1472* (Bartram, 1933a).

MOOREA. Without locality: *Temarii Nadeaud sn* (Bescherelle, 1901, as *Aerobryum vitianum*).

Distribution.—Society Islands (Tahiti, Moorea), Samoa, Fiji, Tonga, New Caledonia, New Guinea, Java, Sri Lanka (Ceylon), Solomon Islands, Hongkong, Philippine Islands, China, Malay Peninsula, India, Himalaya, Caroline Islands (Ponape, Kusaie), Central and South America.

Sullivant (1859) recognized a similarity between *Meteorium vitianum* and *M. longissimum* in his comment: "resembles *Meteorium longissimum* . . . but the leaves of that species are undulate on the margins, have a shorter acumination, and are not papillose." In Fleischer's (1905, p. 304) new genus *Aerobryopsis*, the species *A. longissima* is illustrated with lamina cells which have a single papilla over the lumen, a characteristic which is also illustrated for *A. longissima* var. *dozyana* by Fleischer (1908, 3: 781, f. 142). Mitten (1868, p. 171) wrote: "*Meteorium vitianum* is probably identical with this species [*A. lanosum*]; for, notwithstanding Sullivant's remark that in *Aerobryum longissimum* there are no papillae, I find them present in authentic specimens of that moss as well as in the Samoan specimens; and they in each arise from the middle of the cell." Jaeger and Sauerbeck (1877, p. 252) cited Sullivant's species as a synonym of *Aerobryum lanosum* Mitten.

3. *Floribundaria* Fleischer
  Hedwigia 44: 301. 1905.
Floribundaria aeruginosa (Mitten) Fleischer
  Hedwigia 44: 303. 1905.

> *Meteorium aeruginosum* Mitt., J. Linn. Soc. Bot. 10: 171. 5 B. 1868.
> *Papillaria aeruginosa* (Mitt.) Jaeg., Ber. S. Gall. Naturw. Ges. 1875–1876: 263. 1877.
> *Meteorium floribundum* Sull., 1859, *non* Dozy & Molkenboer. *fide* Paris, Index 3: 350. 1905.

Common on twigs and branches in upper valley forests. The delicate slender stems branch irregularly to form loose, tangled wefts which are pale to yellow-green. Stem leaves erect, ovate-lanceolate, about 1 mm long; costa faint, extending to about midleaf; margins serrulate. Cells of the lamina linear, 30–60 × 2–3 μ, finely seriate-papillose. Sporophytes not found in Society Islands collections.

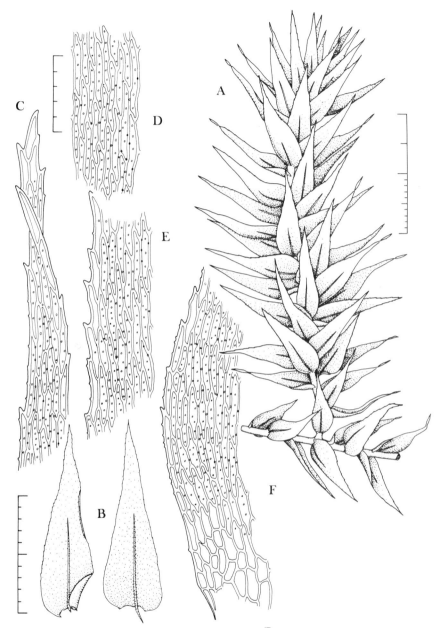

Fɪɢ. 69. *Floribundaria aeruginosa.* (*HOW 2528.*) A. Habit, scale 2 mm. B. Leaves, scale 1 mm. C. Leaf apex. D. Leaf, upper median cells. E. Leaf, upper margin. F. Leaf base, margin and alar cells. C–F, scale 50 µ.

ILLUSTRATIONS. Mitten (1868, 5B), Fleischer (1908, 3: 817, f. 146, *F. floribunda*). Figure 69.

TAHITI. Without locality: *Vernier sn* (Bescherelle, 1895a, as *Papillaria*); 800–1000 m, N side of Tahiti, *Nadeaud 305–308* (Bescherelle, 1898a, as *Papillaria*). Haapape District: Rahi, to 800 m; Miaa, 850 m, *Temarii Nadeaud sn*. Pirae District: Fautaua Valley, *Temarii Nadeaud sn* (Bescherelle, 1901, as *Papillaria*); *Larminat sn* (Potier de la Varde, 1912); *Quayle 213* (Bartram, 1933a).

RAIATEA. Faaroa Bay: N side, 400 m, on mountainside on old *farapepe, Moore 68* (Bartram, 1931).

Distribution.—Society Islands (Tahiti, Raiatea), Samoa (Manua, Upolu), Fiji.

Following the original description of *Meteorium aeruginosum*, Mitten (1868) wrote: "Branches very slender. Foliage, in the young state, pale aeruginous green without gloss; when older, of a pale brown. From *M. floribundum* . . . this species differs in its more compressed divergent foliage, and in the teeth of its external peristome being divided to the mouth of the capsule, and not exserted on a combined base." Fleischer (1908) treated *Floribundaria aeruginosa* as allied to *F. floribunda*, which has a broad distribution in the tropical regions of the world, and which he considered to be polymorphic. In the unusual peristome development, Fleischer found a parallel in the West African species *F. cameruniae*, but noted that it differed vegetatively from *F. aeruginosa*.

XXIII. PHYLLOGONIACEAE

Orthorrhynchium Reichardt
Verh. Zool. Bot. Ges. Wien 18: 115. 1868.
Orthorrhynchium cylindricum (Lindberg) Brotherus
E. & P. Nat. Pfl. 1(3): 835. 1906.

Phyllogonium cylindricum Lindb., Oefv. K. Svensk. Vet. Ak. Foerh. 21: 603. 1864.
Phyllogonium angustifolium Schimp. *ex* Mitt., *in* Seemann, Fl. Vit. 396. 1873. *fide* Mitten, J. Linn. Soc. Bot. 10: 187. 1868. *cf.* Index Muscorum 4: 53. 1967.
Phyllogonium cryptocarpon Schimp., *in* Jardin, Bull. Soc. Linn. Normandie ser. 2, 9: 267. 1875. *cf.* C. Mueller, J. Mus. Godeffroy 3(6): 69. 1873.
Phyllogonium neckeraceum Schimp., *in* Paris, Ind. Bryol. ed. 2. 3: 388. 1905. *nom. nud. in synon. fide* Paris, 1905.
Cryptogonium cylindricum Lindb. *ex* Par., Ind. Bryol. 293. 1894. *err. cit. pro Phyllogonium, cf.* Index Muscorum 2: 520. 1959.
Hypnum novarae Reichdt., Hedwigia 7: 190. 1868. *cf.* Bescherelle, Ann. Sci. Nat. Bot. ser. 7, 20: 54. 1895.

Primary stems prostrate, nearly leafless, secondary stems erect, 4–8 cm long, unbranched to irregularly branched, the branches usually in one plane. Secondary stems and branches 3–4 mm wide, with leaves. Leaves complanate, erect-spreading at an angle between 22° and 45° to the stem, 1.3–1.6 × 0.7–0.9 mm, oblong, abruptly pointed, ecostate, the margins entire; perichaetial leaves to 5 mm long, the apex long-acuminate, the margins minutely denticulate. Cells of the lamina linear, 35–55 × 4–5 μ in the upper leaf, smooth-walled, shorter toward the leaf apex and toward the leaf base; the alar cells undifferentiated but more nearly quadrate, the basal row of cells dark-colored. Sporophytes rare; seta short, to about 0.5 mm; capsule cylindric, to 2.5 × 0.4–0.5 mm; peristome single, the teeth short, blunt, extending to about 65 μ above the rim (according to Bartram, 1933b); operculum conic, apiculate; calyptra with papillae, a few long, erect hairs, slightly lobed at the base.

ILLUSTRATIONS. Bartram (1933b, 175, f. 129). Figure 70A, B.

TAHITI. Without locality: *S. B. Ponten sn*, 1852, *Eugenie* Expedition (Lindberg, 1864, type, as *Phyllogonium*); *Dumont d'Urville sn*, 1825; *Ponten sn*; *Andersson sn* (NY); *Jelinek sn*; *Larminat sn* (Po-

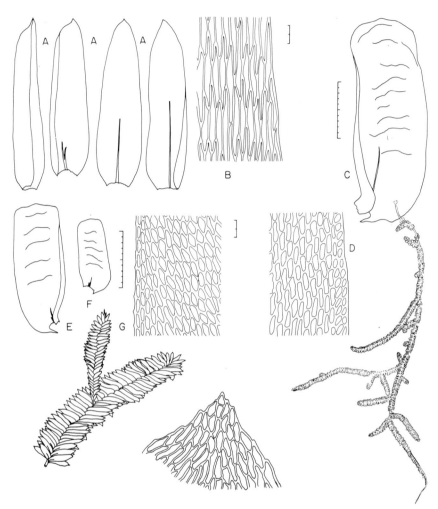

Fig. 70. A, B. *Orthorrhynchium cylindricum*. (*HOW 3395.*) A. Leaves, scale 1 mm. B. Leaf, upper margin and median cells, scale 20 μ. Unlabelled: Left, habit sketch, scale 1 mm. Center, leaf apex, scale 20 μ. C, D. *Neckeropsis lepineana*. C. Leaf, scale 1 mm. D. Leaf, upper margin and median cells, scale 20 μ. Unlabelled: Right, habit sketch, scale 1 mm. E–G. *Himanthocladium cyclophyllum*. (*HOW 3462.*) E. Leaf. F. Branch leaf. E, F, scale 1 mm. G. Upper leaf margin and median cells, scale 20 μ. (*del.* HAM.)

tier de la Varde, 1912); Papeete, *Savatier 1092, 740* (Bescherelle, 1895a, as *Phyllogonium*); common on trees and rocks, rarely in fruit, *Nadeaud 326–329* (Bescherelle, 1898a, as *Phyllogonium*). Haapape District: Rahi, 800 m, *Temarii Nadeaud sn* (Bescherelle, 1901, as *Phyllogonium*). Pirae District: Fautaua Valley, *Jelinek sn, Novara* Expedition (Reichardt, 1868b, as *Hypnum novarae*); *Setchell and Parks 5084* (Brotherus, 1924a, NY, BISH).

MOOREA. Without locality: *Temarii Nadeaud sn*, 1899 (Bescherelle, 1901, as *Phyllogonium*); on trunks in humid forest, *Eriksson 70* (Bartram, 1950b). Paopao Bay: Mt. Matanui, lower slopes, on bark, with *Calymperes hyophilaceum* and *Bazzania, 3395, 3397;* 10–30 m, on bark of mapé, *Inocarpus edulis, 3410.* Mt. Rotui: Between Paopao and Papetoai bays, 10–50 m, on bark, with *Calymperes* and a fern, *Trichomanes omphalodes, 3439.*

Distribution.—Society Islands (Tahiti, Moorea), Marquesas Islands (Nuku Hiva), Hawaii (?), Samoa (Tutuila; Upolu, type locality for *Phyllogonium angustifolium*), Fiji (Viti Levu, Ovalau), Cook Islands (Rarotonga), Mangareva, Austral Islands (Raivavae), Tonga (Eua), New Hebrides, Futuna, Tubuai, Loyalty Islands, New Caledonia.

The only other species with which *Orthorrhynchium cylindricum* might be confused is *O. elegans* (Hook. f. & Wils.) Reich., from New Zealand and Australia, which differs in having much smaller, more obtuse leaves (1.0–1.25 mm), which are more widely diverging, commonly at an angle of 45° to the stem. Lamina cells are slightly larger in *O. elegans,* up to 60 μ long, and the sporophyte has a seta which Sainsbury (1955) has reported as being 2 mm long, the capsule turbinate and wide-mouthed, a marked distinction between the two species.

XXIV. NECKERACEAE

The family Neckeraceae is represented in the Society Islands by four genera: *Neckeropsis, Himanthocladium, Homaliodendron,* and *Pinnatella*. The genus *Calyptothecium*, placed in the Neckeraceae by Bartram, Brotherus, Fleischer, and Dixon, is treated as a member of the closely related family Pterobryaceae, following the evaluation of Noguchi (1965), who found this classification best on the basis of both gametophytic and sporophytic characters.

Plants of the Society Islands taxa are usually horizontally erect, less frequently slightly or wholly pendulous or creeping, and are common on exposed bark or rock. Branching typically is in one plane, and the leaves may be strictly complanate or only slightly so, commonly transversely undulate and with a weak costa.

KEY TO GENERA OF THE NECKERACEAE

1. Plants frondose, pinnately branched; costa ends in leaf apex____4. *Pinnatella*.
1. Plants erect to pendulous, irregularly branched; costa ends in midleaf
    2. Leaves in 8 rows, compressed in one plane, nearly complanate, costa strong, single_____2. *Himanthocladium*.
    2. Leaves in 4 rows, strictly complanate, costa faint
        3. Leafy stems slender, variable in width, to 3 mm, often flagelliform at tips; leaves plane, not undulate, obovate, leaf apices broadly rounded_____3. *Homaliodendron*.
        3. Leafy stems uniformly wide, 3–6 mm, not flagelliform at tips; leaves undulate, leaf apices truncate_____1. *Neckeropsis*.

1. *Neckeropsis* Reichardt
Verh. Zool. Bot. Ges. Wien 18: 191. 1868.

Neckeropsis lepineana (Montagne) Fleischer
Musci Fl. Buitenzorg 3: 879. 1908.

Neckera lepineana Mont., Ann. Sci. Nat. Bot. ser. 3, 10: 107. 1848.
Neckera undulata Mont., *non* Hedwig, Voy. au Pole Sud, Crypt. p. 318.
    1845. *fide* Montagne, Sylloge p. 23, 1856, and 1848; also Touw, 1962.
Neckera comorae C. Muell., Linnaea 268. 1876. *fide* Fleischer, 1908.
Neckera crinita Mitt., 1859, *non* Griff. *fide* Touw, 1962.

Plants yellow-green, erect to suberect on rocks and tree trunks, irregularly branched, 10–15 cm long (to 30 cm in Indomalayan and Philippine Islands specimens, Bartram, 1939), and 3–6 mm wide, uniform in width. Leaves asymmetrical, ligulate to lingulate; apices truncate, 2.5–3.0 × 0.8–1.0 mm; costa absent or short and double, single to forked, the forks unequal, reaching to midleaf. Cells of the lamina 15–30 × 4–6 μ, irregularly thick-walled, smooth, slightly pitted at midleaf, longer, more strongly pitted toward the leaf base. Sporophytes not present in my collections.

ILLUSTRATIONS. Touw (1962, pp. 384, 390), Fleischer (1908, 3: 881, f. 155), Bartram (1939, pl. 18, f. 297). Figure 70C, D.

TAHITI. Without locality: *Lépine sn* (Montagne, 1845, as *Neckera undulata*; 1848, as *N. lepineana*; 1856a); *Jacquinot sn* (Montagne, 1845); *Wilkes 174* (Sullivant, 1859, as *Neckera*); *Andersson sn* (Aongstrom, 1873, as *Neckera*; Bescherelle, 1895a); *Jelinek sn* (BM, G); *Picquenot sn* (BM, G, M; Bescherelle, 1901); *Du Petit-Thouars sn*; *Vesco sn* (BM); *Vernier sn* (BM); Papeete, *Savatier 740, 1037* (Bescherelle, 1895a); *Savatu 1037* (BM); *Bailey sn* (NY); *Poutin sn* (BM); *Brown and Brown* (Touw, 1962; BISH). Taiarapu Peninsula: Frequent on branches of *Cyrtandra*, *Nadeaud 73* (Bescherelle, 1898a); Haavini Valley, with *Ctenidium stellulatum* and *Hypopterygium, 2525*; with *Floribundaria aeruginosa* on *Inocarpus edulis* trunk, *2611*; *2654*. Haapape District: Rahi, 800 m, *Nadeaud sn* (Bescherelle, 1901). Papara District: With *Calyptothecium urvilleanum* and *Papillaria helictophylla*, *Tilden 27*. Paea District: Papehue River Valley, *Tilden 344* (BISH, BM, FH, US). Pirae District: NW ridge of Mt. Aorai in shady ravine by trail, 1232 m, hanging from rocks and tree trunks, *Setchell and Parks 5135* (Brotherus, 1924a; BISH, BM, FH, US); Fautaua Valley, common at 240 m, on rocks and tree bark, with *Racopilum* and *Dumortiera, 2068*; *2063*; *2071*; on rocks next to stream, with *Pinnatella keuhliana* and *Racopilum, 2073*; with *Ectropothecium sodale* on wet rocks and on *Hibiscus tiliaceus* bark, *2095*; 240 m, *2346*; *2348*; with *Bryum billardieri*, *Fissidens mangarevensis*, *Pinnatella keuhliana*, *Hypopterygium*, *Ectropothecium*, *Trichosteleum*, and *Bazzania, 3121*; *3147*; 300 m, with orchid, *3187*; Fare Rau Ape–Mt. Aorai trail, *2661*; 918 m, with *Symphysodontella cylindracea, 2664*; *317, 341, 365* (1960); 1000 m, about 100 m above first shelter along trail, with *Calyptothecium urvilleanum*, *Symphysodontella cylindracea*, *Metzgeria*, *Lopholejeunea*, and *Lejeunea, 2840*; with *Ectropothecium, 2917*.

MOOREA. Paopao Bay: Haring Plantation, *3402*; Paopao and Papetoai bays, 125 m, on *Inocarpus* bark, *3462*.

RAIATEA. Temehani Range: S end, 500 m, among other mosses on shrub branches, *Moore 46g* (Bartram, 1931). Without locality: *Sibbald sn* (Touw, 1962).

Distribution.—Society Islands (Tahiti; Moorea, a new record; Raiatea), Mangareva, Rapa, Tubuai, Raivavae, Hawaii (Kauai, Maui, Oahu), Cook Islands (Rarotonga, Tonga), Samoa (Savaii, Upolu, Apia, Tutuila), Fiji (Viti Levu, Ovalau, Vanua Levu, Taveuni, Vanua Mbalavu, Naviti, Nadarivatu), New Hebrides (Tana, Futuna, Aneityum), New Caledonia, Loyalty Islands (Lifu, Mare), Caroline Islands (Palau, Koror), Mariana Islands (Guam, Saipan), Australia (Queensland, Brisbane), New Guinea, Moluccas (Morotai, Halmaheira, Buru, Kapalamadang, Ceram), Celebes (north and southwest peninsulas), Philippine Islands (Mindoro, Puerto Galera, Luzon, Bataan, Baguio, Ifuagao, Bajaran, Rizal, Laguna, Montalban, etc.), Borneo (Sarawak, North Borneo, Timbun Mata Island, inc. Mt. Kinabalu), Lesser Sunda Islands (Sumbawa, East Timor), Christmas Island, Java (East and West Java), Sumatra, Malay Archipelago (Malay Peninsula, Perak, Kelantan, Selangor, Pulau Penang), Thailand, China, India, Sri Lanka (Ceylon), Mauritius, Malagasy Republic (Madagascar), Comoro Archipelago (Johanna, Mayotte), South Africa (Cape of Good Hope), Tanganyika (Bukoba, Ugombe, Usambara), Uganda (Cameroun), Nicobar Islands, Gambier Archipelago.

Himanthocladium is linked to *Neckeropsis* by transitional forms, (Touw, 1962), the genus *Homaliodendron* related to *Neckeropsis* as plants with fan-like, pinnate stems and glossy, complanate leaves, with the boundaries between the two genera in some cases difficult to define. Touw observed that the greatest concentration of species of *Neckeropsis* occurs in northeast India and the southeast Asiatic peninsula, where, in addition to *N. lepineana*, eight other species have been found. The genus is circumtropical, with *Neckeropsis lepineana* pan-palaeotropical, more common in Malaysia and the Pacific than in Africa and on the Asian continent. Touw found the absence of this species from southwest India to be remarkable, since it could reasonably be expected there, and he commented further that other species with similar ecology are present in its place. In Japan, for example, *N. lepineana* is not found, but in the proper habitats, *N. calcicola* and *N. obtusata* are present.

2. *Himanthocladium* (Mitten) Fleischer
Musci Fl. Buitenzorg 3: 883. 1908.

Key to Species of *Himanthocladium*

1. Leaves in dorsal and ventral series............................1. *H. cyclophyllum.*
1. Leaves all arranged laterally, without dorsal and ventral series.....................
....2. *H. implanum.*

1. *Himanthocladium cyclophyllum* (C. Mueller) Fleischer
Musci Fl. Buitenzorg 3: 887. 1908.

Neckera cyclophylla C. Muell., Syn. 2: 664. 1851.
Neckera rufula C. Muell., *in* Geheeb, Bibl. Bot. 44: 20. 1898. *nom. nud.*
Neckera warburgii Broth., Monsunia 1: 49. 1900. *fide* Bartram, 1939.
Neckera implana Besch., 1898a, *non* Mitten. *fide* Fleischer, 1908.

Plants arising from a prostrate, often leafless rhizome, the erect portions irregularly pinnately branched, yellow-green, slightly glossy, to 10 cm long; leaves flattened, arising in dorsal and ventral lateral rows, complanate, transversely undulate, to 2.5 × 1.0 mm, asymmetrical, smaller on flagelliform branches or on ultimate branches, narrowly lingulate, broadly rounded or truncate at the apex, short-pointed, margins serrulate becoming denticulate near the apex. Cells of the upper lamina oval, obliquely elongate, thick-walled, 25–35 × 5–7 μ, smooth. Costa single or short, double, the branches unequal. Sporophytes not observed. Bartram (1939, p. 241) described sporophytes with the seta 1.5–2 mm long, slightly curved, smooth, the capsule exserted, cylindric, erect, the urn 1.5 mm long, peristome teeth narrow, minutely papillose, the segments of endostome from a low basal membrane.

ILLUSTRATIONS. Bartram (1939, pl. 18, f. 301). Figure 70E–G.

TAHITI. Without locality: *Nadeaud 337* (Bescherelle, 1898a, as *Neckera implana, fide* Fleischer, 1908).

MOOREA. Without locality: *Temarii Nadeaud sn*, previously unreported (BISH, as *H. implanum*, det. Bescherelle). Mt. Rotui: 125 m, on *Inocarpus* bark, *3462.*

Distribution.—Society Islands (Tahiti; Moorea, a new record), Java, Celebes, New Guinea.

Fleischer (1908) reviewed the genus *Himanthocladium* and treated Bescherelle's specimen identified as *H. implanum* under *H. cyclophyllum.* Although Bescherelle (1898a) also reported *H. graeffeana* from Tahiti, Fleischer continued to give only Fiji for its distribution; for *H. implanum*, he gave only Samoa. Furthermore, Fleischer related the former to *H. flaccidum* (C. Muell.) Fleisch., the latter, to *H. loriforme* (Bosch & Lac.) Fleisch. Dixon and Greenwood (1930) wrote: "Much confusion has arisen in this genus (*Himanthocladium*) owing to Mitten having described his *Neckera implana* as dioicous, whereas it is actually synoicous. *N. graeffeana* is quite identical with Mitten's plant." Bartram (1939, p. 243) wrote of *H. loriforme*, "This species is uncomfortably close to *H. cyclophyllum* which occasionally shows some of the branches just as complanate as in *H. loriforme*. I can find no consistent distinctions in the leaf cells or in the dentation of the apex, and I doubt if the difference in the leaf outline is consistent enough to be reliable."

The existing confusion shows a general recognition of the variability which characterizes *Neckeropsis* and *Himanthocladium*, and which can only be resolved by further monographic studies as those already initiated by Touw.

2. *Himanthocladium implanum* (Mitten) Fleischer
Musci Fl. Buitenzorg 3: 886. 1907.

Neckera implana Mitt., J. Linn. Soc. Bot. 10: 169. 1868.
Neckera graeffeana C. Muell., J. Mus. Godeffroy 5. 1873. *fide* Dixon & Greenwood, Proc. Linn. Soc. N. S. Wales 55: 286. 1930.
Himanthocladium graeffeanum (C. Muell.) Fleisch., Musci Fl. Buitenzorg 3: 889. 1908.

Mitten's original description for *Neckera implana* (1868, p. 169):

Dioica; rami ramulis dispersis subplumaeformes, pinnati; folia complanata, lateralia, patentia, ligulata, obtusa, angulo parvo apicali, laevia, plana, nervo crassiusculo infra apicem evanido, marginibus apice minute crenulatis, cellulis apicalibus parvis ovali-rotundis, inferioribus sensim longioribus angustis; folia ramosa conformis, rarius subundulata; perichaetialia parva, a basi convoluta sub-rotunda subulata patentia, apicibus subserrulatis, enervia; theca ovali-cylindracea, in peunculo aequilongo, operculo conico curvirostrato; peristomium dentibus processibusque angustis obscuriusculis minute punctulatis linea media notatis.

This very nearly resembles *Neckera loriformis*, Bryol. Javanica, t. 183; but the leaves are wider and flat.

ILLUSTRATIONS. None.

TAHITI. Mountains of Hitiaa and Faaiti: At foot of Mt. Aorai, *Nadeaud 336* (Bescherelle, 1898a, as *Neckera graeffeana* var. *tahitensis*). Haapape District: Rahi Valley, 800 m, *Temarii Nadeaud sn* (Bescherelle, 1901, as *N. graeffeana*).

Distribution.—Society Islands (Tahiti?), Rapa, Samoa, Fiji. The Society Islands collections are probably best included under *Himanthocladium cyclophyllum.*

3. *Homaliodendron* Fleischer
Hedwigia 45: 72. 1906.
Homaliodendron exiguum (Bosch & Lacoste) Fleischer
Musci Fl. Buitenzorg 3: 897. 1908.

Homalia exigua Bosch & Lac., Bryol. Jav. 2: 55. t. 175. 1863.
Homalia pseudo-exigua Besch., Ann. Sci. Nat. Bot. ser. 7, 20: 42. 1895.
Thamnium exiguum (Bosch & Lac.) Kindb., Hedwigia 41: 240. 1901.
Homalia bibrachiata Geheeb, Bibl. Bot. 13: 6. 1889. *fide* Fleischer, 1908.
?Hypnum bibrachiatum C. Muell., *in* Engler, Bot. Jahrb. 86. 1883. *fide*
Fleischer, 1908.
?Neckera semperiana Hampe mss., C. Muell., *in* Bot. Zeit. 20: 381. 1862.
fide Bartram, p. 244. 1939.
Neckeropsis pseudonitidula Okamura. *fide* Touw, p. 420. 1962.

Plants slender, pale green; stems variable in length and width, to 3–4 cm long, prostrate to suberect, to about 3 mm wide. Leaves obovate, complanate, spreading laterally, the leaf apex broadly rounded, 1.0–1.5 × 0.7–0.8 mm; costa ends near midleaf. Cells of the lamina 10–15 × 5–8 μ, ovoid-elongate, smooth, irregularly thick-walled in the upper blade, longer toward the leaf base. Branch leaves smaller. Sporophytes not found in Society Islands collections.

ILLUSTRATIONS. Dozy and Molkenboer (1863, 2: t. 175), Fleischer (1908, 3: 899, f. 156). Figure 71.

TAHITI. Without locality: *Andersson sn,* 1852 (Aongstrom, 1872, as *Omalia exigua*; Bescherelle, 1895a, as *Homalia pseudo-exigua*; Kindberg, 1902, as *Thamnium exiguum*); associated with *Neckeropsis lepineana, Lépine sn* (Bescherelle, 1895a). Tahiti nui: N side, 800–1100 m, general localities, *Nadeaud 341, 342,* 1896 (Bescherelle, 1898a, as *Homalia pseudo-exigua*); *Larminat sn,* 1911 (Potier de la Varde, 1912). Papenoo District: Papenoo River Valley, associated with *Fissidens mangarevensis* and *Plagiochila, 3061.* Pirae District: Fautaua Valley, about 200 m, *2083*; with *Papillaria, Plagiochila,* and *Calymperes tahitense, 3151; 3125.*

MOOREA. Mt. Matanui: Lower slopes, 200 m, above Haring Plantation, on rock, with *Calymperes tahitense, Fissidens mangarevensis, 3415.* Mt. Rotui: S side, below 200 m, between Paopao and Papetoai bays, *3438.*

Distribution.—Society Islands (Tahiti; Moorea, a new record), New Guinea, Mascarene Islands, Himalayas, Assam, Sri Lanka

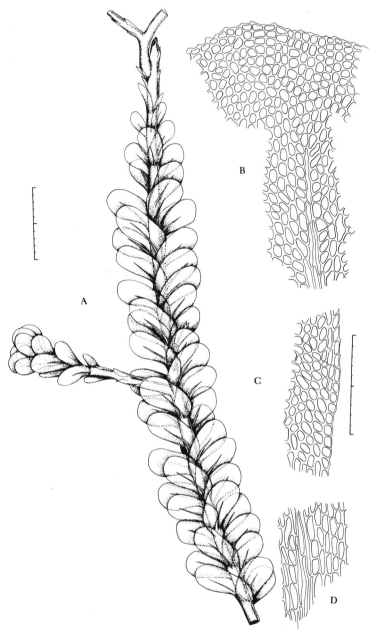

FIG. 71. *Homaliodendron exiguum.* (*HOW 3121.*) A. Plant habit, scale 1 mm.
B. Leaf apex and upper costa cells. C. Leaf, upper margin cells. D. Leaf,
upper median cells. B–D, scale 100 μ.

(Ceylon), Tonkin, Malaya, Formosa, Sumatra, Java, Borneo, Cele-bes, Philippine Islands, Australia (Queensland), New Caledonia, Isle de France, Bourbon, Malacca, Fiji (Vanua Levu), Okinawa, Ryukyu, Japan (Kyushu, Shikoku). The slender habit, flagelliform branches, obovate-spathulate leaves, and the strictly complanate arrangement of the leaves are characteristic of *Homaliodendron exiguum*. It is much more com-mon than the above records indicate, and appears frequently in mixtures with other bryophytes collected in the humid forests.

Excluded species

Homaliodendron flabellatum (Smith) Fleischer
Hedwigia 45: 74. f. 134. 1906.
 Neckera australasica C. Muell., Syn. 2: 42. 1850. *fide* Dixon and Green-
  wood, Proc. Linn. Soc. N. S. Wales 55: 286. 1930.

This species is provisionally listed on the basis of Nadeaud's (1873) report of *Neckera australasica*. Bescherelle (1895a) was unable to verify Nadeaud's determination and I have not yet ex-amined the original collection, which may have been lost. I am familiar with *Homaliodendron flabellatum* as it appears in the Hawaiian Islands, and would have recognized it on sight in the Society Islands had it been encountered. Nadeaud was himself not convinced that his collection from Papeiha was properly the same plant as described by Mueller, and it may be that what Nadeaud described in Latin was in reality a species of *Pinnatella*.

The wide distribution of *Homaliodendron flabellatum* is such that its presence in the Society Islands would pose no great surprise, but for the moment, this species of *Homaliodendron* must be excluded from the flora.

4. *Pinnatella* (C. Mueller) Fleischer
Hedwigia 45: 80. 1906.
Pinnatella kuehliana (Bosch & Lacoste) Fleischer
Hedwigia 45: 80. 1906.
 Thamnium kuehliana Bosch & Lac., Bryol. Jav. 2: 71. t. 189. 1863.
 Porotrichum kuhlianum Bosch & Lac., Bryol. Jav. 2: 71. 1863.
 Thamnium laxum Bosch & Lac., Bryol. Jav. 2: 72. 1863. *fide* Fleischer,
  Hedwigia 45: 53. 1906.
 Porotrichum elegantissimum Mitt., J. Linn. Soc. Bot. 10: 187. 1868.
 Hypnum elegantissimum (Mitt.) C. Muell., J. Mus. Godeffroy 3(6): 90.
  1873.

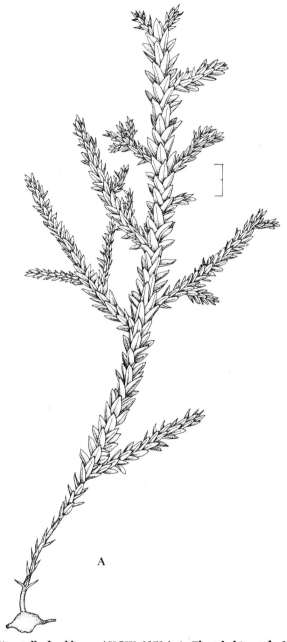

A

FIG. 72. *Pinnatella kuehliana.* (*HOW 3152.*) A. Plant habit, scale 1 mm.

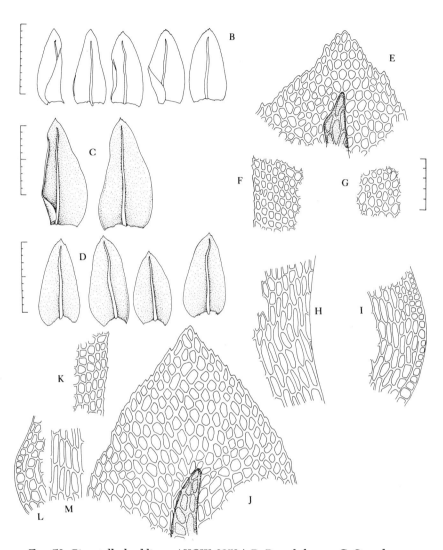

FIG. 73. *Pinnatella kuehliana.* (*HOW 3152.*) B. Branch leaves. C. Stem leaves. D. Branch leaves. B–D, scale 1 mm. E. Leaf apex cells, branch leaf, scale 50 μ. F. Leaf, margin cells. G. Leaf, upper median cells. H. Leaf, basal cells adjacent costa. I. Branch leaf, base margin cells. J. Stem leaf, apex cells. K. Stem leaf, margin cells. L. Stem leaf, basal cells. M. Stem leaf, basal cells (adjacent costa). F–M, scale 50 μ.

Plants yellow-green, frondose above a prostrate primary stem, the erect branch system 3–5 cm tall, branching pinnate, in one plane; leaves ovate-lingulate, abruptly acuminate, 1.0–1.5 × 0.7–0.9 mm; costa ends in the upper leaf about 6–12 cells below the apex. Cells of the lamina smooth, irregularly thick-walled, irregularly quadrate to hexagonal, slightly elongate, 10–15 × 7–10 μ, longer toward the leaf base. Sporophytes not examined. Fleischer (1908, 3: 921) reported sporophytes to be unknown.

ILLUSTRATIONS. Dozy and Molkenboer (1863, 2: t. 189, as *Porotrichum*). Figures 72, 73.

TAHITI. Without locality: Associated with *Papillaria, Homaliodendron exiguum,* and *Floribundaria aeruginosa, Larminat sn,* 1911 (Potier de la Varde, 1912, as *Pinnatella elegantissima*); throughout the interior of the island, especially in the Puaa, Tamarua, and the Tipaearui valleys, in the mountains of Hitiaa, of Faaiti, and at the foot of Mt. Aorai, sterile, *Nadeaud 339* (Bescherelle, 1895a, as *Porotrichum elegantissimum*). Pirae District: Fautaua Valley, 300 m, *2367;* 480 m, with *Ectropothecium sodale, 3041;* with *Homaliodendron exiguum, Fissidens mangarevensis,* and *Porella, 3061;* above third ford above Cascade de Fautaua, with *Calyptothecium urvilleanum, Calymperes tahitense, Fissidens mangarevensis,* and *Neckeropsis lepineana, 3157.*

Distribution.—Society Islands (Tahiti), Fiji, Samoa, New Guinea, Celebes, Ceram, Java, Sumatra, Philippine Islands, New Caledonia, d'Entrecasteaux.

The frondose habit, leaves stiff, pressed against the stems, the costa ending in the upper lamina, are characteristic of *Pinnatella.*

XXV. PILOTRICHACEAE

Following Miller's (1971) review of the Hookeriales, it is appropriate to place the genus *Chaetomitrium* in the family Pilotrichaceae.

Chaetomitrium Dozy & Molkenboer
Musci Fr. Ined. Archip. Indici 117. 1846.
Chaetomitrium tahitense (Sullivant) Mitten
in Seemann, Fl. Vit. 292. 1871.

> *Hookeria tahitense* Sull., Proc. Am. Acad. Arts Sci. 3: 79. 1857.
> *Hookeria deplanchei* C. Muell., *in* Fleischer, Hedwigia 63: 215. 1922.
> *Holoblepharum tahitense* (Sull.) Sull., U.S. Expl. Exped. Wilkes Musci 22. f. 23b. 1859.
> *Holoblepharum deplanchei* Duby, *in* Besch., Ann. Sci. Nat. Bot. ser. 5, 18: 227. 1873.
> *Chaetomitrium deplanchei* (Besch.) Jaeg., Ber. S. Gall. Naturw. Ges. 1875–1876: 369. 1877.

Plants prostrate, 4–5 cm long, with short lateral branches; leaves slightly complanate, 1.3–1.6 × 0.55 mm, ovate-lanceolate, from short- to long-acuminate, the upper margins denticulate; costa short, double, faint, ending in the lower one-quarter to one-third of the leaf. Cells of the lamina thin-walled, linear, 50–60 × 3–5 μ in the upper leaf, slightly larger below, unipapillose, the papilla formed by the projecting cell end wall. No sporophytes were seen, but Sullivant (1859) described the capsule as oblong-cylindric, the mouth oblique, exostome teeth linear-lanceolate, attenuated, very closely articulated, with a narrow median line, prominently lamellose on the interior face; cilia of the inner peristome linear, carinate, imperforate, arising from a narrow membrane, the ciliolae rudimentary. In Sullivant's specimen, the operculum was as long as the capsule, subulate-rostrate, from a subconic base. The calyptra he described as elongated mitriform, densely hispid, with erect, simple or jointed hairs, and ciliate at the base, the basal hairs dentate.

ILLUSTRATIONS. Sullivant (1859, pl. 23b). Figure 74A–D.

TAHITI. Mountains of Tahiti: *Wilkes sn* (Sullivant, 1854, as *Hookeria*; 1859, as *Holoblepharum*; Bescherelle, 1895a). Miaa: 850 m, *Temarii Nadeaud sn* (Bescherelle, 1901). Taiarapu Peninsula:

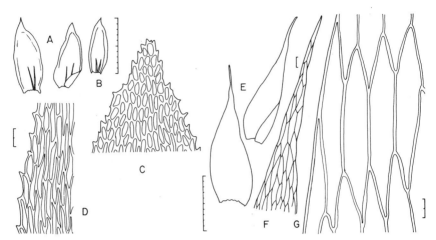

FIG. 74. A–D. *Chaetomitrium tahitense.* (*Hürlimann T 1207.*) A. Stem leaves.
B. Branch leaf. A, B, scale 1 mm. C. Leaf apices. D. Leaf, upper margin and
cells. C, D, scale 20 μ. E–G. *Leucomium aneurodictyon.* (*HOW 2667.*) E.
Leaves, scale 1 mm. F. Leaf apex, scale 50 μ. G. Leaf, upper margin and cells,
scale 20 μ. (*del.* HAM.)

Taravao, above experiment station, 500 m, prostrate on tree trunk, *Hürlimann T 1207* (Hürlimann, 1963, FH).

Distribution.—Society Islands (Tahiti), New Caledonia, Australia (north Queensland), New Guinea (Papua), New Hebrides.

I have not seen Sullivant's original specimen from Tahiti, and was unable to locate it in the U.S. National Herbarium, but have examined a specimen determined by Dixon (16 June 1919, NY) which he observed compared well with the type he studied at the same time.

Dixon (1919) was right in considering *Chaetomitrium deplanchei* and *C. tahitense* to be synonymous, but he became involved with nomenclatural priority in recognizing *C. tahitense* as a variety of *C. deplanchei*. Wijk and Margadant rectified Dixon's error by giving *C. deplanchei* as a variety of *C. tahitense*. Dixon also placed *C. geheebii* Broth. in synonymy with *C. deplanchei*, but related it more closely to *C. tahitense* in the papillose seta, the branches only slightly flattened and in the very concave leaves. Variability in seta length (1.0–2.0 cm), leaf outline, apical acumination, margin denticulation, and degree of cell papillosity is quite considerable.

XXVI. HOOKERIACEAE

As redefined by Miller (1971), the family Hookeriaceae is represented in the Society Islands by the genera *Eriopus, Cyclodictyon,* and *Callicostella.* These taxa commonly appear on bark and dead wood and occasionally on rocks and soil.

1. *Eriopus* Bridel
Bryol. Univ. 2: 788. 1827.
Eriopus pacificus (Bescherelle) Fleischer
Hedwigia 63: 212. 1922.
> *Epipterygium pacificum* Besch., Bull. Soc. Bot. France 45: 66. 1898.
> *Cyathophorella pacifica* (Besch.) C. Muell., *in* Fleischer, Hedwigia 63: 212. 1922.
> *Eriopus samoanus* Mitt., mss. in hb. NY.

Leaves broadly ovate, 1.6–2.3 × 0.8–0.95 mm, ecostate, bordered, the border formed by 2–3 series of elongate, thick-walled cells, entire below, denticulate in the upper one-third of the blade. Cells of the lamina thin-walled, elongate-hexagonal, lax, 60–70 × 24–28 μ, shorter toward the leaf apex, longer toward the base, 80–100 × 25–30 μ; border cells elongate, linear, thick-walled, 80–110 × 10–12 μ. No antheridia, archegonia, or sporophytes found. (Based on *2950.*)

ILLUSTRATIONS. Figure 76.

TAHITI. Without locality: *Nadeaud 279* (Bescherelle, 1898, as *Epipterygium*). Pirae District: Mt. Aorai, 1700 m, valley W of Chalet Fare Ata, with *Trachyloma tahitense* and *Metzgeria, 2950.*

Distribution.—Society Islands (Tahiti), Samoa.

Bescherelle (1898a) compared *Eriopus pacificus* (as *Epipterygium*) with *Epipterygium limbatulum* Besch. (=*Eriopus remotifolius* C. Muell.), from Java, from which it differs in its ecostate

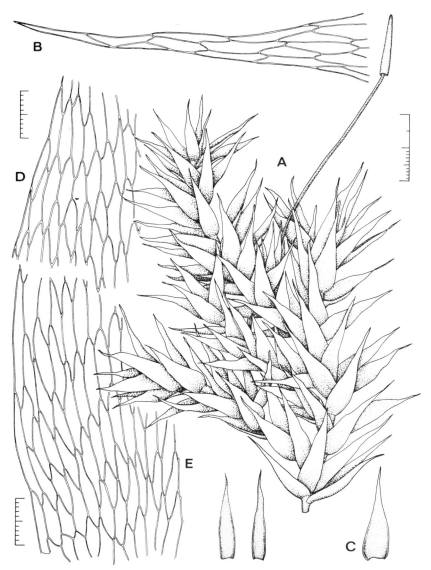

Fig. 75. *Leucomium aneurodictyon.* (*HOW 2667.*) A. Habit, scale 2 mm. B. Leaf apex cells, scale 100 μ. C. Leaves, scale 2 mm. D. Leaf, upper margin and median cells, scale 100 μ. E. Leaf, basal margin and median cells, scale 100 μ.

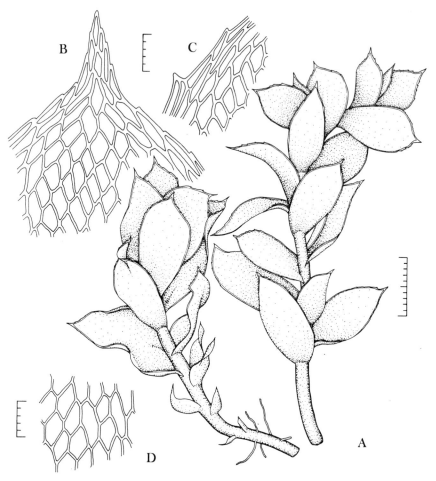

Fig. 76. *Eriopus pacificus.* (*HOW 2950.*) A. Habit, scale 1 mm. B. Leaf apex, cells. C. Lamina, upper margin. B, C, scale 50 μ. D. Lamina, upper median cells, scale 50 μ.

leaves, half as long, and in the borders with weaker teeth in the upper lamina. *Eriopus samoanus* Mitt., msc., from Samoa (Powell, NY!), is a more robust plant, the cells of the lamina larger, but differs primarily in having long, erect-spreading teeth, 12–36 μ, on the upper borders of the lamina. Smaller, less robust forms, agreeing almost exactly with Bescherelle's original description, and identical to my own collection, appear in Mitten's specimens.

It seems appropriate to recognize the taxon with the spinose margins as *E. pacificus* var. *samoanus*, a *E. pacifico* (Besch.) Fleisch. insulae Societatae proximum sed plantis robustioribus; cellulis major; margine cum dentibus erectis vel 12–36 μ longis differt. Specimen typicum leg. Powell ex herb. Mitten, NY! sub. *E. samoano*.

2. *Cyclodictyon* Mitten
J. Linn. Soc. Bot. 7: 163. 1864.
Cyclodictyon blumeanum (C. Mueller) O. Kuntze
Rev. Gen. Pl. 2: 835. 1891.

Hookeria blumeanum C. Muell., Syn. 2: 676. 1851.
Hookeria vescoana Besch., Ann. Sci. Nat. Bot. ser. 7, 20: 44. 1895.
Cyclodictyon vescoanum (Besch.) Broth., E. & P. Nat. Pfl. 1(3): 934. 1907.

Plants prostrate, pale whitish-green, 3–4 cm long, the branches 1–2 cm long; leaves complanate, slightly dimorphous, the upper leaves smaller and more forward pointing than the lateral leaves; leaves oblong, abruptly acuminate, 1.3–1.5 × 0.55 mm, slightly concave, inserted on the stem at an angle, bordered by 1–2 series of elongate, thin-walled cells which converge to form the leaf apex; margins of the upper leaf entire to serrate or denticulate, the teeth formed by projecting ends of border cells; costa double, diverging, quite slender, 1–3 cells wide, ending in the upper one-quarter of the lamina. Cells of the lamina large, thin-walled, regularly to irregularly hexagonal, 40–60 μ, nearly uniform from border to midleaf; border cells to 100 × 4–7 μ. Sporophytes not seen in authentic specimens of *H. vescoanum* (NY!), but reported by Bescherelle (1895a) to be 13 mm long, reddish; capsule horizontal, ovate-cylindric; operculum conic-rostrate, 0.8 mm long. In the isotype of *C. blumeanum* (NY!): seta smooth, to 15 mm; capsule 1.5 × 0.55 mm; horizontal, ovate-cylindric. No calyptra seen. Exothecial cells in immature capsule slightly collenchymatous, quadrate, 16–22 μ in the upper capsule, rectangular below, to 40 × 16 μ; stomata present, with some apparent variations involving 3 and 4 cells about the opening. Leaves of the Javan material were slightly larger, to 1.9 × 0.63 mm, but differed in no other important respect. Specimens of *C. blumeanum* described by Bartram (1939), for the Philippine Islands, have setae 1.5–2.0 cm long, the capsule urn 1.5–2.0 mm long, peristome teeth brownish, with transverse striolations, a wide median furrow, operculum long-beaked, and calyptra naked.

ILLUSTRATIONS. Figure 77.

TAHITI. Without locality: Among thalli of *Dumortiera hirsuta*, *Vesco sn* (Bescherelle, 1895a, as *H. vescoana*); *Larminat sn* (Potier de la Varde, 1912, as *C. vescoana*). Miaa: 850 m, *Temarii Nadeaud sn*, 1899 (Bescherelle, 1901, as *H. vescoana*). Puaa, Papeete to Papara: On trees, *Nadeaud 348–350* (Bescherelle, 1898a, as *H. vescoana*). Hitiaa District: Plateau region, 650 m, *3231*. Taiarapu Peninsula: Haavini Valley, 670–700 m, on bark, *2299*.

Distribution.—Society Islands (Tahiti), Java, Sumatra, Philippine Islands, Formosa, Sri Lanka (Ceylon), New Guinea, Fiji.

Bescherelle (1895a) recognized similarities between his new species *H. vescoana* and *H. blumeanum*, but distinguished them primarily on the basis of larger leaves and a shorter costa on the part of *H. vescoana*, features which Fleischer (1908) considered only of varietal significance, and which led him to treat the Society Islands taxon as *C. blumeanum* var. *vescoanum* (Besch.) Fleisch. Fleischer examined *C. ceylanicum* Broth. and *Hookeria morokae* C. Muell., and included both in synonymy with *C. blumeanum*.

3. *Callicostella* (C. Mueller) Mitten
J. Linn. Soc. Bot. Suppl. 1: 136. 1859.
Callicostella papillata (Montagne) Mitten
J. Linn. Soc. Bot. Suppl. 1: 136. 1859.

> *Hookeria papillata* Mont., London J. Bot. 3: 632. 1844. *non* Taylor, London J. Bot. 7: 283. 1848.
> *Schizomitrium papillatum* (Mont.) Sull., U.S. Expl. Exped. Wilkes Musci 23. 1859.
> *Hookeria oblongifolia* Sull., Proc. Am. Acad. Arts Sci. 3: 80. 1854. *fide* Sullivant, U.S. Expl. Exped. Wilkes Musci 23. 1859.
> *Callicostella oblongifolia* (Sull.) Jaeg., Ber. S. Gall. Naturw. Ges. 1875–1876: 352. 1877.

I have examined a fragment of an isotype (NY!) which consists of sterile plants, 1–2 cm long, with short lateral branches and nearly complanate leaves, the stems thick and wiry. Leaves 1.4–1.7 × 0.55 mm, slightly concave, oblong, the apex obtuse, with an abrupt api-

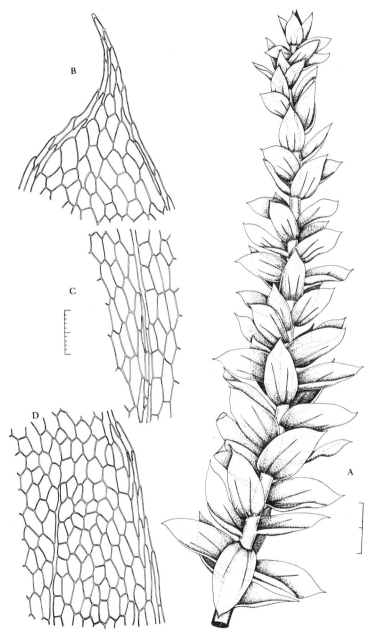

Fig. 77. *Cyclodictyon blumeanum.* (*HOW 2525.*) A. Habit, scale 2 mm. B. Leaf apex, cells. C. Upper lamina cells, adjacent costa. D. Upper lamina and margin cells. B–D, scale 100 μ.

culus; margins serrulate to denticulate in the upper leaf, entire below; costa double, widely diverging, strong (up to 50 μ wide at the leaf base), ending in the upper quarter of the blade, just below the obtuse apex. Cells of the upper leaf irregularly 6–7 sided, irregularly thick-walled, 5–9 μ, rounded- to conic-papillose, a single papilla over the lumen on free surfaces; cells of the leaf base smooth, rectangular, 30–50 × 8–10 μ; margin cells elongate to about midleaf, shorter in the upper leaf, where projecting papillae or entire cells form the margin teeth; the larger, thin-walled margin cells near the leaf base give the margins a bordered appearance. No sporophytes seen.

ILLUSTRATIONS. Fleischer (1908, 3: 1024, f. 174). Figure 78.

TAHITI. Without locality: *Andersson sn*, 1852 (Aongstrom, 1873); in deep humid valleys near water, *Lequerré sn*, 1857. Papeiha Valley: Tatefau, among hepatics on soil and on rotting fern leaves, *Nadeaud 83*, 1859 (Nadeaud, 1873; Bescherelle, 1895a, as *Hookeria oblongifolia*). Hitiaa District: Mountains, about 800 m, *Nadeaud sn*, 1896 (NY); Tamanu Valley, *Nadeaud 122* (NY); frequent collections, numbered by Bescherelle *351–354* (Bescherelle, 1898a, as *Hookeria oblongifolia*). Mataiea District: Vaihiria Valley, on branches, *Eriksson 66* (Bartram, 1950b, as *Hookeria oblongifolia*); Lake Vaihiria, 400 m, with *Vesicularia, Leucobryum tahitense, Rhynchostegium*, and *Trichocolea, Whittier sn*; 100 m, with *Vesicularia* and *Ectropothecium, 3094*; *Setchell and Parks 5365* (Brotherus, 1924a, as *C. oblongifolia*, BISH!, NY!). Taiarapu Peninsula: Taravao, above experiment station, near dam, 400–500 m, on *Aleurites* trunk, *Hürlimann T 1187* (Hürlimann, 1963, FH!); Haavini Valley, 130 m, on bark, with *Fissidens clarkii, Ectropothecium, Leucomium aneurodictyon, Syrrhopodon, Vesicularia*, and *Riccardia, 2538*; 145 m, on rocks in stream, with *Ectropothecium, Vesicularia*, and *Marchantia, 2551*; with *Leucobryum, 2605*. Pirae District: Fare Rau Ape–Mt. Aorai trail, 930 m, on rock with *Leucomium aneurodictyon, 2668*; 1000 m, *2686*; Fautaua Valley, 490 m, with *Leucomium aneurodictyon, Vesicularia, Racopilum*, and *Hypopterygium, 3123*; 500 m, with *Entodon solanderi, Ectropothecium*, and *Plagiochila, 3146*.

MOOREA. Without locality: *Temarii Nadeaud sn*, 1900 (Bescherelle, 1901, as *Hookeria oblongifolia*).

Distribution.—Society Islands (Tahiti, Moorea), Rapa, Marquesas Islands (Nuku Hiva), Pitcairn Island, Fiji (type locality for *Hookeria oblongifolia*), Samoa, New Caledonia, Java (type locality for

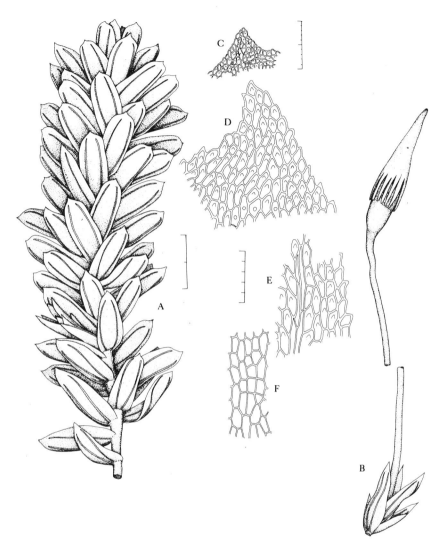

FIG. 78. *Callicostella papillata.* (*Hürlimann T 1187.*) A. Habit, upper side of plant, scale 1 mm. B. Perichaetial leaves and sporophyte with calyptra, scale 1 mm. C. Leaf apex cells, scale 100 μ. D. Leaf apex cells. E. Upper leaf margin and median lamina cells. F. Leaf base cells. D–F, scale 50 μ.

H. papillata), Borneo, Sumatra, Philippine Islands, New Guinea, d'Entrecasteaux, Nepal, Bengal, India, Formosa.

Sullivant (1859) placed *Hookeria oblongifolia* in synonymy with *H. papillata* (as *Schizomitrium papillatum*). Mueller (1873) chose to treat the two as separate species and created a third, *H. vesiculata*, for Samoa. Bescherelle (1895a) did not agree with Aongstrom's use of *H. papillata* for Andersson's Tahitian specimen, but instead cited all the collections he examined as *H. oblongifolia*, either in accord with Mueller's recognition of it as a distinct species, or in ignorance of Sullivant's opinion that *H. oblongifolia* was a synonym of *H. papillata*.

I have examined an isotype of Montagne's *H. papillata* (NY!) as well as an isotype of *H. prabaktiana* (C. Muell.) Bosch & Lac., and consider them to represent extremes in a range of variability which Fleischer (1908) illustrated quite well for *Callicostella papillata* as it is known from Java. The Javan forms are more strongly papillose, the margins irregularly serrate to denticulate, whereas the Tahitian forms are usually less papillose and have more uniformly serrulate margins. Mueller's *Hookeria vesiculata* from Tutuila and Upolu seems, according to the description, to fit into this range of variation and may well be placed in synonymy when authentic specimens can be examined.

Tahitian specimens identified as *Callicostella oblongifolia* (by Brotherus, *Setchell and Parks 5365*; by Bescherelle, *Nadeaud 122*, NY!) compare well in the size of the plants and the leaves, although the costa is not as strong (to 30–35 μ wide at the leaf base), and the cells of the upper lamina are slightly larger (about 12 × 7 μ), more elongate, the papillae lower, less conspicuous; basal cells have nearly identical dimensions; margin cells are more uniform and the serrulations more regular and not as pronounced. Seta smooth, 10–20 mm long; capsule dark, ovoid, constricted beneath the mouth, 1.6 × 0.8 mm; peristome teeth brownish, papillose, about 340 μ long; operculum not seen; calyptra cucullate, laciniate at the base. Exothecial cells collenchymatous, 4–6-sided in the upper capsule, 35–60 × 35–45 μ, the lower cells rectangular, the walls uniformly thickened; stomata present. Spores green, finely papillose, regularly 12–13 μ.

Dubious species

Callicostella vesiculata (C. Mueller) Jaeger

Ber. S. Gall. Naturw. Ges. 1875–1876: 356. 1877.

Hookeria vesiculata C. Muell., J. Mus. Godeffroy 3(6): 76. 1873.

I have not yet examined authentic specimens; Mueller's original description follows:

Caulis perpusillus tener apice curvatulus; folia caulina laxe conferta pallida secunda parva nunquam plana sed magis incumbentia, oblongo-ovata apice obtuse et excavate acuminata, valde inaequalia concava superiora vesiculata, inferne integerrima apice cellulis prominulis erosulo-serrulata, nervis binis pallidis callosulis ante apicem abruptis percurse, e cellulis majusculis levibus apice saepius unipunctatis pellucidis hexagonis basi parum majoribus rectangularibus reticulata. Caetera ignota.

Species distincta quidem, sed propter statum mancum valde incomplete nota, ab omnibus congeneribus foliis incumbenti-curvatis laxiuscule reticulatis leviusculis statim diversa.

ILLUSTRATIONS. None.

TAHITI. Pirae District: Fautaua Valley, 400–500 m, *Quayle 663* (Bartram, 1933a, FH).

Distribution.—Society Islands (Tahiti), Samoa (Tutuila, Upolu), Rapa, Pitcairn Island.

This species may ultimately be proven to belong in the species complex associated with *C. papillata,* but until critical material is examined, it must remain a member of the Society Islands moss flora.

XXVII. DISTICHOPHYLLACEAE

Distichophyllum Dozy & Molkenboer
Musci Fr. Ined. Archip. Indici 4: 99. 1846.

Plants prostrate, complanate, infrequently branched, pale to whitish-green; leaves spathulate to apiculate; costa single, ending one-half to two-thirds the length of the leaf, the cells large, hexagonal, thin-walled. Seta smooth to papillose; capsule erect to pendulous; peristome teeth transversely striate, deeply furrowed along the median line; calyptra cucullate.

Key to Species of *Distichophyllum*

1. Leaf apices broadly rounded, leaves 2.7–3.8 mm; seta rough...3. *D. spathulatum.*
1. Leaf apices pointed, leaves shorter than 2.5 mm; seta smooth
    2. Costa two-thirds length of leaf; submarginal lamina cells markedly smaller than median cells................1. *D. cuspidatum.*
    2. Costa less than one-half length of leaf; submarginal cells nearly as large as median cells ....2. *D. nadeaudii.*

1. *Distichophyllum cuspidatum* (Dozy & Molkenboer) Dozy & Molkenboer
Musci Fr. Ined. Archip. Indici 4: 101. t. 33. 1846.
    Hookeria cuspidatum Dozy & Molk., Ann. Sci. Nat. Bot. ser. 3, 2: 305. 1844.
    Mniadelphus cuspidatus (Dozy & Molk.) C. Muell., Linnaea 21: 196. 1848.
    Distichophyllum mucronatum Thwait. & Mitt., J. Linn. Soc. Bot. 13: 311. 1873. *fide* Fleischer, Musci Fl. Buitenzorg 3: 987, 989. 1908.

Plants prostrate, light yellow-green, 8–10 mm long, about 4–6 mm wide; leaves laterally compressed on the stem in a dorsi-ventral arrangement, spirally twisted when dry, flat and erect-spreading when wet, obovate, the apex rounded to apiculate, 2.1–2.5 × 0.40–0.53 mm; costa slender, about two-thirds the length of the leaf, 1.35–1.65 mm long. Leaf margins bordered, the borders formed by 2–4 series of elongate, thick-walled cells which extend into and form the cuspidate leaf apex. Cells of the upper leaf thin-walled, rounded-hexagonal, to 25 μ near the middle of the lamina, smaller, about 15 μ near the margins; cells of the border are smooth, linear, to 120 × 6 μ. Seta smooth, 5–7 mm long; capsule erect to inclined,

1.0–1.1 × 0.33 mm; operculum conic-rostrate 0.7–0.8 mm long; calyptra cucullate and fringed at the base. Capsule exothecial cells quadrate, the angles thickened, about 20–25 μ. Peristome teeth about 240 μ long. Spores not seen.

ILLUSTRATIONS. Bartram (1939, pl. 19, f. 322).

TAHITI. Without locality: *Wilkes sn* (Sullivant, 1859, as *Mniadelphus*).

Distribution.—Society Islands (Tahiti), Sri Lanka (Ceylon), Sumatra, Java, New Caledonia, New Guinea, Caroline Islands, Philippine Islands (Mindanao), India.

2. *Distichophyllum nadeaudii* Bescherelle
Ann. Sci. Nat. Bot. ser. 7, 20: 43. 1895.

Plants about 10 mm long and 4 mm wide, prostrate, yellow-green; leaves obovate, cuspidate, 2.0–2.5 × 0.7–0.8 mm; costa ends below midleaf, 0.8–1.1 mm long, about 25–30 μ wide at the leaf base; leaf margins bordered by 2–3 rows of thick-walled, elongate cells 90–120 × 4–6 μ, which join to form the cuspidate leaf apex. Cells of the lamina regularly hexagonal and uniform in the upper leaf, 16–22 μ, only slightly smaller near the borders and larger toward the middle of the lamina; cells of the leaf base large, rectangular, 40–70 × 19–24 μ. Seta smooth, 10–12 mm long; capsule inclined to horizontal, 1.1 ×0.68 mm. Calyptra, operculum, and spores not seen. Capsule exothecial cells quadrate, the angles thickened, 20–25 μ, to rectangular, with uniform walls, 50 × 12 μ toward the apophysis; stomata few.

ILLUSTRATIONS. None.

TAHITI. Without locality: On bark of trees, toward 1100 m, *Nadeaud 69* (1873, as *Mniadelphus montagneanus*; Bescherelle, 1895a). Taiarapu Peninsula: On bark, with *Leucomium aneurodictyon, Radula, Riccardia,* and *Fissidens, Nadeaud 8* (343), 1896 (Bescherelle, 1898a, NY!).

Bescherelle (1895a) compared this species with *D. montagneanum* (C. Muell.) Bosch & Lac. (as *Mniadelphus*), from which he distinguished it by the longer leaf apex, the broader leaf border, and the shorter costa. He also related *Distichophyllum nadeaudii* to *D. crispulum* (Hook. f. & Wils.) Mitt., from Australia and New Zealand, which has smaller leaves, a longer leaf apiculus, a more attenuated leaf base, and a border which vanishes in the upper leaf margins. The most similar Society Islands species, *D. cuspidatum*, differs in its more narrow leaves, longer costa, and shorter seta, but in general appearance the two species are quite alike.

3. *Distichophyllum spathulatum* (Dozy & Molkenboer) Dozy & Molkenboer
Musci Fr. Ined. Archip. Indici, p. 103. f. 34, 35a. 1846.

Hookeria spathulata Dozy & Molk., Ann. Sci. Nat. Bot. ser. 3, 2: 305. 1844.
Mniadelphus spathulatus (Dozy & Molk.) C. Muell., Linnaea 21: 196. 1848.
Distichophyllum tahitense Besch., Ann. Sci. Nat. Bot. ser. 7, 20: 43. 1895.

Plants prostrate, common on humus in dense shade, 10–20 mm long, 6 mm wide, markedly compressed or flattened; leaves obovate, plane, broadly rounded at the apex but sometimes with a small "vestigial" apiculus formed by portions of 2 or 3 border cells, 2.7–3.8 × 1.45–1.75 mm; costa ends in upper quarter of the leaf, about 2.5–2.7 mm long, about 70 μ wide at the base. Leaf margins bordered by 1–2 series of elongate, thin-walled cells, 80–120 × 3–5 μ in the upper lamina, and by 3–6 series of cells in the lower lamina. Cells of the lamina small near the margins, 7–12 μ, irregularly hexagonal, becoming elongate-hexagonal and markedly larger toward midleaf, 36–48 × 25–30 μ; basal cells rectangular, 60–90 × 19–38 μ, darkened at insertion of leaf onto stem. Seta scabrous, 8–10 mm long, the projecting papillae to 25 μ high; capsule inclined to horizontal, ovoid, 1.1 × 0.54 mm; operculum conic-rostrate, about 0.8 mm long; calyptra papillose, the base ciliate-fringed. Capsule exothecial cells quadrate, the angles thickened in the upper jacket, about 25 μ, becoming rectangular toward the base; stomata present. Spores not seen. Description based on *Nadeaud 70* (isotype *D. tahitense* Besch., NY).

ILLUSTRATIONS. Dozy and Molkenboer (1846, pls. 34, 35a). Figure 79.

TAHITI. Taiarapu Peninsula: Tatefau Plateau (?), on wet sides of valleys, *Nadeaud 70*, 1859 (Nadeaud, 1873, as *Mniadelphus spathulatus*; Bescherelle, 1895a, as *D. tahitense*, isotype, NY). Tahiti nui: General localities, N side, to 800 m, on soil and tree trunks, *Nadeaud 345–347* (Bescherelle, 1898a, as *D. tahitense*). Miaa: 850 m, *Temarii Nadeaud sn*, 1899 (Bescherelle, 1901, as *D. tahitense*). Pirae District: Pirae–Mt. Aorai trail, *Quayle 697c, 704c, 706a* (Bartram, 1933a, as *D. tahitense*, BISH); 1700–1800 m, with *Rhizogonium spiniforme*, 2876.

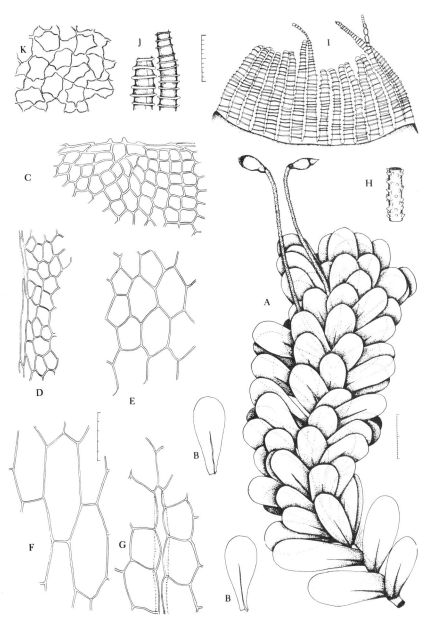

FIG. 79. *Distichophyllum spathulatum*. (*Nadeaud 70.*) A. Habit with sporophytes, scale 2 mm. B. Leaves, scale 2 mm. C. Leaf apex cells. D. Leaf margin
cells. E. Upper leaf cells. F. Leaf base cells. G. Leaf cells, adjacent costa. C–G,
scale 50 μ. H. Seta section, enlarged to show papillae. I. Peristome section,
scale 100 μ. J. Peristome teeth, scale 50 μ. K. Capsule outer wall cells, scale
50 μ.

Distribution.—Society Islands (Tahiti), Java, Sumatra.

I can find no good reason for disagreeing with Nadeaud's (1873) original identification of *D. spathulatum* (as *Mniadelphus*), as Tahitian specimens agree in most important features. Fleischer (1908) noted that this species is very similar to the Javan *D. undulatum* Bosch & Lac., which differs in being monoicous and in having shorter perichaetial leaves.

XXVIII. DALTONIACEAE

Daltonia Hooker & Taylor
Musc. Brit. 80. 1818. *nom. illeg. incl. typ. gen. prior* (*Cryphaea*
Mohr, 1814), *fide* Index Muscorum 2: 1. 1962.
Daltonia sphaerica Bescherelle
Bull. Soc. Bot. France 45: 119. 1898.

I have not examined authentic material of this species, known
only from the original collection. Bescherelle's original description
follows:

> Monoica. Caulis pusillus, vix 4 mill. longus. Folia crispatula,
> madore erecto-patentia, minuta, angustissime lanceolata, in
> acumen attenuatum cuspidatum sensim producta, carinata,
> flavida, haud revoluta, limbo continuo flavido e basi ad medium
> lato (10 cellul.) versus apicem angustiore integerrimo vel
> ob cellulas marginales subtiliter prominulas obsolete dentic-
> ulato marginata, cellulis minutis ovato-hexagonis undique ob-
> scuriusculis inferioribus longioribus oblongis, infima basi fus-
> cescentibus areolata, costa supra carinam evanida. Folia
> perichaetialia caulinis breviora, latiora, laxius reticulata, subito
> breviter acuminata, vix marginata. Capsula in pedicello 3 mill.
> longo purpureo rugoso sinuoso erecta, minuta, sphaerica, collo
> breviusculo sublaevi. Calyptra minuta basi dense fimbriato-
> ciliata.

ILLUSTRATIONS. None.

TAHITI. Marau Falls: In humid valley below falls, on branch of
Cyrtandra pendula, Nadeaud 68, 1859 (Nadeaud, 1873, as *Daltonia
contorta*; Bescherelle, 1898a).

Distribution.—Society Islands (Tahiti), endemic.

On the basis of Bescherelle's observations, *Daltonia contorta*
must be excluded from the Society Islands moss flora for the present. The attenuated leaves and the spherical capsule served to distinguish this species from *D. contorta*, according to Bescherelle,
as well as from *D. pusilla* Hook. & Wils., from Tasmania.

XXIX. LEUCOMIACEAE

Leucomium Mitten
J. Linn. Soc. Bot. 10: 181. 1868.
Leucomium aneurodictyon (C. Mueller) Jaeger
Ber. S. Gall. Naturw. Ges. 1877–1878: 275. 1880.
Hypnum aneurodictyon C. Muell., Syn. 2: 681. 1851.
Hypnum debile (Sull.) C. Muell., J. Mus. Godeffroy 3(6): 81. 1873. *fide* Fleischer, 1923.
Hookeria debilis Sull., Proc. Am. Acad. Arts Sci. 3: 10. 1854. *fide* Fleischer, Musci Fl. Buitenzorg 5(4): 1107. 1923.
Leucomium debile (Sull.) Mitt., J. Linn. Soc. Bot. 10: 181. 1868. *fide* Fleischer, 1923.
Leucomium limpidum Thwait. & Mitt., J. Linn. Soc. Bot. 13: 320. 1873. *fide* Fleischer, 1923.
Leucomium mahorense Besch., Ann. Sci. Nat. Bot. ser. 7, 2: 97. 1885. *fide* Fleischer, 1923.
Leucomium philippinense Broth., Philippine J. Sci. C 8: 91. 1913. *fide* Bartram, Philippine J. Sci. 68: 276. 1939.

Plants usually found on bark or decaying wood, intermixed with other bryophytes, occasionally forming thin, glossy, pale- to whitish-green mats, the primary stems irregularly branched, the branches less than 1 cm long; leaves are complanate or nearly so, spreading laterally, but at stem apices the leaves may be slightly secund. Leaves 1.9–2.5 × 0.54 mm, ecostate, ovate-lanceolate, acuminate, the tips flexuose; margins entire; areolation lax. Cells smooth, thin-walled, fusiform to irregularly hexagonal, 140–200 × 20–33 μ in the upper lamina, slightly shorter toward the leaf apex and toward the base. Seta 1.0–1.5 cm long, reddish, smooth; capsule horizontal; urn about 1.1 × 0.48 mm; operculum conic-rostrate, about 1 mm long. No calyptra was seen. Exothecial cells quadrate to rectangular, thin-walled, 19–48 × 19–25 μ. Spores brownish, finely papillose, 14–19 μ.

ILLUSTRATIONS. Brotherus (1905, 2: 1096, f. 775A–E; 1924a, 2: 268, f. 623A–E), Fleischer (1923, 4: 1108, f. 185). Figures 74E–G, 75.

TAHITI. Without locality: Very common in the interior of the island, *Nadeaud sn*, 1896 (Bescherelle, 1898a, *409–417*, as *Leucomium debile*). Haapape District: Rahi, 800 m, *Temarii Nadeaud*

22; Miaa, 850 m, *Temarii Nadeaud 20* (Bescherelle, 1901, as *L. debile*). Taiarapu Peninsula: Taravao, on decaying wood, *Hürlimann T 1197* (Hürlimann, 1963); above experiment station, 450 m, on N slope, in *Miconia* and *Hibiscus* forest, *2204*; 450 m, associated with *Hypopterygium, Cyclodictyon, Hypnodendron,* and *Vesicularia, 2215*; with *Fissidens clarkii* and *Trichosteleum, 2281*; Haavini Valley, 120 m, near Pueu, above camp on bank, with *Fissidens nanobryoides, F. clarkii, F. zollingeri, Vesicularia,* and *Anthoceros, 2528*. Mataiea District: Vaihiria Valley, 50 m, with *Hypnodendron, Calymperes tahitense,* and *Vesicularia, 3102*; 100–200 m, with *Anthoceros* and *Dumortiera, 3087*. Pirae District: Fare Rau Ape–Mt. Aorai trail, 930 m, *2667*; 1000 m, with *Eurrhynchium, Racopilum, Distichophyllum,* and *Marchantia, 2681*; 1700 m. in valley N of Chalet Fare Ata, with *Trichocolea, 2911*; Fautaua Valley, 220 m, on fern hanging from rocks, *2508*; 400–500 m, with *Ectropothecium* and *Porella, 3144*.

Distribution.—Society Islands (Tahiti), Samoa, Fiji, Marquesas Islands (Nuku Hiva), Sri Lanka (Ceylon), Java, New Caledonia, Sumatra, Borneo, Philippine Islands (Luzon), Malacca, West African Islands (?), South India, Usambara.

This species is much more common than my own records would suggest, and appears frequently in admixtures with other bryophytes. Its Society Islands distribution undoubtedly includes all the high, volcanic islands.

Bartram (1939) observed that there is considerable variation in the leaf apices, and supported Fleischer (1923) in his conclusion that *Hookeria debilis* Sull., from Samoa and Fiji, is synonymous with *L. aneurodictyon*. Specimens I have examined in Society Islands collections agree in all major respects with Bartram's description for Philippines *L. aneurodictyon,* but in Tahitian material, the seta is slightly longer and is smooth, rather than minutely scabrous at the tip as in Philippines specimens examined by Bartram. Bartram provided no spore measurements, and Fleischer's report (7–10 μ, greenish, nearly smooth) suggests immature spores, but in all other features, the Tahitian specimens fit Fleischer's description of *L. aneurodictyon* for Java.

The extremely lax areolation, the short seta, small capsule, and especially the long-beaked operculum, serve to distinguish this genus from *Vesicularia,* and from *Isopterygium,* the only Society Islands genera for which *Leucomium* could be mistaken.

XXX. HYPOPTERYGIACEAE

Common in damp, shaded sites on bark, decomposing organic debris, or rocks, taxa in the family Hypopterygiaceae are characterized by a prostrate primary stem with erect, branched, or unbranched secondary stems, the branches typically in one plane and restricted to the top of the secondary stem, giving the plants a frondose habit. Leaves in 3 ranks, the lateral leaves asymmetrical, the third rank or underleaves (sometimes termed "amphigastria") symmetrical, the leaves bordered by several rows of elongate, thick-walled cells. Leaves are broadly ovate, acute; the costa ends in mid-leaf or in the leaf acumen; lamina cells are large, hexagonal, thin-walled, or rounded, thick-walled.

Key to Genera of the Hypopterygiaceae

1. Stems horizontal, branches pinnate along most of the length of the secondary stem; costa ends in the upper one-fourth to one-fifth of the leaf; lamina cells rounded _____1. *Lopidium.*
1. Stems inclined to erect, the branches restricted to the top of the erect stem; costa ends in or below midleaf; cells hexagonal_____2. *Hypopterygium.*

1. *Lopidium* Hooker f. & Wilson
    Fl. Nov. Zealand 2: 119. 1854.
Lopidium trichocladulum (Bescherelle) Fleischer
    Musci Fl. Buitenzorg 3: 1071. 1908.
    Hypopterygium trichocladulum Besch., Bull. Soc. Bot. France 45: 127. 1898.

I have not yet examined authentic specimens of this species. Bescherelle's original description follows: "A *H. trichoclado* V. d. Bosch et Lac. Javae proximum sed foliis acuminatis minus longe cuspidatis integerrimis, costa supra folii summum evanida, foliis stipuliformibus ecostatis differt."

Illustrations. None. (See Bosch and Lacoste, Bryol. Jav. 2: 9, t. 138, 1861, *Hypopterygium trichocladon,* for reference.)

Tahiti. Without locality: Hitiaa to Aorai and Tipaeaui, *Nadeaud sn,* 1896 (Bescherelle, 1898a; *Nadeaud 441,* as *Hypopterygium*).

Miaa: 850 m, *Temarii Nadeaud sn*, 1899 (Bescherelle, 1901, as *Hypopterygium*).

Distribution.—Society Islands (Tahiti), endemic.

2. *Hypopterygium* Bridel
Bryol. Univ. 2: 709. 1827.

Primary stems creeping, secondary stems erect, with a fan-shaped cluster of tertiary stems arising toward the upper end. Leaves are dimorphous, the lateral leaves obliquely inserted, complanate, the ventral row of leaves transversely inserted, pressed against the stem; both are bordered by 1 or 2 rows of elongate cells. The fan-shaped branching pattern distinguishes this genus from *Lopidium* and from *Cyathophorella*.

Key to Species of *Hypopterygium*

1. Ventral leaves (amphigastria) typically without costa; stipes to 5 cm long; plants dioicous_____1. *H. debile.*
1. Amphigastria costate; stipes to 3 cm long; plants monoicous
  2. Lateral leaf margins entire; stipes to 1.5 cm long_____2. *H. arbusculosum.*
  2. Lateral leaf margins toothed
    3. Fronds to 2.5 cm wide; stipes 1–3 cm long_____3. *H. nadeaudianum.*
    3. Fronds to 1.0 cm wide; stipes 1–2 cm long_____4. *H. tahitense.*

1. *Hypopterygium debile* Reichardt
Verh. Zool. Bot. Ges. Wien 18: 197. 1868.
Reise Oesterr. Freg. *Novara* Bot. 1(3): 194. f. 35. 1870.

Plants dioicous, on damp rock or rotting wood, stems prostrate, leafless or with reduced leaves, secondary stems (stipes) black or dark, tomentose, erect, to 5 cm long, the upper portion branched, limp, weak, the branches 4–7 mm long, dichotomous, themselves simply pinnately branched. Stem leaves widely outspread, flat, asymmetric from a semisheathing base, ovate-acuminate, 0.5 × 0.25 mm, bordered, the margins formed by a single series of elongate thick-walled cells, entire below, serrulate toward the apex. Lamina cells lax, thin-walled, smooth, rhomboidal to hexagonal, uniform. Costa slender, vanishing between midleaf and the leaf apex. No sporophytes or archegoniate plants have been found. Description based upon Reichardt (1868b).

ILLUSTRATIONS. Reichardt (1870, f. 35).

TAHITI. Pirae District: Fautaua Valley, on wet rocks and cliffs,

Jelinek sn (Reichardt, 1868b, 1870; Bescherelle, 1895a; Kindberg, 1901). Mataiea District: Above Lake Vaihiria, 1000 m (?), *Eriksson sn* (Bartram, 1950b).

Distribution.—Society Islands (Tahiti), Samoa.

Kindberg (1901) indicated that the leaves might be short-acuminate and that the costa often ended near midleaf (rather than toward the apex as Reichardt illustrated). Bescherelle (1895a) observed that this species could be distinguished from *H. tahitense* Aongstr. by the oval-acuminate stem leaves without a costa.

2. *Hypopterygium arbusculosum* Bescherelle
   Bull. Soc. Bot. France 45: 127. 1898.

Plants monoicous (synoicous); stems prostrate with erect secondary stems approximately 1.5 cm long; tertiary branches clustered at the stipe apex forming a roughly circular, flattened frond 1.0–1.5 cm wide; branches divided, to 1 cm long; branchlets very short. Leaves small, plane, asymmetrical, to 1.75 × 1.0 mm; margins 1–2 rows of thick-walled, elongate cells, entire (or very nearly so) to their apices; costa ends in midleaf or just above but does not extend into the apex. Stipe leaves short, broadly ovate; costa short; margins serrate toward the apex. Amphigastria symmetrical, circular, often abruptly acuminate; costa ends at midleaf or slightly above. Sporophytes not examined. Bescherelle (1898a) described the seta as 16–20 mm long, smooth, reddish; capsule horizontal to pendulous, globose, smooth; operculum long-rostrate; peristome cilia split, sometimes fused at the tips; calyptra long, smooth, conic; base split to the operculum.

ILLUSTRATIONS. Figure 81L–S.

TAHITI. Without locality: Puaa Valley, ravines of Tearapu, and of Mt. Ereeraoa, above Papeete to 1000 m, *Nadeaud sn* (Bescherelle, 1898a, NY!). Rahi: 800 m, Miaa, 850 m, *Temarii Nadeaud sn* (Bescherelle, 1901). Fare Rau Ape: 750 m, *Hürlimann T 1222* (Hürlimann, 1963, det. Bartram). Taiarapu Peninsula: 440 m, *2207* (illustrated).

RAIATEA. Temehani Range: S end, 500 m, among other mosses on branches of shrubs, *Moore 46d* (Bartram, 1933a, BISH!).

Distribution.—Society Islands (Tahiti, Raiatea), endemic.

Specimens identified as *H. arbusculosum* (*Hürlimann T 1222* and *Whittier 2207*) have lateral leaves with margins mostly entire; lower amphigastrial leaves possess entire margins, but the margins of upper amphigastria may be serrulate. Median lamina cells are irregularly hexagonal, thin-walled, about 45×20 μ, in stem leaves. Bescherelle (1898a) compared this species with *Hypopterygium rotulatum* (Hedw.) Brid., from which it differed in having entire leaves, very short costae, and solitary, quite long setae. Kindberg (1901) examined Bescherelle's material and noted that leaf margins were not always entire, that the amphigastrial costae were sometimes subpercurrent, and that the capsules were subovate, scarcely "globose." Kindberg's treatment of *H. arbusculosum* as an "unterart" of *H. tamariscinum* is not recognized as valid in *Index Muscorum*.

3. *Hypopterygium nadeaudianum* Bescherelle
Ann. Sci. Nat. Bot. ser. 7, 20: 58. 1895.
  Hypopterygium filiculaeforme Nad., 1873, *non* Bridel. *fide* Bescherelle, 1895.

Plants monoicous, prostrate stems reddish tomentose, stipe bases for the most part naked, 1–3 cm long, the upper frondose portion semicircular, to 2.5 cm wide, primary frond branches bifurcate to pinnate, occasionally triangular in outline or the single branch with simple pinnate branching, about 2.5 cm long. Leaves laterally asymmetrical, broadly ovate-acuminate, 2.4×1.4 mm, entire below, toothed above; margins formed by 2 series of elongate thick-walled cells; costa ends below to slightly above midleaf. Amphigastria circular; costa ends from midleaf to the apex. Sporophytes not found. Bescherelle (1895a) described the seta as 20 mm long, smooth, reddish, curved at the apex; capsule horizontal to incurved, large, ovate, with its base comprised of prominent vesciculose cells; operculum needle-shaped, symmetrical; calyptra mitriform, short, lobed at the base.

ILLUSTRATIONS. Figure 81A–K.

TAHITI. Without locality: Humid valleys toward Marau and especially in the crater-valley of Mamano, to 900 m, *Nadeaud sn,* 1859 (Nadeaud, 1873, as *Hypopterygium filiculaeforme*; Bescherelle, 1895a, *Nadeaud 65*). Pirae District: 1100 m, *Nadeaud sn,* 1896 (Nadeaud, unpublished diary, p. 25); general localities on windward Tahiti nui and Tahiti iti (Bescherelle, 1898a, *Nadeaud 433–436;* P); Fautaua Valley, *Temarii Nadeaud sn* (Bescherelle, 1901); Mt. Aorai, *Hürlimann T 1222* (Hürlimann, 1963). Haapape District: Rahi, 800 m, *Temarii Nadeaud sn,* 1899 (Bescherelle, 1901). Maara Valley: *Setchell and Parks sn,* 1922 (Brotherus, 1924a).

MOOREA. Without locality: *Temarii Nadeaud sn*, 1899 (Bescherelle, 1901).

Distribution.—Society Islands (Tahiti, Moorea), Fiji.

Kindberg (1901) indicated this species should be compared with *Hypopterygium rigidulum*, and wrote: "Frons major; stipes altus. Folia magis distantia, minus dentata, paullo majora; limbus biserialis; costa interdum magis abbreviata. Flores interdum synoici." Plants are olive to yellow-green, stems tomentose, leafless, 1–3 cm long, with curved, bifurcate to pinnate branches; sporophytes about 2 cm long.

4. *Hypopterygium tahitense* Aongstrom
Oefv. K. Svensk. Vet. Ak. Foerh. 30(5): 121. 1873.

Plants monoicous (synoicous), prostrate stems reddish-brown tomentose; stipes 10–20 mm long, reddish-brown, leafless; semicircular frond at the top asymmetric, about 1 cm wide, in 3–7 branch divisions, each irregularly pinnately branched. Lateral branch leaves asymmetric, 1.8 × 1.1 mm, bordered; margins of 2 rows of elongate cells, entire below, denticulate above; costa ends at midleaf or just above in most leaves. Amphigastria costate, the costa ends in midleaf, bordered, the borders entire below, denticulate above. Sporophytes in groups of 3–5; setae about 1.5 cm long, smooth, yellow-brown; capsules horizontal.

ILLUSTRATIONS. Figure 80.

TAHITI. Without locality: *Andersson sn* (Aongstrom, 1873; Bescherelle, 1895a); *Vesco sn* (Bescherelle, 1895a); 800–1100 m, N side of Tahiti, *Nadeaud sn* (Bescherelle, 1898a). Pirae District: Pirae–Mt. Aorai trail, *Quayle sn* (Bartram, 1933a); 1700 m, in valley W of Chalet Fare Ata, with *Distichophyllum, Racopilum, Ptychomnion, Plagiochila, Trichocolea, Riccardia,* and *Anthoceros, 2931; 2470.*

Distribution.—Society Islands (Tahiti), endemic.

Common on wet basaltic rocks at elevations over 150 m. Kindberg (1901) has treated this species as a synonym of *Hypopterygium muelleri*, which has a distribution including Fiji, Raivavae, Rapa, Mangareva, and Tonga.

Dubious species

Hypopterygium novae-seelandiae C. Mueller
Bot. Zeit. 9: 562. 1851.

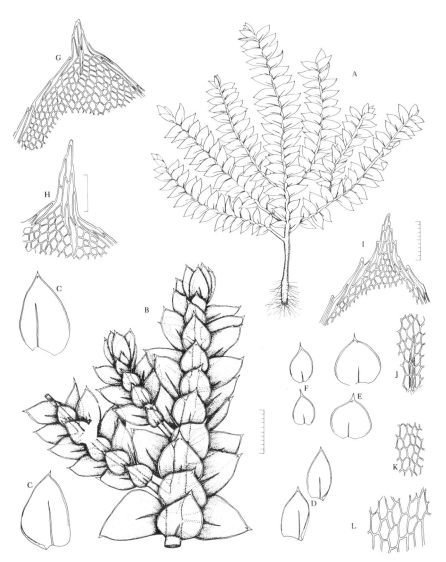

FIG. 80. *Hypopterygium tahitense.* (*HOW 2470.*) A. Habit, upper side of plant, scale 0.5 mm. B. Habit, showing portion of lower surface with amphigastria. C–E. Lateral leaves. F. Amphigastrial leaves. B–F, scale 1 mm. G, H. Lateral leaf apices, cells, scale 100 μ. I. Amphigastrial leaf apex cells. J. Lateral leaf, median cells adjacent to costa. K. Lateral leaf, upper lamina median cells. L. Lateral leaf base, median cells. I–L, scale 100 μ.

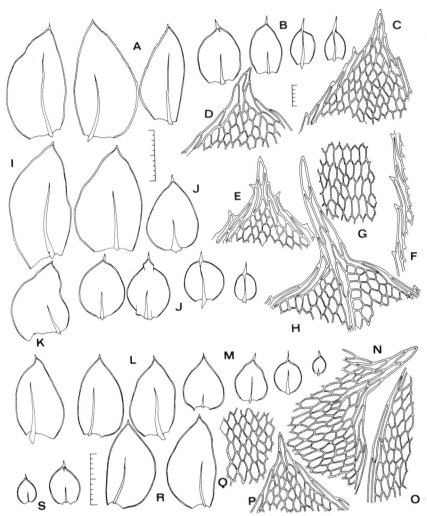

Fig. 81. A–K. *Hypopterygium nadeaudianum*. A, I, K. Lateral leaves, scale 1 mm. B, J. Amphigastrial (ventral) leaves, scale 1 mm. C, D, E. Lateral leaf apices, cells, scale 50 μ. F. Lamina margin cells, lateral leaf, scale 50 μ. G. Lamina, upper median cells, lateral leaf, scale 50 μ. H. Amphigastrial leaf apex, scale 50 μ. L–S. *Hypopterygium arbusculosum*. L, R. Lateral leaves, scale 1 mm. M, S. Amphigastria, scale 1 mm. N. Amphigastrial leaf apex, cells, scale 50 μ. O. Upper margin, cells, amphigastrial leaf, scale 50 μ. P. Apex, cells, lateral leaf, scale 50 μ. Q. Lateral leaf, upper median cells, scale 50 μ.

Hypopterygium smithianum Hooker f. & Wilson, Fl. Nov. Zel. 2: 118. 1854.
Hypopterygium rotulatum sensu C. Muell., Syn. 2: 9. 1851. *fide* Sullivant, 1859.

The confusion existing concerning this and the following species which Sullivant (1859) reported for New Zealand and Tahiti is not new. Sullivant wrote: "Our specimens accord entirely with the description of *H. rotulatum,* in the Flora of New Zealand above cited, and are no doubt the same; but, as there remarked, it is doubtful whether *Leskea rotulata* Hedw. was intended for this species, or for the next, *H. novae-seelandiae.* And indeed, it may be further remarked, there is a doubt whether Hedwig's species was intended for either." I have no further record of *H. novae-seelandiae* from Tahiti beyond the Wilkes Expedition citation by Sullivant; in Kindberg's (1901) monograph, its distribution is given from only New Zealand, and Sainsbury (1955) considers it to be a New Zealand and Tasmanian species only.

Hypopterygium rotulatum (Hedw.) Bridel
    Bryol. Univ. 2: 713. 1827.

The presence of this species in the Society Islands must be questioned. Sullivant (1859) indicated uncertainty in reporting *H. rotulatum* from the Wilkes Expedition Musci, and no further reports of its appearance in the Society Islands have been found. Dixon (1927) wrote that *H. rotulatum* differed from *H. novae-seelandiae* in having nontomentose stipes, the leaves reflexed in both wet and dry states, a less rigid habit, the branching more frequent and irregular. *Hypopterygium novae-seelandiae* was considered by Dixon to be more frequently of a bright- or yellowish-green, with more lax leaves, strongly undulate when dry but not deflexed.

XXXI. CYATHOPHORACEAE

The single representative of this family, *Cyathophorella*, is readily distinguished from its closest allies in the genus *Hypopterygium* by its unbranched habit and by the sack-like modification of amphigastria bases.

Cyathophorella (Brotherus) Fleischer
Musci Fl. Buitenzorg 3: 1088. 1908.
Cyathophorella tahitensis (Bescherelle) Fleischer
Musci Fl. Buitenzorg 3: 1096. f. 184x–z. 1908.
   Cyathophorum tahitense Besch., Ann. Sci. Nat. Bot. ser. 7, 20: 59. 1895.
   Cyathophorum pennatum var. *taitense* Nad., 1873.

Delicate plants found on tree bark or decaying wood where humidity is constantly high. Stems erect, to about 2 cm tall, arising from a prostrate primary stem, unbranched. Leaves are 3-ranked, in 2 lateral series which lie in the same plane, and the third series which forms the underleaves or amphigastria. Lateral leaves asymmetrical, 2–3 × 0.5–0.75 mm; costa short; underleaves symmetrical, ecostate, the uppermost about 1.75–2.0 × 0.5 mm, with unique "water-sacs" at the leaf base. Sporophytes not found.

ILLUSTRATIONS. Fleischer (1908, 3: 1092, f. 184x–z). Figure 82.

TAHITI. Without locality: *Nadeaud sn*, 1859 (Nadeaud, 1873, as *Cyathophorum pennatum* var. *taitense*); "Montagnes des environs de Marciati au fond de la vallée de Papenoo et au fond de la grande vallée de Punarua, au pied de l'Orohena," *Nadeaud 450*, 1896; "Montagnes de Hitiaa et du bord de la mer, celles de Faaiti, au pied de l'Aorai, ainsi que celles de la vallée de Tipaeaui," *Nadeaud 451*; "Vallées de Puaa et de Tearapau, vers 1100 mètres, la premiere a gauche, la deuxieme a droite de la grande vallée de Tipaeaui," *Nadeaud 452* (Bescherelle, 1898a, as *Cyathophorum tahitense*). Taiarapu Peninsula: On W-facing slope above experiment station, 400 m, on dead log, *2187*; on dead *Freycinetia* branches, *2184*; N side of peninsula, Haavini Valley, on *Inocarpus edulis* bark, with *Calymperes*, *Whittier sn*. Mataiea District: Road to Lake Vaihiria, *Eriksson sn* (Bartram, 1950b).

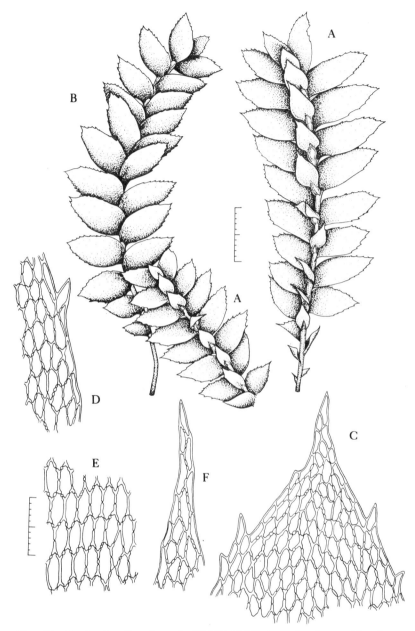

Fig. 82. *Cyathophorella tahitensis.* (*HOW 2187.*) A. Habit, lower side, showing underleaves (amphigastria). B. Habit, upper side. A, B, scale 2 mm. C. Lateral leaf, apex cells. D. Lateral leaf, margin cells. E. Lateral leaf, median cells. F. Amphigastrial leaf, apex cells. C–F, scale 100 μ.

MOOREA. Without locality: *Temarii Nadeaud sn,* 1899 (Besche-relle, 1901, as *Cyathophorum*).

Distribution.—Society Islands (Tahiti, Moorea), Samoa, Fiji.

Bescherelle (1898a) observed only sterile plants and plants with unfertilized archegonia along the length of the stems. As Fleischer (1908) noted, the underleaves have distinctive pouches or water sacs; these serve to separate *Cyathophorella tahitensis* from all other Society Islands mosses. It appears to be closely related to *Cyatho-phorum bulbosum* (Hedwig) C. Mueller of Australia, Tasmania, and New Zealand, which lacks the unique pouches associated with the amphigastria.

XXXII. THUIDIACEAE

Two closely related genera, *Thuidiopsis* and *Thuidium,* are reported from the Society Islands. Neither seems to be very common on Tahiti, and there are no records of their appearance on other islands of the archipelago. Most authorities (Brotherus, 1924b; Dixon, 1927; Bartram, 1933a) have treated *Thuidiopsis* as a subgenus of *Thuidium,* distinguished by branch leaves with long narrow points that become strongly incurved when dry so that the branches are catenulate. Fleischer (1923) recognized *Thuidiopsis* as a distinct genus, differing from the genus *Thuidium* which has branch leaves that do not strongly curve in toward the stem.

KEY TO GENERA OF THE THUIDIACEAE

1. Branch leaves long, narrow-pointed, the points strongly incurved when dry_____1. *Thuidiopsis.*
1. Branch leaves short-pointed, the points erect or only slightly incurved when dry_____2. *Thuidium.*

1. *Thuidiopsis* (Brotherus) Fleischer
   Musci Fl. Buitenzorg 4: 1497, 1515. 1923.
Thuidiopsis furfurosa (Hooker f. & Wilson) Fleischer
   Musci Fl. Buitenzorg 4: 1497. 1923.

> *Hypnum furfurosum* Hook. f. & Wils., Fl. Nov. Zel. 2: 10. f. 88. 1854.
> *Thuidium furfurosum* (Hook. f. & Wils.) Jaeg., Adumbr. 2: 332. 1878.
> *Thuidium denticulosum* (Mitt.) Jaeg., Adumbr. 2: 324. 1878. *fide* Sainsbury, 1955.

Plants yellow-green, not glossy, secondary stems to 10 cm long, creeping to suberect, the branches about 1 cm long. Stems densely covered by unbranched, simple or foliose paraphyllia; stout and woody, bipinnately branched. Stem leaves 1.5–2 mm long, spreading, triangular-ovate or lanceolate, acuminate, the margins of the upper lamina denticulate. The costa ends below the leaf apex in the upper one-half or one-third of the leaf. Branch leaves 0.75–1.0 mm long, imbricated, the leaf bases erect, the upper leaf curved in toward the stem when dry, but erect when moist. Branchlet leaves much smaller, shortly pointed, the costa ends near midleaf, and may be smooth or terminate in a spicule. Cells of stem and branch leaves are unipapillose, isodiametric, about 10 μ in diameter, the leaf apical cell truncate and bipapillose. Perichaetial leaves ovate-lanceolate, long-acuminate, the margins entire. Seta 2–3 cm long, red, flexuose; capsule 2.0–2.3 mm long, oblong-cylindric, cernuous, slightly curved, pale brown; operculum conic-rostrate, the beak inclined. Spores smooth, 10–12 μ. Description after Sainsbury (1955).

ILLUSTRATIONS. Hooker and Wilson (1854, 2: 10, 88, f. 7). Figure 83A–F.

TAHITI. Without locality: *Quayle 77* (Bartram, 1933a, FH). Tai-arapu Peninsula: N side, 150 m, Haavini Valley, with *Racopilum, Oxyrrhynchium, Ectropothecium,* and *Callicostella papillata, 2480.*

Distribution.—Society Islands (Tahiti), Australia, Tasmania, New Zealand, South America, Guatemala, Costa Rica.

Although Sainsbury (1955) and Bartram (1933a) both reported this species under the genus *Thuidium,* it seems appropriate to follow Fleischer's (1923) treatment under the genus *Thuidiopsis.* In personal correspondence with Bartram, Dixon (May, 1933) wrote: "I should have said your 77 [Quayle's collection from Tahiti] was certainly *T.* [*Thuidium*] *furfurosum.* I have many specimens from N.Z. which seem to me very close to it. . . . The broad stem leaves are, I think, a feature of this, though it varies enormously." Dixon recognized considerable variability in this species, indicated by his further comment: "I scarcely think my 260 is a form of this [*T. furfurosum*], though I know there is very little that *T. furfurosum* cannot do." The Society Islands specimens fit Sainsbury's description reasonably well, although the stem leaves are smaller, to about 0.75 mm long, and the lamina cells also tend to be smaller, 5–8 μ (rather than 10 μ) in diameter.

2. *Thuidium* Bruch, Schimper & Guembel
   Bryol. Eur. 5: 157. 1852.

Key to Species of *Thuidium*

1. Dioicous. Primary stem leaves to 0.5 mm long; paraphyllia 1–2 cells wide, usually 3 or more cells long _____1. *T. ramosissimum.*
1. Monoicous. Primary stem leaves to 0.4 mm long; paraphyllia 1 cell wide, 1–2 cells long_____2. *T. tahitense.*

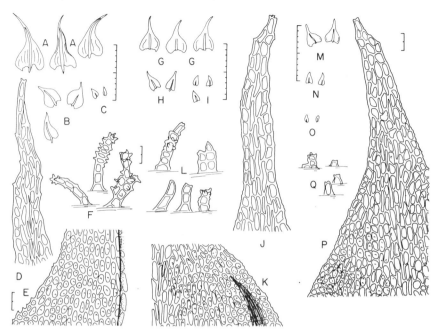

Fig. 83. A–F. *Thuidiopsis furfurosa.* (*HOW 2480.*) A. Leaves. B. Branch leaves. C. Branchlet leaves. A–C, scale 1 mm. D. Leaf tip. E. Upper leaf cells and margin. D, E, scale 20 μ. F. Stem paraphyllia, scale 20 μ. G–L. *Thuidium ramosissimum.* (*Quayle 663,* isotype.) G. Leaves. H. Branch leaves. I. Branchlet leaves. G–I, scale 1 mm. J. Leaf tip. K. Upper leaf cells and margin. L. Stem paraphyllia. J–L, scale 20 μ. M–Q. *Thuidium tahitense.* (*Nadeaud sn,* isotype.) M. Leaves. N. Branch leaves. O. Branchlet leaves. M–O, scale 1 mm. P. Upper leaf cells and tip. Q. Stem paraphyllia. P, Q, scale 20 μ. (*del.* HAM.)

1. *Thuidium ramosissimum* Dixon & Bartram
   Bishop Mus. Occ. Pap. 10(10): 21. f. 9. 1933a.

Dixon and Bartram's (1933a) original description:

Dioicous. Slender plants growing in extensive mats, yellowish-green above, brown below. Stems 4–5 cm long, bipinnately to tripinnately branched, the ultimate branches filiform and minute-leaved, paraphyllia scanty, usually of one row of cells, simple or branched. Stem leaves erect-spreading, about 0.5 mm long, triangular ovate from a subcordate base, rather abruptly short acuminate, concave, faintly plicate below; costa thin and faint, ending near the base of the acumen; margins plane, minutely crenulate with papillae; leaf cells irregularly oval-rhomboidal, with firm, pellucid walls, nearly or quite smooth above, papillose toward the base, branch leaves smaller, ovate, those of the ultimate branches about 0.12 mm long, bluntly pointed, the cells with 2 or 3 short, but very evident papillae.

ILLUSTRATIONS. Bartram (1933a, p. 22, f. 9). Figure 83G–L, from the type specimen, FH.

TAHITI. Pirae District: Fautaua Valley, 400–500 m, *Quayle 663a* (type, FH); *Quayle 663, 662b* (Bartram, 1933a, FH); 916 m, on rock, *2661*; 525 m, on bank, *Whittier sn.*

Distribution.—Society Islands (Tahiti), endemic.

The leaves of ultimate branches (in the type specimen) do tend to have incurved tips when in a dry state, and Bartram originally considered this species as best placed in the section *Thuidiopsis,* but accepted Dixon's advice (personal communication to Bartram, April, 1933) that the specimens were best treated as members of the section *Euthuidium* (*Thuidium*).

2. *Thuidium tahitense* Brotherus
   E. & P. Nat. Pfl. 1(3): 1013. 1908.
   Amblystegium byssoides Besch., Bull. Soc. Bot. France 45: 125. 1898.

Plants yellow-green, very slender, delicate, often found only inter-mixed with other bryophytes in damp, wet, shaded areas on rocks or bark. Branching is irregularly tripinnate, the main stems slender, about 0.13–0.15 mm in diameter; paraphyllia absent or very sparse, when present only 2–3 cells high. Primary stem leaves small, 0.30–0.38 × 0.20–0.24 mm, ovate to triangular ovate-lanceolate; costa ends below the leaf acumen. Secondary branch leaves smaller,

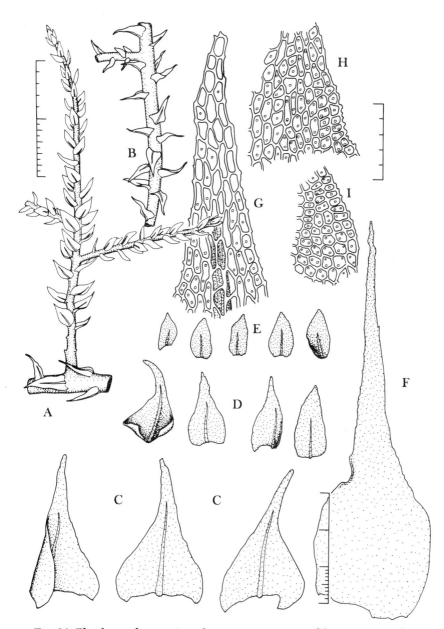

FIG. 84. *Thuidium tahitense*. A. Habit. B. Primary stem and leaves. A, B, scale 2 mm. C. Primary stem leaves. D. Secondary branch leaves. E. Tertiary branch leaves. F. Perichaetial leaf. C–F, scale 300 μ. G. Primary stem, leaf apex. H. Primary stem leaf, upper lamina and median cells. I. Primary stem leaf, basal cells. G–I, scale 50 μ.

ovate, short-acuminate, to 0.22 × 0.13 mm; ultimate branch leaves very small, to 0.12 × 0.07 mm. Cells of primary branch leaves 6–10 × 4–7 μ, irregularly quadrate to hexagonal, isodiametric to elongate. Perichaetial leaves ovate-lanceolate, long-acuminate, to 1.4–1.6 × 0.38 mm. Seta reddish-brown, about 2 cm long, smooth. The single depauperate capsule examined was ovate-cylindric, about 2.5 × 0.9 mm. (From a Nadeaud collection det. Bescherelle as *Amblystegium byssoides* Besch., NY).

ILLUSTRATIONS. Figures 83M–Q, 84.

TAHITI. Puaa and Tearapau valleys: On rocks on the floor of humid ravines, *Nadeaud 421*. Papara District: Temarua Valley, *Nadeaud 420*; Tarutu (Mamano) Valley, to 900 m, *Nadeaud 422* (Bescherelle, 1898a, as *Amblystegium byssoides*). Pirae District: Fautaua Cascade, with *Fissidens nadeaudii*, 2353; Mt. Aorai, 1700 m, in ravine below Chalet Fare Ata, with *Plagiochila*, 2959. Taiarapu Peninsula: Haavini Valley, 145 m, with *Dumortiera*, 2554; 150 m, with *Racopilum spectabile, Cyclodictyon blumeanum, Callicostella papillata*, and *Hypopterygium*, 2557.

Distribution.—Society Islands (Tahiti), endemic.

Bescherelle (1898a) recognized the similarity of Nadeaud's collections to *Thuidium byssoides*, but for some reason chose to identify the specimens not as *Thuidium* sp., but as belonging to the genus *Amblystegium*, and created a new species, *A. byssoides*. Brotherus (1908) properly identified this taxon as belonging to the genus *Thuidium*, and provided it with a new name, *T. tahitense*. In related taxa, Brotherus listed *T. crenulatum* Mitt. from Hawaii, which differs in the much more regular branch pattern, the larger, more papillose leaves, and in the much more abundant paraphyllia present in Mitten's type specimen (*Douglas sn*, Sandwich Islands, NY!), which might be treated more properly as a member of the genus *Thuidiopsis*.

XXXIII. AMBLYSTEGIACEAE

Platyhypnidium Fleischer
Musci Fl. Buitenzorg 4: 1536. 1923.
Platyhypnidium obscurum (Bescherelle) Fleischer
Musci Fl. Buitenzorg 4: 1537. 1923.

Rhynchostegium obscurum Besch., Ann. Sci. Nat. Bot. ser. 7, 20: 48. 1895.
Grimmia scouleri Nadeaud, 1873. *fide* Bescherelle, 1895.

Plants aquatic, on rocks in flowing water, dark green, stems 10–15 cm long, sparingly, irregularly branched, 2–2.5 mm wide with leaves slightly flattened; leaves erect-spreading laterally, ovate, abruptly acuminate, bases clasping the stems, margins decurrent, entire or nearly so toward the base, serrate toward the apex, 1.5–(1.6)–1.7 × 1.0–1.1 mm, costate; costa variably ending below midleaf (0.7 mm) or extending into the apex (1.2 mm), stout at the base, abruptly attenuated, to 120 μ wide, usually single, but with occasional unequal forks. Lamina cells irregularly elongate-hexagonal, the upper ends occasionally blunt, typically pointed, 37–(50)–75 × 2.5–(6.3)–10 μ; cells of the margins distinctively larger, uniformly wider; median basal cells 30–63 × 5–7 μ; alar cells short-rectangular, 10–15 × 5–7 μ. No sporophytes observed.

ILLUSTRATIONS. Figure 85.

TAHITI. Tearapau Peninsula: At the edge of streams, with *Brachythecium tearapense*, *Nadeaud 86*, 1859 (Bescherelle, 1895a, as *Rhynchostegium*).

Distribution.—Society Islands (Tahiti), endemic.

The above description is based upon specimen *2628* from the Conservatoire Botanique Genève, *64* in J. Nadeaud's "Enumération des plantes indigènes de l'ile de Tahiti," originally identified as "*Gumbelia Scouleri* (C. Müll.)??" and later as *Platyhypnidium obscurum* by Fleischer, who based his name upon Bescherelle's *Rhynchostegium obscurum*.

Fleischer (1923) described the genus *Platyhypnidium*: plants monoicous, yellow-green or blackened, aquatic, the branches flagelliferous. Leaves spreading to almost 90° (patent), to compressed, broadly ovate, obtuse to acuminate, the margins more or less dentic-

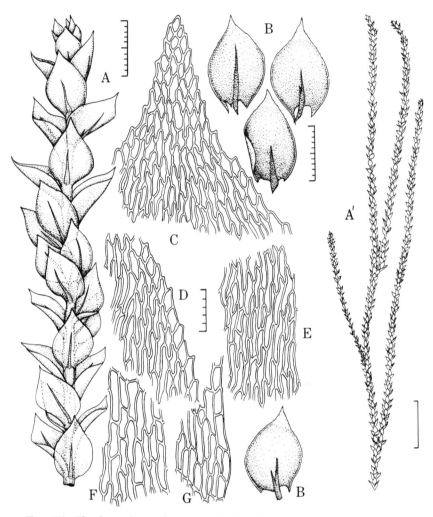

FIG. 85. *Platyhypnidium obscurum.* (*Nadeaud 64,* De Candolle Herb.) A. Habit, scale 1 cm. A'. Habit, scale 1 mm. B. Leaves, scale 1 mm. C. Leaf apex. D. Leaf margin. E. Lamina cells, upper median. F. Lamina cells, lower median. G. Lamina cells, basal angle. C–G, scale 50 μ.

ulate, plane, the costa single. Cells elongate, chlorophyllose, alar cells few, quadrate. Perichaetial leaves oblong-lanceolate, acuminate. Seta elongate, smooth, the capsule oblong, inclined, asymmetrical, the operculum short-rostrate, oblique, the calyptra smooth, cucullate. Peristome double, the endostome cilia short. Fleischer observed that most of the species of *Platyhypnidium* are closely related; his illustration of *P. muelleri* (Lac.) Fleisch. (1923, 4: 1538, f. 242), with nearly orbicular stem leaves and ovate-lanceolate branch leaves, may be of some use in identifying *P. obscurum*. In *Platyhypnidium muelleri*, the leaves are broadly ovate, obtuse to short-acuminate, to 1.6 × 1.3 mm, the margins denticulate. Lamina cells elongate-rhomboidal, 50–70 × 5–7 μ, shorter toward the apex, quadrate toward the leaf base. Seta smooth, 2–5 cm long; capsule ovoid, inclined, constricted beneath the mouth; exothecial cells 5–6-sided, thin-walled, rectangular; operculum conic-rostrate, the beak oblique. Peristome teeth inserted beneath the mouth, the exostome orange to greenish-brown, with narrow lamellae, the midline zigzag. Spores smooth, greenish, 15–20 μ. There can be no doubt that Fleischer intended *Platyhypnidium obscurum* 'Fleisch.' from Tahiti, as a recombination of *Rhynchostegium obscurum* Besch., and that only an error associated with publication could have been responsible for its incorrect citation, instead of *P. obscurum* (Besch.) which is proper and which followed the format Fleischer used in citing other recombinations.

XXXIV. BRACHYTHECIACEAE

In the Society Islands this family is represented by three genera: *Brachythecium, Rhynchostegium,* and *Oxyrrhynchium.* Plants are slender to robust, prostrate, forming mats of variable thickness. Leaves are ovate-lanceolate, usually erect-spreading, the costa single, ending in midleaf, the cells of the lamina linear. The seta is elongate, smooth to papillose, the capsule inclined to horizontal, symmetrical, the peristome double, exostome teeth striate, papillose, the endostome cilia prominent, as long as the peristome teeth.

Key to Genera of the Brachytheciaceae

1. Operculum short-pointed _____1. *Brachythecium.*
1. Operculum with a long beak
    2. Seta smooth; leaves concave; costa without a tooth at its tip on the back of the leaf; plants autoicous_____3. *Rhynchostegium.*
    2. Seta papillose; leaves plane or only slightly concave; costa ends with a tooth at its tip on the back of the leaf; plant dioicous_____
    _____2. *Oxyrrhynchium.*

1. *Brachythecium* Bruch, Schimper & Guembel
Bryol. Eur. 6: 5. 1853 (fasc. 52–54 Mon. 1).

Key to Species of *Brachythecium*

1. Seta scabrous (rough)_____1. *B. tearapense.*
1. Seta smooth_____2. *B. longipes.*

1. *Brachythecium tearapense* Bescherelle
Ann. Sci. Nat. Bot. ser. 7, 20: 47. 1895a.
>*Hypnum plumulosum* Sull., 1859, *nec* Hedwig. *fide* Bescherelle, 1895.
>*Hypnum paradoxum* Nad., 1873, *nec* Hooker f. & Wilson. *fide* Bescherelle, 1895.
>?*Brachythecium longipes* Broth., E. & P. Nat. Pfl. 1(3): 1147. 1908.
>*Brachythecium tarapense* Besch. *ex* Par., Ind. Bryol. Suppl. 51. 1900. *orthogr. pro B. tearapense* Besch.

Leaves to 1.5 × 0.46 mm, ovate-lanceolate, slightly concave, the upper margins serrulate. Cells of the upper median lamina 44–55 × 4–5 μ, linear, fusiform; basal cells enlarged, slightly inflated, about 55 × 13 μ, hyaline, irregularly rectangular, extending across the leaf base. Seta 3–4 cm tall, smooth below, slightly papillose above, reddish; capsule dark brown to black, horizontal, arcuate, broadest at the mouth, 1.2–1.5 × 0.9–1.0 mm; peristome teeth to 450 μ long, transversely striate below, hyaline and papillose toward the tips; inner peristome segments hyaline, papillose, as long as the outer teeth. Exothecial cells irregularly 4–6-sided, mostly 12–17 μ, the walls thickened at the angles. Spores yellow-green, 17–22 μ, smooth. (Based on *Nadeaud 366*, det. Bescherelle, NY.)

ILLUSTRATIONS. Figure 86.

TAHITI. Without locality: *Wilkes sn* (Sullivant, 1859, as *Hypnum plumulosum*); common throughout the interior of the island on trees in humid valleys at the base of Mt. Erereaoe, to Teapiri, Tearapau, and Papeava, *Nadeaud 366–368* (Bescherelle, 1898a); *Quayle 211a* (Bartram, 1933a, BISH!). Miaa: 850 m, *Temarii Nadeaud sn*, 1899 (Bescherelle, 1901).

Distribution.—Society Islands (Tahiti), endemic.

2. Brachythecium longipes Brotherus
E. & P. Nat. Pfl. 1(3): 1147. 1908.

"Autoicous. Pale green, glossy, stems up to 4–5 cm long, irregularly branched, flattened, about 4 mm. wide with leaves. Leaves ovate lanceolate, long acuminate, flattened, plicate, up to 2.5 mm long by 1 mm wide; costa very thin and faint, rarely extending halfway up and often almost entirely lacking; margins plane, denticulate all around; cells very long and narrow, decidedly more lax in a few rows across the extreme base. Seta 2.5–4 cm long, reddish brown to almost black, smooth; capsule short oblong, brown or blackish, arcuate and horizontal; operculum conic" (Bartram, 1933a, based on *Nadeaud 365*).

ILLUSTRATIONS. None.

TAHITI. Without locality: *Nadeaud 365*, 1896 (Bescherelle, 1898a, as *Brachythecium tearapense*; Brotherus, 1908, as *B. longipes*). Pirae District: *Quayle 697*, 1922; *Whitney Expedition 701–706* (Bartram, 1933a, as *B. longipes*).

Distribution.—Society Islands (Tahiti), endemic.

Bartram (1933a) observed that Nadeaud's collection *365* contained both *Brachythecium tearapense* and *B. longipes*, the former with a scabrous seta, the latter with a smooth, long seta, which could be referred to *B. longipes* Broth. These plants were similar to *B. lamprocarpum* (C. Muell.) Jaeg., from Hawaii, but appeared

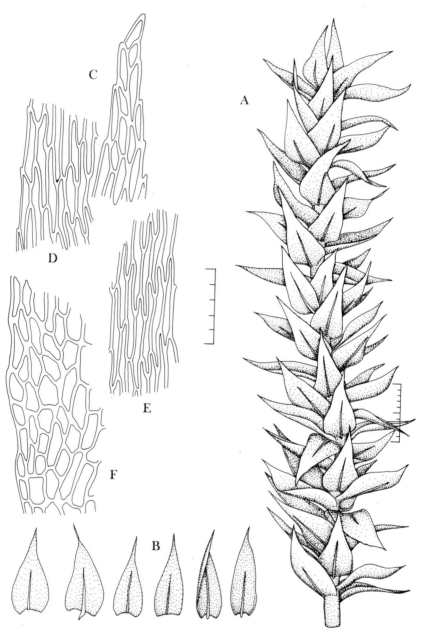

Fig. 86. *Brachythecium tearapense.* (*Nadeaud sn.*) A. Habit. B. Leaves. A, B, scale 1 mm. C. Leaf apex, cells. D. Lamina, upper margin cells. E. Lamina, upper median cells. F. Lamina, cells of basal angle. C–F, scale 50 μ.

to be distinct in the longer seta, larger leaves, and the unusually indistinct costa, according to Bartram. But Nadeaud's collection *366* (NY!) has the shorter leaves of *B. tearapense* (only the perichaetial leaves were as long as 2.5 mm), and the longer seta of *B. longipes,* with distinct papillae below the capsule! Brotherus (1908) referred to Bescherelle's original description in placing *B. tearapense* in his key, and apparently examined only specimens of his new species *B. longipes,* which appeared in one of the collections Bescherelle reported as *B. tearapense.* It seems possible that only one variable species exists in the Society Islands, but only examination of all the known collections will help to resolve the issue.

Among other closely related taxa is *B. oxyrrhynchium* (*Cirriphyllum*), which is known on all major Hawaiian Islands to Java and the Philippines. The costa is less strong and the seta is shorter.

2. *Oxyrrhynchium* (Bruch, Schimper & Guembel) Warnstorf
   Krypt. Fl. Brandenburg 2: 764, 781. 1905.
Oxyrrhynchium rugosipes (Bescherelle) Brotherus
   E. & P. Nat. Pfl. 1(3): 1155. 1905.
   Rhynchostegium rugosipes Besch., Bull. Soc. Bot. France 45: 120. 1898a.

Stem leaves 1.2–1.6 × 0.64–0.7 mm, broadly ovate, abruptly acuminate, slightly concave; costa extends three-fifths to four-fifths the length of the lamina and ends in a prickle or tooth on the leaf back. Cells linear, 80–110 × 4–7 μ, smooth, the ends rounded to pointed. Seta 2–3 cm long, smooth below, papillose in the upper third to half; capsule inclined to horizontal or pendulous, to 1.5 × 0.8 mm; operculum long-rostrate, to 1.9 mm (three-fifths of the length is beak). Perichaetial leaves to about 2 mm long. Exothecial cells 4–6-sided, irregularly rectangular to hexagonal, thin-walled, 24–36 × 12–17 μ. Peristome teeth to 370 μ high, transversely striolate at the base, papillose and hyaline at the tips. Spores smooth, 9–12 μ. (Based on *Nadeaud 306,* det. Bescherelle, NY!)

ILLUSTRATIONS. Figure 87.

TAHITI. Puaa and Tarutu valleys: To 900 m, on humid rock faces, fruiting, *Nadeaud 306, 369, 1859* (Bescherelle, 1898a, as *Rhynchostegium*). Haapape District: Miaa, 850 m, *Temarii Nadeaud 15,* 1899; Rahi, 850 m, *Temarii Nadeaud 19* (Bescherelle, 1901, as *Rhynchostegium*).

Distribution.—Society Islands (Tahiti), endemic.

Bescherelle (1898a) related this species to *Rhynchostegium dis-*

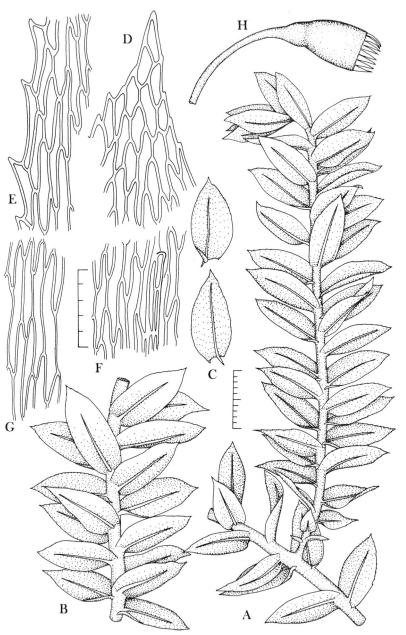

Fig. 87. *Oxyrrhynchium rugosipes.* (*Nadeaud sn.*) A. Habit. B. Habit. C. Leaves. A–C, scale 1 mm. D. Leaf apex cells. E. Lamina, upper margin cells. F. Lamina, cells at top of costa, lower surface of leaf (note prickle at tip of costa). G. Lamina, upper median cells. D–G, scale 50 μ. H. Urn, scale 1 mm.

tans Besch., from Réunion, from which it differs in the length of the seta and especially in the more broadly ovate leaves and the scabrous seta. The synoicous inflorescence, the long, cuspidate perichaetial leaves, and the longer seta distinguish *Oxyrrhynchium rugosipes* from *Hypnum asperipes* Mitt., from Tasmania.

3. **Rhynchostegium** Bruch, Schimper & Guembel
Bryol. Eur. 5: 197. 1852. (Fasc. 49–51 Mon. 1).
Rhynchostegium nigrescens Bescherelle
Bull. Soc. Bot. France 45: 121. 1898a.

Monoicous. Plants prostrate with suberect branches at irregular intervals along the primary stem; leaves spreading, slightly dimorphic, those of the lower series slightly narrower than the lateral leaves, and closer to the stem to give the stems a rather complanate appearance. Leaves broadly ovate, 2.2–2.4 × 0.8–1.1 mm, short-acuminate, apices twisted when dry; costa ends in the upper third to half of the lamina without forming a prickle or tooth at its tip on the back of the leaf; margins denticulate to the lower quarter of the leaf. Perichaetial leaves ecostate; margins entire, to 1.9 mm, long-acuminate. Lamina cells linear, 70–110 × 7–11 μ, smooth, the walls uniform, the ends rounded to pointed. Seta orange-brown, smooth, 2.5–3 cm long; capsule black, inclined, arcuate, asymmetrical, with a well-defined apophysis, and strongly constricted beneath the mouth when dry or empty, ovoid-cylindric when wet, 1.2–1.5 × 0.7–0.8 mm; peristome to about 400 μ high, the inner peristome almost as high; operculum long-rostrate. Exothecial cells 30–60 × 25–35 μ, thin-walled, the angles thickened. Spores smooth, 12–15 μ in diameter.

ILLUSTRATIONS. Figure 88.

TAHITI. Arue District: Teoa, to 1100 m, on wet rocks on valley floor, *Nadeaud sn* (NY). Puaa: To 1000 m, fruiting, *Nadeaud 370, 371* (Bescherelle, 1898a).

Distribution.—Society Islands (Tahiti), endemic.

The much larger leaves, the larger lamina cells, and the smooth seta without a prickle at its tip on the leaf back, serve to distinguish *Rhynchostegium nigrescens* from *Oxyrrhynchium rugosipes*.

Excluded species

Rhynchostegium debile Bescherelle
Bull. Soc. Bot. France 45: 121. 1898a.

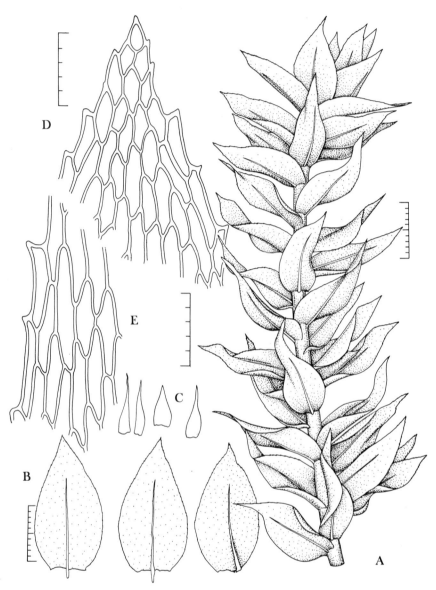

Fig. 88. *Rhynchostegium nigrescens.* (*Nadeaud 306.*) A. Habit, scale 1 mm.
B. Leaves, scale 1 mm. C. Perichaetial leaves, scale 1 mm. D. Leaf apex cells,
scale 50 μ. E. Lamina, upper margin and cells, scale 50 μ.

Brotherus (1908, 1(3): 1165) indicated this is not a *Rhyncho-stegium* but a *Vesicularia*. Only a single specimen, no. 372 (Na-deaud, no. *64*, NY!), was cited by Bescherelle (1898a), and it does exhibit the characters of the genus *Vesicularia*, but it is not in good condition, and many of the leaves have eroded apices. For this reason, I hesitate to refer this specimen to any given species of *Vesicularia*.

Rhynchostegium obscurum Bescherelle
Ann. Sci. Nat. Bot. ser. 7, 20: 48. 1895.

Fleischer (1923, 4: 1537) transferred this species to the genus *Platyhypnidium* in the family Amblystegiaceae. I have followed his treatment.

XXXV. ENTODONTACEAE

Entodon C. Mueller
  Linnaea 18: 704. 1845.
Entodon solanderi (Aongstrom) Jaeger
  Ber. S. Gall. Naturw. Ges. 1876–1877: 292. 1878. Adumbr. 2: 358.
  1879.
  Cylindrothecium solanderi Aongstr., Oefv. K. Svensk. Vet. Ak. Foerh.
    30(5): 122. 1873.
  Neckera macropoda, in hb. Thunberg Academy, Upsala, leg. Solander. *fide*
    Aongstrom, 1873.

Plants prostrate, yellow-green, irregularly branched, the branches
2–4 cm long, to 4 mm wide, with leaves; leaves imbricated, complanate, oblong-lanceolate, short-acuminate, 1.6–1.9 × 0.8–0.9 mm.
Cells of the lamina 80–90 × 4–5 μ, smooth, the walls uniformly
thickened; alar cells numerous, quadrate, 16–20 μ. Seta 2–2.5 cm
long, smooth, yellowish; capsule erect, cylindric, longitudinally furrowed when dry, 2.4–3.0 × 0.62–0.64 mm (Aongstrom, 1873, 3–4.5
mm long); operculum conic, 0.5–1 mm long. Peristome teeth inserted beneath the mouth of the capsule, longitudinally striate near
the base, papillose toward the tips; endostome segments keeled, as
long as the teeth. Calyptra pale yellow, 3–4 mm long.

ILLUSTRATIONS. Figure 89.

TAHITI. Without locality: *Solander sn* (in hb. as *Neckera macropoda*; Aongstrom, 1873, as *Cylindrothecium*); *Jacquinot sn*, 1840,
Astrolabe Expedition (in hb. Montagne as *Neckera cladorrhizans*);
Vesco sn, 1847; fruiting, *Andersson sn*; *Vieillard and Pancher 6*,
1855; fruiting, *Thiébault 529*, 1865; *Vernier sn* (Bescherelle, 1895a);
Menzies sn (Mitten, 1871, as *Entodon pallidus*, in part); *Larminat
sn* (Potier de la Varde, 1912). Papeete: Tamanu Plateau, 800–1000
m, in valleys on trees, and in the Fautaua and Arue valleys, *Nadeaud 360–364*; *Nadeaud 284*, 1896 (Bescherelle, 1898a). Haapape
District: Rahi, 800 m, *Temarii Nadeaud 18*; Miaa, 850 m, *Temarii
Nadeaud 13* (Bescherelle, 1901). Pirae District: Fautaua Canyon,
400–550 m, *Quayle 660, 662, 662a*; without locality, *Whitney Expedition 604*; *Brown and Brown sn* (Bartram, 1933a, BISH!, FH!);
Fautaua Valley, 50 m, on volcanic rock, *Hürlimann T 1120* (Hürli-

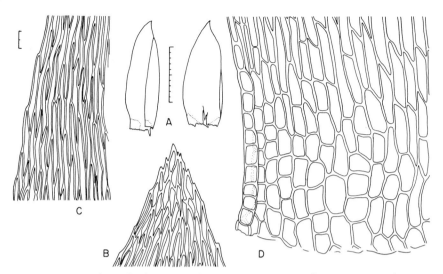

Fɪɢ. 89. *Entodon solanderi.* (*Quayle 604.*) A. Leaves, scale 1 mm. B. Leaf tip. C. Upper leaf cells and margin. D. Leaf base and alar cells. B–D, scale 20 µ. (*del.* HAM.)

mann, 1963, det. Bartram, FH!); 120 m, on exposed rocks, 2336; 310
m, with *Vesicularia, 2365;* 300 m, with *Bryum billardieri, Racopilum cuspidigerum,* and *Taxithelium vernieri, 3188.* Fare Rau Ape,
ca 500 m, *208;* Mt. Aorai trail, slender forms with long-acuminate
leaves, *318.* Papenoo District: Papenoo Valley floor, 150 m, *3015;*
100 m with *Hypopterygium* and *Rhynchostegium nigrescens* on
bark, *2984;* 150 m, on trunk and branches of tree, with *Ectropothecium sodale, 2992.*

MOOREA. Without locality: *Temarii Nadeaud 21, 1899* (Bescherelle, 1901).

Distribution.—Society Islands (Tahiti, Moorea), Austral Islands
(Raivavae), Rapa, Tubuai, Samoa, Hawaii (Oahu, Maui).

In none of the collections ascribed to *Entodon solanderi* which I
examined has the capsule exceeded 3 mm, although Aongstrom
(1873) gave its length as 3–4.5 mm; he cited the width of the plants
as 2 mm, but in none of the specimens studied has the width been
much under 3 mm, the leaves 1.6–1.9 × 0.8–0.9 mm, variable in the
degree of acumination. Aongstrom described the seta as 2–2.5 cm
long, which agrees well with specimens examined, but in *Quayle
604* (determined by Bartram) the seta is nearly 3 cm long. Cells
of the lamina vary in length from 70 to 100 μ, but in some specimens may be as long as 140 μ. *Entodon turgidus* was distinguished
by Aongstrom as pale green, 2.5–3 mm wide with leaves, the leaves
crowded, laterally erect-patent (spreading at an angle of 45° to
the sides of the stem), more closely appressed to the stem above
and below. Bescherelle (1895a, p. 46) described fruiting material
of *E. turgidus* for the first time: seta 20–23 mm long; capsule 3 mm
long, erect, the columella slightly exserted; operculum short, conic-
acuminate, and curved; calyptra long, cylindric, smooth, and straw
yellow. The plants are sometimes dioicous, sometimes monoicous.
The isotype of *E. turgidus* (NY!) differs little from the specimens
determined by various authors as *E. solanderi,* and as *E. solanderi*
is the most widely used name I propose to continue its recognition
as a distinct species, and that *E. turgidus* be treated as a variety,
distinguished by more robust plants, the stems wider, the lamina
cells longer than those of *E. solanderi* var. *solanderi.* Further study
should provide additional supporting information.

Entodon solanderi (Aongstrom) Jaeger var. *turgidus* (Aongstrom)
Whittier *stat. nov.*

Entodon turgidus (Aongstr.) Jaeg., Ber. S. Gall. Naturw. Ges. 1876–1877: 292. 1878. Adumbr. 292. 1879.

Cylindrothecium turgidum Aongstr., Oefv. K. Svensk. Vet. Ak. Foerh. 30(5): 124. 1873.

Rhegmatodon rufus Nad., 1873. *nec* C. Mueller, *fide* Bescherelle, 1895.

ILLUSTRATIONS. None.

TAHITI. Without locality: Fruiting, *Vesco sn,* 1847; with old capsules, *Andersson sn,* 1852 (Aongstrom, 1873, as *Cylindrothecium turgidum,* isotype, NY). Pirae District: Fautaua and Orofero valleys, dry ridges on tree bark, 600 m, *Nadeaud 71,* 1859 (Nadeaud, 1873, as *Rhegmatodon rufus*); *Vernier sn* (Bescherelle, 1895a, as *Entodon turgidus*). Pinai: High valleys, 800 m, *Nadeaud sn* (Bescherelle, 1898a, as *E. turgidus, 356–359;* NY!, *sn*). Papeari District: Maara Valley, *Setchell and Parks 5316* (Brotherus, 1924a, as *E. turgidus*); *Beechey sn* (in hb. Mitten, NY, as *E. turgidus!*).

XXXVI. PLAGIOTHECIACEAE

Catagonium C. Mueller
in Brotherus, E. & P. Nat. Pfl. 1(3): 1087. 1908.
Catagonium gracile (Bescherelle) Brotherus
E. & P. Nat. Pfl. 1(3): 1088. 1908.
Acrocladium gracile Besch., Bull. Soc. Bot. France 48: 15. 1901.
Eucatagonium gracile (Besch.) Broth., E. & P. Nat. Pfl. ed. 2, 11: 178. 1925.

Bescherelle's original description:

Monoicum. Planta gracilis interrupte pinnata, ramis unciali-
bus horizontalibus remotis gracilibus apice decrescentibus.
Folia lutescente viridia, erecto-patentia, basi coarctata, ovato-
concava, apice late acuminata, cellulis marginalibus rectangulis
dentiformibus, ceteris vermicularibus ad basin luteis reticulata,
enervia. Folia perichaetialia anguste perlonga, apice nodoso-
denticulata. Perigonium minutum infra perichaetium positum
foliis concavis apice denticulatis. Capsula in pedicello 15 millim. longo laevi cygnicolla, inclinata vel horizontalis, cylindrica
vel aetate curvatula, operculo crasse rostrato. Peristomii duplicis
dentes externi curvati, dense cristati, interni aequilongi ciliis
duobus brevioribus scaberrimis intermixtis.

ILLUSTRATIONS. None.
MOOREA. Vaianae: *Nadeaud 27,* 1899 (Bescherelle, 1901, as *Acrocladium*).
Distribution.—Society Islands (Moorea), endemic.
Bescherelle (1901) compared this species with *Acrocladium
politum* Hook. f. & Wils. (= *Catagonium*) from New Zealand, distinguishing it on the basis of more slender branches, leaves more
obtusely acuminate and denticulate than in *C. politum.* If there is
a close parallel between these species, the costa of *C. gracile* may
be short and double or absent.

320

XXXVII. SEMATOPHYLLACEAE

Seven genera comprise the family Sematophyllaceae in the Society Islands: *Meiothecium, Sematophyllum, Acroporium, Trichosteleum, Taxithelium, Rhaphidorrhynchium,* and *Glossadelphus. Acroporium* and *Sematophyllum* are erect to suberect and form tufts or turfs, usually on tree bark; the remaining genera form mats or appear as isolated strands on the ground, on rocks, decaying organic debris, and tree trunks and branches. *Taxithelium* is occasionally found on the leaves of ferns or flowering plants.

KEY TO GENERA OF THE SEMATOPHYLLACEAE

1. Plants forming tufts or turfs, erect to suberect
    2. Plants robust, 5–6 cm tall; peristome teeth with a pronounced median furrow_____1. *Acroporium.*
    2. Plants to 2–3 cm tall; peristome teeth with a fine zigzag line_____ _____2. *Sematophyllum.*
1. Plants appearing as thin mats or as isolated strands, prostrate
    2. Costa double, occasionally absent or single in some leaves_____ _____3. *Glossadelphus.*
    2. Costa absent
        3. Peristome single; lamina cells short-ovate, smooth; leaves short-acuminate _____4. *Meiothecium.*
        3. Peristome double; lamina cells ovate-elongate to linear, smooth to seriate-papillose; leaves long-acuminate
            4. Operculum short; lamina cells linear, usually finely seriate-papillose, alar cells quadrate to rectangular, enlarged but not inflated _____6. *Taxithelium.*
            4. Operculum long-rostrate; lamina cells ovate-elongate, coarsely seriate-papillose, or linear and smooth; alar cells inflated
                5. Seta smooth; lamina cells linear, 40–60 $\times$ 4 μ, smooth_____ _____5. *Rhaphidorrhynchium.*
                5. Seta coarsely papillose below capsule, rarely smooth, lamina cells ovate-elongate, 12–40 $\times$ 3–4 μ, coarsely seriate-papillose _____7. *Trichosteleum.*

1. *Acroporium* Mitten
J. Linn. Soc. Bot. 10: 182. 1868.

The erect stems are irregularly branched, and form deep tufts or extensive, loosely compacted turfs several centimeters thick. Leaves are erect-spreading, ovate-lanceolate, the bases slightly auriculate, the basal angles differentiated into inflated, hyaline to yellowish cells; ecostate. Lamina cells are smooth, linear, the walls pitted. The seta is smooth to papillose; capsule erect to horizontal; operculum long.

Key to Species of *Acroporium*

1. Leaves to 2.5 × 0.7 mm, lamina cells 60–100 × 3–4 μ; sporophyte seta 0.6–1.0 cm long..1. *A. sigmatodontium.*
1. Leaves 1–1.5 × 0.6–0.7 mm, lamina cells 50–60 × 2–3 μ; sporophyte seta to 2.0 cm..2. *A. lepinei.*

1. *Acroporium sigmatodontium* (C. Mueller) Fleischer
Musci Fl. Buitenzorg 4: 1281. 1923.

Hypnum sigmatodontium C. Muell., Syn. 2: 687. 1851.
Sematophyllum acutirameum (Mitt.) Jaeg., Ber. S. Gall. Naturw. Ges. 1876–1877: 383. 1878. *fide* Fleischer, 1923.
Sematophyllum sigmatodontium (C. Muell.) Jaeg., Ber. S. Gall. Naturw. Ges. 1876–1877: 382. 1878.
Stereodon acutirameus Mitt., J. Linn. Soc. Bot. Suppl. 1: 106. 1859. *fide* Fleischer, 1923.
Acroporium brachypodum Dix., *in* Bartram, Philippine J. Sci. 68: 335. 1939. *nom. nud.* =var. *brachypodum* Bartr., 1939.
Acroporium robinsonii (Broth.) Broth., E. & P. Nat. Pfl. ed. 2, 11: 437. 1925. = var. *robinsonii* (Broth.) Bartr., 1939.

Plants 4–5 cm long; leaves 2.5 × 0.7 mm. Lamina cells linear, 60–100 × 3–4 μ; alar cells to 150 × 45 μ. Seta 6–10 mm long, red, papillose above; capsule erect to horizontal, 0.8–1 × 0.4–0.5 mm, constricted beneath the mouth when dry; epidermal cells 5–8-sided, thin-walled with thickened angles; outer peristome teeth transversely striate below, papillose toward the tips, to 280–300 μ long. Spores 20–25 μ, minutely papillose, yellow-green.

ILLUSTRATIONS. Dozy and Molkenboer (1861, Bryol. Jav. 2: t. 311), Bartram (1939, pl. 25, f. 427).

RAIATEA. Mt. Temehani: On wet *Pandanus* branches in deep shade, 450 m, *Moore 7*. Highest mountain: W side, 400 m, on wet branches of trees, *Moore 37* (Bartram, 1931, FH).

Distribution.—Society Islands (Raiatea), Sri Lanka (Ceylon), Java, Sumatra, Philippine Islands, New Guinea, Vietnam, d'Entrecasteaux.

2. *Acroporium lepinei* (Bescherelle) Fleischer
Musci Fl. Buitenzorg 4: 1303. 1923.

Sematophyllum lepinei Besch., Ann. Sci. Nat. Bot. ser. 7, 20: 48. 1895a.

Plants 7–8 cm tall; leaves 1–1.5 × 0.6–0.7 mm; lamina cells linear,

50–60 × 2–3 μ; alar cells to 110 × 35 μ. Seta 10–20 mm long, red, smooth; capsule erect to inclined, ovoid, 0.95–1.1 × 0.45–0.55 mm, constricted beneath the mouth; epidermal cells 5–8-sided, 17–25 μ in diameter, the angles thickened; peristome transversely striate below, papillose above, about 250 μ long. Spores 22–25 μ, yellow-green, finely papillose. Fleischer (1923) reported the plants as dioicous, the male plants found as dwarfs on the leaves of archegoniate plants, contrary to Bescherelle's (1895a) observation that the plants are synoicous.

ILLUSTRATIONS. Figure 90.

TAHITI. Taiarapu: About 600 m, *Lépine 15*, 1847 (type, P); *Vesco sn*; as *Hypnum fuscescens*, *Nadeaud 87*, 1859 (Nadeaud, 1873); *Ribourt sn*, 1850 (Bescherelle, 1895a, as *Sematophyllum*). Without locality: 800–1000 m, *Nadeaud 373–376*. Marciati: Fruiting, *Nadeaud 117* (in hb. NY as var. *imbricatulum* Besch. *mss*; Bescherelle, 1898a, as *Sematophyllum*). Pirae District: Trail to summit Mt. Aorai, above 1386 m, *Quayle 147, 149, 155b, 157, 158, 163*; *Whitney Expedition 702, 705c*; S side Mt. Orohena, on tree trunk, *MacDaniels 1553* (Bartram, 1933a, FH, BISH!). Mataiea District: Above Vaihiria, 1000 (840?) m, *Eriksson 62* (Bartram, 1950, FH!). Taiarapu Peninsula: Taravao, above experiment station, 800 m, in *Metrosideros* and *Cyathea* forest, *2155*; 610 m, forming thick cushions on tree branches, *2239*.

RAIATEA. Mt. Temehani: On wet *Pandanus* tree in deep shade, 450 m, *Moore 7a*; 300 m, E side, on wet *Pandanus* branches, *Moore 21*; 500 m, W side, on wet branches of trees in small valley, *Moore 26*; 300 m, E of "hole," on wet *Pandanus* branches, *Moore 29*; 700 m, W side, on wet branches of trees, *Moore 30, 31*. Faaroa Bay: N side, 500 m, on top of mountain, among other mosses, *Moore 54a, 60, 62a, 63, 64a, 69*. Averaiti Valley: Upper end, 400 m, on wet branches of trees in shade, *Moore 55, 58, 81* (Bartram, 1931, FH).

Distribution.—Society Islands (Tahiti, Raiatea), Marquesas Islands (Nuku Hiva), Fiji (Viti Levu), Samoa, Celebes.

Acroporium lepinei is abundantly represented in all damp humid valleys and upper elevations, common on branches, forming pure tufts or intermixed with other bryophytes. It is best distinguished from A. *sigmatodontium* by the longer seta (to 2 cm) and the shorter leaves (to 1.5 mm, as opposed to 2.5 mm in A. *sigmatodontium*).

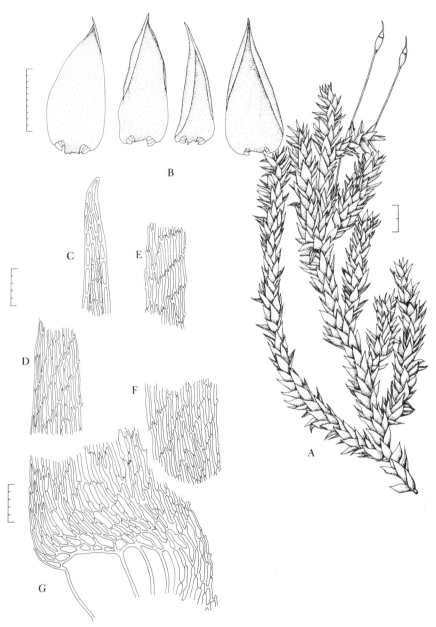

FIG. 90. *Acroporium lepinei*. A. Habit, scale 2 mm. B. Leaves, scale 1 mm. C. Leaf apex cells, scale 50 μ. D. Upper lamina cells. E. Upper lamina, median cells. F. Lower lamina, median cells. G. Leaf base, margin and alar cells. D–G, scale 50 μ.

2. *Sematophyllum* Mitten
J. Linn. Soc. Bot. 8: 5. 1864.

Two species of *Sematophyllum* have been recognized from the Society Islands: *S. entodontoides* and *S. moorei*, the former known only from Tahiti, the latter only from Moorea. Distinctions between the two are minor and I believe *S. moorei* merits recognition only as a variety of *S. entodontoides*.

Sematophyllum entodontoides Bescherelle
Bull. Soc. Bot. France 45: 122. 1898a.

Plants prostrate with branches erect, to 5 cm long, irregularly branched, reddish-green; leaves concave, narrowly ovate-lanceolate, acute, 1.6–1.9 × 0.50–0.54 mm, ecostate, entire; perichaetial leaves denticulate, acuminate, to 2.1 × 0.5 mm, the teeth large, irregular, rounded at the tips. Cells of the lamina (in vegetative leaves) elongate, smooth, 44–55 × 3–5 μ, thick-walled, pitted; alar cells and basal cells orange-brown, the alar cells inflated, thick-walled, 3–4 on each side of the leaf, about 70–90 × 20–25 μ. Seta smooth, to 15 mm long; capsule inclined, 1.2 × 0.65 mm, ovoid; exothecial cells 5–8-sided, the angles thickened, nearly isodiametric, 25–35 μ; peristome teeth strongly papillose, trabeculate, to about 250 μ long. Spores finely papillose, greenish-yellow, spherical to ellipsoidal, 25–35 × 25–30 μ. (Based on *Nadeaud 378*, NY!)

ILLUSTRATIONS. Figure 91A–H.

TAHITI. Pinai and Marciati: Ravines, on branches of trees on elevated ridges, *Nadeaud 377, 378* (NY), 1896 (Bescherelle, 1898a). Haapape District: Rahi, 800 m, *Temarii Nadeaud 20*, 1899 (Bescherelle, 1901).

Distribution.—Society Islands (Tahiti), endemic.

Bescherelle named this species on the basis of its branching pattern, which reminded him of *Entodon flavescens* (Hook.) Jaeg., and he contrasted it with *Acroporium lepinei* in his observation that *Sematophyllum entodontoides* has larger upper stem leaves and strongly dentate perichaetial leaves.

Sematophyllum entodontoides var. *moorei* (Bartr.) Whittier *stat. nov.*
Sematophyllum moorei Bartr., Bishop Mus. Occ. Pap. 9(16): 11. f. 4. 1931.

Plants similar in all major respects to *S. entodontoides*, but

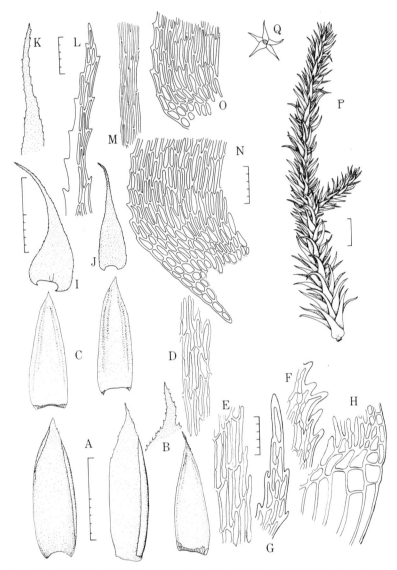

FIG. 91. A–H. *Sematophyllum entodontoides.* (*Nadeaud 378.*) A. Perichaetial leaves. B. Perichaetial leaves, leaf apex. C. Stem leaves. A–C, scale 1 mm. D. Lamina cells, upper median. E. Lamina cells near base. F. Lamina cells, upper margin perichaetial leaf. G. Apex, perichaetial leaf. H. Lamina cells, basal angle. D–H, scale 50 µ I–Q. *Ctenidium stellulatum.* (Type, NY. From an original illustration by Ando, 1960, accompanying the specimen; figures I–O, P, Q by HOW.) I. Stem leaf. J. Branch leaf. K. Branch leaf apex. I–K, scale 1 mm. L. Branch leaf, apex cells. M. Lamina median cells, branch leaf. N. Stem leaf, basal angle. O. Branch leaf, basal angle. L–O, scale 50 µ. P. Habit, scale 1 mm. Q. Stem, cross section showing 5-ranked leaf arrangement.

slightly smaller. Cells of the lamina slightly longer, 60–70 μ, but the alar cells are approximately the same. Perichaetial leaves slightly smaller in the three specimens studied (including Bartram's type specimen). Sporophytes similar: the seta the same length, to 14–15 mm, smooth; capsules identical, differing only slightly in the length of the exostome teeth, which are about 10–20 μ longer than in *S. entodontoides* var. *entodontoides*; exothecial cells and spores are essentially identical in their dimensions.

ILLUSTRATIONS. Bartram (1931, p. 12, f. 4).

RAIATEA. Mt. Temehani: In valley E of mountain, 300 m, on wet *Pandanus* branches, *Moore 23* (type, FH; Bartram, 1931, as *S. Moorei*).

Distribution.—Society Islands (Raiatea), endemic.

Bartram (1931) wrote: "A beautiful species, comparable to no other with which I am familiar. The plants are unusually robust for the genus, rather rigid, densely and compactly matted together and of a brilliant golden-yellow color. The small, short pointed leaves are closely imbricated in a neat trim manner, and frequently, but not always, in distinct spiral rows."

3. *Glossadelphus* Fleischer
Musci Fl. Buitenzorg 4: 1351. 1923.

Key to Species of *Glossadelphus*

1. Leaves 1.0 × 0.5 mm, lamina cells very faintly pluripapillose..1. *G. tahitensis.*
1. Leaves 0.6–0.7 × 0.3–0.4 mm, lamina cells smooth...........2. *G. torrentium.*

1. *Glossadelphus tahitensis* Bartram
Bishop Mus. Occ. Pap. 10(10): 25. f. 11. 1933a.

Plants prostrate, irregularly branched, yellow or yellow-green, the branches tufted, flexuose, ascending, blunt at the tips; leaves ovate, concave, broadly rounded at the apex to obtuse, about 1.0 × 0.5 mm; margins erect, denticulate to the base, papillose-crenulate; costa double, from one-quarter to one-half the length of the leaf. Median lamina cells linear, 40–60 × 4–6 μ, seriate-papillose, marginal cells shorter, rhomboidal toward the apex, becoming shorter and larger toward the base, undifferentiated. Perichaetial leaves ovate-lanceolate, acuminate, to 1.5 mm, ecostate, smooth toward the base, seriate-papillose toward the apex. Antheridial branches short, to 0.25 mm, with 6–8 antheridia and about 6 ovate, obtuse perigonial leaves; cells smooth. Sporophytes with red, smooth seta, to 2.5 cm; capsule asymmetrical, cylindric, horizontal, constricted beneath the mouth when dry; exothecial cells thin-walled; operculum conic, apiculate, to 0.6 mm. Spores smooth, about 15 μ.

ILLUSTRATIONS. Bartram (1933a, p. 26, f. 11).

TAHITI. Pirae District: Pirae–Mt. Aorai trail, *Whitney Expedition sn* (Bartram, 1933a); 1800 m, in valley N of Chalet Fare Ata, with *Leucomium aneurodictyon* and *Fissidens nadeaudii, 2911.*

Distribution.—Society Islands (Tahiti), endemic.

Bartram (1933a) commented: "This is an interesting plant combining the leaf cells of *Taxithelium* with the characteristic blunt, costate leaves of *Glossadelphus*. It will be distinguished at once from *G. torrentium* (Besch.) Fleisch. by the papillose leaf cells." I originally identified my collections as *Taxithelium nepalense*, which has broadly ovate leaves and a broadly acute apex, but the presence of the double costa and the broadly rounded leaf tips will serve at once to distinguish *Glossadelphus tahitensis.*

2. *Glossadelphus torrentium* (Bescherelle) Fleischer
Musci Fl. Buitenzorg 4: 1352. 1923.

Amblystegium torrentium Besch., Bull. Soc. Bot. France 45: 125. 1898a.
Stereophyllum torrentium (Besch.) Besch., Bull. Soc. Bot. France 48(1): 16. 1901.
Ligulina torrentium (Besch.) C. Muell., *mss. fide* Bescherelle, 1898a.

Plants prostrate, slender, stems 3–5 cm long, dark green; branches 6–8 mm long, curved at the apex; leaves elliptical, the apex broadly rounded, 0.59–0.70 × 0.32–0.39 mm, costate, but variable. The costa may be double, the segments short and equal, or markedly unequal so as to appear as a single costa, and in some leaves the costa may be absent. Cells of the lamina fusiform, 36–60 × 4–5 μ, smooth, the walls thin and uniformly thickened; basal cells short-rectangular to quadrate, those of the alar regions slightly smaller and not inflated. Sporophytes not seen.

Bescherelle (1901) amended his original description: "Capsula in pedicello 25 millim. longo laevi purpureo obliqua, arcuata, nigrescens, operculo breviter conico acuminato. Peristomium generis. Folia perichaetilia longe ligulata, obtuse acuminata, apice denticulata, torta."

ILLUSTRATIONS. Figure 92.

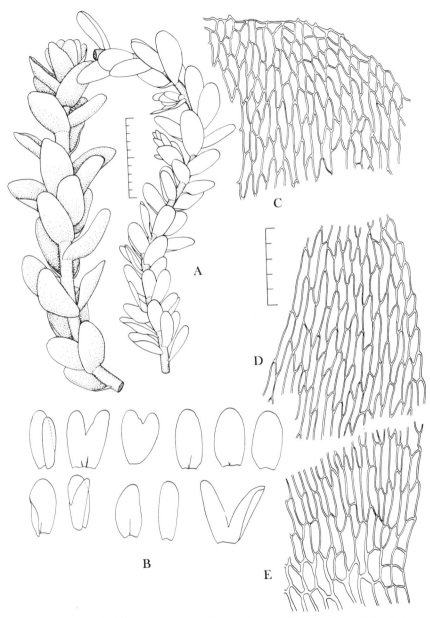

Fig. 92. *Glossadelphus torrentium.* (*Nadeaud sn,* without locality, Tahiti.) A. Habit. B. Leaves (note variability in costa and in leaf outline). A, B, scale 1 mm. C. Leaf apex. D. Lamina, upper margin and median cells. E. Leaf, cells of basal angle. C–E, scale 50 μ.

TAHITI. Pirae District: Faaiti Valley, on basaltic rock and sub-merged stones, and in the Piraa Valley, on rocks, *Nadeaud sn,* 1896 (Bescherelle, 1898a, as *Amblystegium*). Miaa: 850 m, *Temarii Nadeaud sn,* 1899 (Bescherelle, 1901, as *Stereophyllum*).

Distribution.—Society Islands (Tahiti), endemic.

On the basis of fruiting material, Bescherelle (1901) altered his treatment of this species to include it in the genus *Stereophyllum.* The areolation of vegetative leaves suggested the original place-ment of this species in the genus *Amblystegium.* Fleischer (1923) transferred this species to the genus *Glossadelphus,* section *Ana-stigma* Card., without comment. This species is undoubtedly close to *Glossadelphus prostratus* (Dozy & Molk.) Fleisch., from Java, and through further study may prove to be synonymous. Although I have indicated the cells of *G. torrentium* to be smooth, in some leaves the upper end walls seem to project slightly to form minute papillae.

4. *Meiothecium* Mitten
J. Linn. Soc. Bot. 10: 185. 1868.

Plants usually slender, irregularly branched, prostrate, intermixed with other bryophytes on bark; occasionally forming thin, pale green mats; leaves ovate-lanceolate, short-pointed, concave, rather rigid in appearance, ecostate, the margins entire. Cells ovate-elongate, smooth, the walls pitted in the lower lamina; alar cells enlarged, usually inflated. Seta short; capsule erect to inclined; operculum conic-rostrate; peristome single, the teeth papillose.

Key to Species of *Meiothecium*

1. Leaves obtuse or rounded at the apex............................2. M. *rechingeri.*
1. Leaves acute or acuminate at the apex
    2. Leaf apices curved in toward the stem.....................1. M. *hamatulum.*
    2. Leaf apices erect, not curved in toward the stem
        3. Leaves slightly denticulate, 1.25–1.75 mm, keeled, margins narrowly recurved toward the apex.....................3. M. *serrulatum.*
        3. Leaves entire, 0.5–0.8 mm, concave but not keeled, margins broadly recurved................................4. M. *intextum.*

1. *Meiothecium hamatulum* (Bescherelle) Brotherus
E. & P. Nat. Pfl. 1(3): 1103. 1908.

Pterogoniella hamatula Besch., Bull. Soc. Bot. France 48: 15. 1901.
Pterogoniella viahiensis Besch., *nom. nud., loc. cit.*
Neckera madagascariensis Nadeaud, 1873. *nec* C. Mueller Enum. Pl. p. 15. 1873.

I have not seen the original specimen described by Bescherelle (P). In order to avoid problems stemming from differences in translation, the original Latin description follows:

Monoica? Habitu *P. hamatae* similis. Folia anguste et longe ovato-lanceolata, acumine hamato-inflexa, haud reflexa, profunde concava, margine haud revoluta integerrima, cellulis minutissimis elongate ellipticis incrassatis parietibus vix distinctis ad basin infimam majoribus flavidis marginem versus vesiculosis majusculis areolata; costis obsoletis vel nullis. Folia perichaetialia caulinis minora, erecta, infima acute acuminata apice denticulata. Capsula in pedicello brevi purpureo dupliciter geniculato laevi erecta, ovata vel ovato-cylindrica, fusca; operculo conico oblique rostrato. Peristomii simplicis dentes madore erecti, breves, lanceolati, dense, trabeculati, grisei, punctulati, lineamedia exarati. Calyptra basi brevissime laciniata undique scabriuscula.

ILLUSTRATIONS. None.

TAHITI. Pirae District: Ridges of Mts. Aorai and Aramaore, *Nadeaud sn* (Nadeaud, 1873, as *Neckera madagascariensis*). Hitiaa District: Vaihi, among lichen thalli, *Temarii Nadeaud sn*, 1899 (Bescherelle, 1901, as *Pterogoniella*).

Distribution.—Society Islands (Tahiti), endemic.

Bescherelle named this species for its resemblance to *Meiothecium* (*Pterogoniella*) *hamatum*, and noted that it differed in its leaves, which curved in toward the stem at the apex, rather than back toward the base of the stem, and which are more narrow, more gradually acuminate than in *M. hamatum*.

2. *Meiothecium rechingeri* Brotherus *in* Rechinger
Denschr. Ak. Wiss. Wien, Math. Nat. Kl. 84: 399. 1908.

I have not seen authentic specimens of this species. Bartram (1933a) wrote: "Although most of the leaves on these plants are definitely obtuse or rounded at the point, a few from every stem examined show a close approach to *M. hamatum* (C. Muell.) (tab. 219, Bryol. Javanica). The average, however, is constantly shorter and more rounded, so I have tentatively referred these plants to *M. rechingeri* Brotherus, of Samoa, although the color is a golden brown rather than green. At any rate it is a fine addition to the local flora and new to Tahiti."

ILLUSTRATION. None.

TAHITI. Pirae District: Pirae–Mt. Aorai trail, *Quayle sn* (Bartram, 1933a).

Distribution.—Society Islands (Tahiti), Samoa.

3. *Meiothecium serrulatum* Dixon
   in Dixon and Greenwood, Proc. Linn. Soc. N. S. Wales 55: 298. 9 f. 25. 1930.

I have not seen authentic specimens of this species; Dixon's original description follows: "Habitu *M. microcarpi* sed robustius, aureo-viride vel brunnescens. Folia paullos majora 1.25–1.75 mm. longa, minus profunde carinata, apus apicem plerumque marginibus anguste recurvis; ibidem, plus minusve distincte, nonnunquam argute denticulatis. Cellulae superiores paullos majores, anguste ellipticae, subsinuosae, parietibus perincrassatis. Fructus ignotus."

ILLUSTRATIONS. Dixon and Greenwood (1930, pl. 9, f. 25).

RAIATEA. Temehani range: S end, 300 m, on branch of shrub, *Moore 49* (Bartram, 1931, FH).

Distribution.—Society Islands (Raiatea), Fiji (Vanua Levu, type locality).

Only sterile specimens were examined by Dixon, who observed that the larger size and more or less distinctly denticulate, recurved apical margins made this a well-defined species.

4. *Meiothecium intextum* Mitten
   J. Linn. Soc. Bot. 10: 185. 1868.

Plants golden to green, prostrate to suberect, 0.8–1.1 mm wide with leaves; leaves spreading at a 30–40° angle to the stem, ovate-oblong, acute, concave, 0.5–0.8 mm long; margins broadly recurved, entire. Cells smooth, oval-elongate, 12–25 × 5–7 μ in the upper lamina, the walls irregularly thickened, slightly shorter toward the apex, longer toward the leaf base; alar cells 2–3 on each side, inflated, to 25 × 15 μ; leaf base golden- or yellow-brown. No sporophytes seen. Mitten (1868) described the perichaetial leaves as lanceolate, slightly obtuse, serrulate; seta short, reddish; capsule oval, inclined; operculum short-rostrate; peristome single; calyptra scabrous.

ILLUSTRATIONS. Figure 93.

TAHITI. Taiarapu Peninsula: Taravao, above experiment station, on N slope, 610 m, on bark, with *Leucobryum tahitense* and *Rhizo-*

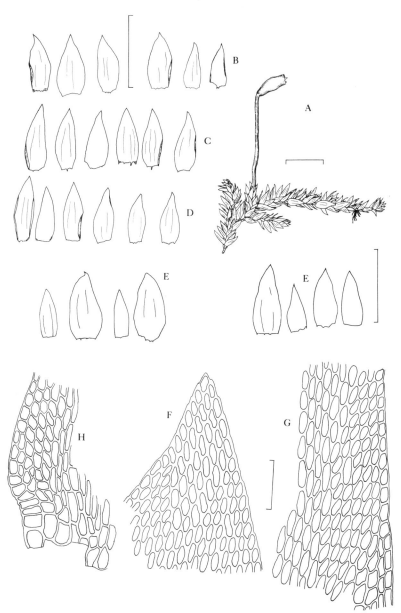

FIG. 93. *Meiothecium intextum.* (*HOW 3380*, Tahiti.) A. Habit, scale 1 mm.
B. Leaves, scale 1 mm (*Powell 42*, Samoa; type, NY). C. Leaves, scale 1 mm
(*Powell 506*, Samoa). D, E. Leaves, scale 1 mm. F. Leaf apex cells. G. Leaf,
upper margin and median cells. H. Leaf base, margin cells. F–H, scale 50 μ.

gonium setosum, 2239. Pirae District: Mt. Aorai–One Tree Hill trail, 180 m, with *Bryum* and other bryophytes on *Mangifera indica, 2837.*

MOOREA. Papetoai Bay: Kellum Plantation, 5 m, on bark, with *Calymperes, 3380.*

Distribution.—Society Islands (Tahiti, Moorea; both new records), Samoa (Manua, type locality).

I have examined the type specimen (*Powell 42,* Samoa; NY!) of this species, and find that my own collections agree so well with it that I have no hesitation in referring them here.

Mitten (1868) wrote: "Obscure, fulvous green, rather rigid, closely interwoven into extensive patches. It is very much less than *M. microcarpum,* and differs from it in the dioecous inflorescence and incomplete peristome." Mitten's *Meiothecium stratosum* is a larger species, 1.5–1.6 mm wide, the leaves longer, to 1.1 × 0.38 mm, the cells more elongate, 36–48 μ, thin-walled, papillose at the upper ends, the papillae formed by projecting end walls (type, NY!).

5. *Rhaphidorrhynchium* (Schimper) Fleischer
Musci Fl. Buitenzorg 4: 1245. 1923.
Rhaphidorrhynchium quaylei Bartram
Bishop Mus. Occ. Pap. 10(10): 23. f. 10. 1933a.

Autoicous. Plants slender, pale or silvery green, glossy, growing in thin mats; stems irregularly pinnately branched, radiculose on the underside, branches short and complanate, closely appressed to the substratum. Leaves ovate-lanceolate, gradually acuminate, 1–1.25 mm long, concave; margin erect, minutely denticulate above, entire below; costa none; leaf cells very long and narrow, about 4 μ wide by 10–14 times as long, smooth; alar cells 3–4, large, oblong, vesiculose, pale yellow; supra-alar cells few, irregularly rhomboidal. Inner perichaetial leaves abruptly contracted to a long, filiform, flexuose, denticulate point; seta very slender, bright red, smooth, 4–5 mm long; capsule ovoid-cylindric, inclined or horizontal, contracted under the mouth when dry; urn about 0.9 mm long; peristome teeth pale yellow, densely transversely striate, segments of the inner peristome carinate, from a basal membrane about half the height of the teeth; cilia 1, slightly shorter than the segments; operculum subulate-rostrate, nearly as long as the urn; calyptra cucullate, extending about halfway down the urn. Spores pale, smooth, 10–12 μ in diameter (Bartram, 1933a, p. 23).

ILLUSTRATIONS. Bartram (1933a, p. 24, f. 10).

TAHITI. Fautaua Canyon: 400–550 m, *Quayle 663* (Bartram, 1933a).

Distribution.—Society Islands (Tahiti), endemic.

Following the description of this species, Bartram wrote: "As far as I know, no species of the section *Microcalpe* has been recorded before from Polynesia or in fact from any of the Pacific Islands. These plants suggest *R. rufulum* Bescherelle, of Guadeloupe, but are apparently quite distinct in the pale color, broader leaves and different perichaetial leaves. My specimen of *R. rufulum* (*Duss 1266*), named by Bescherelle, deviates from the original description in having the setae up to 1 cm. long and the leaf margins sharply denticulate above." Bartram later (*Mosses of Guatemala*, 1949, p. 387) observed that the genus *Rhaphidorrhynchium* is distinguished from *Sematophyllum* principally by the falcate-secund leaves, and that the distinction seemed to be of minor importance. Fleischer (1923) offers little to provide a more satisfactory distinction.

6. *Taxithelium* Spruce *ex* Mitten
J. Linn. Soc. Bot. London 12: 496. 1869.

Plants prostrate, commonly on bark, forming slender, isolated strands or thin mats, pale, brownish- or yellowish-green, the branches irregular; leaves complanate or nearly so, erect-spreading or occasionally falcate-secund, ovate to ovate-lanceolate, ecostate or with a short double costa; margins entire to serrulate; median lamina cells smooth to (more usually) seriate-papillose; alar cells differentiated but usually not inflated. Seta smooth, elongate; capsule inclined to horizontal, asymmetric; peristome double; exostome teeth transversely striolate, papillose above, with a slender zigzag median line; lamellae prominent; endostome with a high basal membrane; segments papillose, keeled; cilia usually single; operculum short and conical. Exothecial cells thin-walled, not collenchymatous. Spores smooth.

Key to Species of *Taxithelium*

1. Leaves indistinctly costate _____3. *T. trachaelocarpum.*
1. Leaves ecostate
    2. Leaves 1.5 × 0.3 mm, cells of the lamina 30–60 × 3–5 μ, seta 2–3 cm long _____2. *T. mundulum.*
    2. Leaves 0.7–1.2 × 0.2–0.3 mm, cells of the lamina 60–80 × 3–4 μ, seta typically less than 1 cm, to as much as 2 cm long _____1. *T. vernieri.*

1. *Taxithelium vernieri* (Duby) Bescherelle
Bull. Soc. Bot. France 45: 123. 1898a.

Hypnum vernieri Duby, Flora 58: 285. 1875.
Trichosteleum vernieri (Duby) Jaeg., Adumbr. 480. 1879.
Hypnum lepineanum Schimp. ex Jard., Bull. Linn. Soc. Normandie ser. 2,
    9: 264, 265. 1875. *nom. nud.* = *Taxithelium lindbergii* (Jaeg.) Ren. &
    Card. *fide* Fleischer, Musci Fl. Buitenzorg 4: 1346. 1923.
Taxithelium lindbergii (Bosch & Lac.) Ren. & Card., Rev. Bryol. 28(6):
    111. 1901.
Hypnum lindbergii Bosch & Lac., Bryol. Jav. 2: 172. t. 271. 1867. *hom.*
    illeg. (*H. lindbergii* Mitt., J. Bot. 2: 123. 1864).
Sigmatella sublaevifolium Par., Ind. Bryol. Suppl. 318. 1900. *nom. nud. cf.*
    Fleischer, Musci Fl. Buitenzorg 4: 1346. 1923.

Monoicous. Stems to 7 cm long, the branches short, to 5 mm,
leaves complanate, hooked at the tips, ovate-lanceolate, long-
acuminate, 0.7–1.2 × 0.2–0.3 mm, concave; margins entire, crenulate
to serrulate in the upper blade, entire toward the leaf base. Lamina
cells linear, to 60–80 × 3–4 μ, shorter toward the apex and base of
the leaf, seriate-papillose, the cell walls thin and uniform; alar cells
differentiated, hyaline, quadrate to oval, only slightly inflated. Seta
1–2 cm long (6–8 mm in the type specimen), smooth; capsule
ovoid, constricted beneath the mouth when dry, erect to horizontal;
exothecial cells quadrate to hexagonal, the walls thin and uniform
to weakly collenchymatous (Fleischer, 1923, 4: 1347). Peristome
teeth to 300 μ long. Spores green, nearly smooth, 13–18 μ (Fleischer,
loc. cit.).

ILLUSTRATIONS. Bosch and Lacoste (1867, Bryol. Jav. 2: t. 271).
Figure 94.

TAHITI. Without locality: On dead wood, *Vernier sn* (Duby, 1875,
as *Hypnum*, isotype, NY!); *Vesco sn*; on ground and on trees in
humid ravines, *Nadeaud 88*, 1859 (Nadeaud, 1873, as *Hypnum*
pycnophyllum Nad., *non* C. Mueller, *fide* Bescherelle, 1895a; Bescherelle, 1895a, as *Trichosteleum*); *Nadeaud 386*, 1896 (Bescherelle, 1898a, as *Trichosteleum*). Rahi: 800 m, *Temarii Nadeaud sn*
(Bescherelle, 1901, as *Trichosteleum*; Renauld and Cardot, 1901).
Paea District: Papehue River, on decaying log, *Setchell and Parks*
5347 (Brotherus, 1924a, BISH, NY!). Pirae District: Fautaua Valley,
400–550 m, on bark in damp, shady location, *Quayle 669a* (Bartram,
1933a, BISH).

MOOREA. Without locality: *Temarii Nadeaud 24* (Bescherelle,
1901, as *Trichosteleum*).

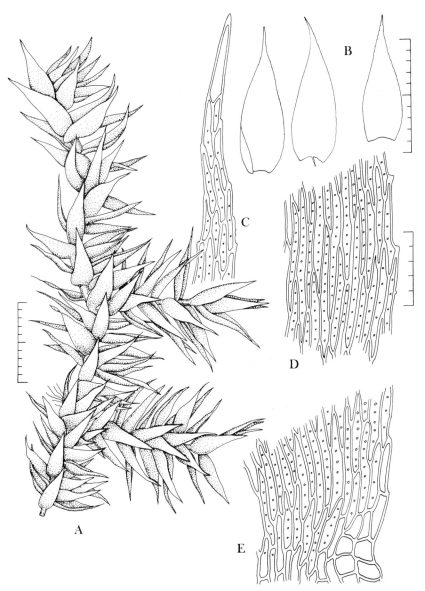

FIG. 94. *Taxithelium vernieri.* (*Vernier sn,* Tahiti, isotype, NY.) A. Habit, scale 1 mm. B. Leaves, scale 1 mm. C. Leaf apex. D. Leaf, upper margin cells. E. Leaf, cells of basal angle. C–E, scale 50 μ.

RAIATEA. Third valley S of Faaroa: On moist rock in shade, 80 m, *Moore 4* (Bartram, 1931).

Distribution.—Society Islands (Tahiti, Moorea, Raiatea, probably common on all islands), Marquesas Islands (Nuku Hiva), Tuamotu Islands (Makatea), Fiji (Viti Levu, Taveuni, Vanua Levu: Thakaundrove), Caroline Islands (Kayangle, Ifaluk, Puluwat, Namonuito; Truk: Etten, Falas; Nukuoro, Mokil, as *T. lindbergii*), Java, Annam, Borneo, Ceram, Amboina, Sumatra, Malaya, Solomon Islands, New Guinea, Sri Lanka (Ceylon), Philippine Islands.

Fleischer (1923, 4: 1347) indicated that *Taxithelium vernieri* was only a more robust form of *T. lindbergii*. Bartram (1933a) followed Brotherus, who treated both as separate species, and observed that "In *T. vernieri* the branch leaves are well-spaced, distinctly complanate and minutely crenulate to nearly entire on the apical margins. In *T. lindbergii* the branch leaves are crowded, falcate-secund, and sharply toothed on the apical margins. These distinctions seem to be constant and are well-marked in a comparison of Duby's illustration (tab. 271, Bryol. Javanica)." Certainly further study is demanded, for if *T. lindbergii* should prove to be distinct, a new name will have to be provided, since the specific epithet was used by Mitten for an American *Hypnum* three years prior to van den Bosch and Lacoste's selection of that name for their Javan specimen.

Duby (1875) compared *Hypnum vernieri* with Sullivant's *H. tenuisetum*, from Samoa, which has flagelliferous stems and leaves with a short double costa, and noted that *H. vernieri* is smaller, the leaves narrower at the base, and that they are much longer-acuminate.

2. *Taxithelium mundulum* (Sullivant) Bartram
Bishop Mus. Bull. 101: 238. 1933b.

Hypnum mundulum Sull., Proc. Am. Acad. Arts Sci. 3: 75. 1854.
Plagiothecium tenerrimum Aongstr., Oefv. K. Svensk. Vet. Ak. Foerh. 4: 16. 1872. *fide* Bartram, Bishop Mus. Bull. 101: 238. 1933b.
Taxicaulis catagonioides C. Muell., Flora 82: 469. 1896. *fide* Bartram, 1933b.
Taxicaulis linearis C. Muell., Bull. Herb. Boiss. 5: 852. 1897. *fide* Bartram, 1933b.
Rhaphidostegium filirameum Broth., Bull. Soc. Bot. Ital. 22. 1904. *fide* Bartram, 1933b.
Rhaphidorrhynchium integrifolium Broth., Bishop Mus. Bull. 40: 29. 1927. *fide* Bartram, 1933b.

Plants to about 1.5 mm wide with leaves; leaves complanate, concave, ovate-lanceolate, to 1.5 × 0.3 mm; margins erect, minutely denticulate to entire; ecostate. Lamina cells linear, thin-walled, 30–60 × 3–5 μ, smooth to seriate-papillose; alar cells rectangular, enlarged but not inflated, 2–4 on each side, hyaline to yellowish. Seta smooth, reddish, 2–3 cm long; capsule inclined; urn 0.5–0.8 mm long, constricted beneath the mouth when dry. Exothecial cells isodiametric, thin-walled, the angles slightly thickened. Peristome teeth as in *T. vernieri*. Operculum conic, with a short, oblique beak, about 0.25 mm long. Spores smooth, to 17 μ in diameter.

ILLUSTRATIONS. Bartram (1933b, p. 238, f. 176).

TAHITI. Taiarapu Peninsula: Taravao, experiment station, 400–500 m, along waterline, on branch of *Psidium guajava* with *Garovaglia tahitensis*, *Hürlimann T 1181* (Hürlimann, 1963, det. Bartram, FH!).

Distribution.—Society Islands (Tahiti), Hawaii (Kauai, Oahu, Lanai; Hawaii, type locality).

Sullivant (1859, p. 14) placed *Hypnum mundulum* Sull. in synonymy with *H. gracilisetum* Hornsch. *ex* Schwaegr. (Spec. Musc. Suppl. 3(1): 220a. 1827), which is currently recognized as *Isopterygium gracilisetum* (Schwaegr.) Jaeg. by Index Muscorum (3: 77. 1964). Bartram (1933b) discussed the taxonomic difficulties with the observation that the papillae of leaf cells provide a variable character, and range from well developed to so minute as to be scarcely visible, or entirely absent. Further, he noted that the denticulation of the leaves is also subject to variation, and that comparative studies with a large series of collections failed to develop any workable plan to distinguish extremes from the chains of intermediate forms. The presence of papillae and the enlarged alar cells distinguish this species from *Isopterygium gracilisetum* and from *I. albescens*, which it closely resembles.

3. *Taxithelium trachaelocarpum* (Aongstrom) Brotherus

E. & P. Nat. Pfl. ed. 2, 11: 443, 1924b.

Hypnum trachaelocarpum Aongstr., Oefv. K. Svensk. Vet. Ak. Foerh. 30(5): 127. 1873.

Trichosteleum trachaelocarpum (Aongstr.) Jaeg., Adumbr. 479. 1879.

Rhaphidostegium trachaelocarpum (Aongstr.) Besch., Ann. Sci. Nat. Bot. ser. 7, 20: 50. 1895a.

To reduce the possibility of confusion, Aongstrom's original Latin description follows:

Monoicum pusillum subflavescens, caulis repens inordinate

pinnatus, ramulis inaequalibus adscendentibus; folia compressa, lateralia laxe patentia oblonge-lanceolata caviuscula parum ad-unca, dorso subtilissime dense papillosa, apice denticulata, costis indistinctis; cellulae pallidae lineares angustissimae, alares minutae paucae hyalinae vesiculiformes vel subnullae; folia perichaetialia longe vaginantia, interna ovato-oblonga longissime acuminata erecta apice flexuosa denticulata; capsula in pedicello longiusculo laevi et collo obconico recto ovalis in-curva, operculo conico, calyptra laevis.

Plantae laxe caespitosae pumilae tenellae in ligno putrido et inter Hypna degentes flavescentes. Caules repens inordinate parce pinnatus, ramulis brevibus inaequalibus adscendentibus. Folia compressa, lateralia laxe disposita patentia parum adunca caviuscula e basi semiamplectente angustata oblongo-lanceolata, margine plana, apice denticulata, costis indistinctis; areolatis foliorum e cellulis pallidis angustissimis linearibus dorso sub-tissime dense punctulatis alaribus paucis minutis hyalinis vesi-culiformibus vel vix nullis. Florescentia monoica. Flos masculus in caule ramisque lateralis gemmiformis parvus. Folia perigoni-alia late ovato-oblonga, interna longius acuminata convaca in-tegerrima; antheridia paraphysibus paucissimis filiformibus longioribus mixta. Flores feminei in caule laterales. Folia peri-chaetii externa ovato-acuminata, interna vaginantia majora e basi laxius reticulata non papillosa. Fructus solitarius. Vaginula oblonga. Pedicellus suberectus tenuis laevis rubescens 1–2 centim. longus. Capsula e basi erecta obconico-ovalis incurva, sicca sub ore constricta fuscescens. Operculum conicum. Ca-lyptra magna laevis pallida. Peristomium duplex, externum e dentibus lanceolato-acuminatis cernis dense trabeculatis, medio linea longitudinali exaratis, internum e membranua subplicata exserta in processus carinatus erectos non pertusos dentibus longitudine aequales fissa, interjectis ciliis solitaris brevibus.

Differt a *Hypno lindbergii* S. Lac. (non Mitt.) statura mi-nore, capsula collo praedita e basi erecta incurva, etc.

ILLUSTRATIONS. None.

TAHITI. Without locality: On decaying wood, intermixed with other bryophytes, *Andersson sn,* 1852 (Aongstrom, 1873, as *Hyp-num*). Mataiea District: Above Vaihiria, 1000 m (feet?), *Eriksson 61* (Bartram, 1950b).

Distribution.—Society Islands (Tahiti), endemic.

Bescherelle (1895a) did not examine this species, and except for Bartram's report (1950b), *Taxithelium trachaelocarpum* has not been reported again. From the original description it can be determined that this species is probably best retained in the genus *Taxithelium*, but it will be necessary to examine the original collection to determine the true affinities of this species.

7. *Trichosteleum* Mitten
J. Linn. Soc. Bot. 10: 181. 1868.

Prostrate stems form pale, brownish to green mats, commonly on dead wood or decaying organic debris, occasionally on rocks; branches irregular; leaves erect-spreading, slightly compressed, to falcate-secund, ovate-lanceolate, acuminate, concave, ecostate; margins denticulate toward the apex. Lamina cells linear, strongly seriate-papillose; alar cells 2–3 on each side of the leaf base, hyaline, inflated. Seta smooth toward base, papillose below the capsule; capsule horizontal to pendulous, ovate, constricted beneath the mouth when dry. Peristome teeth transversely striate, furrowed along the median line; operculum conic, long-rostrate; calyptra cucullate, smooth.

Key to Species of *Trichosteleum*

1. Leaf margins entire, lamina cells unipapillose, seta to about 0.5 cm long....
....3. *T. patens.*
1. Leaf margins serrulate to denticulate, lamina cells seriate-papillose, seta 1–2 cm long
   2. Leaves falcate-secund, 2.2 × 0.5 mm, cells 30–50 × 4–6 μ, seta 1–1.5 cm..1. *T. hamatum.*
   2. Leaves straight, not hooked and curved to one side, 1.5–1.6 × 0.4 mm, cells 12–24 × 2–4 μ..2. *T. orthophyllum.*

1. *Trichosteleum hamatum* (Dozy & Molkenboer) Jaeger
Adumbr. 2: 486. 1879.

Hypnum hamatum Dozy & Molk., Ann. Sci. Nat. Bot. ser. 3, 2: 307. 1844.
Hypnum scaberulum Mont., London J. Bot. 3: 633. 1844. *cf.* C. Mueller, Syn. 2: 307. 1851.
Trichosteleum scaberulum (Mont.) Besch., Ann. Sci. Nat. Bot. ser. 7, 20: 51. 1895a.
Hypnum pickeringii Sull., Proc. Am. Acad. Arts Sci. 3: 74. 1854. *fide* Dixon and Greenwood, Proc. Linn. Soc. N. S. Wales 55: 299. 1930.
Sigmatella pickeringii (Sull.) C. Muell., Flora 82: 469. 1896. *fide* Dixon and Greenwood, 1930.
Sematophyllum (*Sigmatella*) *pickeringii* (Sull.) Besch., Ann. Sci. Nat. Bot. ser. 7, 20: 49. 1895a. *fide* Dixon and Greenwood, 1930.
Pungentella capillariseta C. Muell., Flora 82: 470. 1896. *comb. inval. fide* Bartram, Bishop Mus. Bull. 101: 236. 1933b.

Pungentella lepto-cylindrica C. Muell., Flora 82: 470. 1896. *comb. inval. fide* Bartram, 1933b.

Pungentella semi-asperula C. Muell., Bull. Herb. Boiss. 5: 852. 1897. *comb. inval. fide* Bartram, 1933b.

Sematophyllum microstictum Broth., Bull. Soc. Bot. Italy 1904: 23. 1904. *fide* Bartram, 1933b.

Cupressina luridissima C. Muell., Flora 82: 473. 1896. *fide* Bartram, 1933b.

Rhaphidostegium pickeringii (Sull.) Besch., Bull. Soc. Bot. France 48: 13. 1901.

Acanthocladium hamatum C. Muell. & Broth., Abh. Naturw. Ver. Bremen 16: 507. 1900. *fide* Bartram, 1933b.

Plants pale to dark green or brownish, stems 4–5 cm long, branches irregular; leaves strongly falcate-secund, to 2.2 × 0.5 mm, ovate-lanceolate, acuminate; margins erect, denticulate above; ecostate. Cells of the lamina elongate-elliptic to linear, 30–50 × 4–6 μ, seriate-papillose, walls smooth to slightly pitted, especially toward the leaf base; alar cells large, inflated, 2–3 on each side, hyaline, to 100 μ long, the leaf base and alar cells sometimes yellow-tinged. Perichaetial leaves with a long sheathing base, long-acuminate, to 1.6 mm long. Seta red, 1–1.5 cm long, smooth below and papillose beneath the capsule; capsule horizontal to pendulous; urn 0.8–1 mm long, cylindric, constricted beneath the mouth when dry; operculum conic; beak long and slender, to about 0.9 mm. Peristome teeth to about 300 μ long, papillose at the tips, transversely striate at the base, deeply furrowed along the median line; endostome yellow-green, smooth at the base, papillose above, the segments keeled, the base one-third as high as the teeth. Spores yellowish to green, smooth, 10–18 μ in diameter.

ILLUSTRATIONS. Bartram (1933b, p. 236, f. 175), Dozy and Molkenboer (1855–1870, 2: t. 275), Sullivant (1859, pl. 15a).

TAHITI. Without locality: *Wilkes sn* (Sullivant, 1854; 1859, as *Hypnum pickeringii*). Taiarapu Peninsula: On humid sides of valleys and on the Tatefau Plateau, with *Distichophyllum tahitense, Nadeaud 70,* 1859; *Jardin 10* (Bescherelle, 1895a, as *Sematophyllum pickeringii*); Puaa and Tearapau valleys, vicinity of Marciati to Papenoo, *Nadeaud sn,* 1896 (Bescherelle, 1898a, as *S. pickeringii, 377–379*); experiment station dam, 500 m, on tree fern debris, with *Leucophanes prasiophyllum, Hürlimann T 1238;* Haavini Valley, 115 m, on *Inocarpus edulis* bark with *Ectropothecium, Taxithelium,* and *Calymperes, 2499;* above experiment station, 740 m, with *Hypnodendron vescoanum, Rhizogonium spiniforme, Leucomium aneurodictyon, Metzgeria,* and *Riccardia, 2316;* same locality, 440 m, *2198*. Miaa: 850 m, *Temarii Nadeaud 18*, 1899 (Bescherelle, 1901, as *Rhaphidostegium pickeringii*). Pirae District: Fautaua Valley, 400–550 m, *Quayle 661, 666* (Bartram, 1933a, FH). Mataiea District: Along road to Vaihiria, on soil over 1000 (840?) m, *Eriksson 64*; on trees, *Eriksson 65* (Bartram, 1950b); Vaihiria Valley, 100 m, on coconut trunk, with *Thyridium constrictum, 3066*. Hitiaa District: N side Tahiti nui, 400 m, plateau region, with *Thyridium constrictum, Leucobryum tahitense, Arthrocormus dentatus, Rhizogonium spiniforme, Hypnodendron vescoanum*, and *Bazzania, 3229*.

MOOREA. Without locality: *Temarii Nadeaud sn*, 1899 (Bescherelle, 1901, as *Rhaphidostegium pickeringii*). Papetoai–Paopao trail: S of Mt. Rotui, on decomposing *Cocos* husks on ground, *3441*.

RAIATEA. Small valley W side of mountain: 500 m, on branches of trees, *Moore 32*. Highest mountain: W side of ridge, 800 m, on branches of trees, *Moore 34, 36, 38*. Averaiti Valley: Upper end, 300 m, on *Pandanus* in river bed, *Moore 79*; on branch of tree in shade, *Moore 82, 87* (Bartram, 1931, BISH).

Distribution.—Society Islands (Tahiti, Moorea, Raiatea, probably on all larger islands), Hawaii (all larger islands), Malaysia, New Guinea, New Caledonia, Borneo, Banca, Sumatra, Java (type locality), Celebes, Philippine Islands, Sunda Islands, Caroline Islands (Ponape, Kapingamarangi, Truk), Marshall Islands (Arno), Samoa (Tutuila), Fiji (Viti Levu, Ngau).

After examining authentic specimens, Sullivant (1859) wrote that he considered *Hypnum hamatum* and *H. scaberrulum* to be distinct species. He compared *H. pickeringii* with *H. scaberrulum* to note that his species has only the upper half of the seta tuberculate or papillose, and further that the leaves are much less falcate and only slightly papillose. Sullivant described the leaves of *H. hamatum* as remarkably long, secund, and hamate-falcate, with "cellules" destitute of papillae and shorter than in *H. scaberrulum* or *H. pickeringii*, the seta papillose only on the upper part. Bartram (1933a) observed that in Quayle's collections from the Fautaua Valley, especially no. *666*, the leaves are asymmetrical, broadly ovate-lanceolate, and conspicuously contracted just above the insertion. The upper cells are short-oval, with 2–3 large papillae over the lumens, and Bartram concluded that the specimens were within the range of variation for this variable and widely distributed species. Of the Hawaiian forms Bartram wrote: "The forms of this

plastic species parallel those of *Taxithelium mundulum* as far as
the papillae of the leaf cells are concerned, varying from distinctly
papillose to essentially smooth, and seem to be no more amenable
to satisfactory classification. I agree thoroughly with Dixon (1930)
that no practical distinction can be made between this species and
T. pickeringii Sullivant. *T. hamatum* seems to have a wide range
throughout the islands of the Pacific and no doubt includes a much
more extensive synonymy than that given above, which applies only
to local forms." The following species may prove to be only a
variant of *T. hamatum,* in which the leaves are not markedly
falcate-secund.

2. *Trichosteleum orthophyllum* (Bescherelle) Brotherus
   E. & P. Nat. Pfl. 1(2): 1117. 1908.
   Sematophyllum orthophyllum Besch., Bull. Soc. Bot. France ser. 3, 45: 122.
   1898a.

Leaves erect, not falcate-secund, concave, ovate-lanceolate, 1.5–
1.6 × 0.4–0.42 mm, ecostate; margins erect, denticulate below the
apex. Lamina cells thick-walled, the walls irregularly thickened,
ovate-elongate, 12–24 × 2–4 μ, with 3–4 papillae in a row over the
lumen; alar cells 60–70 μ long, hyaline; basal cells yellow, to about
40 μ long, the walls thick, slightly pitted, as wide as the cell lumen,
which averages about 4 μ. Sporophytes with a red seta to 2 cm
long, smooth below, papillose below the capsule; capsule cylindric,
about 1.3 × 0.54 mm; peristome 290–310 μ high; exostome teeth
transversely striate below, hyaline and strongly papillose at the tips.
Exothecial cells are short-rectangular, the walls uniform, 16–24 ×
12–18 μ. Spores greenish, finely papillose or smooth, about 12 μ in
diameter. Description from Nadeaud collection *108,* Papeava, Tahiti, det. Bescherelle (NY!).

ILLUSTRATIONS. Figure 95.

TAHITI. Pinai: Mountains of Pinai and the Puaa Valley, 800–1000
m, *Nadeaud 284,* 1896; mountains of Pinai and Papeana, with
sporophytes, *Nadeaud 285* (Bescherelle, 1898a, as *Sematophyllum*).
Miaa: 850 m, *Temarii Nadeaud 17,* 1899 (Bescherelle, 1901, as
Sematophyllum).

MOOREA. Without locality: *Temarii Nadeaud 22* (Bescherelle,
1901, as *Sematophyllum*).

RAIATEA. Highest mountain: W side, 600 m, on wet branches of
trees, *Moore 35* (Bartram, 1931, BISH).

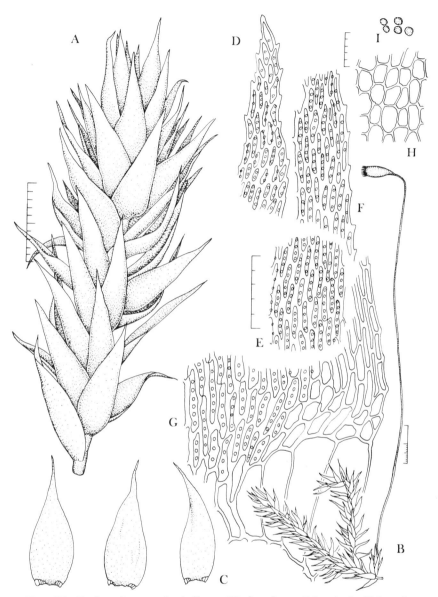

FIG. 95. *Trichosteleum orthophyllum.* (*Nadeaud sn,* Tahiti.) A. Habit. B. Habit, with sporophyte, scale 2 mm. C. Leaves. A, C, scale 1 mm. D. **Leaf apex.** E. Lamina cells, upper median. F. Leaf, upper margin. G. Leaf, basal angle (note enlarged alar cells). D–G, scale 50 μ. H. Capsule exothecial cells. I. Spores. H, I, scale 50 μ.

Distribution.—Society Islands (Tahiti, Moorea, Raiatea), endemic.

Bartram (1931) examined Bescherelle's specimens, and although he referred Moore's collections from Raiatea to *Trichosteleum orthophyllum,* he commented: "The species is far from convincing, and should in all probability, be considered as a form of *T. hamatum.*" The single authentic specimen of *T. orthophyllum* which I have examined seems relatively distinct, the plants much more robust, and easily separated from *T. hamatum* by the erect-spreading, barely secund leaves. *Trichosteleum hamatum* may also be distinguished without a hand lens by the dull, thick appearance of the strongly falcate-secund leaves. Species of the genus *Taxithelium* have a glossy, more delicate appearance.

3. *Trichosteleum patens* Bescherelle
Bull. Soc. Bot. France 48: 16. 1901.

I have not examined authentic specimens. To reduce confusion, Bescherelle's original description follows:

> Monoicum! Planta repens ramosa ramis pinnatis brevibus vix 5 millim. longis apice stellatim foliosis luteo-rufescentibus nitentibus. Folia caulina anguste ovato-lanceolata, erecto-patentia patentiave, cellulis hexagonis elongatis papilla singula dorso prominente ornatis inferioribus ad basin infimam flavidis marginem versus tribus majoribus vesiculosis luteis. Folia perichaetialia flavida, minutissima, anguste ovata, obsolete denticulata. Perigonium minutum infra perichaetia nascens foliis intimis concavis apice elongate lanceolatis denticulatis. Capsula in pedicello 5 millim. longo rubro inferne laevi superne curvulo tuberculoso inclinata, brevis, regularis, ovata, laevis, sub ore angustato, operculo oblique rostrato aciculari torquato. Calyptra minuta, cucullata, apice verrucosa. Peristomii dentes externi linea verticali multangula anguste exarati, interni aequilongi carinati lutei, ciliis nullis.

ILLUSTRATIONS. None.

TAHITI. Puairi: To 900 m, on trees, *Nadeaud sn,* 1898. Miaa: 850 m, *Temarii Nadeaud sn* (Bescherelle, 1901).

MOOREA. Without locality: *Temarii Nadeaud sn* (Bescherelle, 1901).

RAIATEA. Highest mountain: W side, 500 m, on wet clay soil, *Moore 39* (Bartram, 1931).

XXXVIII. HYPNACEAE

Members of the family Hypnaceae are mostly prostrate, shiny plants common on bark, decaying wood, moist rocks, or soil. Branching is pinnate, the leaves ovate-lanceolate, often acuminate, the costa weak, short, and double, or altogether absent, sometimes variably so in the same plant. Leaf margins vary from entire to denticulate. Cells are elongate, linear, smooth to unipapillose, the papilla formed by projecting cell end walls. Alar cells are usually not enlarged, although in the genus *Ectropothecium* there is a single inflated cell on both sides of the leaf base that may remain attached to the stem when the leaf is removed. Sporophytes have a smooth seta, the capsule horizontal or pendulous, ovoid, the operculum conic, apiculate. The calyptra is cucullate. The peristome is double, with 16 teeth in the exostome; the endostome arises from a high basal membrane, and cilia may be present between the endostome segments.

Key to Genera of the Hypnaceae

1. Leaves ranked along the stem giving appearance of 5-pointed star when stem is viewed from apex; leaf margins serrulate to serrate ...... 3. *Ctenidium*.
1. Leaves complanate or irregularly ranked; leaf margins entire to serrate
    2. Leaf cells wide, large; length:width ratio usually less than 5:1; cells smooth, lacking papillae; alar cells quadrate.................4. *Vesicularia*.
    2. Leaf cells narrow, linear; length:width ratio usually over 6:1; cells smooth to unipapillose; alar cells quadrate to elongate
        3. Lamina cells smooth; alar cells quadrate, not elongate or decurrent, leaves ecostate .... 2. *Isopterygium*.
        3. Lamina cells unipapillose by projecting upper end walls; alar cell single, decurrent onto stem; costa short, double, variable
            4. Leaves acuminate; margins usually not serrulate below midleaf....
            ....1. *Ectropothecium*.
            4. Leaves long-acuminate; margins usually serrate to leaf base........
            ....5. *Mittenothamnium*.

1. *Ectropothecium* Mitten
J. Linn. Soc. Bot. 10: 180. 1868.

Plants golden to yellow-green, glossy, prostrate; leaves often falcate-secund (the leaf tips hooked, the leaves curved to one side); costa double and quite faint, sometimes absent. Cells of the lamina are elongate. Leaf margins are entire to denticulate.

Bartram (personal correspondence, 1961) wrote: "As for *Ectropothecium*, it is a sordid mess that is in need of a radical restudy. Like many others, I have sinned in describing new species from ignorance rather than knowledge." Bartram's descriptions call attention to forms which varied to such an extent that they could not be placed conveniently in any known species of *Ectropothecium*; his original specimens await the monographer's consideration in the Farlow Herbarium.

Key to Species of *Ectropothecium*

1. Plants dioicous, leaves 0.9–1.3 × 0.27–0.38 mm; lamina cells 45–50 × 2–4 μ; seta 1.5–3 cm..4. *E. sodale.*
1. Plants monoicous (autoicous)
  2. Leaves asymmetrical, seta to 1 cm................5. *E. venustulum.*
  2. Leaves symmetrical, seta usually more than 1 cm long
    3. Plants slender, branches 3–5 mm long; leaves 0.6–1.0 × 0.22–0.27 mm; lamina cells 35–50 × 3–4 μ .... 3. *E. sandwichense.*
    3. Plants robust, branches to 1 cm or longer
      4. Branching regular, to 1 cm long; leaves 1.1–1.4 × 0.48 mm, falcate-secund; lamina cells to 80 × 3 μ, seta to 2 cm long ......
      ....2. *E. polyandrum.*
      4. Branching irregular, some branches shorter, others much longer than 1 cm .... 1. *E. eccremocladum.*

1. *Ectropothecium eccremocladum* (Bescherelle) Brotherus
E. & P. Nat. Pfl. 1(3): 1065. 1908.
Stereodon eccremocladus Besch., Bull. Soc. Bot. France 45: 126. 1898a.

Bescherelle's original Latin description follows:

Dioicus. Planta longissime pendula; rami biformes nunc biunciales aureo-virides ramulis patentibus vix 5 mill. longis foliis aduncis, nunc longissimi attenuati chrysei nitentes simplices penduli longi (15–20 cent.) interdum divisi foliis erecto-patentibus. Folia anguste ovato-lanceolata, longe cuspidata, apice saepe torta, in ramis longioribus erecta flexuosa e medio ad summum denticulata, cellulis longis linearibus laevibus areolata, costis binis obsoletis. Flos femineus in ramo primario nascens. Perichaetii junioris folia basi late cordato-ovata, lanceolata, erecta, longe cuspidata, apice tortilia, margine e medio remote denticulata, ecostata, cellulis linearibus hyalinis reticulata; archegonia numerosa (circiter 30) paraphysibus longioribus cincta. Cetera desunt.

ILLUSTRATIONS. None.

TAHITI. Puaa Valley: Sterile, *Nadeaud 423* (Bescherelle, 1898a, as *Stereodon*).

Distribution.—Society Islands (Tahiti), endemic.

2. *Ectropothecium polyandrum* (Aongstrom) Jaeger
Ber. S. Gall. Naturw. Ges. 1877–1878: 260. 1880.

Hypnum polyandrum Aongstr., Oefv. K. Svensk. Vet. Ak. Foerh. 30(5): 129. 1873.

Plants golden to yellow-green, prostrate, on bark, the primary stems to 7 cm long, the secondary branches crowded, regularly pinnate, in one plane, 8–10 mm long, tertiary branches infrequent, 3–5 mm. Leaves 1.1–1.4 × 0.48 mm, falcate-secund, lanceolate-acuminate, slightly concave; costa short, faint, double or absent; leaf margins entire near the leaf base, serrulate near the leaf apex. Cells linear, papillose, the papillae formed by projecting cell end walls, the cells about 80 × 3 μ in the upper leaf, shorter and wider near the leaf base, 25–50 × 3–6 μ; alar cells mostly quadrate but with inflated, hyaline cells decurrent onto the stem (and often lost when leaves are removed). Sporophytes not seen. Aongstrom (1873) described the seta as reddish, 1.8–2 cm long, smooth; capsule oblong-ovate, constricted beneath the mouth when dry, and sub-horizontal to pendulous; operculum short, conic, and acute; calyptra pale, smooth, cucullate. Peristome double, external teeth lanceolate-acuminate, densely trabeculate, the median line a longitudinal furrow; the inner peristome of keeled, membranous teeth, with 2–3 cilia arising from the basal membrane between the teeth. The plants are monoicous, according to Aongstrom.

ILLUSTRATIONS. None.

TAHITI. Without locality: *Andersson sn*, 1852 (Aongstrom, 1873, as *Hypnum*, isotype, NY); windward side of Tahiti, numerous collections, *Nadeaud sn* (Bescherelle, 1898a); with *Trichosteleum vernieri*, *Vernier sn* (Bescherelle, 1895a, as *H. polyandrum* var. *fulvo-virens*).

Distribution.—Society Islands (Tahiti), endemic.

Aongstrom (1873) compared *H. polyandrum* with *H.* (*Drepanium*) *buitenzorgii* Bel. (=*Ectropothecium*), from Java, which differed in having a much shorter seta, the capsule only slightly pendulous, but Bartram's (1939) description of *E. buitenzorgii* as it is represented in the Philippines, suggests larger leaves and cells, the seta longer, 2.5–3.5 cm, with a pendulous capsule, and, contrary to Aongstrom's note, reports that the plants are dioicous.

Bescherelle (1895a) described the variety *fulvo-virens*: "A typo differt: colore fulvo-virente, ramis laxius pinnatis, foliis remotis laxis minus falcatis haud serrulatis ob cellulas marginales apice paullo prominentes e basi subdentatis." I have not seen authentic specimens of this variety.

3. *Ectropothecium sandwichense* (Hooker & Arnott) Mitten
   in Seemann, Fl. Vit. 400. 1871.

> *Hypnum sandwichense* Hook. & Arnott, Bot. Capt. Beechey's Voyage 109. 1841.
>
> *Plagiothecium sandwichense* (Hook. & Arnott) Jaeg., Ber. S. Gall. Naturw. Ges. 1876–1877: 454. 1878. Ad. 2: 520.
>
> *Hypnum paucipilum* Sull., Bull. Torr. Bot. Cl. 5: 11. 1874. *fide* Bartram, Bishop Mus. Bull. 101: 248. 1933b.
>
> *Cupressina trachylocarpa* C. Muell., Flora 82: 478. 1896. *fide* Bartram, 1933b.
>
> *Ectropothecium trachylocarpon* (C. Mueller) Paris, Ind. Bryol. Suppl. 139. 1900.

Plants golden, prostrate; leaves falcate-secund, ovate-lanceolate, acuminate, 0.6–1.0 × 0.22–0.27 mm, costate; costa short and double, or sometimes absent; margins of leaves serrulate to the leaf base or nearly so. Cells of the lamina linear, 35–50 × 3–4 μ in the upper leaf, papillose, the papillae formed by the projecting cell distal end wall; in the lower lamina, cells shorter, 25–35 μ near the center of the leaf base, quadrate, about 12 × 12 μ in the basal angle, but with inflated, hyaline cells decurrent onto the stem; margin cells shorter and wider than median lamina cells, 24–35 × 4–6 μ, the outer cell wall thinner than the inner wall. The single seta examined was about 8 mm long, the capsule, no longer present, pendulous (based on isotype, NY).

ILLUSTRATIONS. None.

TAHITI. Paea District: Papehue, on bark, *Tilden 340* (exs. series, BISH!).

RAIATEA. Third valley S of Faaroa Bay: 100 m, on moist rocks in shady mapé (*Inocarpus*) grove, *Moore 3* (Bartram, 1931, BISH!).

BORA BORA. Mt. Temanu: *Phillips sn* (Phillips, 1947, BISH!).

Distribution.—Society Islands (Tahiti, Raiatea, Bora Bora), Hawaii (all larger islands), Makatea, Marquesas Islands (Nuku Hiva), Rapa, Austral Islands (Raivavae, Rurutu, Maria Island), Mangareva, New Zealand, Australia (east), Swains Island, Samoa, Fiji.

Hooker and Arnott originally described this species, "ramis pinnatis, foliis distichis teneris nitidis ovato-lanceolatis falcato-secundis acuminatis concavis undique serrulatis, nervo brevissimo obscuro, capsula brevi-ovata cernua, calyptra juniore apice pilosa," and observed that "this is a small delicate species, in some respects allied to *H. elegans*, Musc. Exot., and in others to *H. circinale*, but differing by the characters above given."

Bartram (1933b) described the seta of *E. sandwichense* as variable in length, averaging 16–20 mm, the capsules as pendulous or abruptly hooked, constricted beneath the mouth and short-oval or oblong, and more or less asymmetrical when dry; the operculum was described as broadly convex and apiculate, the calyptra as usually slightly hairy when young. Leaves were reported by Bartram to be over 1.5 mm long, although the longest I measured from the Beechey collection (the isotype) were not over 1.0 mm. Bartram further indicated that the margins are serrulate only in the upper leaf, but the isotype has leaves in which the serrulations extend to within 3–5 cells of the leaf base. Perichaetial leaves (around an old perichaetium) measured 1.5–1.7 mm. Bartram implied that a costa was not present by comparing *E. sandwichense* to *E. arcuatum*, but as already noted, the isotype has a short, double costa present in some leaves, but absent in others. Bartram's description of *E. viridifolium* compares more closely with the isotype of *E. sandwichense*!

4. *Ectropothecium sodale* (Sullivant) Mitten
J. Linn. Soc. Bot. 10: 180. 1868.

  Hypnum sodale Sull., Proc. Am. Acad. Arts Sci. 3: 78. 1854. Reprint p. 9. 1854.
  Hypnum calpaecarpum Aongstr., Oefv. K. Svensk. Vet. Ak. Foerh. 30(5): 128. 1873. *fide* Aongstrom, 1876.
  Hypnum molluscoides Sull., Proc. Am. Acad. Arts Sci. 3: 73. 1854. *fide* Sullivant, 1859.

Plants golden to yellow-green, prostrate, regularly pinnately branched, the primary stems 5–7 cm long, secondary branches 8–10 mm, occasionally with tertiary branches; leaves falcate-secund, primary stem leaves 0.9–1.3 × 0.27–0.38 mm, lanceolate-acuminate, costate; costa short and double, faint, sometimes absent; branch leaves shorter. Cells of the lamina elongate, sinuose, 40–50 × 2–4 μ, papillose, the distal end walls project to form the papillae; cells of the leaf margins similar to median cells of the upper leaf, the margins finely serrulate in the upper leaf and occasionally to within 3–4 cells of the leaf base, but entire in the alar region; basal cells elongate-rectangular, 20–35 × 2–5 μ near the center, irregularly quadrate and thick-walled at the basal angles, 9–14 μ, with 1–2 inflated hyaline cells, 48 × 14 μ, decurrent onto the stem. Sporophytes were not seen.

ILLUSTRATIONS. Sullivant (1859, pl. 12b). Figures 96, 97.

TAHITI. Without locality: *Lay and Collie sn* (Guillemin, 1836, as *H. chamissonis*; Bescherelle, 1895a); *Jacquinot sn* (Montagne, 1845, as *H. chamissonis*); *Wilkes sn* (Sullivant, 1859, NY); widespread on trees around the island, *Nadeaud 85* (Nadeaud, 1873, as *H. chamissonis*; Bescherelle, 1895a); *Andersson sn* (Aongstrom, 1873, as *H. calpaecarpum, fide* Aongstrom, 1876); *Vesco sn*; *Lépine 17*; *Vieillard and Pancher sn*, 1855 (in hb. Montagne as *H. chamissonis*); *Lequerré sn* (Camus hb.; Bescherelle, 1895a); common in valleys, on trees, from pale yellow to green in different localities, *Nadeaud sn*, 1896 (Bescherelle, 1898a, 399–402); *Larminat sn* (Potier de la Varde, 1912); *Beechy sn* (Mitten, 1871); on trees, *Picquenot sn*, 1897 (NY ex Corbière hb., unreported); *Tilden 71*, 1909 (exs. series, BISH!). Miaa: 850 m, *Temarii Nadeaud sn*, 1899 (Bescherelle, 1901). Paea District: Orofere Valley, *Setchell and Parks 5300, 5302*. Papeari District: Maara Valley, *5364*. Pirae District: Fautaua Valley, *5425, 5426* (Brotherus, 1924a); *Quayle 662c, 666a, 669b* (Bartram, 1933a); Fare Rau Ape–Mt. Aorai, 800 m, on dead roots, *Hürlimann T 1228* (Hürlimann, 1963). Mataiea District: Lake Vaihiria, 650 m, on moist soil at base of a *Polypodium, MacDaniels 1598* (Bartram, 1933a); trail to Lake Vaihiria, *Eriksson 59, 60*; 1000 m (?), above Lake Vaihiria, on trees, *Eriksson 57* (Bartram, 1950b). Taiarapu Peninsula: Taravao, above experiment station, 400–500 m, along new dam on dead wood and branches, *Hürlimann T 1164, T 1170, T 1175* (Hürlimann, 1963).

MOOREA. Without locality: *Wilkes sn* (Sullivant, 1854, as *H. molluscoides*; 1859); *Andersson sn* (Aongstrom, 1873, as *H. calpaecarpum,* Eimeo, NY!); *Temarii Nadeaud sn* (Bescherelle, 1901).

RAIATEA: Faaroa Valley: On moist branches of trees in shade, 100 m, *Moore 12, 13, 15, 16*. W side highest mountain: small valley, 800 m, in shade of shrubs, *Moore 28*. Temehani range: On branches of shrubs in shade, 400 m, *Moore 48* (Bartram, 1931).

Distribution.—Society Islands (Tahiti, Moorea, Raiatea; to be expected on all major islands), Marquesas Islands (Nuku Hiva), Samoa (Manua), New Caledonia, New Guinea, Fiji.

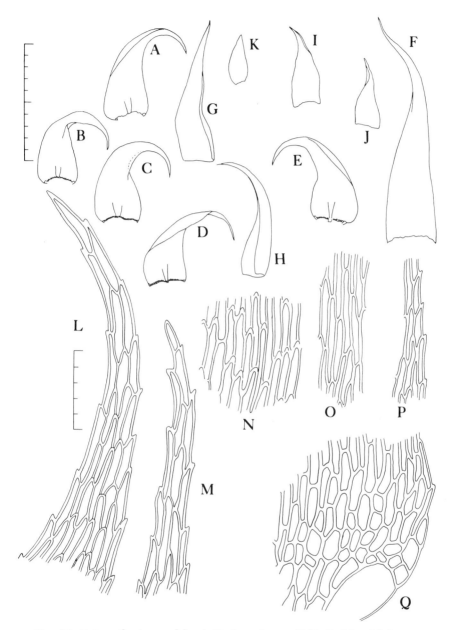

FIG. 96. *Ectropothecium sodale.* **A–E.** Stem leaves. **F–K.** Perichaetial leaves, series from outermost to innermost. A–K, scale 1 mm. **L, M.** Leaf apices. **N.** Upper lamina, cells. **O.** Leaf base, cells near center. **P.** Leaf margin, cells of upper lamina. **Q.** Leaf base, cells of alar region. L–Q, scale 50 μ. (Drawn from authentic material from U.S. Expl. Exp. Wilkes, det. Sullivant, NY.)

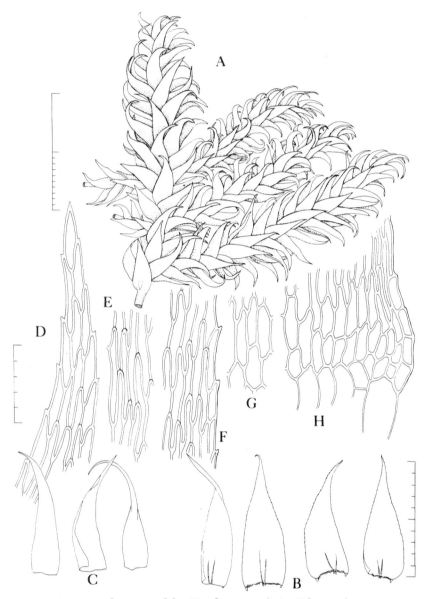

Fig. 97. *Ectropothecium sodale.* (*E. chamissonis.*) A. Habit, scale 2 mm. B. Stem leaves (4). C. Perichaetial leaves (3). B, C, scale 1 mm. D. Stem leaf apices. E. Stem leaf, upper median cells. F. Stem leaf, upper margin cells. G. Stem leaf, basal median cells. H. Stem leaf, alar cells. D–H, scale 50 μ.

Sullivant (1854) noted that plants were dioicous, and described the sporophytes: "Capsula ovato-urceolata exannulata horizontali pendulave; peristomii euhypnoidei ciliolis binis breviusculis; operculo hemisphaerico recte breviter rostellato; pedicello tenuissimo longiusculo." Leaves are not ecostate, as Sullivant reported; a costa, albeit short, double, and faint, is commonly present, but some leaves lack the costa.

This species has a wide distribution, but as its taxonomic position within the genus *Ectropothecium* becomes better understood, the range will be considerably extended. Dixon (1950) treated *E. sodale* as very similar to *E. chamissonis*, the species originally used by Guillemin (1836), Montagne (1845), and Nadeaud (1873) for Society Islands and Marquesas specimens. In *Hypnum chamissonis* Hornsch., from Raddack (isotype, NY!, *ex* Mitten hb.), the plants are quite similar to *E. sodale*, but the fragments are less robust, the secondary branches shorter. Leaves are similar in outline, 1.1–1.2 × 0.35–0.38 mm, the cells of the leaf margin with a bordered appearance, rather hyaline, the outer cell wall thinner than the inner, the cells shorter and wider than median lamina cells, 34–50 × 4–5 μ in the upper leaf, slightly longer toward midleaf, to 50–60 μ, and shorter near the leaf base, 35–45 μ, becoming quadrate at the basal angles of the leaf, 10–15 μ, but with inflated, hyaline cells decurrent onto the stem, 40–70 × 25 μ. The costa is typical: short, faint, and double, or absent. Cells of the lamina faintly unipapillose, the papillae formed by projecting cell distal end walls; cells linear, sinuose, 60–85 × 2–5 μ in the upper leaf, shorter and wider, 25–36 μ just above the insertion of the leaf onto the stem. As in other taxa studied, a row of small hyaline cells extends across the insertion of the leaf base. No sporophytes were seen, but one sketched by Mitten had a seta 8–10 mm long. On the herbarium sheet, next to the isotype of *E. chamissonis*, Mitten noted, "cells easily distinguishable, not as in *H. sandwichense*."

Beyond the observation that the authentic specimens of *E. sandwichense*, *E. sodale*, and *E. chamissonis* provide no mutually exclusive characters, taxonomic judgment must be limited. The variability that exists within the genus *Ectropothecium* is such that *E. sandwichense*, *E. sodale*, and *E. chamissonis* might, in a broad interpretation, be considered synonyms within the range of a single species, represented by *E. chamissonis*! Monographic treatment of the genus *Ectropothecium* will be needed to properly resolve the many taxonomic problems that now exist.

5. *Ectropothecium venustulum* Bescherelle
Bull. Soc. Bot. France ser. 3, 45: 124. 1898a.

I have not seen authentic specimens of this species; Bescherelle's original description follows:

Monoicum. Cespites latissime repentes, densissimi, venustuli, rami pinnati unciales 5–6 mill. lati, pallide chryseo-virides, intricati, inferne radicantes, ramulis plerumque simplicibus 2–3 mill. longis. Folia patentia dein falcata, flexuosa, minuta, ovato-lanceolata, integerrima vel apice falcato subtiliter denticulata, cellulis angustis lineari-hexagonis apice unipapillosis basi ad margines quadratis nonnullis hyalinis. Folia perichaetialia longiora, erecta, apice inflexa, serrulata, ecostata, cellulis oblongis latis areolata. Perigonia infra perichaetium copiosa. Capsula in pedicello laevi rubro 1 cent. longo tenuissimo horizontalis pendulave, minutissima, urceolata, infra os strangulata, operculo brevissime conico.

ILLUSTRATIONS. None.

TAHITI. Papara District: Puté, floor of the Temarua Valley, *Nadeaud sn*, 1896 (Bescherelle, 1898a, no. *408*).

Distribution.—Society Islands (Tahiti), endemic.

2. *Isopterygium* Mitten
J. Linn. Soc. Bot. 12: 21, 497. 1869.
Isopterygium albescens (Hooker) Jaeger
Ber. S. Gall. Naturw. Ges. 1876–1877: 433. 1878.

Hypnum albescens Hook., *in* Schwaegrichen, Spec. Musc. Suppl. 3(1): 226b. 1828.
Isopterygium molliculum (Sull.) Mitt., *in* Seemann, Fl. Vit. 399. 1871. *fide* Dixon and Greenwood, Proc. Linn. Soc. N. S. Wales 55: 295. 1930.
Isopterygium lonchopelma (C. Muell.) Jaeg., Ber. S. Gall. Naturw. Ges. 1876–1877: 432. 1878. *fide* Dixon and Greenwood, 1930.
?*Isopterygium argyrocladum* Besch., Bull. Soc. Bot. France 45: 123. 1898a.
Plagiothecium anderssoni Aongstr., Oefv. K. Svensk. Vet. Ak. Foerh. 4: 15. 1872. *fide* Bartram, 1933b.
Taxicaulis hawaiicus C. Muell., Flora 82: 469. 1896. *fide* Bartram, 1933b.
Taxicaulis filisetaceus C. Muell., *nom. nud. fide* Fleischer, Musci Fl. Buitenzorg 4: 1700. 1923.
?*Isopterygium marquesianum* Bartr., *nom. nud. in* BISH!

Plants slender, thread-like, or forming thin mats on decaying wood or bark, the stems irregularly branched, pale to whitish-green; leaves 0.9–1.2 × 0.24–0.27 mm, more narrow and not as concave as those represented by Schwaegrichen (1828), or as in specimens identified by Fleischer (no. *485*, NY!), from Java. Cells linear, smooth, 60–110 × 2–3 μ in the upper leaf, irregularly rectangular to quadrate in the leaf base, 12–36 × 7–12 μ, only slightly or not at all inflated in the alar region. All Society Islands material I have examined was sterile, but in Javan material (*Fleischer 485*), the seta was 1.5–2.0 cm long, smooth, reddish; capsule constricted beneath the mouth, ovoid, inclined to pendulous, 1.2 × 0.67 mm; peristome outer teeth about 270 μ long, transversely striolate, the median furrow quite pronounced; inner peristome teeth papillose. Exothecial cells irregularly rounded-quadrate to rectangular, 24–48 × 20–28 μ. Stomata are present at the capsule base. Spores green, smooth, 9–10 μ.

ILLUSTRATIONS. Schwaegrichen (1828, pl. 226b). Figure 98.

TAHITI. Mountains of Hitiaa and Faaiti: On tree trunks, *Nadeaud sn*, 1896 (Bescherelle, 1898a, as *I. argyrocladum*). Miaa: 850 m, *Temarii Nadeaud sn*, 1899 (Bescherelle, 1901, as *I. argyrocladum*).

MOOREA. Without locality: *Temarii Nadeaud sn*, 1899 (Bescherelle, 1901, as *I. argyrocladum*).

RAIATEA. Faaroa Bay: N side, 400 m, on mountain, on branch of tree in shade, *Moore 64*. Averaiti Valley: Upper end, 300 m, on moist rock in stream bed, *Moore 72*; 300 m, on tree branches in shade, *Moore 80* (Bartram, 1931, *Moore 80* as var. *applanata* Fleisch.).

Distribution.—Society Islands (Tahiti, Moorea, Raiatea), Hawaii (all larger islands), Australia, New Zealand, Philippine Islands, Java, Borneo, Celebes, Sumatra, Japan, Sri Lanka (Ceylon), Nepal, New Guinea, Himalayas.

Bartram (1931) considered *I. argyrocladum* to be indistinguishable from *I. albescens*; there is nothing in Bescherelle's original description to suggest it is distinct, and I provisionally accept it as a synonym of *I. albescens*. Hawaiian forms of *I. albescens* have slightly smaller leaves and shorter cells, but they compare well in all general features. Specimens from the Marquesas, reported by Bartram (1933a) as *I. minutirameum* var. *brevifolia* Fleisch. (as *I. marquesianum* Bartr., BISH!), seem to fit within the range of variation of *I. albescens*. In Javan specimens, the leaves were broader and more concave, 0.9–1.2 × 0.32–0.38 mm, and the cells slightly longer than in Society Islands materials, to about 130 μ. All specimens examined were without the short double costa which is so common in the Hypnaceae.

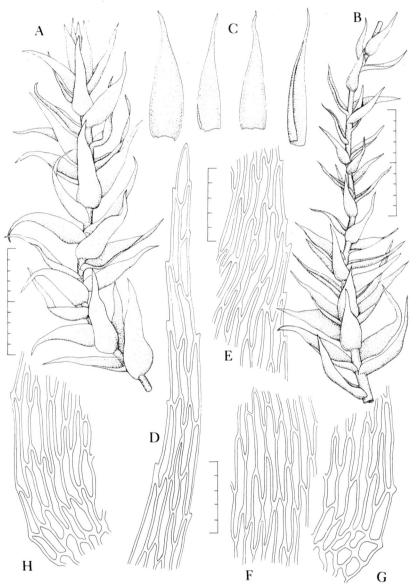

FIG. 98. *Isopterygium albescens.* A. Habit. B. Habit. C. Leaves. A–C, scale 1 mm. D. Leaf apex cells. E. Leaf, upper margin cells. F. Leaf, upper median cells. G, H. Leaf base cells. D–H, scale 50 μ.

3. *Ctenidium* (Schimper) Mitten
J. Linn. Soc. Bot. 12: 509. 1869.
Ctenidium stellulatum Mitten
in Seemann, Fl. Vit. 399. 1871.

The type specimen (NY!) consists of 2 stems 2–3 cm long, golden-brown, about 3.5–4.0 mm wide, irregularly branched, the primary stem with leaves erect, apices flexuose, long-acuminate, from a broad cordate base, 1.3–1.6 × 0.5–0.8 mm, ecostate; secondary branch leaves more slender, not quite as long. Cells linear, smooth-walled, unipapillose, the papilla formed by the projecting cell end wall, the cells of the upper lamina 45–70 × 3–5 μ, those of the margins shorter and wider, 24–36 × 5–7 μ, the outer cell wall thinner than the inner wall to give the margins a hyaline, "bordered" appearance; basal cells, especially those in the basal angles, short-rectangular, 12–25 × 5 μ, decurrent onto the stem. Margins serrate. All specimens examined were sterile.

ILLUSTRATIONS. Figure 91I–Q.

TAHITI. Without locality: *Bidwill sn* (Mitten, 1871; type, NY). High valleys of Puaa and Pinai: 800–1000 m, *Nadeaud 424*, 1896 (Bescherelle, 1898a, NY). Haapape District: Rahi, 800 m, *Nadeaud sn*, 1899 (Bescherelle, 1901). Pirae District: Trail to summit Mt. Aorai, *Quayle 147* (Bartram, 1933a, BISH!).

Distribution.—Society Islands (Tahiti), Formosa.

Dixon (1916) examined the authentic material of *Ctenidium stellulatum* and commented that it was "marvelously like the 125 Nilgiri, Beddome specimen which I have called *Ct. squarrulosum.*" What fate befell Dixon's *C. squarrulosum* is not known; it does not appear in *Index Muscorum*. Plants of *Ctenidium stellulatum* are robust, golden-brown or yellow. Mitten (1871) noted that the species epithet was chosen because the leaves, seen from the stem apex, are arranged in a stellate manner. The type material (NY!) was studied and illustrated by H. Ando in 1960, and a copy of his illustration accompanies the herbarium sheet.

4. *Vesicularia* (C. Mueller) C. Mueller
Flora 82: 407. 1896. Bot. Jahrb. Syst. 23: 330. 1896.

Plants prostrate on rocks, bark, or decaying wood, in wet, humid regions, forming extensive, thin, pale to dark green mats. Primary stems with short lateral branches, the leaves complanate, ovate-acuminate, ecostate; margins entire to faintly serrulate. Cells of the lamina thin-walled, large, elongate-hexagonal, smooth, and chlorophyllose.

Key to Species of *Vesicularia*

1. Leaves 1.4–1.8 mm long; lamina cells to 85 × 20 μ
   2. Lamina cells to 20 μ wide (45–70 × 10–20 μ)_____1. *V. inflectens.*
   2. Lamina cells 10–12 μ wide_____3. *V. tahitensis.*
1. Leaves less than 1.4 mm long; lamina cells mostly less than 60 μ long
   2. Lamina cells 50–60 μ long, seta 2–3 cm long _____ 2. *V. aperta.*
   2. Lamina cells to 48 μ long, seta to 2 cm _____4. *V. calodictyon.*

1. *Vesicularia inflectens* (Bridel) C. Mueller
Bot. Jahrb. Syst. 23: 330. 1896.

Leskea inflectens Brid., Bryol. Univ. 2: 331. 1826–1827.
Hypnum inflectens (Brid.) C. Muell., Syn. 2: 239. 1851.
Hypnum fuscescens Hook. & Arnott, Bot. Capt. Beechey's Voyage 76. f. 19. 1841. *fide* Mitten, *in* C. Mueller, 1873.
Ectropothecium fuscescens (Hook. & Arnott) Mitt., J. Linn. Soc. Bot. 10: 180. 1868.
Hypnum loxocarpum Aongstr., Oefv. K. Svensk. Vet. Ak. Foerh. 30: 126. 1873. *fide* Aongstrom, Oefv. K. Svensk. Vet. Ak. Foerh. 33: 53. 1876.
Hypnum montagnei sensu Mont., 1848, *nec.* Schimp. *fide* Bescherelle, 1895a.

Plants prostrate, green to dark green, common on rocks and bark in shaded, wet regions, primary stems 5–7 cm long, secondary branches to 1 cm; leaves complanate, slightly dimorphic, the upper leaves ovate-acuminate, symmetrical, 1.4–1.8 × 0.68–0.95 mm, the lateral leaves slightly asymmetrical; ecostate; margins entire to slightly serrulate. Perichaetial leaves about the same size as stem leaves, but lanceolate-acuminate. Cells of the lamina 45–70 × 10–20 μ, irregularly elongate-hexagonal, thin-walled, smaller, and more rectangular toward the leaf base and the basal angles, 35–48 × 12 μ. Seta 1.0–2.2 cm long, reddish, smooth; capsule 1.3 × 0.8 mm, ovate-cylindric; operculum conic, with a short apiculus, about 0.6 mm long. Peristome teeth about 290 μ long, transversely papillose-striate, the endostome papillose. Capsule exothecial cells rounded-quadrate, slightly bulging, the angles thickened, 19–30 μ. Spores 12–17 μ, green, smooth.

ILLUSTRATIONS. Sullivant (1859, pl. 16C). Figure 99.

TAHITI. Without locality: *Dumont d'Urville sn* (Bridel, 1826–1827, as *Leskea*); *Beechey sn* (NY!); *Wilkes sn* (Sullivant, 1859, as *Hypnum apertum* var. *condensatum*); *Andersson sn,* 1852 (Aongstrom, 1873, as *H. loxocarpum,* isotype, NY!); *Vesco sn; Lépine 19;*

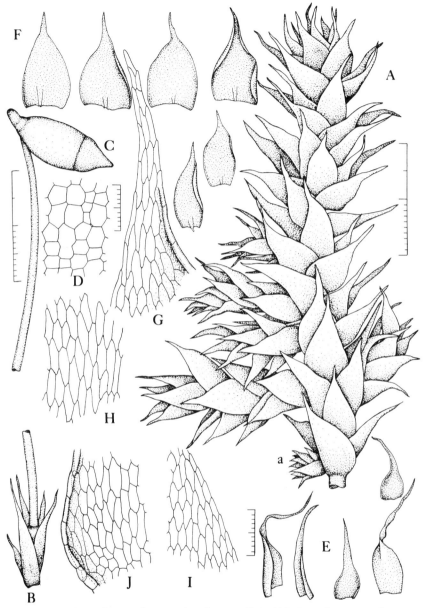

Fig. 99. *Vesicularia inflectens.* (*Hürlimann T 1148.*) A. Habit: a. male inflorescence, perigonial leaves. B, E. Perichaetial leaves. C. Capsule and operculum. A, B, C, E, F, scale 2 mm. D. Capsule, exothecial cells. F. Stem
leaves (6), scale 2 mm. G. Stem leaf, apical cells. H. Stem leaf, upper lamina
cells. D, G, H, scale 100 μ. I. Stem leaf, margin upper lamina cells. J. Stem
leaf, alar and basal cells. I, J, scale 100 μ.

on wet rocks near streams throughout the island, *Nadeaud 84* (Nadeaud, 1873, as *Hypnum*); *Vernier sn*; *Lequerré sn*; *Jardin sn*; *Jelinek sn*; Reine Valley, on trunks of old trees, *Savatier 732* (Bescherelle, 1895a, as *Ectropothecium*); common on wet rocks, several collections, *Nadeaud sn*, 1896 (Bescherelle, 1898a, as *Ectropothecium, 389–393*); *Picquenot sn*, 1897 (*ex* hb. Corbière, unreported, NY!); *Larminat sn* (Potier de la Varde, 1912). Pirae District: Fautaua Valley, 400–500 m, damp, shady site, *Quayle 669* (BISH!); *St. John and Fosberg 14143* (BISH!, unreported); on volcanic rocks and decaying wood, *Hürlimann T 1114, T 1127*; 600 m, trail from Fare Rau Ape to Mt. Aorai, on lateritic cliffs and under thick growth of *Gleichenia* (*Dicranopteris*), *Hürlimann T 1211*. Taiarapu Peninsula: Teahupoo, 10 m, Maire Valley, moist shady site, *MacDaniels 1652* (Bartram, 1933a); Taravao, above experiment station, 500 m, on volcanic rock, *Hürlimann T 1162* (Hürlimann, 1963); 440 m, above experiment station, on bark, with *Vesicularia apertum, Trichosteleum hamatum, Leucomium aneurodictyon, Callicostella papillata*, and *Riccardia, 2205*; 120 m, N side, Haavini Valley, above camp, *2491*; with *Racopilum, Leucomium aneurodictyon, Trichocolea*, and *Porella, 2258*. Paea District: Maraa Grotto, on dripping rocks, *Setchell and Parks 5069*. Papeari District: Maraa Valley, *5413* (Brotherus, 1924a, BISH! NY!). Papenoo District: Papenoo Valley, 180 m, with *Vesicularia apertum, 2457*. Paea District: Papehue, *Tilden 342* (BISH!).

MOOREA. Without locality: *Temarii Nadeaud sn*, 1899 (Bescherelle, 1901, as *Ectropothecium*); on stones in humid forest, *Eriksson 56* (Bartram, 1950b). Mt. Rotui: S side, between Papetoai and Paopao bays, ca 100 m, on fern petiole, with *Calymperes* and hepatics, *3435*.

RAIATEA: Uturoa: On wet wood in stream bed, 50 m, *Moore 1*. Third valley S of Faaroa Bay: 100 m, on moist rocks in damp, shady mapé (*Inocarpus*) grove, *Moore 2*; 80 m, on dripping rocks, *Moore 5*. Faaroa Valley: 100 m, on moist rocks in deep shade, *Moore 11, 14* (Bartram, 1931, BISH!, FH!).

BORA BORA. Very common on rocks and tree bases, *Phillips sn*, 1944 (Phillips, 1947).

Distribution.—Society Islands (Tahiti, Moorea, Raiatea, Bora Bora), Samoa, Fiji, New Caledonia, Admiralty Islands, Caroline Islands (Ponape), Solomon Islands, Tubuai, Rapa, Rotuma, Australia, New Guinea, south China.

2. *Vesicularia aperta* (Sullivant) Thériot

J. Linn. Soc. Bot. 45: 465. 1922.

Hypnum apertum Sull., Proc. Am. Acad. Arts Sci. 3: 73. 1854. U.S. Expl. Exped. Wilkes Musci 18. f. 16b. 1859.

Vesicularia bryifolia (Aongstr.) Broth., E. & P. Nat. Pfl. ed. 2, 11: 465. 1925.

Ectropothecium bryifolia (Aongstr.) Jaeg., Ber. S. Gall. Naturw. Ges. 1877–1878: 269. 1880.

Hypnum bryifolium C. Muell. *ex* Aongstr., Oefv. K. Svensk. Vet. Ak. Foerh. 33(4): 53. 1876.

Hypnum (Ectropothecium) inflectens Aongstr., 1873, *non* C. Mueller, 1896.

Plants pale to dark green, prostrate on bark or decaying wood; leaves closely overlapping on the stems, broadly ovate, short-acuminate, concave, slightly asymmetrical; margins entire or very slightly serrulate; costa typically absent but when present, short, double, and faint. Cells of the lamina smooth, elongate, 50–60 × 10–12 μ in the upper blade; alar cells quadrate, about 20–25 μ. Seta 2–3 cm long; capsule inclined to pendulous, asymmetrical; urn as long as broad, about 1.1–1.3 mm; peristome teeth to 540 μ long. Spores 12–(16)–22 μ, green, finely papillose.

ILLUSTRATIONS. Sullivant (1859, f. 16b, as *Hypnum*). Figure 100P–U.

TAHITI. Without locality: On the ground, *Wilkes sn* (Sullivant, 1859, as *Hypnum*); *Andersson sn* (Aongstrom, 1873, as *Hypnum inflectens*; 1876, as *H. bryifolium*; Bescherelle, 1895a, as *Ectropothecium bryifolium*); common on the banks of streams in humid valleys, on ground and trees, *Nadeaud sn*, 1896 (Bescherelle, 1898a, as *Ectropothecium bryifolium, 394–398*). Papenoo District: Without specific information, *Tilden 70*, 1909 (BISH!). Pirae District: Fautaua Valley, *Setchell and Parks 5304* (Brotherus, 1924a, as *Vesicularia bryifolia*, NY!). Taiarapu Peninsula: Taravao, above experiment station, in guava and *Miconia* forest, with *Vesicularia inflectens, Leucomium aneurodictyon, Trichosteleum hamatum*, and *Riccardia, 2205*. Papenoo District: Papenoo Valley, 150 m, W side, on tree branch near dry spring and Chinese garden, *2329*; with *Fissidens mangarevensis* on bark, *2448*; with *Vesicularia inflectens, 2457*. Without locality: *Moseley sn, Challenger* Expedition (unreported, in hb. Mitten as *Hypnum graminicolor*, NY!).

Distribution.—Society Islands (Tahiti), endemic.

This species may represent a variation of *Vesicularia inflectens*, for what appear to be intergrading forms seem common, and the two extremes appear together in collections. In *Vesicularia in-*

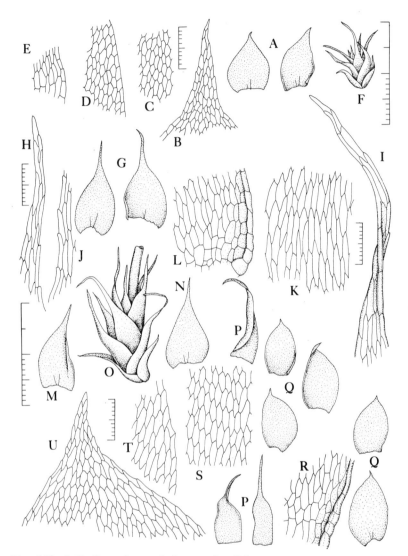

Fig. 100. A–F. *Vesicularia calodictyon.* (*Griffith sn*, Samoa.) A. Leaves, scale 2 mm. B. Stem leaf apex cells. C. Stem leaf median cells. D. Leaf upper margin cells. E. Stem leaf alar and basal cells. B–E, scale 100 μ. F. Perichaetial leaves, scale 100 μ. G–O. *Vesicularia tahitensis.* G, M, N. Leaves, scale 2 mm. H, I. Stem leaf apices, cells. J. Stem leaf, upper lamina margin cells. K. Stem leaf, upper lamina median cells. L. Stem leaf, basal and alar cells. H–L, scale 100 μ. O. Perichaetium, scale 2 mm. P–U. *Vesicularia aperta.* P. Perichaetial leaves (3), scale 2 mm. Q. Stem leaves (5), scale 2 mm. R. Stem leaf, basal and alar cells. S. Stem leaf, upper median cells. T. Stem leaf, upper margin cells. U. Stem leaf, apical cells. R–U, 100 μ.

flectens, the leaves are more transversely inserted on the stem and do not overlap as closely as in *V. aperta;* further, the leaves are narrower and longer-acuminate. Cells are slightly larger in the leaves of *V. inflectens,* and the capsule is longer than broad. Sullivant's *Hypnum apertum* is identical to Mueller's *H. bryifolium,* and is very similar to Mueller's *H. calodictyon* from Samoa, which may also prove to be identical. If further study supports Sullivant's assertion that *H. apertum* var. *condensatum* is a Hawaiian variety, then *Vesicularia perviridis* (C. Muell.) C. Muell. (= *V. graminicolor*) may prove to be synonymous.

3. *Vesicularia tahitensis* (Aongstrom) Brotherus
   E. & P. Nat. Pfl. ed. 2, 11: 465. 1925.

    Hypnum tahitensis Aongstr., Oefv. K. Svensk. Vet. Ak. Foerh. 30: 125. 1873.
    Ectropothecium tahitensis (Aongstr.) Besch., Ann. Sci. Nat. Bot. ser. 7, 20: 53. 1895a.

Plants prostrate on rotting wood or bark, yellow-green, branching pattern regular to irregular, the lateral branches to 1 cm long; leaves 1.5–1.8 × 0.55–0.67 mm, usually without a costa, occasionally with a short, double costa or a single segment of the double costa; concave, ovate-lanceolate, abruptly long-acuminate; margins entire to serrulate. Perichaetial leaves longer, to more than 2 mm long, entire to irregularly serrulate, ecostate. Cells of the upper lamina 60–85 × 10–12 μ, elongate, thin-walled, smooth; at the basal angles, cells nearly quadrate, 20–25 μ, toward the center of the leaf base elongate-hexagonal to rectangular, wider, about 60–85 × 15 μ. Only incomplete sporophytes were seen in the isotype examined (NY!); seta smooth, 1.5–2.0 mm long; capsule pendulous.

    ILLUSTRATIONS. Figure 100G–O.

    TAHITI. Without locality: *Andersson sn,* 1852 (Aongstrom, 1873, as *Hypnum,* isotype, NY!; Bescherelle, 1895a, as *Ectropothecium*). Mt. Orohena: E side of S ridge, 1400 m, on rocks at base of waterfall, *St. John and Fosberg 17130* (unreported, det. Bartram, BISH!). Between Papeava and Puaa: Tarutu (Mamano) and Teapiri, 900–1000 m, *Nadeaud sn,* 1896 (Bescherelle, 1898a, as *Ectropothecium*).

    Distribution.—Society Islands (Tahiti), Rapa, Pitcairn Island, Samoa (Tutuila).

    Aongstrom (1873) compared this species with *Hypnum* (*Vesicularia*) *reticulatum* Dozy & Molk., from Java, which he observed did have a constricted capsule, and which did not have the leaf apices as constricted as those in *H. tahitensis. Vesicularia tahitensis* is close to *V. inflectens,* and may prove to be only a variant with more slender leaves.

4. *Vesicularia calodictyon* (C. Mueller) Brotherus
   E. & P. Nat. Pfl. ed. 2, 11: 465. 1925.
   Hypnum calodictyon C. Muell., J. Mus. Godeffroy 3(6): 80. 1874.
   Ectropothecium calodictyon (C. Muell.) Jaeg., Ber. S. Gall. Naturw. Ges. 1877–1878: 271. 1880.

Plants yellow-green, the lateral branches to 1 cm long, irregular, the stem leaves closely overlapping, 1.0–1.2 × 0.48–0.60 mm, ovate-lanceolate, short-acuminate, the margins entire to slightly serrulate. Cells elongate, 48 × 12 μ in the upper lamina, about the same size in the leaf base but shorter, more nearly quadrate at the basal angles, 20–25 μ. Sporophytes examined from the isotype (NY!) were incomplete; seta smooth, to 2.0 cm; capsules inclined or pendulous. Perichaetial leaves to 2.5 mm long. Mueller (1873) described the leaves as variable ecostate, or with a short, double, but faint costa.

ILLUSTRATIONS. Figure 100A–F.

TAHITI. Without locality: *Beechey 180* (Dixon, 1950).

Distribution.—Society Islands (Tahiti), Samoa (Upolu, type locality).

Known for Tahiti only from the collection by Beechey reported by Dixon (1950), this species, as it was known from Samoa, was compared with *Hypnum reticulatum* Dozy & Molk. by Mueller, who observed that the leaves of his new species were dimorphic, ovate, oblong-acuminate, and not piliferous. The leaf margins (of the isotype from Samoa) have a slightly bordered appearance, for the cells are rhomboidal, and the outer walls quite thin. This species is closely allied to *Vesicularia aperta* (Sull.) Thér., and differs primarily in the bordered appearance of the leaves and in the shorter, more uniform cells of the lamina.

Excluded species

Vesicularia longifolia Herz., *nom. nud.,* Geographie der Moose 357. 1926.

5. *Mittenothamnium* Henn.
   Hedwigia 41 (Beibl.): 225. 1892. *nom. cons.* (*Microthamnium* Mitt., 1869. *hom. illeg.*)
Mittenothamnium macroblepharum (Bescherelle) Cardot
   Rev. Bryol. 40: 21. 1913.

Microthamnium macroblepharum Besch., Ann. Sci. Nat. Bot. ser. 7, 20: 51. 1895a.

Hypnum macroblepharum Schimp., *in* Jardin, Bull. Linn. Soc. Normandie ser. 2, 9: 264, 266. 1875. *nom. nud.*

Macrothamnium macroblepharum (Schimp.) Besch., 1898. *orthogr. pro Microthamnium.*

I have not yet examined the original collection upon which this species is based. Bescherelle's original description:

Monoicum. Cespites laxe intricati, flavo-virides. Stipes brevis ramo primario 4–5 cent. longo ramulis patulis pinnatis ramosis brevibus simplicibus vix 5 mill. longis vel ramosis longioribus simpliciter pinnatis. Folia patula flexuosa, remota, basi concava contracta anguste ovato-lanceolata sensim in acumen longum obliquum tortum protracta, margine ob cellulas marginales prominentes subtiliter e basi serrata, costis brevissimis obsoletis, cellulis anguste hexagonis apice prominentibus subpapillosis reticulata. Perigonium prope perichaetium nascens, minutum, sphaericum, foliis ovatis concavis late acuminatis apice erosulis, antheridiis brevibus crassis. Perichaetium in ramo primario obsitum, longum, foliis erectis parum divaricatis basi truncatis ovato-lanceolatis in cuspidem longissimam apice nodoso-dentatum attenuatis, ecostatis, integris. Capsula in pedicello 10–15 mill. longo rubello tenuissimo levi apice contorquato pendula vel ob torsionem pedicelli horizontalis, minuta, sub apice magis strangulata, operculo? Calyptra? Peristomii magni dentes radiantes apice incurvi, externi sat longi, fusci, interni haud hiantes aequilongi, ciliis 1–2 brevioribus.

ILLUSTRATIONS. None.

TAHITI. Without locality: Mountains of Hitiaa, Faaiti, and at the foot of Mt. Aorai, Tipaeaui Valley: *Nadeaud 387* (Bescherelle, 1898a, as *Macrothamnium*).

Distribution.—Society Islands (Tahiti), Marquesas Islands (Nuku Hiva), type locality.

Brotherus (1908, 1[3]: 1051) wrote that this species was unknown to him and that he could not place it properly in his key. As Fleischer (1923, 4: 1381) treated this genus, the species of *Mittenothamnium* are supposed to be dioicous, a characteristic of the genera in Fleischer's subfamily Ctenidieae.

XXXIX. POLYTRICHACEAE

Pogonatum P. Beauvois
  Mag. Enc. 5: 329. 1804.

The genus *Pogonatum* is characterized by plants forming low turfs of erect, occasionally branched, secondary stems on exposed, clayey banks or on rocks at middle and upper elevations, and is represented by two species in the Society Islands: *P. graeffeanum* and *P. tahitense.* Both species are typical of the genus *Pogonatum,* section *Aloides,* having 4-angled capsules, 32 teeth in the peristome, and prominent, chlorophyllose lamellae 3–8 cells high covering most of the upper portion of the leaf. The rhizomatous, primary stems are often lost when specimens are collected.

Brotherus (1924b) placed *P. tahitense* after *P. aloides* in his key. Diagnostic features for this group are: a light-colored capsule with indistinct ridges, the capsule erect to inclined, the lamellae 5–7 cells high, the terminal lamella cell rounded, rarely flat or indented. Separated from these in Brotherus' key is *P. graeffeanum* (= *P. subtortile, fide* J. Coenen in hb. NY!), grouped with taller (frequently to 8 cm), often branched plants with capsules dark, inclined to horizontal, distinctly ridged and with leaves bearing lower lamellae, 3–4 cells high, the terminal cell larger and rounded. G. L. Smith (personal communications, 1967, 1968) has suggested that *P. tahitense* might be considered *P. aloides sensu latissime,* and that *P. graeffeanum* (or *P. subtortile sensu* Coenen) might similarly be treated as *P. tortile.* These alliances seem to be appropriate, and are worth consideration in more detailed monographic analysis, but for the moment it seems wise to retain the names already in use for the Society Islands taxa.

Key to Species of *Pogonatum*

1. Plants 3–4 cm tall; lamellae on leaves 3–4 cells high, capsules inclined to horizontal, distinctly ridged..1. *P. graeffeanum.*
1. Plants 1–2 cm tall; lamellae on leaves 5–7 cells high, capsules erect to inclined, indistinctly ridged..2. *P. tahitense.*

1. *Pogonatum graeffeanum* (C. Mueller) Jaeger
Ber. S. Gall. Naturw. Ges. 1873–1874: 254. 1875.
Polytrichum (*Catharinella*) *graeffeanum* C. Muell., J. Mus. Godeffroy 3(6): 61. 1873.
Polytrichum virens C. Muell., in hb. Reg. Berol. 1856. *fide* C. Mueller, 1873.

Plants to 3–4 cm tall, light to brownish-green. In a dry state the leaf base stands away from the sheathing basal portion and stem at a 90° angle, and the upper portion of the leaf is variably twisted but usually incurved toward the stem. The capsules may be dark when mature, but this feature does not always hold true; they may be inclined to horizontal, the ridges distinct.

ILLUSTRATIONS. Figure 101A–G.

TAHITI. Pirae District: Fare Rau Ape–Mt. Aorai trail, ca 1000 m, on weathered volcanic rock, *Hürlimann T 1252* (Hürlimann, 1963); *Decker and Decker 91*; on exposed soil, with *Pogonatum tahitense, Bryum billardieri*, and *Campylopus, 2660; 2670*; with *Trematodon longicollis, Campylopus*, and *Notoscyphus paroicus, 2690; 2727, 2844*; 500 m, on banks below old buildings of French Alpine Club (now a military training center), under *Dicranopteris* and *Lycopodium*, associated with *Campylopodium euphorocladum, 201* (1960); with *Pogonatum tahitense, 205; 296; 2033; 2035*; Fautaua Valley, 550 m, above Cascade de Fautaua, on soil banks, with *Pogonatum tahitense, Whittier sn*. Papenoo District: Papenoo Valley, 150 m, road along W side on soil banks, a small form associated with *Campylopodium euphorocladum, 2397*.

Distribution.—Society Islands (Tahiti, probably on all major islands), Samoa (Upolu, type locality), Fiji (Ovalau).

2. *Pogonatum tahitense* Bescherelle
Ann. Sci. Nat. Bot. ser. 7, 20: 31. 1895.

Plants 1–2 cm tall, leaves dark, reddish, erect, apices incurved. Sporophytes to 2 cm tall. The shorter stature of the plants, dark color, and strong, regularly incurved leaves, the apices often reaching nearly to the stem, provide good distinctive diagnostic field characters. Some plants having the characters of this species but which were several centimeters tall have been collected; these may prove to be a distinct species.

ILLUSTRATIONS. Figure 101H–L.

TAHITI. Pirae District: Without locality, *Vesco sn*; 500 m, near Fort Fautaua, *Nadeaud 52* (Bescherelle, 1895a; Nadeaud, 1873, as

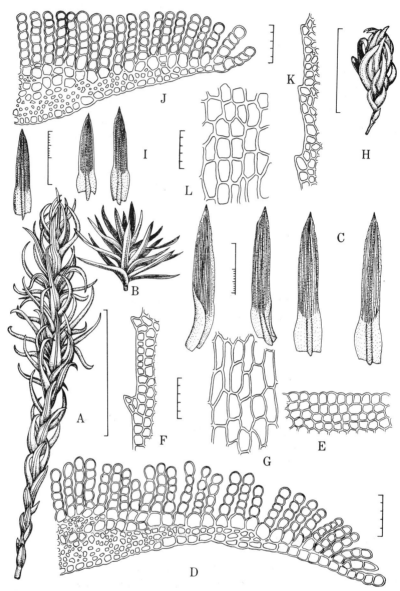

Fɪɢ. 101. A–G. *Pogonatum graeffeanum.* (*HOW 2660.*) A. Habit, dry. B. Habit, upper portion of plant only. A, B, scale 1 cm. C. Leaves, upper surface showing extent of lamellae, scale 2 mm. D. Leaf, cross section. E. Lamella, side view. F. Leaf margin, upper blade. G. Lamina basal cells. D–G, scale 50 μ. H–L. *Pogonatum tahitense.* (*HOW 2025.*) H. Habit, dry, scale 1 cm. I. Leaves, scale 2 mm. J. Leaf, cross section. K. Leaf margin, upper blade. L. Lamina, basal cells. J–L, scale 50 μ.

Polytrichum convolutum var. *cirrhatum*); Fare Rau Ape–Mt. Aorai trail, 750 m, on vertical lateritic face, with *Dicranella hochreutineri, Hürlimann T 1224* (Hürlimann, 1963, det. Bartram, FH!); 500 m, banks below old Alpine Club buildings, under *Dicranopteris* and *Lycopodium*, with *Campylopodium euphorocladum* and *Notoscyphus paroicus, 221* (1960); *2027, 2028; 2031;* 1000 m, along trail to summit, on soil and rock, with *Marchantia, Fissidens nadeaudii,* and *Bryum leptothecium, 2679;* with *Notoscyphus paroicus, Trematodon longicollis,* and *Pogonatum graeffeanum, 2690;* 1800 m, *2747;* 2065 m, summit, Mt. Aorai, on ground in front of shelter, *2789;* Fautaua Valley, 540 m, above Cascade de Fautaua, on soil banks, *3133.* Papeari District: Banks along road, to 50 m, *191* (1960).

RAIATEA. Highest mountain: W side, 600 m, on wet rock, *Moore 40* (Bartram, 1931, BISH!).

Distribution.—Society Islands (Tahiti, Raiatea), Hawaii.

Paris (1905) gave Schimper as the author of *Pogonatum tahitense,* but Bescherelle (1895a) described *P. tahitense* as a new species, reporting Vesco's collection together with Nadeaud's without reference to a prior name by Schimper, although he did cite Schimper as the authority for other names in his paper. It seems probable that Paris was in error, and that the authors of *Index Muscorum* (1967) who cited Schimper as the author of *P. tahitense* relied upon Paris' *Index* for their information.

Bartram (1933b) observed that the Hawaiian species *Pogonatum baldwinii* is "exceedingly close" to *P. tahitense,* contrasting them on the basis of more strongly crisped leaves, the marginal teeth stronger and sharper in *P. baldwinii.* Hoe (1974) includes *P. tahitense* in the Hawaiian bryoflora.

BIBLIOGRAPHY

Andrews, A. L. 1947. Taxonomic notes. 4. The Leucobryaceae. Bryologist 50(4): 319–26.

Aongstrom, J. 1872. Foerteckning och beskrifning oefver mossor, samlade af Professor N. J. Andersson under Fregatten *Eugenies* verldsomsegling aren 1851–53. Oefv. K. Svensk. Vet. Ak. Foerh. 4: 3–29.

———. 1873. Foerteckning och beskrifning oefver mossor, samlade af Professor N. J. Andersson under Fregatten *Eugenies* verldsomsegling aren 1851–53. Fortsattning. Oefv. K. Svensk. Vet. Ak. Foerh. 5: 113–51.

———. 1875. Verzeichniss und Beschreibung der Moose, welche Prof. N. J. Andersson auf der Expedition der Fregatten *Eugenies* Resa im Jahre 1851–53 gesammelt hat. Abstract. Hedwigia 14: 58–63, 76–79, 85–93.

———. 1876. Raettelser och tillaegg till foerteckning och beskrifning oefver mossor, samlade af Professor N. J. Andersson under Fregatten *Eugenies* verldsomsegling 1851–53, i Oefversigt af Kongl. Vetensk.-Akad. Foerhandl. 1872. Oefv. K. Svensk. Vet. Ak. Foerh. 33: 50–55.

Bartram, E. B. 1931. Mosses of Raiatea. Bishop Mus. Occas. Pap. 9: 1–14.

———. 1933a. Polynesian mosses. Bishop Mus. Occas. Pap. 10: 1–28.

———. 1933b. Manual of Hawaiian mosses. Bishop Mus. Bull. 101: 1–275.

———. 1936. Contributions to the mosses of Fiji. Bishop Mus. Occas. Pap. 11: 1–30.

———. 1938. Mosses of the Solomon Islands. Bryologist 41: 127–32.

———. 1939. Mosses of the Philippines. Philippine J. Sci. 68: 1–437.

———. 1940. Mosses of southeastern Polynesia. Bishop Mus. Occas. Pap. 15: 323–49.

———. 1942. Third Archbold Expedition mosses from the Snow Mountains, Netherlands New Guinea. Lloydia 5: 245–92.

———. 1943a. Mosses of Papua, New Guinea. Farlowia 1: 41–47.

———. 1943b. Burma mosses. Farlowia 1: 171–89.

———. 1944a. Additions to the mosses of Fiji. Bryologist 47: 57–61.

———. 1944b. New and noteworthy Philippine mosses. Farlowia 1: 503–13.

———. 1945. Pacific outpost mosses. Bryologist 48: 45–53.

———. 1948. Additional Fijian mosses. Bishop Mus. Occas. Pap. 19: 219–31.

———. 1950a. Additional Fijian mosses. 2. Bishop Mus. Occas. Pap. 20: 27–33.

———. 1950b. Mosses collected by Dr. John Eriksson, during the Swedish *Albatross* Expedition, 1947–48. Acta Horti Gothob. 18: 267–73.

———. 1953. New Caledonian mosses collected by Dr. O. H. Selling. Bot. Not. 106: 197–203.

———. 1956. Additional Fijian mosses. 3. J. Wash. Acad. Sci. 46: 392–96.

———. 1957a. Mosses of eastern Papua, New Guinea. Brittonia 9: 32–56.

———. 1957b. Mosses of Upolu, Western Samoa. Bishop Mus. Occas. Pap. 22: 15–30.

———. 1958. The natural history of Rennell Island, British Solomon Islands. Copenhagen 3: 99–100.

———. 1959. Contributions to the mosses of the highlands of eastern New Guinea. Brittonia 11: 86–97.

————. 1960a. Mosses of d'Entrecasteaux group and Louisade Archipelago, Papua, New Guinea. Blumea 10: 142–50.

————. 1960b. Mosses of Guam, Mariana Islands. Bryologist 63: 101–5.

————. 1960c. Additions to the moss flora of Netherlands New Guinea. Svensk. Bot. Tidskr. 54: 483–87.

————. 1965. Mosses of the eastern highlands, New Guinea, from the 6th Archbold Expedition. Contrib. U.S. Nat. Herb. 37: 43–67.

Bescherelle, E. 1873. Florule bryologique de la Nouvelle-Caledonie. Ann. Sci. Nat. Bot. ser. 5, 18: 184–285.

————. 1878a. Note sur deux especes de mousses du groupes des *Pterobryella* de la Nouvelle-Caledonie. Rev. Bryol. 5: 30–32.

————. 1878b. Note sur trois nouvelles especes de mousses de la Nouvelle-Caledonie appartenant au genre *Pterobryella* C. M. Bull. Soc. Bot. France 25: 64–68.

————. 1881. Note sur les mousses des colonies Francaises. Bull. Soc. Bot. France 28: 187–93.

————. 1895a. Florule bryologique de Tahiti et des iles de Nukahiva et Mangareva. Ann. Sci. Nat. Bot. ser. 7, 20: 1–62.

————. 1895b. Essai sur le genre *Calymperes*. Ann. Sci. Nat. Bot. ser. 8, 1: 247–308.

————. 1898a. Florule bryologique de Tahiti. Supplement. Bull. Soc. Bot. France 45: 52–67, 116–28.

————. 1898b. Note sur le *Rhacopilum pacificum* Besch. J. Bot. Morot. 12: 42–46.

————. 1898c. *Nadeaudia* Besch., *genus novum*. Rev. Bryol. 25: 11.

————. 1898d. Sur le genre *Nadeaudia* Besch. Rev. Bryol. 25: 42–43.

————. 1898e. Note sur le *Philonotula papulans* C. M. Rev. Bryol. 25: 89–90.

————. 1901. Deuxieme supplement a la flore bryologique de Tahiti. Bull. Soc. Bot. France 48: 11–17.

Breen, R. S., and R. A. Pursell. 1959. The genus *Splachnobryum* in the United States, Mexico, Central America and the Caribbean. Rev. Bryol. Lichenol. 28: 280–89.

Bridel, S. E. 1826–1827. Bryologia universa seu systematica ad novam methodum disposito historia et descriptio omnium muscorum frondosorum hucusque cognitorum cum synonymia ex auctoribus probatissimis. 1: i–xxviii, 1–456; 2: 1–846. Lipsiae.

Brigham, W. T. 1900. An index to the islands of the Pacific Ocean. Bishop Mus. Mem. 1: 85–256. Maps 1–24. F. 1–12.

Britton, E. G. 1907. The Mitten collection of mosses and hepatics. J. N.Y. Bot. Gard. 8: 28–32.

Brotherus, V. F. 1905–1908. Musci. *In* A. Engler and K. Prantl, Die Natuerliche Pflanzenfamilien. Ed. 1. Leipzig.

————. 1910. Contributions to the bryological flora of the Philippines. 3. Philippine J. Sci. 5: 137–62.

————. 1918. Contributions to the bryological flora of the Philippines. 5. Philippine J. Sci. 13(4): 201.

————. 1924a. Tahitian mosses collected by W. A. Setchell and H. E. Parks. Univ. Calif. Publ. Bot. 12: 45–48.

————. 1924b. Musci. *In* A. Engler and K. Prantl, Die Natuerliche Pflanzenfamilien. Ed. 2. Leipzig.

Brotherus, V. F., and W. W. Watts. 1915. Mosses of the New Hebrides. J. Proc. Roy. Soc. N. S. Wales 59: 127–57.

Buck, P. H. 1953. Explorers of the Pacific. Bishop Mus. Spec. Publ. 43: 1–125.

Cardot, J. 1899. Nouvelle classification des Leucobryacees basee principale-ment sur les caracteres anatomiques de la feuille. Rev. Bryol. 26: 1–8.
————. 1900. Recherches anatomiques sur les Leucobryacees. Mem. Acad. Sci. Cherbourg 32: 1–84. Pl. 1–19.
————. 1901. Note sur deux collections de mousses de l'Archipel Indien. Rev. Bryol. 28: 112–18.
————. 1908. Sur une petite collection de mousses de la Nouvelle-Caledonie. Bull. Herb. Boissier 2, 8: 166–74.
————. 1912. Musci. *In* B. P. G. Hochreutiner, Plantae Hochreutineranae. Ann. Cons. Jard. Bot. Geneve 15: 157–77.
————. 1916. Note sur une petite collection de mousses de Madagascar. Bull. Mus. Hist. Nat. 6: 342–50. Reprint 1–9.
Copeland, E. B. 1932. Pteridophytes of the Society Islands. Bishop Mus. Bull. 93: 1–86.
Crampton, H. E. 1916. Studies on the variation, distribution and evolution of the genus *Partula*. Carnegie Inst. Washington Publ. 228.
Cranwell, L. M. 1933. Flora of Manihiki, Cook Group. Rec. Auckland Inst. Mus. 1: 169–71.
Crum, H. A., and W. C. Steere. 1957. The mosses of Porto Rico and the Virgin Islands. New York Acad. Sci., Sci. Surv. Porto Rico and the Virgin Islands 7: 395–599.
Dansereau, P. 1957. Biogeography. Pp. i–xiii, 1–394. Ronald Press. New York.
————. 1966. Studies on the vegetation of Porto Rico. Univ. Porto Rico Inst. Caribbean Sci. Pp. 1–287.
Dixon, H. N. 1913–1929. Studies in the bryology of New Zealand. Parts 1–6. New Zealand Inst. Bull. 3: 1–372.
————. 1916. Miscellanea bryologica 5. J. Bot. Brit. For. 54: 352–59.
————. 1919. Miscellanea bryologica. 6. J. Bot. Brit. For. 57: 73–80.
————. 1922a. Miscellanea bryologica. 8. J. Bot. 60: 281–91.
————. 1922b. The mosses of the Wollaston Expedition to Dutch New Guinea, 1912–13, with some additional mosses from British New Guinea. J. Linn. Soc. London 45: 477–510.
————. 1927. Gilbert Islands mosses. J. Bot. Brit. For. 65: 254–57.
————. 1928a. *Splachnobryum pacificum* Dixon *sp. nov.* Rev. Bryol. Lichenol. 1: 12.
————. 1928b. Miscellanea bryologica. 11. J. Bot. Brit. For. 66: 347–54.
————. 1934. Bryophyta nova (17–75). Ann. Bryol. 7: 157–78.
————. 1937. On a small collection of mosses from New Guinea, with a re-vision of the genus *Spiridens* by W. R. Sherrin. Ann. Bryol. 10: 16–19.
————. 1950. Notes on the moss collections of the Royal Botanic Garden, Edinburgh. Notes Roy. Bot. Gard. Edinburgh 20: 93–102.
Dixon H. N., and A. Greenwood. 1930. The mosses of Fiji. Proc. Linn. Soc. N. S. Wales 55: 261–302.
Dozy, F., and J. H. Molkenboer. 1845–1854. Musci Frondosi Inediti Archi-pelagi Indici, descriptio et adumbratio muscorum frondosorum in insulis Java, Borneo, Sumatra, Celebes, Amboina, nec non in Japonia nuper de-tectorum minusve cognitorum. Pp. 1–185. Pl. 60. Batavia.
Dozy, F., and J. H. Molkenboer. 1855–70. Bryologia Javanica, seu descriptio muscorum frondosorum Archipelagi Indici iconibus illustrata. 2 vols. Leiden. grichen. Pp. i–vi, 1–352. Pl. 1–77. 1801. Suppl. 1(1): i–xvi, 1–196. Pl. archipelagi indici iconibus illustrata. 2 vols. Leiden.
Drake del Castillo, E. 1887. Sur la geographie botanique des Iles de la Societe. Bull. Soc. Philom. Paris 7, 11: 146–55.
Duby, J. E. 1875. Choix de mousses exotiques nouvelles ou mal connues. Mem. Soc. Phys. Hist. Nat. Geneve 24: 361–74.

Egler, F. E. 1939. Vegetation zones of Oahu. J. Hawaii Forestry 18: 44–57. Reprint 1–14.

Fleischer, M. 1904–1923. Die Musci. Flora von Buitenzorg 5(1–4): 1–1729. Leiden.

———. 1905. Neue Gattungen und Arten. Hedwigia 44: 301–29.

———. 1906. Neue Familien, Gattungen, und Arten der Laubmoose. Hedwigia 45: 53–87.

———. 1914–1922. Kritische Revision von Carl Muellerschen Laubmoos-Gattungen. 1. Hedwigia 55: 280–85. 1914; 2. 59: 212–19. 1917; 3. 61: 402–8. 1920; 4. 63. 209–16. 1922.

Fosberg, F. R. 1963. (Editor). Man's place in the island ecosystem. Symposium Tenth Pacific Sci. Congr., Honolulu, 1961. Pp. 1–264. Map. B. P. Bishop Museum Press. Honolulu.

Gams, H. 1932. Bryocenology (moss societies). In F. Verdoorn (Editor), Manual of bryology. Pp. 323–66. Nijhoff. Hague, Netherlands.

Gimingham, C. H., and E. T. Robertson. 1950. Preliminary investigations on the structure of bryophytic communities. Trans. British Bryol. Soc. 1: 330–44.

Goodspeed, T. H. (Editor). 1936. Essays in geobotany in honor of William Albert Setchell. Pp. i-xxv, 1–319. University of California Press. Berkeley.

Gressitt, J. L. (Editor). 1963. Pacific Basin biogeography. Symposium Tenth Pacific Sci. Congr., Honolulu. 1961. Pp. i-ix, 1–563. B. P. Bishop Museum Press. Honolulu.

Greville, R. K. 1848. Notice of a new species of Spiridens. Ann. Mag. Nat. Hist. ser. 2, 1: 325–26.

———. 1850. Notice of a new species of Spiridens. Trans. Bot. Soc. Edinburgh 3: 47–48.

Guillaumin, A. 1934. Les regions florales du Pacifique. Mem. Soc. Biogeogr. 4: 255–70. Map.

Guillemin, J. B. A. 1836–1837. Zephyritis Taitensis. Enumeration des plantes decouvertes par les voyageurs, dans les Iles de la Societe, principalement dans cette de Taiti. Ann. Sci. Nat. Bot. ser. 2, 6: 297–320. 1836; 7: 177–92, 241–55, 349–70. 1837.

Guppy, H. B. 1906. Observations of a naturalist in the Pacific, between 1891 and 1899. Vol. 2. Plant dispersal. Pp. i-xxviii, 1–627. Macmillan. New York.

Hedwig, J. 1801–1842. Species muscorum frondosorum descriptae et tabulis aeneis coloratis illustratae. Opus posthumum, editum a Friedrich Schwaegrichen. Pp. i–vi, 1–352. Pl. 1–77. 1801. Suppl. 1(1): i–xvi, 1–196. Pl. 1–49. 1811; 1(2): i–vii, 1–374. Pl. 50–100. 1816; 2(1): i–vi, 1–86. Pl. 100–125. 1823; 2(1): 87–179. Pl. 126–50. 1824; 2(2–1): 1–79. Pl. 151–75. 1826; 2(2–2): 81–210. Pl. 176–200. 1827; 3(1): no pagination. Pl. 201–25. 1827; 3(2): no pagination. Pl. 226–50. 1828; 3(2–1): no pagination. Pl. 251–75. 1829; 4(1): no pagination. Pl. 276–300. 1830; 4(2): no pagination. Pl. 301–25. 1842. Lipsiae.

Herzog, T. 1926. Geographie der Moose. Pp. i–xi, 1–439. F. 151. 8 photos. Jena.

Hoe, W. J. 1974. Annotated checklist of Hawaiian mosses. Lyonia 1(1): 1–45.

Holtum, R. E. 1964. The tree ferns of the genus Cyathea in Australasia and the Pacific. Blumea 12: 242–74.

Hooker, W. J. 1818–1820. Musci exotici; containing figures and descriptions of new or little known foreign mosses and other cryptogamic subjects. 1: i–viii. Pl. 1–96. 1818; 2: 97–176. Appendix, 1–31. 1820. London.

Hooker, W. J., and G. A. Walker-Arnott. 1830–1841. The botany of Captain

Beechey's voyage, comprising an account of the plants collected by Messrs. Lay & Collie, and other officers of the expedition during the voyage to the Pacific and Bering's Straits performed in His Majesty's ship, *Blossom*, under the command of Captain F. W. Beechey . . . in the years 1825, 26, 27, and 28. Pp. i–ii, 1–485. London.

Horikawa, Y. 1951. Tropical bryophytes in the Japanese Archipelago. J. Sci. Hiroshima Univ., ser. B, div. 2, Bot. 6: 27–38.

———. 1952. Tropical bryophytes in the Japanese Archipelago. 2. J. Sci. Hiroshima Univ., ser. B, div. 2, Bot. 6: 63–103.

———. 1954. Tropical bryophytes in the Japanese Archipelago. 3. J. Sci. Hiroshima Univ., ser. B, div. 2, Bot. 6: 273–79.

Hosokawa, T. 1952. A plant sociological study in the mossy forests of the Micronesian islands. Mem. Fac. Sci. Kyushu Univ., ser. E, Biol. 1: 65–82.

———. 1959. On Hosokawa's line and the response. Acta Phytotax. Geobot. 18: 14–19.

Hürlimann, H. 1963. Laubmoosfunde von den Fidschi- und Tonga-Inseln und von Tahiti. Bauhinia 2: 167–76.

———. 1965. Weitere Laubmoose von den Tonga-Inseln. Bauhinia 2: 288–94.

Jaeger, A. 1869. Enumeratio generum et specierum Fissidentacearum adjectis nonnullis adnotionibus de earum litteratura et distributione geographica. Pp. 1–36. Sangalli.

Jaeger, A., and F. Sauerbeck. 1875–1878. Genera et species muscorum systematico disposita seu Adumbratio florae muscorum totius orbis terrarum. Ber. S. Gall. Naturw. Ges. Reprint 1: i–xl, 1–740. 1870–75; 2: i–iv, 1–778. 1876–80.

Jardin, E. 1860. Supplement au Zephyritis Taitensis de M. Guillemin. Mem. Soc. Sci. Nat. Cherbourg 7: 239–44.

———. 1875. Enumeration de nouvelles plantes phanerogames et cryptogames decouvertes dans l'ancien et le nouveau continent et recuellies par Edelestan Jardin. Bull. Linn. Soc. Normandie ser. 2, 9: 247–339. Reprint 1–95.

Johnson, A. 1964. An account of the Malaysian Leucobryaceae. Gard. Bull. Straits Settlem. 3, 20: 315–60.

Kindberg, N. C. 1901. Gruendzuge einer Monographie ueber die Laubmoos-Familie Hypopterygiaceae. Hedwigia 40: 275–303.

———. 1902. Gruendzuge einer Monographie der Laubmoos-Gattung *Thamnium*. Hedwigia 41: 203–68.

Koponen, T. 1968. Generic revision of Mniaceae Mitt. Ann. Bot. Fennici 5(2): 117–51.

Lindberg, S. O. 1864. Upstallning af familjen Funariaceae. Oefv. K. Svensk. Vet. Ak. Foerh. (Stockholm) 21: 589–608.

MacArthur, R. H., and E. O. Wilson. 1967. The theory of island biogeography. Pp. i–xi, 1–203. Princeton University Press. New Jersey.

Malta, N. 1926. Die Gattung *Zygodon* Hook. et Tayl. Eine Monographische Studie. Latvijas Univ. Bot. Darma Darbi 1: 1–185.

Merrill, E. D. 1936. Malaysian phytogeography in relation to the Polynesian flora. *In* T. Goodspeed, Essays on geobotany. Pp. 247–61. Berkeley.

Merrill, E. D., and E. H. Walker. 1947. A botanical bibliography of the islands of the Pacific, and a subject index to Elmer D. Merrill's bibliography. Contr. U.S. Natl. Herb. 30: 1–404.

Miller, H. A. 1953. Moss societies on Oahu. Proc. Hawaiian Acad. Sci. 1952–53: 8.

———. 1954. Field observations on associations of Hawaiian mosses. Bryologist 57: 167–72.

————. 1957. "A phytogeographical study of Hawaiian Hepaticae." Dissertation, Stanford University. Pp. i–x, 1–123. Univ. Microfilms No. Mic 57–1166. Ann Arbor, Michigan.

————. 1959. Distribution patterns of Pacific Island Bryophyta. Abstract. Ninth Internat. Bot. Congress, Montreal 2: 263.

————. 1960. A preliminary list of Micronesian bryophytes. Bryologist 63: 116–25.

————. 1967. Oddments of Hawaiian bryology. J. Hattori Bot. Lab 30: 270–76.

————. 1971. An overview of the Hookeriales. Phytologia 21(4): 243–52.

Miller, H. A., H. O. Whittier, and C. E. B. Bonner. 1963. Bryoflora of the atolls of Micronesia. Beih. Nova Hedwigia 11: 1–89. Pl. 1–31.

Miller, H. A. (Editor), H. O. Whittier, R. del Rosario, and D. R. Smith. 1971. Bryological bibliography of the tropical Pacific islands. Pacific Scientific Information Center, Bernice P. Bishop Museum, Honolulu. Pp. 1–51.

Mitten, W. 1859. Musci Indiae Orientalis; an enumeration of the mosses of the East Indies. J. Proc. Linn. Soc. Bot. 1: 1–96.

————. 1861–1862. Musci et Hepaticae Vitiensis. Bonplandia 9: 365–67. 1861; 10: 19. 1862.

————. 1868. A list of the Musci collected by the Rev. Thomas Powell in the Samoa or Navigator's Islands. J. Linn. Soc. Bot. 10: 166–95.

————. 1871. Musci, Jungermanniae, Marchantieae. Pp. 378–419. In B. Seemann, Flora Vitiensis. London.

————. 1882. Record of new localities of Polynesian mosses, with descriptions of some hitherto undefined species. Proc. Linn. Soc. N. S. Wales 7: 98–104.

————. 1885. Musci and Hepaticae. In Report on the scientific results of the voyage of H. M. S. Challenger during the years 1873–76. Botany 1: 78–79, 212–14, 258–63. London.

Montagne, J. F. C. 1842–1845. Plantes cellulaires. In Hombron and Jacquinot, Voyage au Pole Sud et dans l'Oceanie sur les corvettes l'Astrolabe et la Zelee execute par ordre du roi pendant les annees 1837–1840, sous le commandement de M. J. Dumont d'Urville. Botanique 1: i–xiv, 1–349. Paris.

————. 1843. Quatrieme centurie de plantes cellulaires exotiques nouvelles. Decades 1–6. Ann. Sci. Nat. 2, 19: 238–66. Pl. 8, 9. Decade 7. 20: 294–306.

————. 1845. Cinquieme centurie de plantes cellulaires exotiques nouvelles. Decades 1–7, 10. Ann. Sci. Nat. Bot. ser. 3, 4: 86–123.

————. 1848. Sixieme centurie de plantes cellulaires exotiques nouvelles. Ann. Sci. Nat. Bot. ser. 3, 10: 106–36.

————. 1856a. Sylloge generum specierumque cryptogamarum quas in varii operibus descriptas iconibusque illustratas, nunc ad diagnosum reductas, non nullasque novas interjectas ordine systematico disposuit. i–xxiv, 1–498. Paris.

————. 1856b. Huitieme centurie de plantes cellulaires nouvelles tant indigenes qu'exotiques. Decades 1–3. Ann. Sci. Nat. Bot. ser. 4, 6: 179–99.

Mueller, C. 1845. Synopsis Macromitriorum hactenus cognitorum. Bot. Zeit. (Berlin) 3: 521–26, 539–45.

————. 1849–1851. Synopsis muscorum frondosorum omnium hucusque cognitorum. 1: i–viii, 1–812. 1849; 2: 1–772. 1850–51. Berlin.

————. 1857. Decas muscorum Oceani Pacifici. Bot. Zeit. (Berlin) 15: 777–82.

————. 1858–1862. Additamenta nova ad Synopsis muscorum. Bot. Zeit. (Berlin) 16: 161–65. 1858; 20: 327–29, 337–39, 361–62. 1862.

————. 1859. Supplementum novum ad Synopsis muscorum. Bot. Zeit. (Berlin) 17: 205–7, 219–21.

———. 1874. Musci Polynesiaci praesertim Vitiani et Samoani Graffeani. J. Mus. Godeffroy 3(6): 51–90.

———. 1896. Bryologica Hawaiica, adjectis nonnullis musci novis Oceanicis. Flora 82: 434–79.

———. 1896. Musci. *In* F. Reinecke, Die Flora der Samoa Inseln. Bot. Jahrb. Syst. 23: 317–32.

———. 1901. Genera muscorum frondosorum, classes Schistocarporum, Cleistocarporum, Stegocarporum complectentia, exceptis Orthotrichaceis et Pleurocarpis. Pp. i–vi, 1–474. Berlin.

Mueller, C., and V. F. Brotherus. 1900. Musci Schauinslandiani, ein Beitrag zur Kenntniss der Moosflora der Pacifischen Inseln. Ergebnisse einer Reise nach dem Pacific (H. Schauinsland 1896–97). Abh. Naturw. Ver. Bremen 16: 493–512.

Nadeaud, J. 1864. Plantes Usuelles des Tahitiens. These presentee publiquement soutenue a la Faculte de Medicine de Montepellier le 11 Juillet 1864, Pour obtenir le Grad le Docteur en Medicine. No. 52. Montpellier.

———. 1873. Enumeration des plantes indigenes de l'ile de Tahiti. Pp. i–v, 1–86. F. Savy, Libraire de la Societe Botanique de France, Paris.

———. 1896. Diary (Unpublished manuscript field notes), partial transcript in Musee de Papeete, Tahiti, prepared by Mlle. Aurora Natua.

———. 1897. Note sur quelques plantes rares ou peu connues de Tahiti. J. Bot. Morot 11: 103–20.

Nees von Esenbeck, C. G. 1823a. *Spiridens,* novum Muscorum Diplaperistomiorum genus detexit. Dr. C. S. C. Reinwart. Nova Acta Acad. Leop.-Carol. 11: 143–46.

———. 1823b. Pugillus Plantarum Javanicarum e cryptogamicarum variis ordinibus selectus communicavit C. F. Blume. Nova Acta Acad. Leop.-Carol. 11: 119–40.

Noguchi, A. 1962. Mosses of Phyllogoniaceae. Misc. Bryol. Lichenol. 2: 157–58.

———. 1965a. Notulae bryologicae. 7. Some transfers of names of the Asiatic mosses. J. Hattori Bot. Lab. 28: 147–54.

———. 1965b. On some species of the moss genus *Calyptothecium.* Bot. Mag. Tokyo 78: 63–67.

———. 1967. Musci Japonici. 7. The genus *Macromitrium.* J. Hattori Bot. Lab. 30: 205–30.

Ochi, H. 1957. *Bryum ramosum* and some of its allies in Pan-Pacific and Indo-Malayan areas. Bryologist 60: 1–11.

Osada, T. 1965. Japanese Polytrichaceae. 1. Introduction and the genus *Pogonatum.* J. Hattori Bot. Lab. 28: 171–201.

Papy, H. R. 1948–1958. Tahiti et les iles voisines. Travaux du Lab. Forest. Toulouse 5 (2), 1: 1–8. 1948; 2: 1–8. 1950; 3: 1–386. 1951–54; 4: 1–32. 1957; 5: 1–21. 1958.

Paris, E. G. 1893. Monographie des Cryphaeacees. Rev. Bryol. 20: 45–46.

———. 1900. Index bryologicus sive enumeratio muscorum hucusque cognitorum adjunctis synonymia distributionesque geographica locupletissimus. Supplementum primum. 1–334. Paris.

———. 1901. Muscinees du Tonkin 2e Article. Rev. Bryol. 28: 123–27.

———. 1903–1906. Index bryologicus sive enumeratio muscorum ad diem ultimam anni 1900 cognitorum adjunctis synonymia distributionesque geographica locupletissimus. Editio secunda 1: 1–384. 1903–4; 2: 1–375. 1904; 3: 1–400. 1904–5; 5: 1–160(1–31). 1906. Paris.

Phillips, E. 1917. Notes on Borabora, Society Islands, and a small collection of mosses from Mt. Temanu. Bryologist 50: 166–67.

Pocs, T., and P. Tixier. 1967. On the ciliferous *Syrrhopodon* species in Asia. Ann. Hist. Nat. Mus. Natl. Hung. 59: 125–34.

Potier de la Varde, R. 1912. Contribution a la florule de Taiti. Rev. Bryol. 39: 20–23.

Reese, W. D. 1961. The genus *Calymperes* in the Americas. Bryologist 64: 89–140.

Reichardt, H. W. 1868a. *Orthorhynchium*, eine neue Laubmoos-Gattung. Verh. Zool. Bot. Ges. Wien 18: 115–16.

―――. 1868b. Diagnosen der neuen Arten von Laubmoosen welche die *Novara*-Expedition mitbrachte. Verh. Zool.-Bot. Ges. Wien 18: 193–98.

―――. 1870. Fungi, Hepaticae et Musci frondosi. *In* E. Fenzl, Reise der Osterreichischen Fregatte *Novara* um die Erde. . . . Botanischer Theil 1: 133–96. Pl. 20–36.

―――. 1877. Beitrag zur Kryptogamenflora der Hawaiischen Inseln. Sitzungs-ber. Kaiserl. Akad. Wiss., Math.-Naturwiss. Cl., Abt. 1, 75: 133–96.

Reinecke, F. 1896–1898. Die Flora der Samoa-Inseln. Bot. Jahrb. Syst. 23: 237–368. 1896; 25: 578–708. 1898.

Reinwardt, K. G. K., and C. F. Hornschuch. 1829. Musci Frondosi Javanici. Nova Acta Acad. Leop.-Carol. 14: 699–732.

Renauld, F. 1901. Nouvelle classification des *Leucoloma*. Rev. Bryol. 28: 66–70; 85–87.

Renauld, F., and J. Cardot. 1901. Note sur le genre *Taxithelium*, R. Spruce. Rev. Bryol. 28: 109–12.

―――. 1905. Musci exotici novi vel minus cogniti. Bull. Soc. Roy. Bot. Belgique 41: 1–148.

Richards, P. W. 1938. Ecology. *In* F. Verdoorn (Editor), Manual of bryology. Pp. 367–95. Hague.

―――. 1940. Literature on the ecology of bryophytes published since 1932. Ecology 28: 245–48.

―――. 1954. Notes on the bryophyte communities of lowland tropical rain-forest, with special reference to Moraballi Creek, British Guiana. Vegetatio 5–6: 319–28.

Robinson, C. B. 1914. The geographic distribution of Philippine mosses. Philippine J. Sci. Bot. 9: 199–218.

Roth, G. 1912. Oebersicht ueber die Gattung *Calymperes*. Hedwigia 51: 122–34.

Sachet, M. H., and F. R. Fosberg. 1955. Island bibliographies. Micronesian botany. Natl. Res. Council Publ. 335: i–iv; 1–577.

Sainsbury, G. O. K. 1955. A handbook of New Zealand mosses. Bull. Roy. Soc. New Zealand 5: 1–490.

Salmon, E. S. 1902. Bryological notes. J. Bot. Brit. For. 40: 1–9.

Schimper, W. P. 1865. *Euptychium*, muscorum Neocaledonicorum genus no-vum et genus *Spiridens* revisum specieque nova auctum. Nova Acta Acad. Leop-Carol. 32: 1–10. Pl. 1–3.

―――. 1867. Nachtrag zu der Genus *Spiridens*. *Spiridens flagellosus* Schpr. species nova descripta et iconibus illustrata. Nova Acta Acad. Leop.-Carol. 33(5): 1–6. Pl. 4.

Schultze-Motel, W. 1963a. Beitrag zur Kenntnis der Laubmoose der Hawaii-Inseln. Willdenowia 3(1): 97–107.

―――. 1963b. Vorlaeufiges Verzeichnis der Laubmoose von Neu-guinea. Willdenowia 3: 399–549.

―――. 1973. Katalog der Laubmoose von Melanesien. Willdenowia 7: 47–82.

Schwaegrichen, C. F. 1801–1842. (See Hedwig, J.)

Seemann, B. 1865–1873. Flora Vitiensis: A description of the plants of the Viti or Fiji Islands with an account of their history, uses and properties. Pp. i–xxxiii, 1–453. Pl. 1–100. (Musci by W. Mitten.) London.

Setchell, W. A. 1926. Phytogeographical notes on Tahiti. 1. Land Vegetation. Univ. California Publ. Bot. 12: 241–90.

———. 1928. Migration and endemism with reference to Pacific insular floras. Proc. Third Pan-Pacific Sci. Congr. Tokyo 1: 869–75.

Sherrin, W. R. 1938. Revision of the genus *Spiridens. In* H. N. Dixon, On a small collection of mosses from New Guinea. Ann. Bryol. 10: 16–19.

Shin, T. 1958a. Miscellaneous notes on mosses from Southwestern Japan. 2. Sci. Rep. Kagoshima Univ. 7: 67–68.

———. 1958b. Studies on the mosses of Entodontaceae in Japan and its adjacent regions. 1. Sci. Rep. Kagoshima Univ. 7: 57–66.

———. 1961. Mosses of Ryukyu Islands. 1. Sci. Rep. Kagoshima Univ. 10: 47–64.

———. 1962. Mosses of the Ryukyu Islands. 2. Sci. Rep. Kagoshima Univ. 11: 93–107.

———. 1964. Fissidentaceae of Japan. Sci. Rep. Kagoshima Univ. 13: 35–149.

Skottsberg, C. 1928. Remarks on the relative independency of Pacific floras. Proc. Third Pan-Pacific Sci. Congr. Tokyo 1: 914–20.

———. 1936. Antarctic plants in Polynesia. *In* T. H. Goodspeed (Editor), Essays on geobotany. Pp. 291–310. F. 1.

———. 1938. Geographical isolation as a factor in species formation, and its relation to certain insular floras. Proc. Linn. Soc. 150: 286–92.

———. 1941. The flora of the Hawaiian Islands and the history of the Pacific Islands. Proc. Sixth Pacific Sci. Congr. 4: 685–707.

Smith, D. R. 1969. "Mosses of Micronesia." Ph.D. dissertation, Washington State University, Pullman.

Stark, J. T., and A. L. Howland. 1941. Geology of Bora Bora, Society Islands. Bishop Mus. Bull. 169: 1–43. Pl. 4.

Sullivant, W. S. 1854. Notices of some new species of mosses from the Pacific Islands, in the collection of the United States Exploring Expedition under Captain Wilkes. Proc. Amer. Ac. Arts Sci. 3: 1–16. Reprint, pp. 1–12. Metcalf & Co., Cambridge.

———. 1857. Notices of new species of mosses from the Pacific Islands. Proc. Am. Acad. Arts Sci. 3: 73–81, 181–85.

———. 1859. Musci. United States Exploring Expedition . . . under the command of Charles Wilkes, U.S.N. 17: 1–32. (Pl. 1–20 in unofficial issue only.)

Takaki, N. 1967. A revision of Japanese *Campylopus.* J. Hattori Bot. Lab. 30: 231–48.

Thériot, I. 1911. *Holomitrium vaginatum* (Hook.) et especes affines. Bull. Soc. Bot. Geneve ser. 2, 3: 245–52. F. 1–7.

———. 1936. Reliquiae Boissieranae. Bull. Soc. Bot. Geneve 26: 76–91.

———. 1937. Mousses de l'ile-de-Paques. Rev. Bryol. Lichenol. 10: 74–77.

Thériot, I., H. N. Dixon, and H. Buch. 1934. Bryophyta nova (17–25). Ann. Bryol. 7: 157–62. 1f.

Tixier, P. 1966. La biogeographie du genre *Thyridium* (Muscinees). Compt. Rend. Sommaire Seances Soc. Biogeogr. 379: 146–51.

Touw, A. 1962. Revision of the moss-genus *Neckeropsis* (Neckeraceae). 1. Asiatic and Pacific species. Blumea 11: 373–425.

———. 1971. A taxonomic revision of the Hypnodendraceae (Musci). Blumea 19: 211–354.

Van Balgooy, M. M. J. 1960. Preliminary plant geographical analysis of the Pacific. Blumea 10: 385–430.

———. 1969. A study on the diversity of island floras. Blumea 17: 139–78.

Van Steenis, C. G. G. J. 1963. Pacific plant areas. 1. Nat. Inst. Sci. Tech. Manila 8: i–iii, 1–297.

———. 1962. The land-bridge theory in botany, with particular reference to tropical plants. Blumea 11: 235–542.

Van Steenis, C. G. G. J., and M. M. J. Van Balgooy. 1966. Pacific plant areas. 2. Blumea Suppl. 5: 1–312.

Whittier, H. O. 1968. "Mosses of the Society Islands: Preliminary studies on their taxonomy, ecology and geography." Ph.D. dissertation, Columbia University, New York.

———. 1973. Mosses of the Marquesas Islands, French Polynesia. Bryologist 76(1): 174–77.

———. 1975. The amphigenous moss flora of French Polynesia. Proceedings of the International Bryological Colloquium, Lille, France, 1973. Accepted for publication.

Whittier, H. O., H. A. Miller, and C. E. B. Bonner. 1963. Musci. In Miller, Whittier, and Bonner, Bryoflora of the atolls of Micronesia. Beih. Nova Hedwigia 11: 7–41. Pl. 5–14.

Whittier, H. O., and H. A. Miller. 1967. Mosses of the Society Islands: Fissidens. Bryologist 70: 76–92.

Whittier, H. O., and B. A. Whittier. 1974. List of mosses of southeastern Polynesia. Bryologist 77(3): 427–46.

Wiens, H. 1965. Atoll environment and ecology. Pp. i–xxii, 1–532. Yale University Press. New Haven, Conn.

Wijk, R. van der, W. D. Margadant, and P. A. Florschutz. 1959–69. Index Muscorum 1–5. 1. A–C 548 p., 1959; 2. D–H (Hypno), 535 p., 1962; 3. H (Hypnum)–O, 529 p., 1964; 4. P–S, 604 p., 1967; 5. T–Z (Addenda), 922 p., 1969. Int. Bur. Plant Taxon Utrecht, Netherlands.

Wilder, G. P. 1934. The flora of Makatea. Bishop Mus. Bull. 120: 1–49. Pl. 1–5. F. 1.

Williams, H. 1933. Geology of Tahiti, Moorea and Maiao. Bishop Mus. Bull. 105: 1–89. 19 f. 8 pl.

Willis, J. C. 1922. Age and area, a study in geographical distribution and origin of species. Pp. i–x, 1–259. Cambridge University Press. London.

Yuncker, T. G. 1945. Plants of the Manua Islands. Bishop Mus. Bull. 184: 1–13.

Zanten, B. O. van. 1959. Trachypodaceae. A critical revision. Blumea 9: 477–575.

———. 1964. Mosses of the Star Mountains Expedition. Scientific results of the Netherlands New Guinea Expedition 1959. Nova Guinea Bot. 16: 263–368.

———. 1968. Mosses of the Danish Noona Dan Expedition to the Philippines, Bismarck Archipelago and the British Solomon Islands. J. Hattori Bot. Lab. 31: 135–51.

Zimmerman, E. C. 1948. Insects of Hawaii. Vol. 1. Introduction. Pp. 1–206. University of Hawaii Press. Honolulu.

GLOSSARY

This glossary incorporates the technical definitions of important terms as they are used in this book. Although it is not an exhaustive guide, it should help the student understand the most commonly used terms. When possible the Latin or Greek origins have been included for the convenience of the reader.

A-: Greek prefix. Not, without.

AB-: Latin prefix. Away from.

ABAXIAL: Away from the axis. The abaxial side of a leaf or leaf-like organ is the side away from the stem. Opposite of adaxial.

ACROCARPOUS: Having the archegonia, and hence the sporophyte, at the tip of the stem or ordinary branch. Acrocarpous mosses can usually be distinguished by their erect habit. Even though the classification of mosses as acrocarpous and pleurocarpous may not show a natural relationship, it is a convenient method for grouping these plants.

ACUMEN: Slenderly tapering point or apex of a leaf.

ACUMINATE: With a slender, gradually tapering point or apex (the margins often with inward curvature). The angle formed by the apex should be 10° or less. Latin *acuminatus*, sharpened.

ACUTE: Ending in a point of more than 10°, but less than a right angle. With a short, sharp point.

ADAXIAL: Toward the axis. The side of a leaf or other organ that is toward the stem, properly the ventral side. Opposite of abaxial or dorsal.

AGGREGATE: Clustered. Often applied to two or more sporophytes from one perichaetium.

ALA (pl. ALAE): Latin for wing, or flat part.

ALAR: Applied to the cells of the angles of the base of the leaf which often differ in size, shape, color, or wall thickness from other cells and may be of taxonomic importance.

AMPHIGASTRIA: Leaves on the underside of the stem (often differentiated), as contrasted with lateral leaves. Greek *amphi-*, around, and *-gaster*, stomach.

ANDROECIUM: "Male inflorescence" comprised of the antheridia and related structures. Greek *andros,* male, and *oikos,* house.

ANNULUS: Ring of specialized cells between the rim of the mouth and the lid (operculum) in the capsule. These cells aid in removing the lid when the spores are mature. Latin *annulus,* a ring.

ANTHERIDIUM (pl. ANTHERIDIA): Male reproductive structure in which sperm or antherozoids are formed. Its sexual opposite is the archegonium.

APEX: Tip of a structure; end opposite the place of attachment.

APICAL: Belonging to the tip or apex. Apical cells of leaves are often broader and shorter than the cells in the middle of the leaf.

APICULATE: Tipped with a small point, or ending in a short, abrupt, sharp point, as the tip of a leaf or the apex of the capsule lid.

APICULUS: Small point at the tip of a leaf or other body.

APOPHYSIS: Swelling of the seta just beneath the capsule. Hypophysis.

APPENDAGE: A minor part, attached to something larger. Latin *ad-,* to, and *pendere,* to hang.

APPENDICULAE: Small transverse spurs attached at intervals to the edges of the cilia of the inner peristome.

APPRESSED: Lying close to or flat against something; descriptive of leaves lying flat on the stem.

AQUATIC: Growing in water or very wet places.

ARCHEGONIUM (pl. ARCHEGONIA): Typically flask-shaped female reproductive structure containing the egg. The corresponding male organ is the antheridium. Greek *archegonos,* the first of a race.

ARCUATE: Bent in a curve as a bow; often used in describing capsules and setae. Latin *arcus,* a bow.

AREOLATION: Network formed by the cell walls of a leaf as seen in surface view through a microscope. Latin diminutive of *area,* an open space.

ARISTA: Fine, bristle-shaped or awn-like point.

ARISTATE: Possessing a bristle-like point.

ARTICULATE: Jointed, or possessing cross bars; with reference to peristome teeth. Latin *articulus,* diminutive of *artus,* a joint.

ASCENDING: Pointing upward or forward. Latin *ad-,* to, and *scandere,* to climb.

ASEXUAL: Possessing neither male nor female structures.

ATTENUATE: Thinned, narrowed, tapered, or long, drawn-out. Latin *attenuare*, to make thin.

AURICLE: One of the small "ear-like" lobes at the basal angles of the leaf; a bulge at the base of a leaf. Auriculate. Latin *auricula*, diminutive of *auris*, the ear.

AUTOICOUS (also AUTOECIOUS): Having antheridia and archegonia on the same plant but on separate shoots or in separate clusters (inflorescences). Greek *autos*, same, self, and *oikos*, house.

AXIL: Angle at the base of a leaf, formed between the leaf and the stem. Latin *axilla*, armpit.

AXILLARY: With reference to a structure found in the angle between the leaf and the stem.

AXIS: Imaginary line around which parts or organs develop. Latin *axis*, axle.

BASAL: Belonging to the base. Basal cells of leaves or those which appear where the leaf is attached to the stem often differ in shape and color from those in the middle of the leaf and may be of taxonomic importance.

BEAK: Elongated, narrow tip of the lid (operculum).

BI-: Latin prefix. Twice, two.

BICOSTATE: Having a double midrib or costa. In bicostate leaves the costa is usually shorter than in leaves with a single costa; in addition, some taxa possessing bicostate leaves may variably lack the double midrib, sometimes showing this variation on a single plant.

BIDENTATE: Having two teeth, or having paired teeth. Latin *dens*, a tooth.

BISTRATOSE: With two layers of cells. Applicable to portions of leaf blades, as seen in cross section, in some species such as *Leucobryum*.

CAESPITOSE: Tufted.

CALYPTRA: Cap or hood covering the capsule, either partially or completely. The upper, enlarged portion of the archegonium; the calyptra characteristically becomes lost as the capsule matures. Greek *kalyptra*, a cover for the head.

CAMPANULATE: Bell-shaped. The form of a calyptra in some species of mosses. Latin *campanula*, the diminutive of *campana*, a bell.

CANALICULATE: Channeled. Applicable to leaves with margins so strongly incurved that the blades have the cross section of a channel. Latin *canaliculus,* the diminutive of *canalis,* a channel or canal.

CANCELLATE: Latticed, lattice-like.

CANCELLINEAE: Lattice-like region of hyaline cells at the leaf base of certain genera of Calymperaceae (*Calymperes, Syrrhopodon, Thyridium*).

CAPSULE: Spore-bearing portion of the moss sporophyte, consisting of neck, urn, and operculum. "Fruit" of a moss. Capsule, seta, and foot normally comprise the sporophyte.

CARINATE: Keeled, as in the segments of the inner peristome, or as in the leaves of certain genera.

CAULINE: Belonging to the stem or arising from it.

CENTRAL STRAND: Region of narrow and elongated cells found in the middle of the stems of some mosses, in some instances continuous with the midrib or costa of the leaves.

CERNUOUS: Capsules which are drooping, nodding, or slightly inclined (as opposed to "erect"). Latin *cernuus,* stooping.

CHLOROCYSTS: Chloroplast-containing "green" cells of moss leaves, especially applied to the centrally located, median cells seen in cross sections of leaves of members of the family Leucobryaceae. Containing chlorophyll or chloroplasts. (Contrast with leucocysts.) Greek *chloros,* light green, and *phyllon,* leaf.

CILIA (sing. CILIUM): Delicate, fine, hair-like or thread-like structures or processes of the inner peristome in some mosses, appearing between the segments, as in some species of *Bryum.* Numbers regarding cilia refer to the number which appear between two adjacent segments of the inner peristome. In a second application of the term, reference is made to long, slender teeth along the margins and possibly along the midrib of leaves, as in *Syrrhopodon ciliatus.*

CIRCINATE: Coiled or bent into a partial or complete ring or circle.

CLAVATE: Club-shaped, as in the propagula of *Calymperes tenerum.*

COLUMELLA: Central axis of sterile tissue in the moss capsule, around which the spores are produced. Diminutive of the Latin *columna,* pillar.

COMA: Tuft of leaves or branches forming the crown of the stem. Latin *coma,* hair.

COMOSE: Ending in hairs. Tufted at the tips, as in *Campylopus introflexus.*

COMPLANATE: Flattened or compressed; with leaves so arranged that the plant or branches appear to be flattened. Latin *com-*, together, and *planare*, to make level or plane.

COMPLICATE: Folded together, lengthwise. Latin *com-*, together, and *plicare*, to fold.

CONCAVE: Hollow.

CONDUPLICATE: Folded lengthwise along the midrib, the upper surface being within, or face-to-face. The moss genus *Fissidens* is characterized by conduplicate leaves. Latin *con-*, together, and *duplicare*, to duplicate.

CONSTRICTED: Contracted. Referring to capsules abruptly narrowed beneath the mouth when dry.

CONTORTED: Twisted. Latin *contorquere*, to twist.

CONVOLUTE: Applied to leaves with rolled up or rolled together margins. Latin *con-*, together, and *volvere*, to roll.

CORTEX: In bryophytes, which have no bark, it is the outer layer, including the epidermis, when such a layer is differentiated from the interior. Latin for bark.

COSTA: Midvein, nerve, or midrib of the leaf. Leaves having one or more primary longitudinal midribs or veins are termed costate. Latin *costa*, rib.

COTYPE: Material of a species gathered at the same place as the type. The term is being supplanted by the somewhat more specific words topotype and isotype.

CRENATE: Having rounded or convex teeth or projections. Latin *crenatus*, notched, scalloped.

CRENULATE: Applicable to margins of leaves toothed with small, rounded projections; minutely crenate.

CRISPATE: Curled and twisted in various ways; true of many moss leaves in a dry condition. Latin *crispus*, curled.

CUCULLATE: Hood-like, usually cone-shaped calyptra, slit on one side only; also applicable to leaves with the apex curved inward like a slipper. Latin *cucullus*, cap.

CUSP: Sharp, rigid point. Leaves tipped with a sharp, rigid point are described as cuspidate. Latin *cuspis*, a point.

CYGNEOUS: Abruptly curved downward, as the neck of a swan. Latin *cygnus*, swan.

DECUMBENT: Prostrate with ascending tips. Latin *de-*, from, down, and *cumbere*, to lie, recline.

DECURRENT: Applicable to a leaf with margins extending down the stem below the point of attachment, as a ridge or wing. Latin *de-*, from, down, and *currere*, to run.

DENDROID: Tree-like, arborescent; a habit in which the main secondary stem resembles a minute tree. Greek *dendron*, tree, and *-oid*, like, resembling, having the form of.

DENTATE: Toothed, the teeth extending outward, sharp. Latin *dens*, tooth.

DENTICULATE: Possessing minute or obscure teeth.

DEOPERCULATE: Applied to a capsule after its lid (operculum) has fallen off.

DI-: Greek *di-* or *dis-*, twice, double; a common prefix.

DICHOTOMOUS: Forked; parted or divided in pairs. Greek *dicha*, in two, and *temnein*, to cut.

DIMORPHOUS: Plants, leaves, and other organs having two forms. Leaves of *Racopilum, Hypopterygium*, and *Cyathophorella* are dimorphic. Greek *di-*, two, and *morphē*, form.

DIOICOUS (also DIOECIOUS): With the antheridia and archegonia (or male and female inflorescences) on separate plants. Unisexual plants.

DISTANT: Leaves arranged far apart, with little or no overlap; as opposed to imbricate, in which the leaves overlap.

DISTICHOUS: Leaves arranged on opposite sides of a stem in two vertical rows or ranks as in *Fissidens*. Greek *dis-*, twice, and *stichos*, a row.

DIVARICATE: With reference to stems or branches which spread widely from each other. Divergent. Latin *dis-*, apart, and *varicare*, to straddle.

DIVISURAL LINE: Vertical median line on the teeth of the peristome, often zigzag; also the vertical median line of the endostome segments. Latin *dividere*, to divide.

DORSAL: Surface facing away from the axis when parallel with the stem. In the case of the leaf this is the lower surface. Latin *dorsum*, back.

DORSIVENTRAL: Having distinct upper and lower surfaces.

ECOSTATE: Without a costa, midrib, or nerve.

ECOTYPE: Taxonomic unit within a species; often characterized by minor morphological differences and always by restriction to a particular set of ecological conditions.

ELLIPTIC: Oblong, with regularly rounded ends; a long oval; shaped as an ellipse.

ELONGATE: Considerably longer than wide.

EMERGENT: Capsules extending slightly beyond the perichaetial leaves, half uncovered. Latin *emergere*, to come forth.

ENDEMIC: Confined to a single country or region.

ENDOSTOME: Internal peristome; inner row of the peristome, consisting usually of as many projections as the outer, with the projections characteristically alternating with the outer teeth. These projections are known as segments or processes; between the segments there are often one or more hair-like processes known as cilia.

ENTIRE: Leaf margins even, not toothed or notched.

EPIDERMIS: Outer layer of cells.

EPIPHRAGM: Membrane covering the mouth of the capsule, formed by the dilated top of the columella in the Polytrichaceae (*Pogonatum*).

EPIPHYTE: A plant growing upon another plant, as mosses growing on bark (corticolous epiphytes) or on leaves (epiphyllous epiphytes).

EQUITANT: Leaves whose bases are folded so as to overlap and cover the leaves within or above them.

ERECT: Leaves diverging from the stem at an angle of 45°.

ERECT-SPREADING: Leaves extending from the stem at an angle of less than 45°.

EXCURRENT: With the costa extending beyond the apex or tip of the leaf.

EXOSTOME: Outer row of teeth in a peristome.

EXOTHECIAL: Referring to the outer layer of cells of the capsule wall.

EXSERTED: Applicable to a capsule extending beyond the perichaetial leaves. Latin *exserere*, to thrust out.

FALCATE: Curved like a sickle. Latin *falx, falcis*, sickle or scythe.

FALCATE-SECUND: Each leaf curved like a sickle, and all leaves turning to one side of the stem, extending in the same direction, as if windswept.

FASCICLE: Closed cluster; a bundle or a bunch of leaves or branches. Fasciculate. Latin *fasciculus*, diminutive of *fascis*, a bundle.

FASTIGIATE: Erect branches, close together, and approximately equal in height; having branches in tufts closely narrowed at the base.

Especially characteristic of the genus *Philonotis*. Latin *fastigium*, gable.

FLABELLATE: Small, fan-shaped branch pattern. Latin *flabellum*, a fan.

FLACCID: Soft, limp, not firm or rigid. Latin *flaccidus*, limp.

FLAGELLIFORM: Shaped like a whiplash; branchlets which are long, slender, and commonly tapering. Latin *flagellum*, a whip.

FLEXUOSE: Irregularly wavy; bending alternately backward and forward. Latin *flexus*, a bending or turning.

FOOT: Part of the sporophyte at the base of the seta, embedded in gametophyte tissue, functioning in anchorage and nutrient absorption for the sporophyte.

FRONDOSE: Fan-shaped, flattened branch system suggestive of a leaf. Latin *frons*, *frondis*, a leaf.

FRUIT: Bryologist's term for the sporophyte or capsule.

FUSIFORM: Spindle-shaped; narrowly oval with narrow, tapering ends; applicable to the cells of some moss leaves, especially in the families Sematophyllaceae and Hypnaceae; also applicable to the propagula of some species of *Calymperes* and *Syrrhopodon* (Calymperaceae).

GAMETOPHYTE: Plant-bearing gametes; the sexual generation. In the mosses the gametophyte is the leafy plant, exclusive of the foot, seta, and capsule which comprise the sporophyte generation.

GLABROUS: Smooth, neither hairy nor papillose. Latin *glaber*, smooth.

GLAUCOUS: Bluish gray or bluish white; whitened with a bloom; a light green color tinged with bluish gray. Greek *glaukos*, silvery or gray.

GLOBOSE: Rounded like a ball or globe; spherical; applicable to capsules of some mosses, especially in the family Bartramiaceae.

GUARD CELLS: Two cells which surround (and which may control the size and shape of) stomata; may be present on the capsules of some moss genera, absent in others.

GYMNOSTOMOUS: Capsules lacking a peristome. Greek *gymnos*, naked, and *stoma*, mouth.

GYNOECIUM: Archegoniate ("female") inflorescence.

HABIT: General appearance or aspect of a plant. Latin *habitus*, condition or dress.

HABITAT: Where a plant grows; its ecological niche. Latin *habitare*, to dwell.

HAIR POINT: Leaf tip differing from the rest of the blade, drawn out into a slender, characteristically colorless point, as in *Tortula* or *Racopilum.*

HETEROGENEOUS: Not uniform in kind. For example, a heterogeneous costa consists of more than one kind of cell, including guide cells, stereid cells, and accompanying cells.

HETEROICOUS (also HETEROECIOUS): With more than one form of inflorescence in the same species, so that antheridia and archegonia may appear together and/or separately on the same plant; both monoicous and paroicous. Greek *heteros,* different or other, and *oikos,* house or household.

HIRSUTE: Hairy, with coarse, stiff hairs. Latin *hirsutus,* shaggy or bristly.

HISPID: Rough, with short, stiff hairs. Latin *hispidus,* spiny or bristly.

HOMOGENEOUS: Uniform in kind or nature; for example, a homogeneous costa has one type of cell.

HYALINE: Transparent and colorless, like water or glass. Greek *hyalinos,* glassy.

HYGROSCOPIC: Altering form or position with change in moisture; especially applicable to setae and to the peristome mechanisms which regulate spore dispersal.

HYPOPHYSIS: Apophysis or swelling of the seta at the base of the capsule. Greek *hypo-,* under, and *phyein,* to grow.

IMBRICATE: Closely overlapping like the shingles or tiles of a roof, with reference especially to leaves and their distribution along a stem. Latin *imbricare,* to cover with tiles.

IMMERSED: With the capsule hidden within the leaves of the perichaetium; also applicable to stomata in capsules of some species of *Orthotrichum* in which the guard cells are concealed beneath adjacent cells of the capsule wall.

INCLINED: Capsule positions between erect and pendulous.

INCRASSATE: Thickened; thick-walled cells. A feature of diagnostic importance, especially in leaf cells and particularly in basal cells. Latin *in-,* in, and *crassare,* to make thick.

INCURVED: Curved toward the stem.

INFLATED: Referring to alar cells of leaves, enlarged much beyond the size of neighboring cells.

INFLEXED: Incurved. Latin *in-,* in, and *flectare,* to bend.

INFLORESCENCE: Clusters of antheridia or archegonia and their attendant paraphysis and bracts. Latin *in-*, in, and *florescere,* to begin to blossom.

INNOVATION: A young offshoot from the stem. Latin *in-*, in, and *novare,* to make new.

INSERTION: Attachment of leaves to stem.

INTERCALARY INFLORESCENCE: Inflorescence neither apical nor basal, appearing on shoot or branch. Latin *inter-*, between, and *-calare,* to call.

INTRICATE: Tangled. Latin *intricare,* to tangle.

INVOLUTE: Leaf margins rolled up and inward. Latin *in-*, in, and *volvare,* to roll.

ISODIAMETRIC: Descriptive of cells having an equal diameter in any direction (although most usually in length and width). Greek *isos-*, equal, *dia-*, through, and *metron,* a measure.

JULACEOUS: Smooth, slender, and cylindrical; worm- or catkin-like, with leaves uniformly erect or appressed. Greek *ioulos,* down or beard; Latin *iulus,* catkin.

KEEL: Sharp ridge, as on the longitudinal folds of some leaves.

LAMELLAE (sing. LAMELLA): Longitudinal strips of tissue in the form of a thin blade or blades, standing on edge and extending parallel with one another along the costa, as in *Pogonatum.* Also thin plates, particularly the flat plates on the dorsal surface of many peristome teeth. Latin diminutive of *lamina,* a plate or leaf.

LAMINA: Blade of the leaf, as distinct from the costa, midrib, or nerve. Characteristically of one cell layer (unistratose) in most mosses. Latin *lamina,* a plate or leaf.

LANCEOLATE: Lance-shaped; characteristically four to six times longer than wide, broadened at the base, and tapering to a point. Latin *lanceola,* diminutive of *lancera,* lance.

LATERALLY COMPRESSED: Flattened from left to right (as distinct from dorsiventrally compressed).

LEUCOCYSTS: Cells without chloroplasts (contrast with chlorocysts); the upper and lower tiers of cells as seen in cross sections of leaves of *Leucobryum.*

LID: Operculum. The upper portion of the sporophyte capsule which covers the peristome teeth and capsule mouth.

LIGULATE: Strap-shaped; longer and narrower than lingulate. Latin *ligula,* diminutive of *lingua,* tongue.

LIMB: Upper part of the leaf (as distinct from the leaf base), e.g., *Pogonatum,* in which the base is sheathing and membranous.

LINEAR: Very narrow, with very nearly parallel margins, applied to the shapes of cells and of leaves. Latin *linea,* a line.

LINGULATE: Tongue-shaped.

LUMEN: Cavity of a cell; often the basis for cell length-width measurements. Latin, *lumin,* an opening for light.

LUNATE: Crescent-shaped. Basal cells of some species of *Macromitrium* are distinctively crescent-shaped. Latin *luna,* moon.

MAMMILLATE: Pertaining to a convex lid or operculum with a short, nipple-like point. Also referring to a single large, rounded papilla covering a cell.

MARGINED: Bordered. Possessing a bordering band of cells of different shape or color from the others.

MEDIAN: Those cells in the middle of the lamina, between the margin and the costa, as distinguished from alar, basal, and apical cells; also applicable to the leaves of the middle portion of stems and branches.

MICRON (pl. MICRA): 1/1000 of a millimeter, represented by the Greek letter μ. Greek *mikron,* small.

MICROPHYLLOUS: Bearing minute leaves. Greek *mikros,* small, and *phyllon,* leaf.

MIDRIB: Costa, nerve, or midvein of moss leaves.

MITRATE: A calyptra shaped like a peaked cap with the lower margin undivided or with several equal clefts.

MITRIFORM: Miter-shaped, symmetrical calyptra, cleft on several sides; conical with slightly narrowed mouth or opening.

MONOICOUS (also MONOECIOUS): With antheridia and archegonia on the same plant. See also: AUTOICOUS, PAROICOUS, and SYNOICOUS. Greek *monos,* one, and *oikos,* house.

MUCRO: A very short, small, abrupt point, usually stout.

MUCRONATE: Tipped with a mucro, the costa percurrent as a short, small, abrupt tip.

NECK: Base of capsule just above seta but below the spore sac; also the elongated part of the archegonium just above the swollen venter which contains the egg.

NERVE: Costa, midrib.

OB-: Prefix frequently used to indicate some kind of inversion.

OBLONG: Elliptic, obtuse at each end, three or four times longer than wide.

OBOVATE: Inversely ovate, with the narrowed end toward the base, broadest toward the apex.

OBTUSE: Blunt or rounded at the end; a leaf ending in an angle of from 90° to nearly 180°.

OPERCULUM: Lid covering the mouth of the capsule.

ORBICULAR: Almost circular leaf outline.

OVAL: Broadly elliptical.

OVATE: Descriptive of a plane figure having the silhouette of an egg; in moss leaves, the broadest point is toward the leaf base. Latin *ovum*, egg.

OVATE-LANCEOLATE: Between ovate and lanceolate.

OVATE-OBLONG: Leaf outline between ovate and oblong.

PAPILLA (pl. PAPILLAE): Nipple-shaped, rounded or acute projections on cell surfaces, especially leaf cells, and occasionally on the seta and peristome teeth; of especially important diagnostic value.

PAPILLATE: Papillose. Rough with papillae.

PARAPHYLLIA (sing. PARAPHYLLIUM): Minute leaf-like or thread-like and sometimes much-branched organs among leaves on a stem, as in *Thuidium*.

PARAPHYSES (sing. PARAPHYSIS): Jointed, hyaline hairs or minute threads among the antheridia and archegonia in an inflorescence.

PAROICOUS: Antheridia and archegonia appear on the same plant, but not intermixed; if in the same inflorescence, the antheridia appear in the axils of bracts below those surrounding the archegonia. Monoicous or bisexual.

PATENT: Spreading. Leaves spreading from the stem at an angle of 26–45°.

PATULOUS: Leaves spreading from the stem at an angle of 46–90°.

PELLUCID: Partially to completely transparent, but not hyaline.

PENDENT: Hanging down from its support; pendulous. The capsule drooping or nodding more than when cernuous, as in some species of *Bryum*.

PERCURRENT: Costa extends throughout the entire length of the leaf to terminate in the apex, but does not extend beyond the blade.

PERICHAETIUM: Special leaves which enclose the cluster of archegonia and which surround the base of the seta.

PERIGONIUM: Special leaves which enclose the antheridia. Greek *peri-*, around, and *gonos*, reproductive organs.

PERISTOME: Ring of teeth surrounding the mouth of the capsule, visible upon removal of the lid or operculum. Especially important in diagnostic distinctions between families and genera, these basic patterns should be noted. Double peristome, consisting of an outer row of teeth (the exostome) and an inner row of segments or processes (the endostome), with one or more cilia occurring between the segments. Frequently a basal membrane of varying height will be noted, with its upper part cleft into the segments and cilia. The hypnaceous peristome consists of sixteen strongly articulate teeth, keeled segments, and cilia, with the basal plates of the teeth marked between articulations with close, fine, transverse lines. The single peristome consists of one row of teeth. Greek *peri-*, around, and *stoma*, mouth.

PILIFEROUS: Possessing a hair-like prolongation or hair-like points, characteristic of leaves and calyptrae.

PINNATE: Branching pattern which is feather-like, with numerous spreading branches on each side of the stem in two opposite rows. Latin *pinna*, a feather.

PITTED: Cell walls marked with small openings or depressions; porose, as in *Acroporium*, certain members of Leucobryaceae and Calymperaceae.

PLANE: Flat. The margin of a leaf which is not involute or revolute.

PLANTS: General reference to the leafy gametophyte of the moss, as opposed to the sporophyte.

PLEUROCARPOUS: Having archegonia (and later, sporophytes) which appear on short, lateral, special branches. Pleurocarpous mosses usually can be distinguished by their creeping habit. See also: ACROCARPOUS.

PLICAE (sing. PLICA): Folds, usually lengthwise, in moss leaves. Such folded leaves are described as plicate. Latin *plicare*, to fold.

PLUMOSE: Regularly and closely pinnate like a plume or feather. Latin *pluma*, feather.

PLURIPAPILLOSE: With two or more papillae per cell surface.

POLYGAMOUS: With antheridia and archegonia disposed in various ways on the same plant.

POLYOICOUS (also POLYOECIOUS): Combination of autoicous and heteroicous or synoicous, with dioicous; at least some stems bearing antheridia the first year and only archegonia in succeeding years.

PORES: Perforations or thin places in a cell wall. Porose.

PRIMARY: First growth of stem, usually prostrate or creeping, with more or less erect branches called secondary stems.

PROCESSES: Segments and cilia of the inner peristome, applied especially to the segments or principal divisions.

PROCUMBENT: Trailing along the ground, lying flat upon the substratum.

PROPAGULA (sing. PROPAGULUM): Small structures, often club-shaped, comprised of a few cells capable of reproducing the plant vegetatively. Propagula often appear clustered in leaf axils, or, in the family Calymperaceae, along the costa or at its apex.

PROPAGULIFEROUS: Bearing propagula.

PROTONEMA (pl. PROTONEMATA): Green filamentous or alga-like phase of the gametophyte generation. It develops from the germinating spore and eventually produces the leafy stem. Greek *protos*, first, and *nema*, thread.

PYRIFORM: Pear-shaped.

QUADRATE: Square, or nearly so, referring to cells of mosses in surface view. Latin *quadrare*, to make square.

RADICLES: Rhizoids growing from the lower part of the stem, extending into the ground; in mass, known as tomentum.

RADICULOSE: Covered with radicles.

REFLEXED: Bent backward.

REPAND: Leaf margins which are sinuate or wavy. Latin *re-*, back again, and *pandus*, crooked.

RETICULATE: In the form of a net; with reference to cell areolation patterns in leaves. Latin *reticulum*, diminutive of *rete*, a net.

REVOLUTE: Leaf margins rolled backward and under.

RHIZOIDS: Thread-like, multicellular outgrowths from stems and sometimes leaf bases, either simple or branched, which serve for absorption and anchorage. Greek *rhiza-*, a root, and *-oides*, like.

RHIZOME: Elongate, horizontal, surface or subsurface, root-like stem.

RHOMBOIDAL: Cells shaped like a diamond, forming a four-sided figure having only the opposite sides equal, their length and width different.

ROSETTE: Arrangement of terminal leaves to resemble or imitate a rose.

ROSTELLATE: Operculum with a short beak.

ROSTRATE: Operculum with a long beak. Latin *rostrum*, beak.

RUGOSE: Roughened with transverse wrinkles; characteristic of some moss leaves. Latin *ruga*, a wrinkle.

SACCATE: Sac-like leaves, as in *Cyathophorella*.

SAPROPHYTIC: Living on, and obtaining nourishment from, dead organic matter.

SCABROUS: Rough or harsh to the touch; warty. Latin *scaber*, rough.

SCARIOSE: Dry, thin, membranous, and not green; of a scaly consistency.

SECONDARY (STEMS): Branches arising from the main or primary stem; they may be prostrate (*Thuidium*) or erect (*Macromitrium*), and may frequently divide again (*Hypopterygium*).

SECUND: Leaves all turned to one side, or in the same direction. Latin *secundus*, following.

SEGMENTS: Projections composing the inner row of a peristome which is double, usually alternating with the teeth or projections in the outer row.

SEPTATE: Divided by a partition. Latin *septum*, a fence having transverse walls.

SERIATE: In a series of rows, either transverse or longitudinal.

SERRATE: Toothed; referring to leaf margins with close, regular, sharp, forward-projecting teeth, resembling the teeth of a saw. Latin *serra*, a saw.

SERRULATE: Minutely serrate.

SESSILE: Not stalked; often referring to a sporophyte having no seta. Latin *sedere*, to sit.

SETA: Stalk of the sporophyte which bears the capsule. Latin *seta*, bristle.

SEXUAL: Having male and female organs.

SHEATHING: Referring to the bases of leaves more or less surrounding and clasping the stem, and to perichaetial bracts (or leaves) surrounding the base of the seta.

SINUOSE: Wavy. Cell walls appear in waves rather than straight.

SPATULATE: Leaves spatula-shaped, bluntly and narrowly obovate, narrower toward the base.

SPINOSE: Leaf margins with long, sharp teeth.

SPORANGIUM (pl. SPORANGIA): Capsule of the sporophyte. Greek *spora-*, spore or seed, and *angeion*, vessel.

SPORES: Small spherical structures produced in the capsule, germinating to form the protonema; minute asexual reproductive structures, usually consisting of a single cell.

SPOROPHYTE: Leafless, dependent moss generation which produces spores. It develops as the result of fusion of sperm and egg (syngamy), and when mature typically consists of foot, seta, and capsule. The calyptra which covers the capsule is derived from the archegonium of the leafy gametophyte generation. Greek *spora-*, spore or seed, and *phyton*, plant.

SPREADING (LEAVES): Leaves extending from the stem at an angle greater than 45°.

SQUARROSE (LEAVES): Leaves spreading abruptly and widely, with the upper portion of the leaf forming approximately a right angle to the stem.

STELLATE: Star-like leaf pattern, suggested by the leaf arrangement as it may be seen from the shoot tip of certain mosses as *Ctenidium stellulatum*. Latin *stella*, star.

STEREID CELLS: Small, thick-walled cells of the costa.

STOLONIFEROUS: Slender, creeping, usually minutely leaved secondary stems or branches.

STOMATA (sing. STOMA): Pores in the epidermis or wall of the capsule, surrounded by two special guard cells. Greek *stoma*, mouth.

STRATOSE: In distinct layers or strata.

STRIAE: Very faint furrows; fine longitudinal lines or ridges, especially characteristic of certain moss capsules. Latin *stria*, a channel.

STRUMA: Asymmetrical swelling on one side of the base of the capsule or hypophysis.

STRUMOSE: Bearing a struma or goiter-like swelling on one side of the hypophysis of the capsule.

SUBULA: Very fine point like a needle or an awl. Latin *subula*, awl.

SUBULATE: Leaves having a subula or very fine pointed tip.

SYNOICOUS (also SYNOECIOUS): With antheridia and archegonia intermingled in the same inflorescence. Greek *syn-*, together, and *oikos*, a house.

TEETH (sing. TOOTH): Projections which compose the peristome if it consists of a single row of processes, or the outer row, if there are two rows of processes.

TENIOLAE: Intra-marginal border of differentiated cells in the leaves of certain members of the family Calymperaceae.

TERETE: Cylindrical; round in cross section. Characteristic of certain moss capsules. Latin *teres, teretis*, rounded off.

TERRESTRIAL: Growing on earth; on the land or ground.

THECA: The capsule of mosses.

TOMENTOSE: Covered with soft, matted hairs, with a thick felt of radicles or rhizoids, usually, but not always referring to lower portions of stems. The mat may be referred to as a tomentum.

TOPOTYPE: Material of a species collected at the same place but not at the same time that the type specimen was gathered.

TRABECULAE: Projecting plates on the inner side of the peristome teeth.

TRANSLUCENT: Semi-transparent. Latin *trans-*, through, and *lucere*, to shine.

TUBULOSE: Pertaining to leaves with margins so strongly inrolled that they meet, causing the blades to have the shape of a tube.

TURGID: Swollen or inflated.

TYPE: Plant (or packet of plants) on which a species description and name is based and which serves to represent or characterize that species.

UNDULATE: With a wavy margin or surface, alternately concave and convex. Latin *undula*, the diminutive of *unda*, a wave.

UNIPAPILLATE: With one papilla per cell surface.

UNISTRATOSE: In one layer of cells.

URCEOLATE: Urn- or pitcher-shaped. Latin *urceola*, small urn.

INDEX

401

INDEX

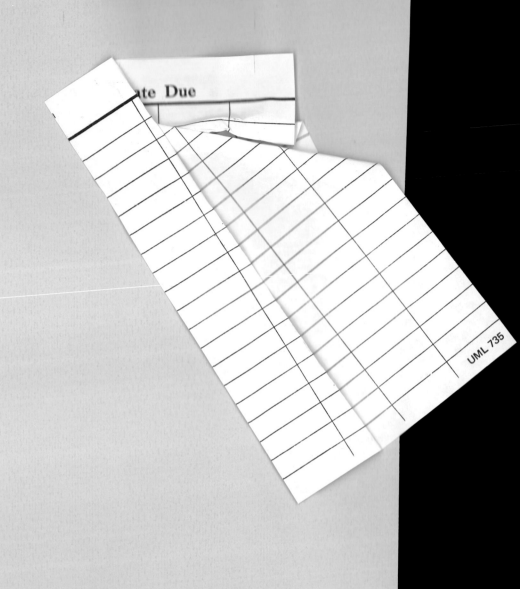

ate Due

UML 735